# Stockholm Arbitration Yearbook 2020

**Stockholm Arbitration Yearbook**

---

VOLUME 2

---

*Editors*

Axel Calissendorff is a partner in and founder of the law firm Calissendorff Advokatbyrå. Prior to that he was a partner in major Swedish law firms. He is the Solicitor to H.M. the King of Sweden and former President of the Swedish Bar Association. His focus is on Corporate and Public M&A. He often sits as an arbitrator. He has authored numerous articles.

Patrik Schöldström is a Judge of Appeal of the Svea Court of Appeal. He is also an Associate Professor of the Faculty of Law of Stockholm University. He has a doctorate in arbitration law and is a former member of the Swedish Bar. He regularly writes articles and case notes. He has extensive experience as an arbitrator – chairman, sole arbitrator, co-arbitrator and emergency arbitrator – in international and domestic disputes, ad hoc and institutional.

*Introduction*

The Yearbook is published under the auspices of the Stockholm Centre for Commercial Law, a part of the Stockholm University Faculty of Law. It is designed to meet the information needs of arbitration practitioners and parties from all over the world. The first volume was published in 2019.

*Objective*

The Yearbook is designed to meet the information needs of arbitration practitioners and parties from all over the world. It provides authoritative articles, some of them with a Swedish angle, that address current matters of global concern in arbitration. Each volume includes one or more chapters accounting for developments in Swedish case law and legislation since the previous volume.

*Frequency*

The publication is annual.

*The titles published in this series are listed at the end of this volume.*

# Stockholm Arbitration Yearbook 2020

Edited by

Axel Calissendorff
Patrik Schöldström

Assistant Editor

Bruno Gustafsson

Editorial Committee



**Stockholm Centre for Commercial Law**
**Faculty of Law**

Stockholm University

Wolters Kluwer

*Published by:*
Kluwer Law International B.V.
PO Box 316
2400 AH Alphen aan den Rijn
The Netherlands
E-mail: international-sales@wolterskluwer.com
Website: lrus.wolterskluwer.com

*Sold and distributed by:*
Wolters Kluwer Legal & Regulatory U.S.
7201 McKinney Circle
Frederick, MD 21704
United States of America
Email: customer.service@wolterskluwer.com

ISBN 978-94-035-2410-8

e-Book: ISBN 978-94-035-2411-5
web-PDF: ISBN 978-94-035-2412-2

# Editors

**Axel Calissendorff** is partner in and founder of Calissendorff Advokatbyrå. Prior to that he was at major law firms, Mannheimer Swartling (1981–2005) as Executive Partner in 2003 and 2004, and Roschier (2005–2013), as a Senior Partner from 2009 to 2012. He is since 2009 the Solicitor to H.M. The King of Sweden and former President of the Swedish Bar Association (2001–2004). His focus is on Corporate and M&A. He is a frequently appointed arbitrator. He has authored numerous articles.

**Patrik Schöldström** is a Judge of Appeal of the Svea Court of Appeal and an Associate Professor of the Faculty of Law at Stockholm University, Sweden. He has a doctorate in arbitration law and is a former member of the Swedish Bar. He regularly writes articles and case notes. He also sits as an arbitrator and has participated in a number of domestic and international arbitrations (ad hoc and institutional) as chair of arbitral tribunal, sole arbitrator, wing arbitrator, and counsel.

# Contributors

**Shreya Aren** is a dual-qualified (India and England and Wales) associate in the London office of Debevoise & Plimpton LLP. Her practice focuses on international commercial and investment treaty arbitration. Ms Aren has acted for corporate and state clients under a wide range of institutional rules as well as in ad hoc arbitrations. She has also acted in arbitration-related court proceedings, such as anti-suit injunctions and challenges to awards, before the English courts. She has experience in a number of different sectors and across jurisdictions (including continental Europe).

**Dr Crina Baltag** is Senior Lecturer in International Arbitration at Stockholm University and qualified attorney-at-law since 2004, with extensive practice in various aspects on international dispute resolution, private and public international law. Crina is member of the Stockholm Chamber of Commerce Arbitration Institute (SCC) Board. Crina is the editor of Kluwer Arbitration Blog, co-managing editor of ITA Arbitration Report and member of editorial boards of prestigious journals in the field, including of the *Journal of International Arbitration*. Crina has been appointed in numerous arbitrations, as sole arbitrator and co-arbitrator under the rules of the ICC, LCIA, SIAC, and CCIR-Romania. Crina holds a PhD in International Arbitration from Queen Mary University of London, UK.

**Giuditta Cordero-Moss,** Dr. juris (Oslo), PhD (Moscow), is a professor at the University of Oslo, Norway. She publishes and lectures in Norway and internationally within the fields of contract law, private international law and arbitration. A former corporate lawyer, she has been acting as arbitrator in international disputes since 2002. She is, i.a.: Delegate for Norway, UNCITRAL Working Group on Arbitration (since 2007); Alternate Member of the ICC Court of Arbitration (since 2018); Member of the Curatorium of the Hague Academy of International Law (since 2019); President (2017–2020) and Judge (2007–2020) of the European Bank for Reconstruction and Development Administrative Tribunal.

**Christer Danielsson** is Advokat, Danielsson & Nyberg Advokatbyrå in Stockholm, President of the Swedish Bar Association and Former President of the Swedish Arbitration Association.

**Ylli Dautaj** is a lecturer at O.P. Jindal Global University, Jindal Global Law School, India. Managing Partner, DER Juridik, Stockholm. PhD Candidate, University of Edinburgh.

**Jacob Frank** is an associate at White & Case in Stockholm and specializes in arbitration and commercial litigation. He has previously worked for other law firms and has also been working as a legal clerk/junior judge at the District Court of Stockholm. He also serves as tribunal secretary.

**Jeffrey Golden** is Joint Head of Chambers at 3 Hare Court; Founder and Chair Emeritus of The P.R.I.M.E. Finance Foundation in The Hague; a member of the Foundation's Panel of Recognised International Market Experts in Finance; and an Honorary Fellow and Member of Court at the London School of Economics and Political Science, where he has also been Visiting Professor in the Law Department (2010–2013). He previously retired from international law firm Allen & Overy LLP, where he was the founder partner of Allen & Overy's U.S. law practice and senior partner in the firm's global derivatives practice. He has acted extensively for the International Swaps and Derivatives Association, was a principal author of ISDA's master agreements and has acted as an arbitrator and appeared as an expert witness in several high-profile derivatives cases. In 2017, he was called as an Honorary Master of the Bench at the Honourable Society of Middle Temple, and, in 2019, he was awarded the American Bar Association International Lifetime Achievement Award.

**Kirsi Kannaste** is Partner at Krogerus Attorneys Ltd's (Helsinki) dispute resolution practice.

**Daria Kozlowska-Rautiainen** is Doctor of Laws, Senior Lecturer at the Stockholm University, Director of the International Commercial Arbitration Law, LLM.

**Alma M. Mozetič** is an associate in the London office of Debevoise & Plimpton LLP. Her practice focuses on international commercial and investment treaty arbitration, corporate investigations and regulatory compliance, and international litigation. Ms Mozetič has a particular focus on multi-jurisdictional and cross-border matters and has represented clients across a wide range of industries in different jurisdictions. She previously worked as a litigator in New York and now often handles European aspects of large US litigations and investigations.

**Ola Ø. Nisja** is a partner at Wikborg Rein and is the firm's Global Head of Disputes. He is admitted to the Supreme Court of Norway. Nisja is also the Chairperson of the Arbitration and Dispute Resolution Institute of the Oslo Chamber of Commerce (OCC), and one of Norway's two representatives to the ICC International Court of Arbitration.

**Ville Pönkä** is Professor of Private Law at the University of Helsinki, Finland.

**Anders Reldén** is a partner with White & Case in Stockholm and specializes in arbitration and commercial litigation. He has represented Swedish and foreign corporations and state entities in complex Swedish and international arbitration matters. He also regularly serves as arbitrator.

**Eric M. Runesson** is Justice of the Swedish Supreme Court, LLD, FCIArb, former member of the Swedish Bar Association.

**Matthew Saunders** is a partner in the London office of Ashurst and leads the firm's global international arbitration practice. His practice focuses upon disputes in the energy sector, particularly gas and renewables, both contract and investment treaty based. Before arriving at Ashurst in 2016 he led teams acting for Gazprom in its various Stockholm-seated disputes arising from sale and transit of gas involving Ukraine. Other significant recent matters include acting for Australian LNG exporters in reportedly the largest gas dispute involving Australian parties and for a Spanish operator of a liquefaction plant in Egypt in one of the longest running supply disputes involving Egypt.

**Sarah Schæffer** is Associate at Plesner (Copenhagen) in the firm's dispute resolution practice group and board member of Young Arbitrators Copenhagen.

**Eva Storskrubb** is a Dispute Resolution Counsel at Roschier Attorneys Ltd. as well as Associate Professor (docent) in Procedural Law and researcher at Uppsala University, Sweden. She has extensive experience of international arbitration proceedings and complex cross-border litigation matters. Storskrubb is also an internationally recognized specialist in EU procedural law. Her research focuses on the impact of EU law on civil justice and commercial dispute resolution including arbitration.

**Patrick Taylor** is a partner in the London and Paris offices of Debevoise & Plimpton LLP. His practice focuses on commercial and investment treaty arbitration, both as counsel and arbitrator. Mr Taylor's practice is geared towards advising clients in the most high-stakes, complex and valuable disputes, and he has developed particular experience in advising on investment protection and investment disputes in emerging markets, the enforcement of fiscal and legislative stabilization clauses, production sharing and shareholder/joint venture disputes, post-M&A disputes, and complex damages analysis. He regularly represents clients in arbitrations seated in Sweden.

**Laura Tuure** is Associate at Krogerus Attorneys Ltd's (Helsinki) dispute resolution practice.

# Contributions to the Yearbook

The editors will be happy to receive contributions at any time. Contributions may be in the form of completed articles or abstracts of 700 words maximum. They will then go through the normal selection and editing process.

For inclusion in the next yearbook, abstracts will usually have to be submitted by early December of the preceding year. Articles – whether or not developed abstracts – usually have to be finished by the authors at the end of March, the year of publication.

A contribution, together with the author's CV, should be submitted to: patrik.scholdstrom@gmail.com and bruno.gustafsson@roschier.com

# Summary of Contents

# Table of Contents

# Preface

Welcome to the second edition of the Stockholm Arbitration Yearbook!

You will find articles on arbitration law in general and Swedish arbitration law in particular. Some contributions are by senior and well-known authors, and others by more junior ones.

We are happy to receive – at any time of the year – proposals for future contributions in the form of a short abstract.

*Axel Calissendorff*
*Patrik Schöldström*

CHAPTER 1

# Swedish Arbitration-Related Case Law 2019–2020

*Christer Danielsson*

## §1.01 INTRODUCTION

This chapter will account for court cases relevant to arbitration law from Swedish appellate courts for the period 1 May 2019–30 April 2020.[1] It does not purport to be exhaustive; the aim is to highlight cases that can be assumed to be of interest to a non-Swedish reader.

## §1.02 BACKGROUND

The Swedish Arbitration Act of 1999[2] (the 'Act') applies to all arbitration proceedings seated in Sweden, whether the parties have any connection to Sweden or not.[3] The Act also sets out the requirements for foreign arbitral awards to be recognized and enforced in Sweden.[4]

Sweden has a three-tier court system: district courts, six regional appellate courts and the Supreme Court. However, district courts are only rarely involved in arbitration cases since the Court of Appeal is the Court of First Instance for invalidity and set-aside cases as well as for enforcement cases.

A Swedish arbitral award can be *declared invalid* if it determines an issue which under Swedish law cannot be decided by arbitrators, or if the award, or the manner in

1. The Supreme Court has not decided any arbitration related cases in the period covered herein.
2. Lagen (1999:116) om skiljeförfarande.
3. The Act, section 46.
4. The Act, sections 52 et seq.

which it came about, is clearly incompatible with the basic principles of the Swedish legal system, i.e., ordre public.[5]

An arbitral award can be *set aside* at the request of a party *inter alia* when the arbitrators have exceeded their mandate and when, without fault of the party, an irregularity has occurred in the course of the proceedings which probably influenced the outcome of the case.[6]

An action to invalidate or set aside an arbitration award shall be considered by the Court of Appeal within whose district the arbitral proceedings were seated.[7] The Court of Appeal's permission is required in order to appeal its judgment.[8] Such leave to appeal is denied in the large majority of cases. For the case to be tried by the Supreme Court, leave is also required from that court.[9]

Historically, invalidity and set-aside actions have very rarely been successful. A statistical survey for the period 1 January 2004–31 May 2014 shows that seven arbitral awards were set aside pursuant to section 34 of the Act while one award was declared invalid pursuant to section 33 of the Act.[10] In the period covered by this chapter, no award was declared invalid or set aside.

## §1.03 *REPUBLIC OF POLAND V. PL HOLDINGS S.A.R.L.*

As reported in the 2019 Stockholm Arbitration Yearbook,[11] the Svea Court of Appeal in February 2019 rendered a judgment in a case similar to *Achmea,*[12] *the Republic of Poland v. PL Holdings S.a.r.l.* ('PL Holdings').[13] The Court of Appeals' judgment was appealed to the Supreme Court. The Supreme Court granted leave. On 4 February 2020, the Supreme Court decided to request a preliminary ruling from the Court of Justice of the European Union (CJEU).

In summary (for further detail, *see* the 2019 Stockholm Arbitration Yearbook) the facts are the following.

In 1987, Poland, on the one hand, and Luxembourg and Belgium, on the other hand, entered into an investment treaty (the 'Investment Treaty') with a dispute resolution clause (section 9) pursuant to which investors in any of the states party to

5. The Act, section 33. In addition, under this provision an award is invalid if it does not fulfil the Act's requirements with regard to written form and signature.
6. The Act, section 34(1), items 3 and 7. Section 34 provides for five other grounds for setting aside an arbitral award but the two mentioned are those most frequently invoked in set aside proceedings.
7. The Act, section 43(1). The large majority of invalidity and set aside proceedings are brought before the Svea Court of Appeal. The reason for this is that most Swedish arbitrations are seated in Stockholm.
8. The Act, section 43(2), which provides that leave to appeal shall be granted 'where it is of importance, as a matter of precedent, that the appeal be considered by the Supreme Court'.
9. The Act, section 43(2). Such requirement was introduced in an amendment to the Act which entered into force on 1 Mar. 2019.
10. Översyn av lagen om skiljeförfarande ('Review of the arbitration act'), SOU 2015:37, p. 81.
11. Stockholm Arbitration Yearbook 2019, pp. 9 et seq.
12. Judgment by the European Court of Justice of 6 Mar. 2018, *Slovak Republic v. Achmea BV*, Case No. C-284/16.
13. Judgment by the Svea Court of Appeal dated 22 Feb. 2019 in Case Nos T 8538-17 and T 12033-7.

the treaty have the right to initiate arbitration proceedings in accordance with three different options, one of which is the Arbitration Rules of the Arbitration Institute of the Stockholm Chamber of Commerce (SCC Rules). Thus, the Investment Treaty is an intra-EU (European Union) bilateral investment treaty.

PL Holdings, a company registered in Luxembourg, initiated arbitration proceedings against Poland in accordance with the SCC Rules with Stockholm as the seat of arbitration. This was prior to the CJEU's judgment in *Achmea*. PL Holdings submitted that Poland had violated its obligations under the Investment Treaty by expropriating assets of PL Holding in Poland. PL Holdings claimed damages from Poland.

In June 2017, the arbitration tribunal rendered a partial arbitral award in which it found that Poland had violated its obligations under the Investment Treaty by expropriating PL Holdings' shareholding in a bank and that PL Holdings was entitled to damages. In the final award in September 2017, the arbitration tribunal ordered Poland to pay substantial damages (approx. EUR 150 million).

Poland filed actions with the Svea Court of Appeal with regard to both the partial award and the final award. Poland requested that the awards be declared invalid (section 33 of the Act) or be set aside (section 34 of the Act) in light of *Achmea*. With regard to the set-aside claim, Poland submitted that the awards should be set aside since they were not based on a valid arbitration agreement.

The Court of Appeal made the following statement with regard to the meaning of *Achmea*:

> The conclusion from the Achmea ruling is therefore that articles 267 and 344 TFEU[14] would not as such preclude Poland and PL Holdings from entering into an arbitration agreement and participating in arbitral proceedings regarding an investment-related dispute. What the TFEU precludes is that Member States conclude agreements with each other meaning that one Member State is obligated to accept subsequent arbitral proceeding with an investor and that the Member States thereby establish a system where they have excluded disputes from the possibility of requesting a preliminary ruling, even though the disputes may involve interpretation and application of EU law. Since the TFEU thus does not preclude arbitration agreements between a Member State and an investor in a particular case, a Member State is, based on party autonomy, free – even though the Member State is not bound by a standing offer as such as that in article 8 of the Achmea case or article 9 in this case – to enter into an arbitration agreement with an investor regarding the same dispute at a later stage, e.g. when the investor has initiated arbitral proceedings. An arbitration agreement and arbitral proceedings between, on the one hand, an investor from a Member State and, on the other hand, a Member State, is therefore as such not in violation of the TFEU.

The Court of Appeal found that the awards should not be declared invalid pursuant to section 33 of the Act.

With regard to setting aside of the awards pursuant to section 34 of the Act, PL Holdings *inter alia* argued that Poland was precluded from invoking that the arbitral awards were not covered by a valid arbitration agreement since Poland had participated in the arbitral proceedings without raising this objection. Under the applicable

14. The Treaty on the Functioning of the European Union.

rules for the proceedings, PL Holdings argued that Poland was obligated to raise an objection concerning the alleged invalidity of the arbitration agreement no later than in its statement of defence, which Poland did not do.

The Court of Appeal found that pursuant to the applicable SCC Rules the objection should have been made no later than in the statement of defence. Since it was not made until in the statement of rejoinder the court concluded, with reference to section 34(2) of the Act, that Poland must be considered to have waived its right to raise the objection.

As noted, the Supreme Court has now requested a preliminary ruling from the CJEU. In its decision the Supreme Court stated the following under the heading 'The need for a preliminary ruling':[15]

> The question is what the implications of the principles elaborated by the CJEU in *Achmea* have for the outcome of the case before the Supreme Court.
>
> It is clear that the provision regarding dispute resolution in the investment agreement of relevance in this case before the Supreme Court is invalid. Thus, a possible conclusion is that the standing offer to initiate arbitration proceedings, which the state can be said to have extended to an investor through the dispute resolution provision, is also invalid, considering that the offer is closely linked to the investment agreement.
>
> In the case before the Supreme Court, it has also been argued that the situation is different in this case since it is the request for arbitration that constitutes an offer. The state would then, as a result of its freely expressed wishes, expressly or tacitly, be able to accept the jurisdiction of the arbitral tribunal, in accordance with the principles explained by the CJEU with regard to commercial arbitration.
>
> The Supreme Court does not consider it to be clear, or clarified, how EU law shall be interpreted with regard to the issues that arise in this case. Therefore, there are reasons for requesting a preliminary ruling from the CJEU in order to avoid the risk of an incorrect interpretation of EU law.

The Supreme Court formulated the question to the CJEU as follows:

> Do Articles 267 and 344 TFEU, as interpreted in *Achmea*, mean that an arbitration agreement is invalid if it has been entered into by a member state and an investor – when there is an arbitration clause in an investment treaty which is invalid because the treaty was entered into by two member states – when the member State, after the investor having requested arbitration, as a result of the state's free will refrain from objecting to jurisdiction?

## §1.04 *PUBLIC JOINT STOCK COMPANY GAZPROM V. NATIONAL JOINT STOCK COMPANY NAFTOGAZ OF UKRAINE*

An SCC arbitration tribunal seated in Stockholm issued three awards in 2017 and 2018 relating to disputes over long-term gas supply and transit contracts entered into in 2009 between Gazprom and Naftogaz, an oil and gas company wholly owned by the state of

15. Decision by the Supreme Court 21 Feb. 2020 in Case No. 1568-19.

Ukraine. The value in dispute was in excess of USD 100 billion, making it the largest known commercial arbitration ever.

Gazprom applied to the Svea Court of Appeal to set aside all three awards.

In November 2019, the Court of Appeal rendered judgment in relation to the claim to set aside one of these, a separate award in the supply dispute.[16] Gazprom argued that the tribunal had committed several errors that qualified as excess of mandate or as an irregularity in the course of the proceedings which probably influenced the outcome of the case. The alleged errors were that the tribunal had exceeded the framework of the dispute as laid down by the parties, that the tribunal had failed to inform the parties that it intended to go down a certain path in the interim award, and that the tribunal's reasons for its findings were incomplete. The Court of Appeal found that there was no merit to any of the allegations made by Gazprom and rejected the challenge.

At the time of the Court of Appeals' judgment the two other challenges (against the final award in the supply dispute and the final award in the transit dispute) were pending. With regard to the award in the transit dispute Gazprom *inter alia* alleged that a substantial part of the tribunal's reasons had been drafted by its administrative secretary.

However, neither this nor any other allegation made by Gazprom in the two pending challenges were examined by the Court of Appeal since Gazprom and Naftogaz in December 2019 entered into a comprehensive settlement covering these and other disputes between the parties.

## §1.05 *REPUBLIC OF LITHUANIA V. OAO GAZPROM*

AB Lietuvos Dujos is a Lithuanian gas company that originally was wholly owned by the Republic of Lithuania. In the 1990s the company was partially privatized when E.ON bought part of the shares. In a second stage of privatization, Gazprom bought into the company in 2004. In connection therewith Lithuania and Gazprom entered into a Share Sale and Purchase Agreement (SPA). Together with E.ON, Gazprom and Lithuania also concluded a Shareholders Agreement (SHA). Also, Gazprom and AB Lietuvos Dujos were parties to a Gas Supply Agreement (GSA) since 1999.

The purpose of the SPA was to govern Lithuania's sale of shares to Gazprom. However, some provisions in the SPA were aimed at Gazprom's existing obligation to deliver gas to AB Lietuvos Dujos, including a provision (Article 7.4.1) pursuant to which Gazprom for a ten-year period undertook to deliver gas at reasonable prices. The GSA was amended accordingly.

In 2012, Lithuania requested arbitration under the SCC Rules against Gazprom, referring both to the SPA and the SHA. According to the claimant, Gazprom had abused its double roles as both shareholder and supplier and had delivered gas to AB Lietuvos Dujos at prices which were not reasonable. Lithuania sought both monetary and declaratory relief. In 2016 the arbitral tribunal rejected the claims.

16. Judgment by the Svea Court of Appeal dated 27 Nov. 2019 in Case No. T 10191-17.

Lithuania initiated proceedings before the Svea Court of Appeal to have the arbitral award declared invalid or set aside. All claims were rejected in a judgment in 2019.[17]

Several grounds for setting aside the award were invoked by Lithuania. Here, focus will be on the claim that the award should be declared invalid pursuant to section 33 of the Act.

According to Lithuania, the tribunal had an obligation to take into account what constitutes a reasonable price under EU competition law when assessing the pricing under Article 7.4.1 of the SPA. The tribunal did not do so. Moreover, as a separate ground for invalidity Lithuania argued that the consequence of the tribunal's failure to take EU competition law into account was that the award upheld gas prices that violated EU competition law. For these reasons, the award and the manner in which it came about was clearly incompatible with the basic principles of the Swedish legal system, i.e., in violation of ordre public.

Gazprom's primary objection was that the dispute before the tribunal was of no competition law relevance which according to Gazprom meant that the arbitrators were under no obligation to take into account EU competition law.

In order to determine if the arbitrated dispute was of relevance from a competition law perspective the Court of Appeal analysed the requests for relief sought by Lithuania and the grounds invoked in support thereof. The Court of Appeal concluded that none of the reliefs sought was aimed at imposing or upholding any violation of competition law. Instead, the requests for relief concerned compensation due to Gazprom having violated the SPA and the SHA, and declaratory relief that Gazprom had violated such agreements.

The Court of Appeal noted that it was common ground between the parties that Lithuania in the arbitration proceedings had not, as an independent ground, invoked that the SPA and the SHA violated EU competition law. Moreover, it had not been demonstrated, the Court of Appeal found that Lithuania had based its claims on circumstances that made the dispute competition law relevant.

The Court of Appeal concluded that the dispute before the tribunal had been purely contractual in nature which meant that the tribunal, having jurisdiction under section 1(1) of the Act,[18] was under no obligation to take into account what constituted a reasonable price according to EU competition law, as alleged by Gazprom. Nor, added the Court of Appeal, did the award uphold gas prices that violated EU competition law or were otherwise in conflict with such rules.

Consequently, there was no violation of ordre public, and since Lithuania also failed with respect to its set-aside motions the arbitral award was upheld.

The Court of Appeal gave permission to appeal its judgment to the Supreme Court. As noted above, this is rare. The Republic appealed, but the Supreme Court did not grant leave.

17. Judgment by the Svea Court of Appeal on 4 Jul. 2019 in Case No. T 7931-16.
18. 'Disputes concerning matters in respect of which the parties may reach a settlement may, by agreement, be referred to one or several arbitrators for resolution'.

## §1.06 *CORALINE LIMITED V. WALTER HÖFT*

In a 2015 SCC award Cypriot company Coraline had been ordered to pay EUR 9.2 million to Walter Höft, a German national. In the arbitration, Mr Höft's case was that he had personally lent more than EUR 12 million to Coraline under a loan agreement and was now requesting repayment.

Coraline initiated proceedings before the Svea Court of Appeal in 2017. In such proceedings Coraline requested that the 2015 award be set aside on three separate grounds, only one of which will be discussed here. The Court of Appeal rendered its judgment in December 2019, rejecting all grounds for appeal and thus upholding the arbitral award.[19] Leave to appeal to the Supreme Court was not given by the Court of Appeal.

The loan agreement under which Coraline was ordered to repay Walter Höft contained two dispute resolution clauses.

Article 9: 'This agreement shall be governed by and interpreted in accordance with the laws of Cyprus and the parties hereby agree that all actions or proceedings arising hereunder, or in connection with this agreement shall be brought in first instance before the competent court in Nicosia, Cyprus.'

Article 6: 'All disputes and differences which may arise out of the present Agreement or in connection with the same are to bet settled by the parties in an amicable way to the maximum possible extent. Should the parties fail to reach an agreement a case shall be submitted, without recourse to courts of law, to the International arbitration court in Stockholm with the rules for procedure of the said court.'

Before the Court of Appeal Coraline argued that the tribunal had lacked jurisdiction to hear the case since the parties had agreed on the exclusive competence of a Cypriotic court and since there was no agreement between the parties which unambiguously stated that they had decided to settle disputes by way of arbitration instead of in court. According to Coraline, this issue should be decided by application of Cypriotic law, alternatively by Swedish law. Since there was no valid arbitration agreement under either law the 2015 award should be set aside.

Walter Höft argued that the validity of the arbitration clause should be assessed under Swedish law. According to him, at the time of entering into the loan agreement the parties had the joint will that disputes should be resolved by arbitration, and under Swedish law the joint will take precedence even over the wording of the agreement.

The Court of Appeal started by referring to a statement made by the Supreme Court in the well-known 2019 *Belgor* case[20] according to which courts in set-aside proceedings, when assessing jurisdiction, shall take into account that the tribunal typically is best suited to determine jurisdiction. For this reason, as explained by the Supreme Court, the starting point for a court in set-aside proceedings shall be that the arbitration tribunal's interpretation and assessment of evidence are correct.

19. Judgment by the Svea Court of Appeal on 19 Dec. 2019 in Case No. T 7929-17.
20. Judgment by the Supreme Court 20 Mar. 2019 in Case No. T 5437-17, *see* the 2019 Stockholm Arbitration Yearbook, pp. 2 et seq.

With regard to applicable law to the arbitration agreement, the arbitration tribunal had found that Swedish law applied and that Article 6 of the loan agreement constituted a valid arbitration agreement.

The Court of Appeal started its assessment by noting that the arbitration agreement constituted an agreement separate from the main agreement (as provided in section 3 of the Act).

The Court of Appeal went on to note that if parties have not made a choice of the law applicable to the arbitration agreement section 48 of the Act provides that the law at the seat shall apply. The choice of the parties must explicitly point to the arbitration agreement - a general choice of law clause is not enough.

The Court of Appeal found that the only provision in the loan agreement which contained any choice of law element was Article 9. However, the Court of Appeal concluded that the reference to Cypriotic law in this provision does not specifically aim at the choice of law for the arbitration agreement. Instead, as drafted section 9 indicates that it refers to the choice of law for the main agreement. Therefore, there is no provision in the loan agreement which specifically deals with the choice of law for the arbitration agreement. Accordingly, Swedish law shall apply as provided in section 48 of the Act.

In the Court of Appeal's opinion Article 6 of the loan agreement contained what, under Swedish law, must be deemed to be an arbitration agreement. The Court of Appeal acknowledged that Article 9 contains a different dispute resolution clause, pointing to a court in Cyprus. 'However', the Court of Appeal stated, 'the content of Article 9 gives no guidance with regard to the interpretation of the arbitration clause in Article 6'.

The loan agreement had been signed by Walter Höft and by Elpida Papastylianou for Coraline, both testified in the set-aside proceedings. Ms Papastylianou stated that she had inserted an arbitration clause in the agreement because Mr Höft wanted disputes to be settled by arbitration. Both Ms Papastylianou and Mr Höft further testified that Article 9 remained in the loan agreement because of an oversight.

The Court of Appeal concluded, taking all circumstances into account, that it had been demonstrated that the parties had a joint will to settle disputes by way of arbitration and that they had entered into an arbitration agreement which did not contain any specific limitations.

## §1.07 *REPUBLIC OF KAZAKHSTAN V. ASCOM GROUP S.A. ET AL*

In 2013, an SCC tribunal issued an award in a dispute between, on the one hand, the Republic of Kazakhstan and, on the other hand, the Moldovan company Ascom Group, investors Anatolie and Gabriel Stati, and a Gibraltar registered company. Shortly thereafter, Kazakhstan initiated proceedings before the Svea Court of Appeal to have the arbitral award declared invalid or set aside. Kazakhstan claimed, as concerning invalidity, that the award and the manner in which came about was incompatible with basic principles of the Swedish legal system (section 33(1) item 2 of the Act). In a judgment in 2016 the Court of Appeal rejected Kazakhstan's claims.

In 2019 Kazakhstan again filed suit with the Svea Court of Appeal, claiming that the 2013 arbitral award be declared invalid. Reference was again made to ordre public but now also to the provision according to which an award is invalid if it includes determination of an issue which, under Swedish law, may not be decided by arbitrators (section 33(1), item 1 of the Act).

By decision of 9 March 2020, the Court of Appeal dismissed Kazakhstan's case, finding that its earlier judgment had res judicata effect.[21]

The Court of Appeal stated that it is the relief sought which determines the res judicata effect of a previous judgment. This is a general rule in Swedish procedural law and, the Court of Appeal argued, there is no reason to take a different approach when it comes to a claim to invalidate an arbitral award. On the contrary, the fact that such claim can be brought without any time limit calls for a strict application of the res judicata principle.

The Court of Appeal noted that Kazakhstan in both actions before the court sought invalidity, that both actions concerned the same arbitral award and that the parties were identical. On the basis of this the Court of Appeal concluded that the 2019 action shall be dismissed for res judicata.

21. Decision by the Svea Court of Appeal on 9 Mar. 2020 in Case No. T 12462-19.

CHAPTER 2

# ISDA and ADR: A Brief History of a Long Relationship

*Jeffrey Golden*[*]

ISDA[1] has been an effective proponent of, and exercised thought leadership regarding, alternative dispute resolution (ADR) for more than three and a half decades – since the formation (actually before that) of ISDA itself.

That may surprise many. When ISDA first published its Arbitration Guide in 2013, it was said to offer a window on a potential change in thinking; an *alternative* to the more traditional preference in the financial markets for court determination of party disputes.[2]

* The author gratefully acknowledges the assistance of Hannah Fry, LLB, LLM, a barrister at 3 Hare Court Chambers, in preparing this chapter for publication.

1. The International Swaps and Derivatives Association, Inc. (and until 1993 the International Swap Dealers Association, Inc.). ISDA was founded in 1985 by a group of commercial, investment and merchant banks for the purpose of standardising contracts and contractual language for OTC derivatives.
2. ISDA, *2013 ISDA Arbitration Guide* (9 September 2013), http://www2.isda.org/functional-areas/public-policy/financial-law-reform/, at 2.2. 'Historically, international financial transactions have tended to be documented under agreements governed by English or New York law and which contain jurisdiction clauses conferring jurisdiction on the English or New York courts.' For more background on this Guide, *see also* Jeffrey Golden and Peter Werner, *The Modern Role of Arbitration in Banking and Finance*, in Golden and Lamm (eds.), *International Financial Disputes: Arbitration and Mediation* (Oxford University Press, 2015).

   The Guide, when it first appeared in 2013, captured a lot of attention. *See*, e.g., client bulletins such as Slaughter and May, https://www.slaughterandmay.com/what-we-do/publications-and-seminars/publications/client-publications-and-articles/i/isda-arbitration-the-final-lap/; Clifford Chance, https://www.cliffordchance.com/content/dam/cliffordchance/briefings/2013/09/arbitration-in-swaps-and-derivatives-new-guidance-from-isda-17-september-2013.pdf; Allen & Overy, https://www.allenovery.com/en-gb/global/news-and-insights/european-finance-litigation-review/eu-developments/idsa-drafts-model-arbitration-clauses-for-use-with-master-agreements. Much of that commentary viewed the Guide as offering a possible

But in fact, ISDA and its documentation represent a long effort by the derivatives markets to minimize the role of courts,[3] at least for any disputes related to the terms or operation of the parties' agreement itself[4] – certainty, speedily delivered, often being preferred even, at least in the abstract, over justice.[5]

Why did this embrace of ADR go unnoticed for so long? For years, relatively few derivatives market disputes were reported. And those that did arise tended to relate to matters outside the contract, which did not trigger the ADR mechanisms in it. For example, in *Hazell v. Hammersmith and Fulham London Borough Council*, one of the more significant early decisions that came before the UK House of Lords, the case was not so much a dispute about how the parties' swap agreements should be interpreted or the measure of any payment under them but rather whether the swaps were beyond the legal capacity of a local authority such that their swap agreements were unenforceable and any transactions contemplated by them were *void ab initio.*[6]

That changed with the global financial crisis that began in 2008, and particularly the Lehman litigation (with the considerable focus on interpretation of contractual damages provisions) that flowed from it.[7] And there can be little doubt that a growing interest in arbitration throughout the ISDA world in the early part of the last decade was a reaction to the cost and expense of the cases arising from that crisis.

change in direction. *See*, e.g., Latham & Watkins, https://www.lw.com/thoughtLeadership/lw-ISDA-Arbitration-Guide-2013 ('Whereas financial institutions historically took a more conservative approach – clearly preferring litigation in state courts over arbitration – the introduction of the optional arbitration clauses represents yet another milestone showcasing that the financial industry is discovering arbitration as an alternative to litigation.'); IFLR.com, https://www.iflr.com/Article/3437078/Rise-of-alternative-OTC-dispute-venues.html ('Traditionally litigation has been the preferred form of dispute resolution in international finance.')

The popularity of the 2013 ISDA Arbitration Guide incentivized ISDA to publish a second, expanded version in 2018. *2018 ISDA Arbitration Guide*, https://www.isda.org/a/5kDME/ISDA-2018-Arbitration-Guide.pdf.

3. *For example,* through binding party self-determinations (contractual privilege), the role of the calculation and valuation agents (especially as mediators 'after consultation') and screen and published pricing sources (that often fall back to reference banks to resolve pricing issues). *See* discussion at *infra* nn. 24–26 and accompanying text.
4. In fact, the earliest court cases raised issues outside of the parties' contractual terms, relating to formation, contract validity, party relationships and taxation. The markets were comfortable referring issues of this kind to the courts. The greater concern related to disputes about the interpretation of language within the contract.
5. *See* discussion at *infra* n. 23 and accompanying text.
6. *Hazell v. Hammersmith and Fulham London Borough Council* [1992] 2 A.C. 1. There has been an evolution in the kinds of cases that we see coming to the courts. As reported in *supra* n. 4, the earliest cases raised issues that judges were often familiar with from other cases: e.g., authority, capacity, duty of care, contract formation. These cases continue. However, more recently the battle has focused on language within the contract itself and its application, often a very highly technical and scientific business, to market practices (which in turn have varied over time): e.g., valuation, formulaic calculations, assessment of 'commercial reasonableness' of operations/procedures in the markets or subsets of them.
7. A research project conducted by Dr Joanne Braithwaite at the London School of Economics and Political Science confirmed that a total of seventy-eight decisions involving ISDA documentation were handed down by the English courts alone during the period 1 January 1993 to 5 August 2011 but of these 60% occurred between 2009 and 2011. Joanne P. Braithwaite, *Derivatives, the Courts and Regulatory Reform*, Capital Markets Law Journal 7(4) (2012), 1–22, available at: http://cmlj.oxfordjournals.org/content/early/2012/09/21/cmlj.kms033.full?keytype=ref&ijkey=uwjPs64CzTOXiza.

Around this time interest increased as well in specialist financial courts and the need for more training in finance for judges – the markets just could not wait many years for answers, as they had done with much of the Lehman court litigation.

## §2.01 AN EARLY COURTSHIP: DEVELOPMENT OF THE CONCEPT OF 'AGREEMENT VALUE'

Little appreciated though it may be, the fact is that from the start (or before the start, depending upon from when you count) the early architects of the derivatives marketplace who became the founders of ISDA hoped to achieve a scheme of things that would, as best possible, keep things out of courts. The aim was to look instead to the markets themselves, and to market participants, for market-sensitive answers to matters of potential or actual disputes, particularly where the answers would directly impact market behaviours and practice.

One particular ambition, at least in the pre-ISDA dollar interest rate market, was to avoid the time and expense of having to *prove* damages. But how, for example, to keep any measure of a claim for post-default damages from being capable of being second-guessed by a court? The answer was thought to be to pre-empt the court by having the parties agree *at the time of contracting* and as a 'pre-estimate' on the approach as to just how any such damages following default would best be calculated or, in other words, to insert a 'liquidated damages' provision.

When it first appeared in the mid-1980s, ISDA documentation began not as a master agreement or a contract but rather as a 'code': publication of standard wording for terms and definitions that the parties could incorporate, in whole or in part, in their own individual agreements.[8]

An article[9] based on interviews with a working group of the founders of ISDA (but before ISDA's incorporation) that produced the code gives insights into this search for an alternative to more traditional methods of determining what one party owes the other on the premature termination of a swap.

Coming into those meetings, the small group of financial institutions in the room had taken a variety of approaches in their bespoke institutional documentation, and achieving a consensus as to the best way forward was going to be difficult without offering a menu approach. Where the article noted agreement could found was in the concept of a formula for liquidating damages. If such a formula could be achieved, it was thought to be preferable to general damages or indemnification provisions – the

8. ISDA was formed and first published documentation in 1985. Called the Code of Standard Wording, Assumptions and Provisions for Swaps (the '1985 Code of Swaps'), that publication was a collection of terms and provisions that functioned more like a dictionary and was intended to 'establish a uniform vocabulary for dollar rate swaps'. 1985 Code of Swaps at iv. Following the positive reception of the 1985 Code of Swaps, ISDA published a second expanded version in 1986 (the '1986 Code of Swaps' and, together with the 1985 Code of Swaps, the 'Codes'), which 'addresse[d] a number of subjects on which the 1985 Edition was silent'. 1986 Code of Swaps at v.
9. Christopher Stoakes, *Standardising Swaps Documentation*, International Financial Law Review IV(3) March 1985) at 11–15.

problem with such provisions being that 'they may have to be proved [in court], which can be expensive and time-consuming'.[10]

One idea that attracted particular interest and attention in the group was a somewhat innovative approach for *market*-determined liquidated damages, being championed by First Boston and Salomon Brothers, called 'agreement value'. As Thomas Jasper, the then Vice President at Salomon Brothers who went on to become the first Chairman of ISDA, explained: 'You find the cost of cover by calling certain dealers in the interest-exchange market to find the price for a buyer or seller swap.'[11] And as another banker also quoted in the article confirmed, 'You terminate the transaction and get quotes from leading swaps participants to assume the rights and obligations of the defaulting party.'[12]

The result of such discussions, as reported from that working group and introduced by ISDA in its codes, was what became the defined concept of 'Agreement Value'.[13] It was based on third-party resolution of the post-default damages issue but was initially thought, for reasons of wider market illiquidity, to have limited relevance beyond the universe of straightforward 'plain vanilla' dollar interest rate swaps.[14] However, as markets for other derivatives products grew over time, so too grew a wider interest in this approach.

As a result, though perhaps underappreciated as an ADR mechanism, Agreement Value put down a marker thirty-five years ago for the relevance of non-judicial, third-party determinations in fixing post-default damages. Reliance in this way on

10. *Id.* at 12.
11. *Id.*
12. *Id.*
13. '*Measure of Damages.* For purposes of determining the amount payable on an Early Termination Date:

    "Agreement Value" means that on the Early Termination Date, if there is a Defaulting Party ... that party will be obligated to make a payment to the other party in the amount, if any, by which the 'Market Quotation determined by the other party exceeds zero ... .

    "Market Quotation" means ... an amount determined on the basis of quotations from Reference Market-makers ... .'

    Sections 12.1 and 12.2 of the 1986 Code of SWAPS.
14. Other issues that the working group had grappled with related to ensuring the quality and validity of the quotations to be relied upon and next steps in the absence on a relevant day of the quotations sought; in other words, according to Patrick de Saint-Aignan of Morgan Stanley (and later ISDA's first Vice Chairman): 'Who should be quoting and on what basis; can you shop the market to your advantage; and what is the fallback if there is no market?' *Id.* at 13. Another 'formula' for liquidated damages, which was to become the fallback in the Codes for occasions when requested quotations were not forthcoming, was based on replacement or redeployment costs by reference to (i) the actual borrowing costs the non-defaulting party would incur to put in place an alternative asset that would produce the lost (fixed or floating) income stream and (ii) a discounting of the expected replacement payments based on a pre-agreed source for a suitable discount rate. However, the working group realised that the enforceability of these formula approaches to liquidated damages was untested in court, especially in a bankruptcy context when default was likely and the formula might matter most. In due course this would send ISDA on a world bankruptcy law tour seeking legal opinions, and where necessary law reform, in support of the enforcement of its close-out mechanics. Court support for the enforcement of ISDA's market-determined liquidated damages was also forthcoming. *See*, e.g., *Drexel Burnham Lambert Products Corp. v. Midland Bank PLX*, 1992 U.S. Dist. LEXIS 21223 (S.D.N.Y.); *BNP Paribas v. Wockhardt EU Operations (Swiss) AG*, [2009] EWHC 3116 (Comm); *Videocon Global Ltd. v. Goldman Sachs International*, [2016] EWCA Civ. 130.

leading market makers with a long-term interest in the credibility and commercial attractiveness of the marketplace itself increased the likelihood of practical and acceptable results on technical issues.

And it proved to be only the beginning of a commitment by ISDA members and the derivatives markets generally to explore alternatives to courts for resolving market disputes or matters with the potential of becoming disputes (and often of sizeable proportion because of the multiplicity of market participants trading on the basis of the same standard terms) in an expeditious, commercial and cost-efficient way.

## §2.02 ENGAGEMENT AND MARRIAGE: THE ISDA MASTER AGREEMENTS

Following the publication of the Codes, ISDA turned its attention to other projects, including 'the development of standard documentation for currency swap transactions and suggested standard form agreements and confirmation telexes for various types of rate swap and currency swap transactions'.[15] In 1987, these projects culminated in the publication of two standard forms, entitled 'Interest Rate Swap Agreement' and 'Interest Rate and Currency Exchange Agreement' (collectively, the '1987 Forms'). These 'master agreements' have been revised and re-published twice since then: in 1992 (the '1992 Forms') and in a single consolidated form in 2002 (the '2002 Form' and sometimes referred to in this chapter collectively with the 1987 Forms and the 1992 Forms as the 'ISDA Master').[16]

15. 1986 Code of Swaps at v.
16. The ISDA Master is widely used as an industry standard and receives considerable attention in all leading treatises on law and practice in the derivatives markets. It has also been reported on and analysed in numerous articles, and increasingly it is the subject of graduate study and thesis writing. ISDA publishes user guidance for its forms in multiple languages. Schuyler K. Henderson, *Henderson on Derivatives* (2d ed., LexisNexis 2010) at 803 concludes that '[t]he ISDA master is perhaps the most successful financial form document ever, anywhere'. The author goes on to write: 'There cannot be any other standard document which governs as many transactions, with as much credit exposure among as many different parties with such beneficial results. This did not happen by chance.' *Id.* Hannes Schneider, former senior partner at the German law firm Hengeler Mueller, expresses, from a civil code perspective, the view that 'ISDA's master agreements have been widely accepted and used throughout the world. What has been accomplished may be described as no less than the creation of a global law by contractual consensus.' Daniel P. Cunningham & Craig T. Abruzzo, *Multibranch Netting – A Solution to the Problem of Cross-Border Bank Insolvencies 1* (International Bar Association 1995). And from the United States, Professors Choi and Gulati argue that '[e]ven in the absence of an ideal legislative body capable of incorporating the interests of all relevant industry participants for any given decision, sophisticated contracting parties may find close alternatives. ISDA, for example, provides a close approximation in the swaps and derivatives markets'. Stephen J. Choi & G. Mitu Gulati, *Contract As Statute*, Michigan Law Review 104 (2006), 1129, 1162. The ISDA Master Agreement's status as the industry standard has also been widely recognized by both domestic and foreign courts.

Whereas the Codes had provided standardized provisions and terminology that could be incorporated into bespoke contracts, each of the 1987 Forms offered derivatives counterparties standardized, off-the-shelf contracts that were intended to further 'simplify and accelerate the process of documenting swaps'.[17]

The concept of Agreement Value in the Codes had included the term 'Market Quotation', which described in largest measure the methodology for referring the question of termination damages to third-party dealers for determination. Market Quotation replaced Agreement Value as the term of art in both the 1987 Forms and the 1992 Forms and moved from being a choice on the menu to a preferred way of dealing – a 'default' mechanism which was presumed applicable absent the express election of the parties for it not to be. The idea of resolving what might otherwise have been disputed valuations in this way had clearly taken root in the markets at the time and so had the interest in characterizing, and achieving the status for, this approach as 'liquidated damages'.

As with its antecedent Agreement Value, Market Quotation reflects a desire to establish, at the time the parties enter into their agreement, a liquidated damages *formula* (i.e., as a reasonable pre-estimate of a methodology for later calculating losses) predicated on a payment measure determined to resolve valuations that might otherwise give rise to disputes – not by referral of these to a court for resolution on this basis, but rather on the basis of an averaging of quotations for replacement transactions from leading dealers. In other words, this is ADR by party agreement and in reliance on ADR by reference market makers.

There are certain mechanical aspects to the Market Quotation measure that must be followed, but the Market Quotation arrived at is intended to be a final and binding expert determination. And whereas a judge rendering such a determination of quantum might be expected to set out in his or her judgment the basis for such a determination, there is, for example, nothing in the Market Quotation contractual language that requires a dealer making its third-party valuation as a reference market maker to base its quote on any particular source or sources of information or data, or indeed to give an explanation of or justification for how its decision was reached.

Certainty, speed and finality were all thought to be key, and all in reliance on market expertise and reputation. Viewed at the time as a novel but creative way of providing for liquidated damages, it was also expected that these reference market makers would function as gatekeepers as well as perform a judge-like function.

They knew the workings of the ISDA Master and brought context and relevant experience to the task. Like arbitration, they offered the prospect of specialist determination and were thought to eliminate the need for cross-checking by more generalist courts. They also could be expected to add a measure of objectivity, if not fairness. That objectivity was expected to be grounded in commerciality too and not driven solely by

17. User's Guide to the Standard Form Agreements – 1987 Edition (ISDA) at 1. The intention was to allow counterparties to enter into one 'master agreement' that would set out the general terms of their trading relationship (e.g., representations and warranties, events of default and termination events, payment mechanics, *etc.*), and then execute letters of confirmation governed by the master agreement that would set out the business terms for each individual transaction.

stand-alone, naked pricing. Most importantly, leading dealers of the highest credit standing could be expected to be particularly sensitive to reputational risk, competitive pressures and regulatory concerns. In short, since the dealers asked to decide these matters had invested a lot in the system, they could be expected as a result to have a lot at stake and hopefully the system's best interests at heart.[18]

## §2.03 THE VOWS: COMMERCIAL PURPOSES THAT ANIMATED THE DRAFTING OF, AND WERE INTENDED TO BE SERVED BY, ADR PROVISIONS IN THE ISDA MASTER

To understand this particular interest in, or even partial preference for, ADR by the derivatives markets in this way, several commercial drivers behind ISDA documentation need to be appreciated, and it may be useful at this juncture to try to summarize a couple of these.

### [A] Mitigation of Costly and Lengthy Litigation

The status of the ISDA Master as a global industry standard these days is taken for granted.[19] However, its initial focus was exclusively on interest rate and currency products, and when it started to reach out to a wider derivatives marketplace – e.g., commodity-, equity- and credit-linked products – it, had to be a 'selling' document, intended to attract and grow the business being placed under it. Moreover, it must also be appreciated that the audience to which it was appealing in that earlier period needed both convincing and assurances.

Geographical and linguistic dividing lines were being crossed. For risk management purposes, financial institutions were asking many of their trading desks to 'cross the street', to use the ISDA Master to achieve for the wider institution the benefits of contractual netting and preferential capital treatment. That often meant abandoning historically more favoured forms, and there were also concerns about exposure to expensive and protracted litigation because of the 'tick-the-box' choice of New York or English law as the governing law of the contract and submission to the jurisdiction of New York or English courts that followed from that.

In relevant ISDA documentation working groups, especially among ISDA members and their counsel in meetings outside the US, there was particular concern voiced

18. Although the Market Quotation remedy had established its popularity, a more general indemnification alternative also stayed on the menu for use both as a fallback when quotations were unavailable or it was thought that any available quotation might produce a commercially unreasonable approach and where parties elected it often because they were trading illiquid products and it was thought that third-party quotations would not serve such thin markets.
19. The latest survey results from the Bank for International Settlements put the outstanding notional amount of trading for the global OTC derivatives market at more than USD 550 trillion, and it is thought that the largest part of it – perhaps more than 90% – trades pursuant to ISDA documentation and terms. *See* Statistical release: Semiannual OTC derivatives statistics at end-December 2019, Bank for International Settlements: Monetary and Economic Department, May 2020. https://www.bis.org/publ/otc_hy2005.pdf.

about extensive US-style discovery procedures and concomitant delays and costs. As a practical matter, if such concerns were not seen to be addressed or mitigated in the documentation, it might have been a serious impediment to the widespread and international buy-in to, and adoption of, the ISDA forms. In turn, that might have lost the economies, liquidity, wider market risk protection and other benefits of scale that have in fact been achieved over time. Accordingly, it was the drafters' ambition that the scope of the issues to be court determined, rather than party or leading dealer determined, would be narrow.

In short, ISDA wanted buy-in from a very diverse group - and that buy-in was by no means assured. Accordingly, Market Quotation (and the replacement remedy of Close-out Amount in the 2002 Form, which embraces and accommodates dealer quotations and also aims at liquidated damages[20]) represented a practical attempt by the ISDA drafters - a selling tool - to enhance the attractiveness of the use of the ISDA Master in the global derivatives markets by mitigating the risk of costly and protracted international discovery and litigation. A fear of crippling expenses that threatened the business model and unacceptable delays loomed large if instead the test required was to reach more of a fact-intensive, objective and court-instructed result.[21]

### [B] Promotion of Certainty in the Global Markets

Market Quotation and Close-out Amount[22] also represent a practical attempt by the ISDA drafters to meet an equally compelling and overarching aim of fostering the ability of market participants to have certainty about their market risk position.

The marked reluctance to allow second-guessing by a court of any quotation received from a leading dealer acting as a reference market maker can only be understood if market interest in 'certainty' and the perceived difficulties, delays and

20. 2002 Form at s. 6(e)(v).
21. Counterparties are organized in many different jurisdictions around the world. In my opinion, the markets, by agreeing to the ISDA Master model, demonstrated a preference for the scope of the issues to be considered by the courts to be relatively narrow (e.g., good faith) in order, as the courts move from the ISDA Master between one set of parties to the next, not to have judges and juries micro-manage and align parties' behaviour and to avoid extensive and, given the international nature of the markets, inevitably expensive factual inquiries. Deference to determinations made absent a showing that they ignored expressly prescribed procedures or that they were capricious (i.e., a decision so irrational that no rational person could have taken it) or made in bad faith is part and parcel of the scheme of things. The commercial attractiveness of this way of doing business itself is paramount, for which a pre-agreed and bargained-for basis that even empowers one party to self-determine and liquidate any contractual claims without resort to the courts, if achievable, was seen as a real plus.
22. As drafters, our intention and instructions were that Close-out Amount should not so much change as borrow from the Market Quotation methodology a measure of damage based on replacement value but offer greater flexibility to the party making the determination. The need for flexibility had been highlighted in the market crises in 1998 and 1999 when many determining parties faced difficulty in obtaining the requisite third-party quotations. A wider source of relevant data was contemplated by the Close-out Amount definition, but it remained the intention of the ISDA working groups that the methodology contemplated would be treated, and qualify, as good liquidated damages.

costs encountered in otherwise discovering facts and confirming consensus in a global marketplace are fully appreciated.

In this author's experience, the markets have a marked preference for certainty even sometimes above justice and almost everything else. You can trade around a position that you know to be certain, however undesirable that position may be and whether or not you believe it to be fair. What is abhorred is not knowing where you stand. Eventually being told that you were correct in your earlier view, or a third-party view that you relied upon at the time, does not give a lot of comfort if you stand 'naked' to a market which has moved on and significantly against you while you waited for that answer or if you fixed a replacement hedge or transaction unnecessarily or at the wrong time.[23]

## §2.04 THE WEDDING PARTY: CONTRACTUAL PRIVILEGE, CALCULATION AGENTS, VALUATION AGENTS, SCREENS AND REFERENCE BANKS

But there is more in the wider ISDA documentation library in support of these business purposes than just liquidated damages. Third-party dealers acting as reference market makers in the calculation of damages on close-out under the ISDA Master keep company with other third parties and third-party sources, introduced through the parties' trade confirmations and schedules, in a broader effort by the ISDA world to 'hermetically seal' the trading universe. In this universe, decisions are expected to be made to the largest extent for market participants by market participants with the commercial objective of keeping things out of court and mitigating the risk of expensive and protracted litigation.

While external pressures (reputational, commercial, regulatory) are expected to play their part, and non-defaulting parties enjoy considerable contractual privilege (i.e., the legal capacity afforded by the contract to make certain determinations choose the sources of data for certain calculations or do as one pleases in a certain matter), also relevant are 'calculation agents', who may be third parties tasked with pricing or valuing or otherwise exercising judgment, but very often after performing a mediation or conciliation role (i.e., 'after consultation with the parties').[24] Similarly, in separate

23. This commercial objective for certainty was, in my view, a fundamental rationale for the considerable discretion that the ISDA Master allows a non-defaulting party and the reference market makers when called upon to quote in a close-out situation. It was fully appreciated by the relevant ISDA documentation working groups that, by this point in time, an ISDA Master might be the umbrella for tens of thousands of trades. Setting specific times or prices was not the game. Neither was searching for correct or perfect (or even 'best') answers. If it turned out that, with the benefit of hindsight or more accurate information, a different (or more 'just') result might have been reached, that was unfortunate - but irrelevant.

24. The calculation agent's role usually sits outside the main body of the ISDA Master but comes in through the incorporation of definitional booklets or other product-specific terms in the confirmations of individual transactions. The duties of calculation agents, while largely ministerial in nature, can have significant consequence to the economics of trading between counterparties. A practice has evolved in which both parties can 'share' the role of calculation agent but provide for a dispute resolution process when agreement cannot be reached. The 2000

ISDA documentation for credit support, the role of the so-called valuation agent (and reference market makers) in connection with dispute settlement when margin calls are challenged is even more explicitly recognized.[25]

Similarly, the pricing and valuation mechanics in ISDA documentation for a great many products look to third parties (screen and published sources, reference banks (often as a fallback when a screen or published price is unavailable) and the like) for final and binding decisions, and without the involvement of courts even if the outcome may be perceived by one of the parties to be 'unfair'.[26]

---

ISDA Definitions contained a brief dispute resolution clause of this sort in the form of confirmation that is included as an exhibit – another example of ISDA embracing ADR along the way.

25. *See*, e.g., 1995 ISDA Credit Support Annex (Bilateral Form – Transfer) – *English Law* at para. 4:

> (a) *Disputed Calculations or Valuations.* If a party (a "Disputing Party") reasonably disputes (I) the Valuation Agent's calculation of a Delivery Amount or a Return Amount or (II) the Value of any transfer of Eligible Credit Support or Equivalent Credit Support, then:
> (1) the Disputing Party will notify the other party and the Valuation Agent ... ;
> (2) in the case of (I) above, the appropriate party will transfer the undisputed amount to the other party ...;
> (3) the parties will consult with each other in an attempt to resolve the dispute; and
> (4) if they fail to resolve the dispute ..., then:
> (i) in the case of a dispute involving a Delivery Amount or Return Amount, unless otherwise specified ... the Valuation Agent will recalculate the Exposure and the Value as of the Recalculation Date by:
> (A) utilising any calculations of that part of the Exposure attributable to the Transactions that the parties have agreed are not in dispute;
> (B) calculating that part of the Exposure attributable to the Transactions in dispute by seeking four actual quotations at mid-market from Reference Market-makers for purposes of calculating Market Quotation, and taking the arithmetic average of those obtained ...; and
> (C) utilising the procedures specified [by the parties in their schedule] for calculating the Value, if disputed, of the outstanding Credit Support Balance;
> (ii) in the case of a dispute involving the Value of any transfer of Eligible Credit Support or Equivalent Credit Support, the Valuation Agent will recalculate the Value as of the date of transfer pursuant to [party agreed variables in the schedule].

26. This tolerance for unfairness and preference for certainty can be seen in a number of embraced market practices embedded in ISDA documentation. *See*, e.g., 2000 ISDA Definitions, s. 7.6. The referenced provision sets out the parties' agreement regarding corrections to published and displayed pricing sources. For example, where a relevant rate for a reset date is based on information from certain sources such as a Reuters screen page that rate is subject to corrections made by that source *but only if the correction is made within one hour of the time when such rate is first displayed*. After that, even if the displayed rate has an extra zero in it, and even if it is later corrected, it becomes the irrevocable basis for the relevant pricing of the transaction. That is the potentially harsh but, in order to ensure certainty, market preferred position!

## §2.05 AN UNREQUITED LOVE AFFAIR[27]

In the period 1992–1993, ISDA actually flirted with the idea of going further and establishing its own arbitration/ADR facility. This was to stand alone, outside the agreement, and its remit would not just be limited to disputes about the ISDA Master or ISDA documentation.

In May 1992, at the behest of one of the Directors, the ISDA Board first discussed the potential role it could play as an arbiter of market disputes. After a brief preliminary discussion at the Board level, the matter was referred to ISDA's staff for a 'feasibility study', which was to include a review with ISDA's outside counsel of issues relating to liability.

Further consideration of this proposal was initially postponed, but two months later, at a dinner with US banking regulators, ISDA was urged to take a more active role in promoting good market practices. When the Board met the next day, ISDA's Chairman suggested that an arbitration service might be one way to respond to this suggestion from the regulators. As he envisioned it, the arbitration process would be informal and would not seek to produce legally binding decisions that would be enforceable in court. The suggestion was made that perhaps the Board should consider market practice statements as an alternative to an 'arbitration' service. It was the consensus of the Directors at the time that at the very least the arbitration service proposal should be refined further before reconsideration by the Board.

Momentum grew for some form of market practice dispute resolution facility in order to ensure that market practice issues were most likely to be decided by market practitioners in accordance with market expectation. However, it was thought that the service should only be on offer where at least one of the parties to the dispute was an ISDA member. One possibility would have been for the ISDA Board itself to take up any such issue, but it was thought that involving the full Board to consider every dispute and at every stage was impractical. Instead, consideration was given to the idea that a dispute would be referred to ISDA's Executive Director in the first instance, who in turn would refer the matter to a sub-committee of the Board. That smaller group of Board members would complete the bulk of the preparatory work for any dispute that was accepted for resolution.

Mechanics aside, the idea of the service had support among the ISDA Directors, not least because of the important message that it was hoped it would convey that ISDA was doing something responsible to reduce the potential for conflict or crisis in the markets. It was suggested that, in part to this end, the results of settled disputes be noticed in ISDA's newsletter[28] or otherwise be published.

Several Directors expressed willingness to serve as arbitrators. However, points of detail remained to be worked out. The approaches taken by one or more of the

27. The history that follows in this section of the article largely draws on the author's files and notes of contemporaneous and non-privileged discussions with members of ISDA's Board of Directors at a time when the author served as outside counsel to that Board.
28. It must be remembered that this was a discussion taking place at a time that pre-dates websites and emails!

exchanges that offered dispute settlement services were to be investigated, not least with a view to getting guidance on fees and the allocation of costs. And concerns about director liability in connection with the proposal still lingered. It was thought that outside counsel should be brought in to advise on the matter before any final decision on implementation was reached.

By January 1993, the search had started for a suitable market dispute that might test the procedures under consideration. That effort was being encouraged by concurrent consideration that was being given to settlement risk and disruption by a crisis management working group that ISDA had also created. It was thought that issues like these could easily ripen into market disputes and justified the attention being given to an ADR service dedicated to market practice issues. And again, it was also thought that the service under review would convey an important message to the regulators that ISDA was doing something responsible to reduce the potential for market conflict or crisis.

However, by the spring of 1993, consideration of a more formal dispute resolution mechanism for parties had given way to a more general proposal for a market practice advisory service, and this latter proposal was given wide circulation, including in materials distributed to ISDA members and attendees at ISDA conferences.

In turn, a Market Practice Advisory Service was reported out by ISDA's Board, complete with guidelines. Fees for issues brought were initially set at USD 1,000. However, this service does not appear to have ever acted in any formal way. Several fact patterns were discussed, and it was reported that live disputes had been promised. But agreed procedure called for a published result (without identifying the parties in the interest of confidentiality), and there does not appear to be any such result.

## §2.06 THE PROGENY: SHARIA-COMPLIANT MASTER; ARBITRATION GUIDES; FRENCH AND IRISH LAW MASTERS; DETERMINATION COMMITTEES AND EXTERNAL REVIEWS; PROTOCOLS AND P.R.I.M.E. FINANCE

Nevertheless, the idea of the relevance of arbitration that inspired the just-described Board level discussions more than a quarter of a century ago has picked up again in the last decade. Indeed, ISDA's cutting edge support for ADR solutions has continued since publication and re-publication of the original ISDA Master itself. It can also be found outside the four corners of that ISDA Master form and the product-specific documentation that it incorporates.

### [A] Islamic Finance

On 1 March 2010, ISDA, in collaboration with the International Islamic Financial Market (IIFM), announced the publication of its innovative ISDA/IIFM Tahawwut Master Agreement (the 'Islamic Finance Master'). Designed to advance trading relationships involving *Shari'a*-compliant hedging activity based on *murabaha* transactions, the Islamic Finance Master included, when benchmarked against the ISDA

Master, a number of new features. Though its form and structure are very much based on the 2002 Form, and a traditional jurisdiction clause providing for referral to English or New York courts is included, this appears as an alternative choice for the first time in ISDA standard form documentation since an arbitration alternative is also included. The parties can, if they so elect, provide for arbitration of their disputes under the ICC Rules or such other rules as may be specified by the parties in their schedule.

Enforcement was a key consideration in this case, in anticipation of certain jurisdictions in which the Islamic Finance Master was likely to be used. It was thought for that reason that arbitration may be advantageous in jurisdictions such as these where an arbitral award is perceived to be more easily recognized than would be a judgment from English or New York courts.

### [B] The Arbitration Guides

Reference has already been made in this chapter to the two editions of the *ISDA Arbitration Guide,* which report evidence of growing interest in the possible broader relevance of arbitration to financial market disputes.[29] Publication of each Arbitration Guide followed an extensive consultation with ISDA members.[30]

As a result, the arbitration clause that first appeared in the Islamic Finance Master now keeps company with model clauses in the Arbitration Guides for use with the 2002 Form and the 1992 Forms for referrals to a menu of arbitral institutions (expanded to a dozen in the second edition of the Arbitration Guide[31]) and seats. The focus in the guidance provided was primarily on key reasons ISDA members had given for possible benefits of arbitration, including competence and enforcement.

### [C] French and Irish Law ISDA Master Agreements

In contemplation of Brexit, ISDA published for the first time French and Irish law versions of the ISDA Master Agreement in July 2018. The move was 'intended to provide options for those institutions that would prefer to continue trading under a European Union (EU) member-state law with EU court jurisdiction clauses once the UK leaves the EU'.[32]

29. *See supra* n. 2 and accompanying text.
30. Each followed also the circulation of memoranda outlining the issues and arguments supporting greater consideration of this form of ADR. A round-robin of meetings with ISDA members and other stakeholders in financial centres around the world preceded publication of the first edition of the Arbitration Guide, a series of conference calls preceded the second, and further comments were invited and received by ISDA staff in advance of publication of both. The surveys of views had demonstrated strong and growing market interest in arbitration and ADR and support for the Arbitration Guides and the guidance offered by them.
31. Including for the first time the Arbitration Institute of the Stockholm Chamber of Commerce.
32. ISDA Press Release, *ISDA Publishes French and Irish Law Master Agreements,* 3 July 2018 at https://www.isda.org/2018/07/03/isda-publishes-french-and-irish-law-master-agreements/ ('English law may become a third-country law after the UK withdraws from the EU, which means English court decisions would no longer be automatically recognized and enforced across the EU and European Economic Area (EEA). That wouldn't be the case for French or Irish law

Both forms are patterned on the 2002 Form of the ISDA Master, including the format of the more traditional jurisdiction clauses there, although interestingly the French law version, like the Islamic Finance Master, gives an arbitration option and contains a model clause in Part 4 of the form of its Schedule providing for arbitration under the ICC Rules with a seat in Paris. A model arbitration clause for use with the 2002 ISDA Master Agreement (Irish law), which provides for arbitration under the LCIA Rules with a seat in Dublin, was separately included in the second edition of ISDA's Arbitration Guide, which appeared around the same time.

### [D] Credit Derivatives Determinations Committees and External Review

Perhaps the most striking embrace of ADR by ISDA and users of ISDA documentation can be seen in the Credit Derivatives Determinations Committees structure that makes binding contractual determinations for issues relating to credit default swaps.

Originally established by ISDA in 2009 but now independently administered,[33] the Determinations Committees are regional committees of experienced market participants, drawn from both the dealer and the non-dealer communities, tasked with comparing facts of specific events, based on publicly available information, with the provisions of standard credit derivatives contracts to make determinations regarding key provisions of those contracts. The Determinations Committees derive their authority from rules incorporated by ISDA documentation for credit derivatives (including those incorporating the ISDA Credit Derivatives Definitions).

The role that the Determinations Committees play is unique in the credit derivatives markets that they serve. Where there is a disputed interpretation, they make factual determinations of issues such as whether (i) a credit event meriting a pay-out under outstanding credit protection has occurred; (ii) whether an auction to determine the final price of any credit protection settlement should be held; and (iii) which reference entity obligations are eligible for delivery when physical settlement is contemplated.

The Determinations Committee process represents a form of ADR in itself. The challenge when one of the described decisions is presented to the relevant regional committee is for that decision to be made quickly and based on limited information in order to aid the efficient functioning of the market. The process is intentionally designed to ensure that trading conventions and commercial expectation are respected. However, the participating representative decision makers may have their own positions that will be impacted by the determinations they make, and part of the challenge is also to mitigate conflicts of interest. Not surprisingly, the results are closely watched and attract a great deal of attention in the media as well as in the markets themselves.

court judgements under the new Master Agreements, reducing the steps involved in settling a contractual dispute with an EU/EEA counterparty.')

33. As of 9 October 2018, ISDA appointed DC Administration Services, Inc. as DC Secretary with responsibility for administering the governing rules. The website for the Determinations Committee can be found at the following URL: https://www.cdsdeterminationscommittees.org/.

Both the dealer and buy sides of the market are represented among the voting representatives on the committees. One way of seeking to ensure fairness and minimize conflicts of interest is to require supermajority votes (at least 80% of those participating) for key issues.[34] In situations where the requisite vote fails to be achieved, the question gets re-formulated as possible 'presented positions' and referred to an external review, another form of ADR, for a final and binding decision.

That has only happened four times in more than a decade that the Determinations Committees have been up and running.[35] External reviewers (usually independent legal experts, QCs, experienced market practitioners or academics) are selected from a panel. The process involves an expert determination by a panel of three external reviewers after arbitration-style arguments, with written submissions and a hearing all made public.[36] The decision deadline for the external reviewers is an extremely tight one: five business days after submission of the question for external review. As with all Determinations Committee decisions, the results of the external review process are published promptly[37] and bind all market participants whether or not they participated in the proceedings.

### [E] Protocols

Reference should also be made to the development by ISDA of its revolutionary alternative 'pre-dispute' resolution (ApreDR) mechanism, the ISDA Protocols.[38] ISDA's

34. The 80% requirement ensures that a decision reflects support from *both* dealer and buy side representatives. For an early history of the Determinations Committees, *see* ISDA Press Release, *ISDA Paper Examines Three-Year History of the ISDA Credit Derivatives Determinations Committees*, 1 May 2012 at https://www.isda.org/2012/05/01/isda-paper-examines-three-year-history-of-the-isda-credit-derivatives-determinations-committees/.
35. The author has had the privilege of serving as an external reviewer on two of these occasions.
36. The decision-making process in an external review is a little complicated. If in the original vote of the Determinations Committee more than 60% of the voting members (but less than the 80% supermajority required) voted for a specific outcome, the question is decided in accordance with that majority vote unless the external reviewers unanimously conclude that another presented position is 'the better answer', in which case the question is decided by that decision of the external reviewers. If the original vote had been less than or equal to 60% of the voting members participating, the question is decided by that vote unless at least two out of the three external reviewers conclude that another presented position is 'the better answer', in which case the question is decided in accordance with the majority vote of the external reviewers.
37. Speed is of the essence. The markets need to know. At the last external review session in which I participated, the briefs in the matter were first filed on a Thursday, supplemental briefs on the Tuesday that followed, a hearing was held on the Wednesday, our decision (as it turned out our unanimous decision) announced later that same day – the markets had been trading and in effect 'betting' on the outcome in the course of the day – and we published that decision with seven pages of reasoning on the Friday. Litigation, on the other hand, can play out over years and involve fulsome discovery. Whenever a party enters into a credit default swap on ISDA terms, it is in effect putting its faith in the hands of the Determinations Committee procedures, which will ultimately decide whether or not a contested credit event that would require a pay-out has occurred – and that decision will bind the relevant market regardless of whether a court later decides in a dispute between private litigants that the Determinations Committee decision, or a follow on decision by external reviewers, was wrong.
38. ISDA's Protocol library can be found at: https://www.isda.org/protocols/.

Protocol project started as an exercise in crisis management in 1998 with the impending introduction of the euro and the resulting disappearance of eleven legacy currencies and related price sources and conventions.[39] It ended up heralding an unprecedented approach to international contract renegotiation and dispute resolution and avoidance taking advantage of what at the time of its first operation was ground-breaking use of the internet. Independent commentators have estimated that the successful promulgation of the original (European Monetary Union) EMU Protocol alone had potentially saved millions in negotiating time and reduced the risk of time-consuming and expensive litigation between swap counterparties. Indeed, a number of these commentators were of the view that, but for the Protocol, the necessary changes to derivatives contracts would not have been achieved in a timely fashion and litigation resulting from the introduction of the euro would have been rampant.

The first Protocol, which received awards and accolades at the time, has since become the model prototype for other Protocols used repeatedly since, and for multiple purposes, by the financial industry and its regulators.

### [F] P.R.I.M.E. Finance

Although ISDA's own proposed arbitration facility (discussed at note 27 *supra* and the accompanying text) never operated, a number of those involved in the discussions at the time were instrumental in establishing an independent Panel of Recognised International Market Experts in Finance ('P.R.I.M.E. Finance') as a specialized institution formed for the specific purpose of facilitating the resolution of complex financial disputes, including by means of arbitration, mediation and other forms of ADR.[40]

Though not an ISDA project, P.R.I.M.E. Finance was set up in the wake of the 2008 global financial crisis with a mission to ensure that the best expertise was available for the settlement of complex market disputes and not least those relating to ISDA documentation and the considerable trading under it that the derivatives markets represent. P.R.I.M.E. Finance now comprises a panel of more than 200 pre-eminent lawyers, judges, bankers, regulators, academics and market participants with collectively more than 6,000 years of relevant experience. All are world leaders in the field of

39. Imagine that Party A and Party B had entered into a currency swap providing for the exchange of Deutschmarks for French francs at an exchange rate periodically set by a screen source, and the parties wake up the morning after the euro is introduced to find that neither legacy currency exists nor does any agreed future screen rate for fixing their exchange. Has their contract been commercially frustrated in a way that would permit one of the parties unilaterally to walk away from the trade? If not, what happens next? The Protocol, to which virtually all the major banks and financial institutions (and a great many others) had adhered, provided answers pursuant to a matching system of preferences, thereby settling the matter as between adhering parties and with the effect of removing most of the risk of litigation from the situation.

40. *See* the P.R.I.M.E. Finance website at: https://primefinancedisputes.org. P.R.I.M.E. Finance is housed at the Permanent Court of Arbitration in The Hague. ADR services, including arbitration, mediation and the provision of expert witnesses and expert opinions, determinations and risk assessment is a core activity and one of the three pillars upon which the project is based. The other two core activities are judicial training and the compilation of a central database of relevant financial market case materials and precedents.

finance or financial market dispute settlement and can provide effective and expeditious resolution of disputes as arbitrators, mediators or experts. Most draw on experience in particular of the ISDA world.[41]

The P.R.I.M.E. Finance project reflects recognition that specialist dispute resolution has a part to play as a complement to the more traditional role of courts - especially as matters in dispute between market participants get more technical and complex and the need for certain answers quickly achieved becomes greater. Formed against the backdrop of the last financial market crisis, the project also reflects a recognition that regulatory reform alone is not the best guarantee of global financial stability. Facts will change, and facts will always be important - they may also be unanticipated. When disputes happen as a result, possibly on a large scale, and speedy, authoritative and expert answers are required, ADR may be a particularly attractive option for reducing legal uncertainty.

## §2.07 CONCLUSION

Despite considerable reliance on innovative and market-driven solutions for resolving actual and potential disputes in the derivatives markets, and the effectiveness of the mechanics employed for keeping such matters out of court, the role of ADR in the ISDA scheme of things has probably been underappreciated.

The evolution of the underlying methodology behind the concepts of Agreement Value, Market Quotation and Close-out Amount represents an ongoing attempt in the ISDA Master to achieve formulaic liquidated damages in order to limit the role of judges (and in New York court cases possibly the role of juries!) and, as an alternative, favour the role of market experts in order that often technical market issues can be determined for the markets by experienced market participants - and in a timely fashion.

Two commercial objectives were key in providing the inspiration for that approach: (i) mitigating the risk of costly and lengthy litigation and (ii) promoting certainty in the markets.

That has also led to an ever-broadening embrace of ADR techniques in the day-to-day operation of these markets in order to resolve or avoid disputes, and not just when assessing damages after default. Reference market makers and reference banks, calculation agents and valuation agents, Determinations Committees and external reviewers have all played their part.

Publication in the past decade by ISDA of Arbitration Guides with guidance, model arbitration clauses and new master agreements that expressly contemplate the possible election of arbitration has understandably attracted considerable attention and discussion. However, the role played by ADR in ISDA documentation and the derivatives market is more extensive than the place that arbitration alone plays, and

41. P.R.I.M.E. Finance experts include those who have previously served as Chair, CEO, General Counsel, director or officer, senior staff, outside or local counsel of ISDA and others who have participated in the ISDA working groups that have reported out ISDA documentation. All the external reviews of the Determinations Committee decisions have been decided by panels that included P.R.I.M.E. Finance experts.

the legacy of ADR and reliance by ISDA members on it similarly more established over a much longer period than is usually acknowledged. As this chapter has shown, mediation, conciliation, expert determinations and reliance on settlement through protocols are also contemplated by many relevant ISDA terms and practices, and each has contributed.

Perhaps not surprisingly, many ISDA 'alumni', seeped in this tradition, have been behind the drive for specialist ADR offerings like P.R.I.M.E. Finance. P.R.I.M.E. Finance was created against the backdrop of a prior global financial crisis and reflected a view that ADR had an important, if complementary, role to play alongside both the courts and global regulatory reform to ensure long-term financial market stability – and correct answers when complex financial disputes do arise!

Which may all be particularly telling at this moment in time. Writing as this author is amidst the COVID-19 pandemic, and with another potential financial crisis looming in its wake, there is mounting talk of a wave of resulting legal disputes[42] – claims of contractual frustration, force majeure, margin calls and valuation issues, practical issues arising from attempts to deliver notices or otherwise perform during lockdown, and close-out issues flowing from counterparty insolvencies to name just a few.

It can only be expected that ISDA and its membership will again seek cost-efficient and timely answers to the issues posed. Given the possible scale of the problem, it may also be expected that such an unprecedented challenge may require creative solutions.[43] On these facts and the brief record provided in this chapter there is every reason to expect that, as a result, the relationship between the ISDA world and ADR may expand, and so will its history.

---

42. *See*, e.g., *Coronavirus Contract Disputes Start Hitting the Courts*, The Wall Street Journal (20 April 2020) at https://www.wsj.com/articles/coronavirus-contract-disputes-start-hitting-the-courts-11587375001; *Private Investors Prepare Legal Action to Recover Losses over Margin Calls*, Financial Times (7 April 2020) at https://www.ft.com/content/a64a1535-f518-4465-b67f-44b19aa97ff3.
43. Interestingly, a note from the UK Cabinet Office issued during the coronavirus crisis seems to invite a creative and extra-court approach to contract disputes arising out of the pandemic. *See Guidance on Responsible Contractual Behaviour in the Performance and Enforcement of Contracts Impacted by the Covid-19 Emergency*, U.K. Government Cabinet Office (7 May 2020) at [14]) at https://assets.publishing.service.gov.uk/government/uploads/system/uploads/attachment_data/file/883737/_Covid-19_and_Responsible_Contractual_Behaviour__web_final___7_May_.pdf. ('Responsible and fair behaviour is strongly encouraged in performing and enforcing contracts where there has been a material impact from Covid-19. This includes being reasonable and proportionate in responding to performance issues and enforcing contracts (including dealing with any disputes), acting in a spirit of co-operation and aiming to achieve practical, just and equitable contractual outcomes having regard to the impact on the other party (or parties), the availability of financial resources, the protection of public health and the national interest.' *See also* a concept note issued by a group of eminent U.K. jurists, including two former Presidents of the U.K. Supreme Court, which calls for conciliation as a form of ADR in such situations, emphasises the possible benefits of a comparative law approach and suggests a search for outcomes which avoid leaving 'one party a winner, and the other party a loser'. *Breathing space – a Concept Note on the Effect of the Pandemic on Commercial Contracts*, British Institute on International and Comparative Law (7 April 2020) at https://www.biicl.org/breathing-space.

CHAPTER 3

# A Negotiation Perspective on the Agreement to Arbitrate and Its Completion

*Eric M. Runesson*

## §3.01 INTRODUCTION

Looking at the 2018 International Arbitration Survey[1] it seems that users of arbitration rank flexibility of procedure as one of the most attractive features of international arbitration. The word 'flexibility' seems to be used in a relative sense, meaning more flexible than court proceedings. Users simultaneously point out lack of speed and lack of effective sanctions as being among the least attractive features of the arbitral process. This would presumably be in comparison to user expectations.

The flexibility of arbitration is due to its consensual basis. The parties may choose their arbitrators, the place and the language of the proceedings. The procedural rules are considerably less comprehensive than the ones in the rule book that the courts have to follow. This gives the parties wide opportunities to agree on the procedural design, including the scope of the proceedings, the rules for taking of evidence and the use of interlocutory and partial awards. In principle, the freedom to agree on the procedure extends to the point where the agreement violates the requirements of fair and equal treatment, the right to be heard and the right to be represented by an attorney or to the point where the agreed procedure does not qualify as 'arbitration' at all, in which case the outcome of the procedure may not be recognized and enforced as an arbitral award (although the agreement and its outcome may have other legal effects).

Standard ad hoc arbitration agreements have little to say about the proceedings as such; the agreement basically says that the parties shall settle their dispute by way of arbitration, also perhaps specifying the place and the language of the proceedings.

1. Queen Mary University of London and White & Case, 2018 International Arbitration Survey: The Evolution of International Arbitration (2018).

When the parties settle for such a 'naked' arbitration agreement, they have opted out from the opportunity to agree *ex ante* how to use the flexibility afforded to them. Instead they will have to try to reach an agreement *ex post*. What might have been considered as reasonable for a party *ex ante* does not always appear 'reasonable' *ex post*.

Usually the procedural agreement has to be hammered out after the fact in a three-party negotiation involving the arbitrators who happens to have a great deal of discretionary power unless the parties unite. In fact, to a certain extent, the arbitrators may have to write the details of agreement for the parties. In other words, they may have to invent an agreement that reasonable parties of the same kind as the parties would have made *ex ante* behind a 'veil of ignorance' regarding who is going to be the claimant and who is going to be the respondent.

Speaking of discretionary power, complaints about lack of speed in court proceedings is common. One of the reasons for lack of speed in civil proceedings is taken to be the failure of the courts to use the discretionary power that it already possesses according to the applicable procedural rules.[2] One might try the hypothesis that the perceived lack of speed in arbitration is due to the same cause. The complaints about lack of sanctions against obstruction seem to be regarded a special case of a general hesitance to use the powers that are already in hand.

## §3.02 THE ENFORCEABILITY INTEREST

For the arbitrators the question will often be how much of the discretionary power they shall dare to use to achieve speedy flexibility in demand without risking the enforceability of the award.

In considering creative ideas to tailor the proceedings to the case at hand, applying sanctions against obstruction, preventing an unnecessary round of lengthy submissions and inefficient presentation of evidence, the arbitrators can be expected to prioritize the interest that the proceedings will result in an enforceable award. For the award to be enforceable under the 1958 New York Convention Article V(d) the proceedings must be in accordance with the agreement of the parties or, where an agreement is missing, in accordance with the law of the country where the arbitration takes place.

Procedural shortcomings may lead to the setting aside of an award rendered in Sweden under section 34 item 7 of the Swedish Arbitration Act (1999:116). More specifically, the award shall be wholly or partially set aside if the arbitrators erred in the handling of the case, provided that the error was not due to a fault of the requesting party and that it is probable that the error influenced the outcome.

2. *See*, e.g., European Commission for the Efficiency of Justice, Length of court proceedings in the Member States of the Council of Europe based on the case law of the European Court of Human Rights, CEPJ (2018) 26 by (Françoise Calvez and Nicolas Regis, 3rd ed. by Nicolas Regis), Strasbourg, 3–4 Dec. 2018.

## §3.03 THE SKELETON AGREEMENT

Using a naked ad hoc arbitration agreement as a starting point it can be inferred that the parties' common intent was and is that the dispute shall be submitted to a non-governmental decision maker, selected by or for the parties, to render a binding decision resolving the dispute in accordance with neutral adjudicatory procedures affording the parties an opportunity to be heard.[3]

Obviously, such an agreement has to be supplemented by a subsequent agreement regarding details or otherwise by the procedural provisions of the Swedish Arbitration Act when the arbitration takes place in Sweden. The requirement for 'neutral adjudicatory procedures affording the parties an opportunity to be heard' should then be understood as follows:

(1) The arbitrators shall handle the dispute in an impartial[4] manner (section 21).
(2) The arbitrators shall afford the parties, an equal opportunity to be heard by allowing them to present their respective cases in writing or orally to their reasonable satisfaction (section 24 paragraph 1[5]). The claimant shall be given the opportunity to state its claims and the respondent shall be given the opportunity to state its position regarding the claims and the parties shall, in doing so, have the opportunity to invoke the circumstances that they wish in order to support the claims and the positions (section 23 paragraph 1). The parties shall also have the opportunity to proffer evidence for consideration by the arbitrators as far as such evidence is not manifestly irrelevant to the dispute (section 25 paragraph 2).
(3) The arbitrators shall give each party an opportunity to review (and be heard about) all documents and all other materials pertaining to the dispute which are supplied to the arbitrators by an opposing party or another person (section 24 paragraph 2).

In addition to these basic procedural features one should add that the arbitrators may not exceed the claims and that they may not resolve the dispute based on factual circumstances which have not been invoked or on

3. The meaning of the term 'arbitration' is taken from the synthesis in Born, Gary B., International Commercial Arbitration (Wolters Kluwer 2 ed. 2014) 247.
4. Impartial in the sense that an arbitrator's actions and views should stand a role reversal test and be the same even if respondent stepped into claimant's shoes or vice versa. *See* Lindskog, Stefan, Skiljeförfarande. En kommentar (Norstedts 2 ed. 2012) 599.
5. Cf. the Swedish expression '*i all behövlig omfattning*'. The word '*behövlig*' can be translated into 'needed' in order to suit a certain end. The end cannot be 'to be heard' since 'needed' would then be redundant. The end must rather be 'to the party's satisfaction', but under an objective test. A party may not demand to be heard by burdening the proceedings with requests that the arbitrators shall consider material that they think is clearly irrelevant. Cf. prop. 1998/99:35 p. 227 (Government Bill). The provision should therefore be understood to say 'to the parties' reasonable satisfaction'. What is clearly irrelevant is for the arbitrators to determine and their determination, wrong as it may be, regards the substance of the case. Cf. Lindskog, *supra* n. 4, at 881 et seq.

evidence which has not been introduced by the parties.[6] Such authority may be given to, e.g., an expert in expert determination procedures, but not to arbitrators as a matter of semantics.

An agreement that does not live up to these general standards would not qualify as an agreement regarding an adjudicative procedure. The resulting decision may thus not be recognized as an arbitral award and hence not be enforceable.

But there is more to the default arbitration agreement.

(4) The arbitrators shall grant a party's requests to have recourse to courts for court administered testimonies and court administered evidence production when such requests are deemed to be justified having regard to the evidence of the case (section 26[7]).

And further, unless the parties agree otherwise - in my experience they are usually not inclined to do so *ex post* - the following also applies.

(5) The claimant may submit new claims, and the respondent may submit claims of its own, provided that the arbitrators do not consider it inappropriate to adjudicate such claims. Subject to the same condition each party may also amend or supplement previously presented claims and may invoke new circumstances and proffer new evidence in support of theirs claims and positions (section 23 paragraph 2 and section 25 paragraph 2).

(6) An oral hearing shall be held upon request by a party (section 24 paragraph 1).

(7) Subject to the provisions above, the arbitrators shall handle the dispute in a practical and speedy manner and, unless impeded, act as instructed by the parties (section 21).

If the arbitrators deviate from the agreement as now construed they have made a procedural error.

6. For the sake of clarity, an arbitrator may rely on his or her expert knowledge (which obviously must be based on educated assumptions about facts) when evaluating the evidence proffered. Cf. Born, *supra* n. 3, at 264.

7. From the wording of the provision it can be inferred that it is mandatory. *See also* Lindskog, *supra* n. 4, at 697. Cf. Heuman, Lars, Skiljemannarätt (Norstedts 1999) at 273 et seq. The better approach would be to presume that an agreement to oust the courts is valid but open a reasonability test; the agreement can be adjusted or set aside if deemed to be unreasonable in a particular context. The parties may for instance find that there are good reasons to exclude court assisted document production aiming for documents in a party's possession but leave way for it when it comes to documents in a third-party possession. Cf. IBA Rules on the Taking of Evidence in International Arbitration (2010) Art. 3(9) and the 'adverse inference rule' in Art. 9 (5) regarding a party's refusal to produce documents in its possession. Cf. Born, *supra* n. 3, at 2421. Dupeyron, Carine, Shall National Courts Assist Arbitral Tribunals in Gathering Evidence?, ICCA Congress Series No. 19 (Kluwer 2017).

## §3.04 NEGOTIATING THE OPERATIVE AGREEMENT

As indicated above, procedural flexibility is a matter of three-party negotiation; however, it is a negotiation without a walk-away option. The arbitrators will bring their interests to the table and consequently act as a party, yet the arbitrators may simultaneously find that they act as mediators between two other parties. So, it is a peculiar kind of negotiation. The context is even more complex since there can be a great deal of internal negotiations among the arbitrators to clarify and determine the interests of the arbitral tribunal as a party.

If a mutually accepted way cannot be negotiated the parties can come to an agreement between themselves and issue joint instructions regarding the procedure; the parties trump the arbitrators. But, absent such instruction, the arbitrators will have it their way (subject to list items (1)–(7) above). It is inevitable that the outcome often will make one of the parties happier than the other unless the arbitrators seek a compromise that will leave the parties more or less equally unhappy. In order for the arbitrators to maintain the parties' confidence that the arbitrators will handle the case in impartial way, a great deal of up-front transparency on the side of the tribunal is a good thing.

A negotiation perspective on procedural decision-making may help to bring attention to the 'real problems'.

## §3.05 THE INTERESTS

As in any sensible negotiation, legitimate interests and needs should be the starting point. The interest that the proceedings shall result in an award that will be recognized and/or be enforceable is predominant, so that it can be taken out of the equation. Without implying any particular order of priorities, it can be assumed that the following legitimate interests will be pivotal:

(a) Finality: The procedure should deal with the dispute in an economic way. This means that the arbitration should be used in order to resolve as many contentious issues as possible, provided that arbitration is an adequate forum. The interest that the dispute is dealt with in an economic way has a bearing on how the arbitrators interpret the scope of the arbitration agreement. In particular the question whether it shall be taken to include issues that are intertwined with the disputed contract.[8] But it also affects how the arbitrators consider the appropriateness of adjudicating new claims by the claimant or claims that are introduced by the respondent. The same goes when it comes to amended or supplemented claims. If finality is a heavy priority, the consequence is that the parties should be allowed to introduce new claims during the proceedings broadening their scope. The possibility to introduce

8. Cf. The Swedish Supreme Court in 'Belgor' NJA 2019 p. 171 para. 18.

claims and to amend them also relates to the interest to achieve justice when the claims cannot be brought up in new proceedings due to res judicata.

(b) Justice: The procedure should lead to a result which is correct as regards the substance of the dispute; i.e., correct pursuant to the applicable substantive law and the invoked facts that have been proved to exist. This interest carries particular weight since an arbitral award cannot be subject to an appeal on the merits or be reopened. Thus, if a party has not been able to invoke a circumstance or to proffer evidence during the proceedings and the circumstance or evidence probably would have led to a different outcome, the award still stands, even when the unhappy party is perfectly excused for his inability. If substantive justice is a heavy priority the consequence is that the parties should be allowed to invoke new circumstances and to introduce new evidence during the proceedings at least when it cannot be ruled out in advance that there is a probability that such new material can influence the outcome. A further consequence is that the parties shall have recourse to courts for court administered evidence production (and perhaps also for testimonies under oath).

(c) Speed: The procedure should be speedy. Speed has no value of its own. The desire for speed is instead explained mainly by two underlying motives. The motive for speed can be that the parties do not like uncertainty; uncertainty is a cost.[9] Uncertainty regarding the outcome is an unavoidable detrimental fact with any form of dispute resolution that is based on a binding third-party decision. To this comes the uncertainty which the prevailing party can feel regarding the auspices that the enforcement of award will have any practical value when (and if) the day comes. Sensitivity to uncertainty correlates to a large extent on a party's degree of risk aversion. Risk aversion in its turn depends much on how big a portion of his wealth (in a very general sense) a party stands to lose should the worst-case scenario be realized with the award. On this theory one can assume that the 'little fish' is more sensitive to uncertainty than 'the bigger fish' on the other side of the table, and consequently, the less wealthy party would normally also be more interested in speed and settlement.

Leaving uncertainty aside, speed may also be desirable due to the time value of what is at stake. Generalizing from the meaning of 'time value of money' one can think of the time value of a claim from the claimant's as well as from the respondents' perspective. For the claimant the concept draws on the insight that a resource that the claimant has now is worth more than the possession of the same resource in the future. This is due to the potential earning capacity of the resource. For the respondent it generally works the other way around; as long as the respondent is in possession of the disputed resource he will enjoy the earning capacity. The problem is accelerated when

9. *See generally* Robert J. Rhee, A Price Theory of Legal Bargaining: An Inquiry into the Selection of Settlement and Litigation under Uncertainty, 56 Emory L.J. 619 (2006) with further references. The article is available at http://scholarship.law.ufl.edu/facultypub/494.

the award of an interest rate cannot compensate for the time value loss. A monetary claim (discounting for uncertainty regarding the respondent's solvency) may however also be a good capital investment when the agreed or statutory interest rate beats the rates offered on the capital market.

Either way, it is apparent that the question regarding how speedy the proceedings should be is likely to define a number of distributive bargaining issues rather than blissful win-win issues.

(d) Cost-efficiency: The procedure should be cost-efficient. That is to say that the arbitration may cost a lot in absolute numbers, but it must not be expensive. From a party's perspective, the costs do not only include fees payable to lawyers and other advisors - and to the other party's advisors where (as in Sweden) the loser generally pays. Costs also include internal costs of various kinds that may not be easy to quantify, such as organizational and investor relations disturbances. It can generally be assumed that costs can be regarded as an investment in avoiding the risk for injustice (and sometimes lack of finality).

What is cost-efficient can normally be related to the value of the dispute. It may be worthwhile to remember that the perceived value at stake can be very different for the parties. To one of the parties the outcome may set a precedent that can be used in other contexts - i.e., the award can have a precedent value beyond the monetary claim - whereas the other party sees the award just as a way to settle an isolated dispute. In effect costly propositions may be more efficient for one side than the other.

The arbitrators are free to consider 'cost sanctions' against a party who turn out to act in ways that reduce cost-efficiency. The principle should be that expenses that were inefficient or unnecessary will not be reimbursed to the winning party: expenses caused by the need to respond to inefficient or unnecessary measures will be recoverable irrespective of the outcome in substance.[10]

## §3.06 THE ISSUES

The above interests naturally define a number of issues to negotiate in a pre-hearing conference: issues that we usually find under well-known heads in an early procedural order. Let me mention a few of the central issues just by way of illustration:

(i) Number of submissions.
(ii) New claims, circumstances and evidence.
(iii) Evidence production and recourse to courts.
(iv) Oral evidence.
(v) Hearings.

10. Cf. Born, *supra* n. 3, at 3101 et seq.

Each party is likely to assign different priorities (often by way of intuition and not articulated) to each of the issues. One can think of it as if they are assigning weights to each of the issues. Each issue has a number of possible solutions (more or less acceptable to each party). The priorities are usually redefined and emerge as the range of possible solutions becomes clearer.

The solutions will be evaluated by each party according to the preferences between the best solution, the worst acceptable solution (acceptable depending on the outcome of the remaining issues) and the other solutions ranked in between. If for example one can conceive of three possible solutions (of course in reality there may be many more issues and solution) there will be 243 ways (the number of conceivable negotiation packages) to structure the proceedings given just five issues. Each package will have an attraction value (again usually given by means of intuition) which is a function of the party's priority of each issue addressed and the preference for the given solution to each issue. Usually the parties perceive the attractiveness in different ways, but they should be able to eliminate inferior packages and replace them with a package that is more attractive to both; a win-win package as the saying goes rather than a series of zero-sum negotiations over separate issues.

Since the arbitrators are somehow sitting in the middle, they should at some point be ready to articulate a default package to speed things up. The package will of course have to be adapted to the case at hand, and here we assume that we are not looking at a mega-case that would normally require hearings for months if taken all together. The proposed solutions can serve as anchor points for the parties' further negotiations. They are free to settle for another package which they both prefer.

If the demand for procedural flexibility shall be met, the arbitrators can hardly sit back and regard the Swedish Procedural Code (Sw. *rättegångsbalken*) as a default standard[11] for handling the case in a practical and speedy manner that should apply unless the parties jointly suggest another way. Instead it should be the other way around. The arbitrators should be proactive in the negotiation. After all, they can normally be expected to have superior experience of how to fit the forum to the fuzz, as the specialists they should be. They should be ready to suggest what they think is a practical and speedy way to handle the case at hand. Although the Procedural Code is not a standard it can be said that what courts can do the arbitrators can also do if they cannot come up with anything better.

The arbitrators' proposition can only to a limited extent be derived from the procedural provisions of the Swedish Arbitration Act. The provisions tend to be too general to be useful (but there are exceptions). Instead the arbitrators can, for inspiration and ideas, have a look at other standards, e.g., International Chamber of Commerce (ICC) Commission Report: Controlling time and costs in arbitration (2nd ed. March 2018)[12] even in an ad hoc arbitration.

The arbitrators could go about it and propose a package deal as suggested below.

11. *See* however Lindskog, *supra* n. 4, at 602.
12. The report is available at https://iccwbo.org/content/uploads/sites/3/2018/03/icc-arbitration-commission-report-on-techniques-for-controlling-time-and-costs-in-arbitration-english-version.pdf.

## §3.07 NUMBER OF SUBMISSIONS

Looking at the dispute at a very early stage, the arbitrators might ask themselves what it would take for them to be duly educated by the parties about the dispute, i.e., how many rounds of submissions will there have to be to arrive at an adequate level of education. They realize that there are two teachers and that the teachers will try to sell very different narratives. Therefore, there is a need to let each party correct the other party's perceived misunderstandings and omissions. Beyond that, it should be for the arbitrators to say what they require.

The default position according to the Swedish Arbitration Act is that there is a need for at least one round of submissions; the statement of claims and the response. But the requirement that the parties shall have an equal opportunity to be heard demands that the claimant is given the chance to rebut what the defendant says in the response and that the respondent has an opportunity to have its say on what the claimant says in its rebuttal and so on. A minimum of two rounds may therefore be necessary. The requirement is an outflow of the justice interest. Speed and cost-efficiency may however push the arbitrators to put an end to a further exchange of written submissions (unless the parties jointly agree otherwise). A party's chances to be heard should normally not be considered as unduly limited if the arbitrators give the parties an opportunity to make their conclusive remarks orally.[13] Telephone or video conferencing may work wonders in speeding things up and save costs.

## §3.08 NEW CLAIMS, CIRCUMSTANCES AND EVIDENCE

The plan made up thus far may be demolished by new, amended or supplemented claims and new circumstances or new evidence. The arbitrators might say that the principle shall be that the party who introduces news shall bear the costs for it irrespective of the outcome of the dispute unless the arbitrators deem that the costs are insignificant. If the costs are not separable, the costs can be set at a pre-determined standard amount that is presumed to correspond to the actual costs. It can be pertinent to consider the possibility to deal with a new (or amended or supplemented) claim in a separate award (after a separate hearing when necessary) if including the new claim would put the original time plan at jeopardy. The same can be said regarding the late introduction of new circumstances or evidence which relate to a claim made by the belated party. For this to work it may require that a party makes a claim for cost compensation and the arbitration agreement does not preclude such compensation (cf. section 42).

The issue regarding the right to introduce new evidence should leave way to consider the International Bar Association (IBA) Rules on the Taking of Evidence in International Arbitration (2010) Article 4.6 where applicable:

> If Witness Statements are submitted, any Party may, within the time ordered by the Arbitral Tribunal, submit to the Arbitral Tribunal and to the other Parties

13. *See* Lindskog, *supra* n. 4, at 648.

> revised or additional Witness Statements, including statements from persons not previously named as witnesses, so long as any such revisions or additions respond only to matters contained in another Party's Witness Statements, Expert Reports or other submissions that have not been previously presented in the arbitration.

The same applies as regards party-appointed experts pursuant to the Rules Article 5.3.

## §3.09 EVIDENCE PRODUCTION AND RECOURSE TO COURTS

It may be helpful to suggest that a party's request for document production shall be handled with due regard to the IBA Rules on the Taking of Evidence in International Arbitration (2010). If the arbitrators are inclined to do so although one of the parties objects, it should be observed that the IBA Rules will have to be applied subject to section 26 of the Swedish Arbitration Act if the arbitrators want to avoid the risk of a 'procedural irregularity'. This may compel them to try to mimic what state court judges would do in the same situation under the Procedural Code, since some say that an arbitration agreement may not lead to any limitation as regards the possibility to introduce evidence compared to court proceedings[14] (unless it follows by the inappropriateness test according to section 23 paragraph 2 of the Swedish Arbitration Act). One of the problems that the arbitrators often will have to address regards the materiality of the documents requested. In principle the IBA Rules say that all documents requested shall be material to the outcome (*See* Article 3.3(b).) whereas section 26 of the Swedish Arbitration Act read in the light of Chapter 38 section 2 paragraph 1 of the Procedural Code says that documents shall be produced if it can be assumed that they have significance as evidence. This is not the place to go further into the deeper meaning of these provisions. It suffices to say that it could be brought up with the parties whether 'relevance' shall mean significance for an invoked circumstance or significance for the significance of a document (affecting the evidentiary value of a document introduced as evidence). In the name of transparency, the arbitrators should make their position clear beforehand since it may save the parties a lot of unnecessary time and energy in subsequent document production efforts.

## §3.10 ORAL EVIDENCE

The arbitrators can propose that, unless the parties agree otherwise, Articles 4 and 5 of the IBA Rules on the Taking of Evidence in International Arbitration (2010) shall apply. Such an order cannot be taken to violate due process. The consequence is that as a default most fact witnesses, and party-appointed experts shall produce written statements. It adds to the expenses, but the good thing is that the uncertainty value may be lower, and cost-efficiency enhanced if the evidentiary hearing can be concentrated on cross-examinations.

14. *See* Lindskog, *supra* n. 4, at 698.

## §3.11 HEARINGS

Disregarding agreements on 'documents only arbitrations', the proposed package would anticipate that at least one party requests an oral hearing. An oral hearing which requires a physical meeting is expensive, and it usually requires scheduling the event long into the future and rescheduling is painful. Nevertheless, it has been noted that the opportunity for a party to present its case in person and in the physical presence of the arbitrators is a basic, irreducible aspect of the adjudicatory process which ought in virtually all cases be fully respected.[15]

In most cases the parties will be able to set a time for the hearings and agree on the structure and scheduling of hearing time although agreement may not come easy. Where the parties cannot agree the arbitrators may have to do it for the parties.[16] The same goes when it comes to opportunities to arrange several hearings, e.g., to deal separately with jurisdiction, preliminary matters, liability, quantum, etc. The situation may then be that one of the parties says that it cannot be present at the venue on the time set by the arbitrators or that one or several of the witnesses cannot attend and that the arbitrators' decision does not give the party a fair chance to be heard.

The default proposition should be that each party shall have an opportunity to present its case in person and in the physical presence of the arbitrators. Where however this would lead to costs or delays that are not reasonable considering the significance of physical presence it must be possible for the arbitrators to decide (unless the parties agree otherwise) that the hearings shall be arranged by way of video conferencing. Courts have the same prerogative pursuant to Chapter 5 section 10 (presence of a party) and Chapter 36 section 19 (presence of a witness) of the Procedural Code. It would hardly be a procedural irregularity if the arbitrators were to give themselves the same prerogative. Furthermore, it can be expected that reasonable parties would not be opposed to it *ex ante*.[17] The principle of equal treatment seems to require however that both parties shall participate at remote venues and that the physical or video presence of the tribunal is balanced so as not to give a party an undue advantage (unless the parties agree otherwise).

There are a plethora of questions to address in conjunction with such a decision, but the arbitrators do not have to invent the wheel right from the beginning. Reference can be made, e.g., to the Seoul Protocol on Video Conferencing in International

15. *See* Born, *supra* n. 3, at 2266.
16. Scheduling sub-issues will be left aside here with the remark that the default proposition would be that the parties be allotted equal time and that the chess-clock method be used. *See*, further e.g., Böckstiegel, Karl Heinz, Case Management by Arbitrators: Experiences and Suggestions, in Aksen, Gerald (ed.), Global Reflections on International Law, Commerce and Dispute Resolution: Liber Amicorum in Honour of Robert Briner, at 23 (ICC 2005) and Jan Paulson, The Timely Arbitrator: Reflections on the Böckstiegel Method, 2(1) Arb. Int'l. 19 (2006).
17. Cf. Queen Mary University of London and White & Case, *supra* n. 1: 43% of respondents used videoconferencing 'frequently' during arbitrations, 17% 'always' used it, and 30% used it 'sometimes'. Around 89% said that videoconferencing should be used more often in arbitration. *See also* ICC Commission Report: Controlling time and costs in arbitration paras 22 and 71.

Arbitration.[18] The Protocol addresses due process, confidentiality and practical issues that will not be further discussed here. Suffice it to say that a reference to the Protocol can be part of the parcel.

## §3.12 THE DEFAULT PACKAGE

The arbitrators would now be ready to place the basics of a default procedural agreement on the table. The proposition stands unless the parties are able to agree on how to better it by making trade-offs across the issues. It should be stressed that in real life, the package would have to be adapted much more to the specifics of the given case as known in the planning phase:

> ***Submissions**: The claimant shall state his claims in writing. The respondent shall then state his position in respect of the claims in writing and state all claims of its own. If the respondent has presented claims of its own, the claimant shall state its position concerning such claims in a separate written submission. Each party shall in their written submissions invoke all the facts and proffer all evidence they wish to rely on in support of the claims respective the position. The arbitrators may decide that a party shall respond to the arbitrators' questions or the other party's questions in respect of a submission. The arbitrators may decide that the response to questions shall be given in writing or orally in a preparatory telephone or video conference. The arbitrators may on their own motion or upon a party's reasoned request decide to convene a preparatory conference in order to give the parties an opportunity to give final comments on his or the other party's case.*
>
> ***New claims, circumstances and evidence**: A party may request that the arbitrators shall decide new, amended or supplemented claims. A party may also request that the arbitrators shall consider new circumstances and new evidence. The arbitrators will allow such claims, circumstances and evidence if it is not inappropriate having regard to the finality of the award, the interest of justice, the time plan and the possibility to render a separate award. The party who introduces such claims, circumstances or evidence shall bear all additional arbitration costs and costs for the other party which are due to the late introduction unless the introducing party shows that his request was due to a fault by the other party or it is made pursuant to the IBA Rules on the Taking of Evidence in International Arbitration (2010) Articles 4.6 or 5.3.*
>
> ***Evidence production and recourse to courts**: A request for evidence production shall be directed to the possessor of the evidence without undue delay. A party shall make any request to have recourse to courts for court administered testimonies or court administered evidence production in its first submission. A party may also make such request at a later stage in which case the arbitrators will consider it as a request to introduce new evidence. Article 3 of*

18. The Protocol is available at http://www.kcabinternational.or.kr/user/Board/comm_notice.do?BD_NO=172&CURRENT_MENU_CODE=MENU0015&TOP_MENU_CODE=MENU0014.

*the IBA Rules on the Taking of Evidence in International Arbitration (2010) shall apply subject to section 26 of the Swedish Arbitration Act.*
**Oral evidence**: *Articles 4 and 5 of the IBA Rules on the Taking of Evidence in International Arbitration (2010) shall apply.*
**Hearings**: *The hearings will be arranged at a place and on the dates set out by the arbitrators below. If a party cannot attend in person at the venue and the hearings cannot be re-scheduled subject to agreement between the parties and the arbitrators, the hearings will be conducted by way of videoconferencing using the Seoul Protocol on Video Conferencing in International Arbitration as a steering document. The arbitrators may issue further directions. If a party proffers oral evidence by a person who cannot attend, the same shall apply as regards the examinations of the person.*
**Note**: *If a party, without valid cause, fails to appear at a hearing or otherwise fails to comply with an order of the arbitrators, such failure shall not prevent a continuation of the proceedings and a resolution of the dispute on the basis of the existing materials pursuant to section 24 paragraph 3 of the Swedish Arbitration Act.*

Further details to be agreed on in round two of the negotiations.

CHAPTER 4

# Harmonising Cultural Differences in International Arbitration: The Role of Parties' Reasonable Expectations and Counsel's Ethical Rules

*Patrick Taylor, Shreya Aren & Alma M. Mozetič*

## §4.01 INTRODUCTION

*You can take your English car to France, but that doesn't mean that you can drive on the left-hand side.*

The essence of this analogy guided a Stockholm Chamber of Commerce ('SCC') Tribunal's treatment of a binding party agreement to apply certain international rules of evidence in a Stockholm-seated arbitration. As a result, the Tribunal qualified those international rules and the parties' agreement by reference to Swedish domestic rules of procedure - much to the dissatisfaction of one of the parties. The Tribunal's approach in that case raises an interesting question of how to address and resolve cultural differences in arbitral proceedings, and the role of parties' expectations in guiding arbitral proceedings.

In this chapter, we discuss the role of culture in international arbitration, particularly in the context of issues of procedure and ethics. With respect to procedural issues, we conclude that recent attempts by the arbitration community to harness the benefit of cultural divergences are laudable, but they have not been without challenges, and we suggest that there is space for further consideration of how culture ought properly to influence procedural matters, and what role the parties' reasonable expectations should play in striking the right balance.

With respect to ethics, we observe that these are closely connected with arbitrators' and counsel's legal culture. Those actors import their ethical standards into the conduct of arbitration. However, ethics are not divorced from procedural consid erations. To the contrary, national ethical rules have often evolved as a direct result of national procedural norms. When you import national procedures into international arbitration without also importing corresponding ethical standards, asymmetry can result between the parties because of their counsel's unequal ethical footing, which in turn can undermine procedural fairness and effectiveness. We therefore suggest that further harmonisation of ethical standards applicable in international arbitration would enhance the process of arbitration in the longer term even though it might limit the influence of cultural diversity on the arbitral process.

## §4.02 ROLE OF CULTURE IN INTERNATIONAL ARBITRATION

When we refer to culture in international arbitration, we mean the set of values and instincts that individual parties, counsel, or arbitrators bring into the arbitration by virtue of their experience and background. As regards these participants, their culture flows from their nationalities, place of legal or commercial training, the nature of the professional practice that they have developed, and any judicial or other adjudicatory experience that they may have had. It has also been suggested that arbitral institutions are influenced by cultural factors such as the legal tradition of their local system.[1]

The expectations of parties, arbitrators and counsel in arbitration vary depending on their respective cultures. Participants often expect the arbitration process to be similar to the domestic processes familiar to them and the legal system or national litigation framework that they are accustomed to. While participants in arbitration do not usually expect a specific substantive outcome based on their familiarity with a particular legal tradition, they do expect the arbitration process to be predictable. That is not an unreasonable expectation given that party consent is the lifeblood of arbitration, and arbitration promises customisable procedures that reflect the parties' agreement.

Globalisation has ushered in an era of greater cultural diversity in transnational legal practices.[2] And nowhere has that been more evident than in international commercial arbitration. That is an overwhelmingly good thing too. Cultural diversity reflects arbitration's spirit of inclusivity. That spirit has allowed arbitration to expand and accommodate new perspectives from different legal traditions. Moreover, the flexibility of arbitration allows parties to influence the cultural make-up of a tribunal to allow for a variety of views among the people who will be deciding their dispute. This in turn guarantees that the further development of arbitration will be rooted in a multiplicity of cultural perspectives. As Professors Jan Paulsson and John Barkett have remarked, '[a]s the arbitral process has become global in its reach, new participants demand opportunities to participate in the process - indeed to shape it - rather than

1. W. Kidane, *China-Africa Dispute Settlement: The Law, Economics and Culture of Arbitration*, International Arbitration Law Library, vol. 23, 289-290 (Kluwer Law International 2011).
2. M. D'Silva, *A New Legal Ethics Education Paradigm: Culture and Values in International Arbitration*, 23 Legal Educ. Rev. 83, 98 (2013) https://www.researchgate.net/publication/256064138_A_New_Paradigm_for_Legal_Ethics_Education_Culture_and_Values_in_International_Commercial_Arbitration (accessed 30 April 2020).

accept its consequences in silence. No one can seriously imagine that the process could thrive, or even survive, as a closed shop'.[3]

Cultural diversity is therefore a desirable and inevitable consequence of arbitration's success as a global means of international dispute resolution. That presents both opportunities and challenges.

However, if the influence of cultural diversity is not anticipated by participants in the arbitral process, it can lead to difficulties. Participants could unintentionally misunderstand or misinterpret actions or omissions by parties, counsel or arbitrators on the basis of the practice in their own national jurisdiction. Parties might deploy strategies acceptable in their national legal traditions that in arbitration are considered 'guerilla tactics'.[4] Moreover, the infusion by a tribunal of its own cultural norms to supplant the expectations of the parties could leave some parties cold on their experience of the arbitral process. These negative aspects of cultural diversity can be damaging to the legitimacy of arbitration because while they are often imperceptible, they can undermine certainty and user confidence in the process.

To better understand the impact of culture on arbitration, in the next section, we explore the challenges that arise out of differences in procedure between common law and civil law jurisdictions. We then go on to consider the challenges that arise out of differences in ethical obligations for counsel in different jurisdictions.

## §4.03 PROCEDURE: THE DIVERGENCE BETWEEN COMMON LAW AND CIVIL LAW APPROACHES

The primary driver of cultural difference in international arbitration, certainly in terms of procedural instincts, is whether a participant has a civil law or common law background, or experience of some other system, such as Islamic law. This particularly affects evidentiary issues and expectations regarding the role and responsibilities of the arbitrators.

In this section, we explore some of the differences between common law and civil law traditions. While we identify certain generic differences, national legal systems are not identical and the general observations in this chapter are not, therefore, necessarily true of all individual civil or common law systems.

The general approach of civil and common law traditions to dispute adjudication is different. In common law traditions, the system tends to be 'adversarial'. Parties' counsel advocate their clients' respective cases in opposition to each other, while serving an overriding duty to the court or tribunal not to mislead it and to ensure that the adjudicator has all of the facts and legal points necessary to her in order to apply the law correctly and make a determination. By contrast, the civil law tradition tends to follow an 'inquisitorial' system. In the civil law system, the adjudicator is presumed to know the law. She is tasked with investigating the case and establishing the relevant

3. J.M. Barkett & J. Paulsson, *The Myth of Culture Clash in International Commercial Arbitration*, 5 FIU L. Rev. 1, 11 (2009).
4. *See*, e.g., G.J. Horvath & S. Wilske (eds), *Guerrilla Tactics in International Arbitration* (Kluwer Law International 2013).

factual and legal matrix, with the assistance of the parties and the counsel as directed by the adjudicator.

That distinction between the systems informs respective attitudes to certain procedural issues. For example, in an adversarial system, parties are usually obliged to disclose all relevant evidence in their possession, including evidence adverse to them. The same may apply to legal precedents: in England, a party must bring all relevant legal precedents to the court's attention, including precedents adverse to its case. In addition, the common law adversarial system relies heavily on witness examinations and in-person hearings to present the parties' cases to the adjudicator, explain the evidence and the law, and test the truthfulness and credibility of witnesses. In a civil law inquisitorial system, on the other hand, parties are not required to disclose all relevant evidence: they can pick and choose which documents they present to the court, and it is for the adjudicator to determine whether she has everything that she wants to see. Moreover, there is a general view that a witness cannot be relied upon to give reliable evidence, and that contemporaneous documents therefore constitute weightier evidence.[5] The adjudicator in a civil law tradition is, therefore, likely to value the objective information provided by documentary evidence and expert opinions over the relatively more subjective information provided by the parties and their witnesses.

It follows that whether an arbitrator is more familiar with an inquisitorial or adversarial process could influence how such an arbitrator would seek to shape the procedure of the arbitration that she presides over.

In a recent speech, Professor Bernard Hanotiau expressed the view that it may be common law arbitrators who tend to be more inquisitorial in their approach, as he observes them to be more interventionist during oral submissions.[6] However, whether or not an arbitrator asks questions and tests the submissions and evidence at an oral hearing is not a hallmark of the distinction between adversarial and inquisitorial processes. Indeed, in the English courts – a quintessentially adversarial forum – it is common for judges to intervene during the oral submissions in order to indicate the points that they may be sceptical of or otherwise struggling to rationalise with the facts and the law. That is an exercise in ensuring that the adjudicator understands the case presented by a party; it is not intended to usurp the role of the parties in presenting their own case. Perhaps most interesting in the context of this chapter is Professor Hanotiau's citation of a survey by the Swiss Arbitration Association in which Swiss in-house lawyers unanimously said that truth 'was not their primary concern'.[7] What they instead wanted was for arbitrators 'to impose a peace treaty on commercial warfare'.[8] Professor Hanotiau went on to identify the parties' control of the evidence

5. A.M. Kubalczyk, *Evidentiary Rules in International Arbitration – A Comparative Analysis of Approaches and the Need for Regulation*, 3(1) Groningen J. Int'l L., 85, 90 (2015).
6. C. Sanderson, *Hanotiau on an Arbitrator's Duty*, GAR (2019), https://globalarbitrationreview.com/article/1211462/hanotiau-on-an-arbitrator%E2%80%99s-duty (accessed 30 April 2020).
7. C. Sanderson, *Hanotiau on an Arbitrator's Duty*, GAR (2019), https://globalarbitrationreview.com/article/1211462/hanotiau-on-an-arbitrator%E2%80%99s-duty (accessed 30 April 2020).
8. C. Sanderson, *Hanotiau on an Arbitrator's Duty*, GAR (2019), https://globalarbitrationreview.com/article/1211462/hanotiau-on-an-arbitrator%E2%80%99s-duty (accessed 30 April 2020), citing the 2009 annual meeting of the Swiss Arbitration Association held in Zürich, Switzerland.

produced in arbitral proceedings as an impediment to a search for the truth, contrasting arbitration and English court litigation in this respect.

Establishing truth may be too lofty an ambition for the typical arbitral process. However, what an arbitral process must do is to live up to the parties' expectations. After all, they are the ones paying for the process. That means giving each party an opportunity to present its case in the most efficient manner possible and to reach a correct and enforceable outcome based on a well-reasoned and internally-consistent award.

So how, principally, do the differences between inquisitorial and adversarial instincts impact arbitral processes?

*First*, pursuant to the emphasis on oral evidence and hearings, common law traditions have brief pleadings, often with no evidence or legal arguments. The details and evidence are provided subsequently and tied together with the submissions in skeleton arguments and orally during the hearing. These are often referred to in international arbitration as 'pleading-style' submissions. In contrast, civil law traditions have lengthy pleadings which include facts and legal arguments along with exhibits. These are referred to as 'memorial-style' submissions. Memorial-style submissions dominate the arbitral landscape.[9]

The overall process of an arbitration will vary widely depending on which submission model is followed, and imposing one against the expectations of one of the parties is likely to leave that party displeased. Establishing which of those expectations is reasonable is therefore important for promoting the popularity and legitimacy of arbitration as a means of dispute resolution.

*Second*, by extension of the emphasis on oral evidence, hearings and trials in common law traditions are much longer than in civil law traditions. Where crucial facts can be established on the basis of written documents, hearings are often not necessary in civil law jurisdictions. Moreover, scepticism as to the value of witness evidence deprioritises the examination of witnesses in the processes of civil courts, and the judges tend to lead any examination that may occur. By contrast, common law jurisdictions place great importance on witness testimony, and allow for extensive questioning by the parties of witnesses during the oral hearing to establish their credibility or lack thereof. It takes time in cross-examination to extract objective answers from a witness predisposed to give highly spun and subjective accounts of events or to expose falsehoods, fabrication or exaggeration presented by a witness. A civil law judge who is agnostic as to the outcome of a civil case (as long as it is an objectively correct outcome) is not motivated in the same way as a party to test the evidence of a witness, which may explain why in civil law systems the solution has been to marginalise witness evidence rather than to develop time-consuming processes to test such evidence.

International arbitration has settled on a half-way house when it comes to the examination of witnesses. Hearings are typically much shorter than English or US court hearings, and the examination of witnesses is targeted and more restrained in tone. The

9. Although parties to an all-English arbitration seated in London are still likely to deploy pleading-style submissions and a process more akin to the English court process.

questioning tends to be led by the parties rather than the tribunals, and cross-examination is generally accepted as a means of testing witness evidence. However, this compromise between civil and common law traditions does not meet with universal approval. In the authors' experience, many civil practitioners deem that established practice is too common-law-centric, while some common lawyers bristle at the instinct of civil law arbitrators to discount witness evidence. Again, managing the parties' expectations and determining which expectations are reasonable and legitimate help ensure that the parties come away satisfied with the fairness of the process even if they do not like the substantive outcome.

*Third*, in common law jurisdictions, experts are usually appointed by the parties. In civil law jurisdictions, they tend to be appointed by the adjudicator, either upon the request of the parties or ex officio. The prevailing view of counsel in arbitration (but certainly not the unanimous one) appears to be that parties and their counsel prefer to keep control over the appointment of experts. One of the criticisms of encouraging tribunals to appoint their own experts is that it usually leads to the proliferation of experts as parties cannot be prohibited in arbitration from appointing their own experts in addition to the tribunal's expert.[10] Tribunal-appointed experts therefore usually result in higher overall costs.[11]

*Fourth*, in terms of documentary evidence, because of the duty on parties under common law systems to produce any relevant document, including internal documents and documents contrary to the party's interests, discovery procedures in the adversarial system are key. Contrary to this, discovery procedures are limited in civil law proceedings, as the dispute is usually determined on the basis of evidence voluntarily produced by the parties. In addition, privilege is a common law concept which, by and large, has no direct equivalent in civil law traditions. Lawyer confidentiality is used in civil law jurisdictions instead.

On documentary evidence, arbitration has again broadly settled on a compromise between the prevailing common law and civil law traditions. Critics of disclosure complain that it is costly and wasteful, adding little to the process, while supporters of disclosure complain that the limited power of arbitrators to sanction parties and counsel enables unscrupulous parties to hide documents damaging to their cases, undermining the effectiveness and value of the disclosure process.

As the paragraphs above illustrate, there are a number of fundamental differences in procedure between civil and common law traditions. It follows that legal proceedings between Swedish parties before a Swedish adjudicator in Stockholm look different from legal proceedings between English parties before an English adjudicator in London. These differences can come to a head when the traditions collide in

10. *See* CIArb, *Party-Appointed and Tribunal-Appointed Experts,* International Arbitration Practice Guidelines, 1–3 (2015), *see also* p. 3 ('It is widely accepted that a party's right to be given a fair opportunity to present their case includes a right to call independent experts'), (accessed 1 May 2020), https://www.ciarb.org/media/4200/guideline-7-party-appointed-and-tribunal-appointed-expert-witnesses-in-international-arbitration-2015.pdf.
11. *See* N. Schmidt-Ahrendts, *Expert Teaming – Bridging the Divide Between Party-Appointed and Tribunal-Appointed Experts,* 43 Victoria U. Wellington L. Rev. 653, 655 (2012), http://www.nzlii.org/nz/journals/VUWLawRw/2012/34.pdf (accessed 1 May 2020).

arbitration, as they might if you had, say, an arbitration seated in London, between a US party represented by US counsel and a French party represented by French counsel, presided over by a Swedish arbitrator.

We believe that one of the key reasons giving rise to the dissatisfaction on both sides of the debate is the different ethical obligations placed on counsel in different jurisdictions as a result of the legal system within which they operate, which have a significant impact on procedural compliance and performance. That subject is addressed later in this piece.

At this stage, we observe simply that where the parties' expectations are not met in procedural matters, it can lead to feelings of injustice or complaints about costs that can undermine user satisfaction in the process. A tribunal must therefore be careful not to allow its own cultural views on document production – and other procedural aspects – to supplant the *reasonable* expectations of the parties. Of course, determining the reasonable expectations of the parties on questions of procedure can be challenging, but it is suggested that arbitrators should resist defaulting to their own national systems for guidance unless that outcome is understood to have been within the range of outcomes that the parties reasonably expected.

Before looking at factors that tribunals consider to ascertain the parties' reasonable expectation, we examine in the following section attempts by the arbitration community to harmonise differing procedural traditions.

## §4.04 HARMONISATION IN INTERNATIONAL ARBITRATION

Due to the differences in procedural traditions across the world, harmonising the rules of international arbitration has been a challenge. Institutional rules usually address only the powers of tribunals to set procedure, without prescribing the procedures themselves. This leaves it up to the tribunal to set appropriate procedures guided by any agreements of the parties and subject to the norms of due process, fairness and any mandatory rules of *lex arbitri*. For example, the London Court of International Arbitration ('LCIA'),[12] International Centre for Settlement of Investment Disputes ('ICSID'),[13] International Chamber of Commerce ('ICC'),[14] United Nations Commission on International Trade Law ('UNCITRAL'),[15] SCC,[16] Singapore International Arbitration Centre ('SIAC')[17] and Hong Kong International Arbitration Centre ('HKIAC')

12. LCIA Arbitration Rules, Art. 14 (2014), https://www.lcia.org/Dispute_Resolution_Services/lcia-arbitration-rules-2014.aspx#Article%2014 (accessed 30 April 2020).
13. ICSID Arbitration Rules, rule 19 (2006), http://icsidfiles.worldbank org/icsid/icsid/staticfiles/basicdoc/partf-chap03.htm (accessed 30 April 2020).
14. ICC Arbitration Rules, Art. 22 (2017), https://iccwbo.org/dispute-resolution-services/arbitration/rules-of-arbitration/ (accessed 30 April 2020).
15. UNCITRAL Arbitration Rules, Art. 17 (as adopted in 2013), https://uncitral.un.org/sites/uncitral.un.org/files/media-documents/uncitral/en/uncitral-arbitration-rules-2013-e.pdf (accessed 30 April 2020).
16. SCC Arbitration Rules, Art. 23 (2017), https://sccinstitute.com/media/1407444/arbitrationrules_eng_2020.pdf (accessed 30 April 2020).
17. SIAC Rules, Art. 19 (2016), https://www.siac.org.sg/our-rules/rules/siac-rules-2016 (accessed 30 April 2020).

Rules[18] all provide wide discretion for the tribunal to conduct the proceedings as they think best.

Due process in arbitration is embodied in the duties of tribunals, for example, to 'conduct the arbitration in an impartial, efficient and expeditious manner, giving each party an equal and reasonable opportunity to present its case' (SCC Rules, Article 23(2)),[19] or to 'act fairly and impartially and ensure that each party has a reasonable opportunity to present its case' (ICC Rules, Article 22.4),[20] or to 'act fairly and impartially as between all parties, giving each a reasonable opportunity of putting its case and dealing with that of its opponent(s)' (LCIA Rules, Article 14.4(i)).[21] However, what constitutes a 'reasonable opportunity to present its case' is likely to be understood differently by parties and counsel based on cultural differences between them. What might be due process for the common lawyer in respect of document disclosure might be unduly burdensome and costly in the eyes of a civil lawyer.

In the past, some of these cultural differences have been resolved through the harmonisation of procedural and evidentiary processes. The process of harmonisation in the context of international arbitration started with the New York Convention and the UNCITRAL Model Law[22] and has continued with, for example, various guides issued by the International Bar Association ('IBA') Arbitration Committee, including most notably the 2010 IBA Rules on the Taking of Evidence in International Arbitration (the 'IBA Rules'). Professor Gabrielle Kauffman-Kohler has noted that there has been convergence of practice in international arbitration on a number of procedural points outside the ambit of the IBA Rules too.[23] Having certainty about procedures helps to de-bias decision-making and eliminate what has been referred to as the 'dark side of arbitral discretion'.[24]

Much of the recent debate on soft law in international arbitration has, however, revolved around the December 2018 launch of the Rules on the Efficient Conduct of Proceedings in International Arbitration (the 'Prague Rules') that are seen as a civil law

18. HKIAC Arbitration Rules, Art. 13 (2018), https://www.hkiac.org/arbitration/rules-practice-notes/hkiac-administered-2018 (accessed 30 April 2020).
19. SCC Arbitration Rules, Art. 23(2).
20. ICC Arbitration Rules, Art. 22(4).
21. LCIA Arbitration Rules, Art. 14(4)(i).
22. G. Kaufmann-Kohler, *Globalization of Arbitral Procedure*, 36 Vand. J. Transnat'l L. 1312, 1321 (2003); *See, also*, T.T Landau & R. Weeramantry, *A Pause for Thought*, in *International Arbitration: The Coming of a New Age?*, ICCA Congress Series, vol. 17 (Albert Jan Van den Berg ed. Kluwer Law International 2013), 496 adding the UNCITRAL Rules of 1976 as another ground-breaking instrument in the harmonisation process.
23. G. Kaufmann-Kohler, *Globalization of Arbitral Procedure*, 36 Vand. J. Transnat'l L. 1312, 1325–1330 (2003).
24. K.P. Berger, *Common Law vs. Civil Law in International Arbitration: The Beginning or the End?* 36 J. Int'l Arb. 295, 304–305, citing W. Park, *The 2002 Freshfields Lecture – Arbitration's Protean Nature: The Value of Rules and the Risks of Discretion*, in *Arbitration Insights: Twenty Years of the Annual Lecture of the School of International Arbitration, Sponsored by Freshfields Bruckhaus Deringer*, 331, paras 17–91 et seq. (Julian Lew & Loukas Mistelis eds Kluwer Law International 2006).

response to what is perceived by some as the common law approach enshrined in the IBA Rules.[25] This development therefore justifies a brief detour.

Intended to provide 'an efficient, economical and fair process for the taking of evidence in international arbitrations, particularly those between [p]arties from different legal traditions',[26] the IBA Rules are supposed to bridge the gap between common and civil law approaches to document production. They do not provide for broad discovery but instead contemplate the disclosure of specific documents or narrow categories of documents that are relevant and material to the outcome of the case and that are in the possession, custody or control of the opposing party. Due to their transcultural nature and high levels of acceptance, tribunals often look to the IBA Rules for guidance even in the absence of a positive agreement between the parties to apply the rules.

However, some participants in international arbitration believe that there is a direct link between the adoption of the IBA Rules and the increasing cost and time inefficiencies of arbitration proceedings. They consider that the IBA Rules adhere too closely to the common law approach to evidence and have led to the importation of techniques associated with the adversarial system such as extensive discovery phases and lengthy cross-examination of witnesses.[27] As will be explored later in this chapter, these criticisms appear to emanate most prominently from civil lawyers whose national systems do not have specific or wide-ranging ethical rules designed to control and safeguard the disclosure and witness examination processes typical for a common law system. That is not surprising given that extensive discovery is not part of those legal traditions – if you do not have wide-ranging disclosure rules, you do not need wide-ranging ethical rules to govern such processes.

The pockets of criticism of the IBA Rules led to the development of the Prague Rules, conceptualised predominantly by Russian and Eastern European lawyers. The Prague Rules provide a 'menu of options said to be more palatable to civil lawyers'.[28] The Prague Rules' civil law lilt is revealed by their original name: 'Inquisitorial Rules on the Taking of Evidence in International Arbitration'. Article 4.2 of the Prague Rules

25. A. Rombach & H. Shalbanava, *The Prague Rules: A New Era of Procedure in Arbitration or Much Ado about Nothing?* 17 SchiedsVZ, 53, 53–60 (2019); D.G. Henriques, *The Prague Rules: Competitor, Alternative or Addition to the IBA Rules on the Taking of Evidence in International Arbitration*, in *ASA Bulletin*, vol. 36 Issue 2, (Matthias Scherer ed. Kluwer Law International 2018), 351–363; M. McIlwrath, *The Prague Rules: The Real Cultural War Isn't Over Civil vs Common Law*, Kluwer Arbitration Blog (2018), http://arbitrationblog.kluwerarbitration.com/2018/12/12/the-prague-rules-the-real-cultural-war-isnt-over-civil-vs-common-law/?print=pdf (accessed 30 April 2020); P. Costa e Silva, *Arbitration, Jurisdiction and Culture: Apropos the Rules of Prague*, Kluwer Arbitration Blog (2018), http://arbitrationblog.kluwerarbitration.com/2018/07/16/arbitration-jurisdiction-culture-apropos-rules-prague-part/ (accessed 30 April 2020).
26. IBA Rules on the Taking of Evidence in International Arbitration, Preamble, p. 4 (29 May 2010) ('IBA Rules'), https://www.ibanet.org/ENews_Archive/IBA_30June_2010_Enews_Taking_of_Evidence_new_rules.aspx (accessed 4 May 2020).
27. A. Rombach & H. Shalbanava, *The Prague Rules: A New Era of Procedure in Arbitration or Much Ado about Nothing?* 17 SchiedsVZ, 53, 54 (2019).
28. F. Singarajah, *Cultural Differences in International Arbitration*, PLC Arbitration Blog (2020), http://arbitrationblog.practicallaw.com/cultural-differences-in-international-arbitration/ (accessed 30 April 2020).

demonstrates the fundamental difference in approach promoted by these new rules, encouraging the tribunal and parties to 'avoid any form of document production, including e-discovery'.

Some practitioners argue that users of arbitration are not harmed by having the ability to choose between different sets of evidentiary guidelines leaning more or less towards civil or common law traditions, while others say that the Prague Rules create more problems than they solve.[29] A detailed assessment of the Prague Rules vis-à-vis the IBA Rules is beyond the scope of this chapter but their launch demonstrates that even with the IBA Rules, which have enjoyed near-universal acceptance, there are critics who consider that arbitration should look to different cultural influences for guidance.

The 2018 Queen Mary Survey on the Evolution of Arbitration indicates that stakeholders want clarity on provisions ranging from independence and impartiality of arbitrators to the conduct of parties and their advisors.[30] Most stakeholders consider arbitral institutions and arbitration interest groups (such as the Chartered Institute of Arbitrators ('CIArb'), International Council for Commercial Arbitration ('ICCA') and IBA to be best placed to influence future harmonisation in these areas.[31]

As a practical matter, certainty in arbitration can be achieved through harmonising standards, guidelines and approaches and through the consensual procedural agreements and the clarity of tribunal interventions in their procedural orders, especially the initial Procedural Order No. 1. It is also important not to lose sight of the fact that diversity and flexibility are among the strengths of arbitration. The legitimate and reasonable expectations of parties to arbitration should allow us to chart a course balancing the twin goals of harmonisation and diversity.

## §4.05 THE CASE IN FAVOUR OF THE PARTIES' REASONABLE EXPECTATIONS

The exercise of a tribunal's discretion on questions of procedure undoubtedly has the potential to cause party dissatisfaction, especially where unexpected cultural influences drive an outcome that is unpopular with one or more of the parties. Procedural harmonisation helps to limit unexpected outcomes, but harmonisation can

29. M. McIlwrath, *The Prague Rules: The Real Cultural War Isn't Over Civil vs Common Law*, Kluwer Arbitration Blog (2018), http://arbitrationblog.kluwerarbitration.com/2018/12/12/the-prague-rules-the-real-cultural-war-isnt-over-civil-vs-common-law/?print=pdf (accessed 30 April 2020).

30. *See* Queen Mary University of London, White & Case, '2018 International Arbitration Survey: The Evolution of International Arbitration' Chart 38, p. 34, http://www.arbitration.qmul.ac.uk/media/arbitration/docs/2018-International-Arbitration-Survey---The-Evolution-of-International-Arbitration-(2).PDF (accessed 30 April 2020).

31. *See* Queen Mary University of London, White & Case, '2018 International Arbitration Survey: The Evolution of International Arbitration' Chart 39, p. 36, http://www.arbitration.qmul.ac.uk/media/arbitration/docs/2018-International-Arbitration-Survey---The-Evolution-of-International-Arbitration-(2).PDF (accessed 30 April 2020).

only go so far if arbitration wishes to preserve the flexibility that is one of its hallmarks. The risk of unexpected procedural outcomes will therefore persist.

To limit that risk, arbitrators should be sensitive to differences in the parties' legal cultures. Tribunals should consider what may constitute due process and fairness in different jurisdictions, and whether it is reasonable for a party to expect such cultural influences to be taken into account in respect of any given procedural issue. The consensual nature of arbitration and the market-driven system in which it operates dictates that a tribunal's ultimate focus should be on user satisfaction: users must feel the benefits of pursuing arbitration over court litigation and of using an international procedure over a national one. In order to do so, tribunals must determine the parties' reasonable expectations in the conduct of the proceedings against the overarching principle of fairness. The parties' culture will inform those expectations.

Objective factors including, for instance, the seat of the arbitration, governing law of the relevant agreement, nationality of the parties, and place of performance of the contract could be considered in evaluating parties' reasonable procedural expectations. In all instances, this assessment will require consideration of all the circumstances of the case.

It is not possible to be prescriptive about all the relevant circumstances that could drive parties' reasonable procedural expectations, but experienced practitioners and arbitrators will have a strong sense of what is *not* a reasonable expectation. One such example that raised a few smiles was the claim by a party from a south Asian jurisdiction that the merits hearing in their arbitration should be delayed because that party had a reasonable expectation not to be subjected to the risk of catching a cold by having to travel to London for hearings in winter, even though it had agreed to London-seated arbitration.

But sometimes the question of what is or is not a reasonable expectation is not so easy to determine. For example, is it reasonable for an arbitrator to consider that the reason she was appointed for a matter was to bring to the table her own specific cultural and legal perspectives, even if those diverge from the governing law and the *lex arbitri*, and if so, should that be treated as part of a party's reasonable expectations?

At a recent closed-door conference, a number of eminent arbitrators debated that question. Specifically, they considered whether, when appointed to adjudicate an English law governed dispute, non-English arbitrators should consider themselves bound by precedent in the same manner as an English judge would be. It was surprising that there was substantial support for both 'yes' and 'no' answers to that question. Some clearly considered that the binding nature of precedent was part of English law and must therefore be adhered to, while others considered that as a foreign lawyer it was proper for them to bring their foreign perspective into the adjudication process and to apply their experience to interpret what they considered English law to be, even if that view might differ from the leading court decision on that question. The reason given for this was that it is in the nature of law to evolve, and an arbitrator ought to be free to propose that evolution in the same manner as the Supreme Court can do in England.

While the position of arbitrators on this topic is not uniform, the English courts have held that arbitrators in English-law governed disputes are bound by the doctrine of precedent, and that failure to abide by it may give grounds to the setting aside of an award.[32] But what if one is sitting in a foreign-seated arbitration where the governing law of the contract is English law? Thus, while arbitrators in English-law governed proceedings seated in England may find themselves bound by precedent or risk their award being set aside, their counterparts in a foreign-seated arbitration may not feel compelled to operate under such constraints. Given the divergence of views among arbitrators as to how much of their own legal tradition they should import into cases they adjudicate, this is an important factor for parties and appointing authorities to bear in mind when selecting arbitrators for specific disputes. It is a dynamic that complicates efforts to identify what the parties' reasonable expectations of their tribunal might be in any given case, and it is a dynamic that therefore risks provoking dissatisfaction among one or more of the parties in the face of any unexpected procedural or, indeed, merits decision. What this serves to highlight is that having regard to the parties' expectations will not guarantee user satisfaction. Where parties' expectations conflict, there will always be a risk of discord. But the parties' reasonable expectations should play some role in guiding the tribunal's perspective.

## §4.06 DIFFERENCES IN ETHICAL RULES

If procedural decisions should be informed by the parties' reasonable expectations as to the conduct of proceedings, what role do professional ethical rules play in shaping the conduct of arbitral proceedings?

Professional ethical rules guide counsel's approach to the procedure of international arbitration. Where procedures are the same or similar to those that counsel are accustomed to in their home jurisdiction, it is likely that they will import the same ethical standards to their performance of such procedures in arbitration, unless their national systems exempt them from doing so. English lawyers, for example, have prominent professional obligations preventing them from suppressing disclosure of damaging documents, and rules preventing them from accusing opposing parties, counsel or witnesses of dishonesty in the absence of clear evidence.[33] Such ethical traditions safeguard the proper performance of evidentiary processes in England.

32. *John Sisk & Son Ltd v. Carmel Building Services Ltd* [2016] EWHC 806 (TCC) (15 April 2016) (refusal to set aside on the basis that the arbitrator correctly followed precedent in relation to a costs claim); *Carboex SA v. Louis Dreyfus Commodities Suisse SA* [2011] EWHC 1165 (Comm) (setting aside on basis that, among other errors of law, the tribunal disregarded English Court of Appeal precedent); *Ocean Marine Navigation Ltd v. Koch Carbon Inc.* [2003] All ER 564 (remarking that the principles set forth by precedent were 'binding on the arbitrator'). *See generally*, G. Rizzo Amaral, *Judicial Precedent and Arbitration – Are Arbitrators Bound by Judicial Precedent? A Comparative Study among England, Scotland, the United States and Brazil* in *Rev. Brasileira de Arbitragem* vol. 14 (J.B. Lee & D. de Andrade Levy eds Kluwer Law International 2017), 49, 63–68.

33. *Medcalf v. Mardell* [2002] UKHL 27 ('This particular professional duty sometimes poses difficult problems for practitioners. Making allegations of dishonesty without adequate grounds for doing so may be improper conduct. Not making allegation of dishonesty where it is proper to make such allegations may amount to dereliction of duty.'); *see also* the Bar Standards Board ('BSB') Misconduct, Rule C7 (read in conjunction with gC96), https://www.barstandardsboard

But where counsel's home court system does not contain procedural concepts that the arbitral process has introduced, such counsel will find no guidance in their national ethical rules to guide their conduct in arbitration. This can give rise to difficulties.

For one thing, it can create situations where parties find themselves fighting on unequal terms, with their respective counsel bound by different ethical restrictions. This can happen in two ways: either opposing counsel's ethical rules differ in a way that allows for a different interpretation of procedural rules – with one interpretation inevitably being more advantageous than the other, such as the US approach to witness preparation; or the opposing counsel is subject to no national ethical rules at all that would restrict certain activities that could favour her client, such as where there is no assumed restriction on unilateral communications with an opponent's witnesses.

Ethical culture is an important element of a party's expectations of the arbitral process. A perception of inequality because the opponent's conduct would be unethical in the party's home jurisdiction, can undermine confidence in the arbitral process and cause dissatisfaction among its users. Putting the parties on an equal ethical footing in arbitration would therefore reduce the scope for conflict and increase fairness and predictability in the process.

In this section, we examine four areas of procedure impacted by ethical obligations on counsel, and we consider whether arbitraging ethical culture in arbitration is fair game or whether it undermines the legitimacy of arbitration as a means of resolving disputes fairly and should therefore be tackled by the arbitral community. The four areas of procedure considered in this section are: (i) witness preparation, (ii) constitution of the tribunal and the appointment of counsel, (iii) disclosure, and (iv) alleging counsel misconduct.

### [A] Witness Preparation

Perhaps the most well-known procedural issue giving rise to ethical conflict in the context of international arbitration is the preparation of witnesses for oral examination. Much has been written about this topic.[34] There is general agreement in international arbitration that *some* pre-testimonial interaction with a witness is permissible. But within the parameters set by the applicable arbitral rules, parties and their counsel can position themselves on various points of the spectrum depending on the ethical rules of their place of legal qualification.

In the United States, failure to prepare a witness to the fullest allowable degree may constitute ethical misconduct or malpractice.[35] But while US attorneys can

---

.org.uk/uploads/assets/de77ead9-9400-4c9d-bef91353ca9e5345/da444eba-fa2e-40c2-b9ff7f705f462807/second-edition-test31072019104713.pdf (accessed 29 September 2020),

34. *See, e.g.*, C.A. Rogers, *Ethics in International Arbitration*, 100 (OUP 2014).

35. C.A. Rogers, *Ethics in International Arbitration*, 108 (OUP 2014) (citing, among other, discussion in District of Columbia Bar, *Opinion No. 79: Limitations on a Lawyer's Participation in the Preparation of Witness Testimony*, Code Prof. Resp. & Opinion D.C. Bar Legal Ethics Comm. (1991) 138, 139). *See* J. Gaal & L.P DiLorenzo, *Ten Degrees of Separation, How to Avoid Crossing the Line on Witness Preparation*, 2018 NYSBA Journal 26, 26 (2018) ('the failure to [prepare a

conduct a mock cross-examination on the evidence as a means of preparing a witness, solicitors and barristers preparing a witness to give evidence in the English court may not do so.[36] The court in *R v. Momodou*[37] aptly summarised the position under English law 'There is no place for witness training in this country, we do not do it. It is unlawful.' By contrast, some European lawyers are prohibited altogether from pre-testimonial communications with witnesses[38] and could even be subject to criminal sanctions for non-compliance,[39] while other European systems allow a certain degree of pre-testimonial interaction with a witness, subject to restrictions.[40] Some national systems have identified the risk of an uneven playing field in arbitration, and while restricting witness interaction in court proceedings they contain lighter restrictions for witness preparation in arbitration proceedings.[41]

The international arbitration community recognised the risk of unfair advantages being secured by one party over another by virtue of its counsel being permitted to

---

witness] can constitute a breach of an attorney's professional responsibility, as attorneys are required to 'competently' represent their clients'), https://www.bsk.com/uploads/Ten-Degrees-Feb-2018.pdf (accessed 1 May 2020). *See also*, S.V. Vasilev, *From Liberal Extremity to Safe Mainstream? The Comparative Controversies of Witness Preparation in the United States*, 9 Int'l Commentary on Evidence, 1, 7–8 (2011) ('the failure to adequately prepare a witness might qualify as malpractice'), https://pure.uva.nl/ws/files/1198357/104946_Comparative_Controversies_of_Witness_Preparation_in_the_United_States.pdf (accessed 1 May 2020).

36. In concrete terms, it is believed that familiarising a witness with the process and conducting a mock cross-examination in respect of a hypothetical set of facts is generally permitted but training witnesses with mock cross-examination on the specific subject of their evidence is not. There are serious personal consequences for those who breach the rules. Due to the fine line between witness familiarisation (allowed) and witness training (not allowed), English lawyers sometimes abstain from preparing witnesses altogether lest they be seen to cross that line. *See* Code of Conduct for Solicitors, Arts 2.1–2.3; *see also* SRA website, stating that a 'serious failure to meet our standards or a serious breach of our regulatory requirements may result in our taking regulatory action against you', SRA Code of Conduct for Solicitors, https://www.sra.org.uk/solicitors/standards-regulations/code-conduct-solicitors/ (accessed 4 May 2020). *See also* the Bar Standards Board, Written Standards for the Conduct of Professional Work, s. 3, [6.1.2.]–[6.1.3.]; Bar Standards Board, Code of Conduct of the Bar of England and Wales and Written Standards for the Conduct of Professional Work (8th edition, adopted by the Bar Council on 18 September 2004, effective from 31 October 2004), [705], [705(b)].
37. [2005] 2 All ER 571, at [584].
38. C.A. Rogers, *Ethics in International Arbitration*, 112 (OUP 2014) (compare, for example, Netherlands that allows a degree of witness preparation and Belgium that prohibits it completely).
39. C.A. Rogers, *Ethics in International Arbitration*, 108 n. 40 (OUP 2014), citing *See* Mirjan Damaska, *Presentation of Evidence and Fact Finding Precision*, 123 U. Pa. L. Rev. 1083, 1088–1089 (1975).
40. In Germany, for example, witness preparation is in theory allowed, but a lawyer must not act in a way that leads to a deliberate dissemination of untruthful statements. *See* s. 43a(3) *Bundesrechtsanwaltsordnung* (BRAO) (The German Federal Lawyers' Act). Further, intentionally encouraging a witness to give untruthful testimony in court or produce a knowingly false statement intended to mislead the tribunal may give rise to a host of criminal offences. For example, a lawyer may be charged with fraud (*Prozessbetrug*, § 263 Criminal Code), participation in providing false unsworn testimony (*Teilnahme an einer uneidlichen Falschaussage*, § 153 Criminal Code), perjury (*Meineid*, § 154 Criminal Code), or obstruction of justice (*Teilnahme an einer Strafvereitelung*, § 258 Criminal Code). *See also* R. Harbst, *A Counsel's Guide to Examining and Preparing Witnesses in International Arbitration*, 175–212 (Kluwer Law International 2015).
41. These countries include France, Belgium and Switzerland. C.A. Rogers, *Ethics in International Arbitration*, 115–116 (OUP 2014).

operate under less stringent ethical restrictions, and it has moved to address the problem. Thus the IBA Rules[42] and the IBA Guidelines on Party Representation[43] both suggest that parties may discuss the prospective evidence of witnesses in preparation for cross-examination, as long as they do not seek to influence the witnesses' own account of relevant facts. There does remain, however, a significant lack of guidance on what is or is not permitted in practice, not least because of an absence of clarity as to what practitioners who are bound to adhere to their national rules on witness preparation should do when acting in an international arbitration that may well be seated outside of their national jurisdiction.

The interpretation of these rules is inevitably informed by the particular counsel's own ethical rules. For example, the IBA Rules state that '*it* [is] *not improper*' for counsel to '*discuss* [the witness's] *prospective testimony with them*'.[44] It is not inconceivable that an American lawyer may read this with the background of their own ethical rules in mind to interpret 'discuss' as allowing mock cross-examination of the witness on the evidence, whereas an English lawyer may read 'discuss' to mean something considerably less than that. On the other hand, for a lawyer whose national ethical rules prohibit all pre-testimony contact and make no exemption for arbitral proceedings, this rule may not make any sense.

Divergence in this area therefore continues to pose a problem for practitioners. In addition to generating the possibility of an inequality of arms, the lack of clarity over which rules apply (national professional ethics rules, ethical rules of the seat, or both?) creates another problem. Professor Rogers calls it a 'double deontology' problem – a situation where an attorney is subject to two sets of ethical rules that are in conflict, so that she will inevitably find herself in violation of one set of rules whichever set she follows. A notorious example from 2007 is a fine of EUR 10,000 that an American-qualified attorney and French national, who was employed with a major U.S. law firm, had to pay after being criminally convicted in France for interviewing a witness in France for the purpose of obtaining information for a court proceeding in the US.[45] He was stuck between a rock and a hard place – had he followed French rules and abstained from interviewing the witness, he would have fallen foul of US rules requiring active preparation of witnesses.

It remains an open question to what extent national bar associations will consider themselves to have the power to police ethical duties extraterritorially in foreign-seated

42. IBA Rules, Art. 4(3) ('It shall not be improper for a Party, its officers, employees, legal advisors or other representatives to interview its witnesses or potential witnesses and to discuss their prospective testimony with them.').
43. IBA Guidelines on Party Representation in International Arbitration (25 May 2013) ('IBA Guidelines on Party Representation'), Guideline 24 (Witnesses and Experts): ('A Party Representative may, consistent with the principle that the evidence given should reflect the Witness's own account of relevant facts, events or circumstances, or the Expert's own analysis or opinion, meet or interact with Witnesses and Experts in order to discuss and prepare their prospective testimony.'), https://www.ibanet.org/Publications/publications_IBA_guides_and_free_materials.aspx (accessed 30 April 2020).
44. IBA Rules, Art. 4(3).
45. C.A. Rogers, *Ethics in International Arbitration*, 107 (OUP 2014) (*citing* Paris Court of Appeals, File n. 06/06272, Judgment of 28 March 2007).

arbitration. As discussed above, some national ethics rules expressly exempt foreign attorneys appearing in local arbitral proceedings from the application of local ethical rules, but not all do. In those cases, where for example the ethical rules of the arbitral seat, or the arbitral tribunal's rules, require a lawyer to prepare a witness - even if this is inimical to the rules of the national bar association in which the attorney is qualified - counsel will find herself in violation of one set of rules regardless of which set of rules she decides to follow. Finally, counsel are also exposed to the possibility of an 'ethical vacuum' in a situation where domestic rules under which counsel are regulated mandate that the rules of the seat of the arbitration apply to issues of ethics and professional conduct but the local ethical regulations of the seat exempt foreign attorneys appearing in arbitral proceedings from the application of the local rules.[46]

### [B] Appointment of Counsel and Arbitrators

The appointment of counsel and arbitrators is another procedural step where ethical rules can create inequalities.

In civil law systems, a personal conflict of interest is considered to be a personal matter rather than a matter subject to regulatory oversight. Individual counsel therefore has wide discretion to ascertain whether or not such conflicts exist and to reach their own conclusion unconcerned by the risk of regulatory sanction for reaching the wrong conclusion. By contrast, in most common law systems, rules pertaining to conflicts of interests are regulated and subject of strict professional conduct rules.

In view of the divergence in national professional rules on the conceptualisation of a conflict of interest, various institutional rules and societies have sought to develop guidance on issues such as the appointment of arbitrators,[47] including, for example, the IBA,[48] and LCIA[49] and ICC Rules,[50] and most recently at the time of writing the draft Code of Conduct for investor-state dispute settlement ('ISDS') adjudicators released by ICSID and UNCITRAL.[51]

46. C.A. Rogers, *Ethics in International Arbitration*, 109 (OUP 2014).
47. P. Halprin & S. Wah, *Ethics in International Arbitration*, 2018 J. Disp Resol. 1 (2018), https://scholarship.law.missouri.edu/cgi/viewcontent.cgi?article=1789&context=jdr (accessed 30 April 2020).
48. IBA Guidelines on Conflicts of Interest in International Arbitration (23 October 2014) ('IBA Guidelines on Conflicts of Interest), Guidelines 2-3, and *see* Appendices that include the Green, Orange and Red Lists; and *see* IBA Guidelines on Party Representation, Guideline 5: 'Once the Arbitral Tribunal has been constituted, a person should not accept representation of a Party in the arbitration when a relationship exists between the person and an Arbitrator that would create a conflict of interest, unless none of the Parties objects after proper disclosure.'
49. LCIA Arbitration Rules, Art. 5(4); and *see* Annex on General Guidelines for the Parties' Legal Representatives.
50. ICC Arbitration Rules, Art. 11(2).
51. Article 12 of the Draft Code that deals with enforcement envisages primarily voluntary compliance, and preserves any applicable institutional rules on sanctions that may apply. Interestingly, Commentary to Article 12 suggests we may see potential additional sanctions (relating to remuneration, disciplinary measures, reputational sanctions and notifications to professional associations) and the creation of an advisory centre or a standing body to enforce the Code, depending on the means of the implementation of the Code. *See* ICSID and UNCITRAL,

Harmonisation in this area has undoubtedly assisted in safeguarding the legitimacy of arbitration as a fair means of dispute resolution, but there is still a lot of uncertainty when it comes to ascertaining how a tribunal will deal with a challenge to an arbitrator or counsel on the basis of an alleged conflict of interest. The proliferation of such challenges has led to complaints about 'guerilla tactics' and the high costs of arbitration. On the other hand, very restrictive interpretations of situations of conflict damage arbitration's image. For that reason, all eyes will be on *Halliburton* that is pending before the UK Supreme Court at the time of writing.[52] The Court heard oral argument in November 2019 on the issue of whether or not an arbitrator's failure to disclose circumstances that should have been disclosed would, by itself, give rise to justifiable doubts as to their impartiality. The decision of the Court of Appeal was criticised for setting the bar to the exclusion of an arbitrator too high. Given the importance of the case, the LCIA, ICC, Chartered Institute of Arbitrators and the Grain and Free Trade Association ('GAFTA') all intervened in the Supreme Court proceedings to make submissions on behalf of the arbitration community.

### [C] Disclosure

There is general agreement that some ability to request document disclosure in international arbitration is valuable.[53] But within the allowable parameters, the question of where parties and their counsel stand on the spectrum varies widely and may again be informed by their domestic ethical traditions.

In both the US and the UK, failure to produce documents that undermine the producing party's case or that are in some way contrary to the producing party's interests constitutes severe misconduct.[54] This approach contrasts sharply with the general approach to discovery in civil law jurisdictions where the judge is responsible for gathering evidence that she deems is necessary to reach a just decision. The parties can propose evidence to be considered by the court, but counsel need not voluntarily disclose documents adverse to its client – in fact, proactive disclosure of such documents may put such counsel in breach of professional rules in their jurisdiction.

A strong consensus emerged on a common standard for document production under the IBA Rules. However, as discussed above, criticism of the IBA Rules by a group of practitioners gave rise to the development of the Prague Rules. The question foreshadowed earlier is whether any shortcomings in the disclosure process in arbitration under the IBA Rules arises from the rules themselves or the different ethical standards binding counsel and parties applying those rules. The relatively more common law-focused IBA Rules work because of the strict duty on counsel to turn over

*Draft Code of Conduct for Adjudicators in Investor-State Dispute Settlement*, World Bank (2020),https://icsid.worldbank.org/en/Documents/Draft_Code_Conduct_Adjudicators_ISDS.pdf (accessed 4 May 2020).

52. *Halliburton Company v. Chubb Bermuda Insurance Ltd & Ors* [2018] EWCA Civ 817.
53. C.A. Rogers, *Ethics in International Arbitration*, 100 (OUP 2014).
54. Civil Procedure Rules, Part 31 (Disclosure and Inspection of Documents) (U.K.); Federal Rules of Civil Procedure (U.S.), rule 26 (Duty to disclose: General Provisions Governing Discovery); Rules of Professional Conduct (N.Y), rules 3.3 and 3.4.

all responsive documents, whether helpful or damaging to the case. The U.S. and English parties know this to be a feature of domestic litigation, which may often drive parties towards settlement. The consequence of being found to have suppressed damaging documents is invariably far more severe than the consequence of disclosing harmful documents, and any counsel complicit in document suppression could have their practising certificates permanently revoked. However, if parties and counsel from different legal traditions do not approach document production process applying the same ethical standards, trust in the process is put at risk, undermining the utility of the process to the fair and just resolution of the dispute, while still costing the parties significant time and money. This divergence is likely a driver of a dissatisfaction among counsel with document disclosure processes in arbitration.

One sometimes hears concerns expressed by lawyers that opposing counsel not bound by the same ethical obligations in respect of document disclosure are less likely to comply with the letter and spirit of disclosure rules. Further, the concern becomes that such counsel may turn a blind eye to certain documents that are damaging for their clients' cases. In fact, it is not inconceivable that a prospective party - should it turn its mind to the issue - may be discouraged from engaging counsel who are bound by strict disclosure obligations, if such party knows that it has certain damaging materials in its possession.

The penalty in arbitration for the failure to produce all documents ordered to be produced is often the drawing of adverse inferences. This is arguably insufficient, either because the sanction itself does not provide sufficient redress or its enforcement is lacking. Counsel frequently raise complaints that tribunals are not quick enough to apply the adverse inferences sanction decisively, and in any event that this is not a tangible sanction to apply. The deterrent effect of adverse inferences is certainly less than the deterrent effect of serious ethical sanctions against lawyers in their personal capacity for complicity in the suppression of documents.

The divergence in ethical cultures therefore may drive inequality of arms in respect of document production. Efforts to address this issue to date are laudable, but there may be scope for further improvement in this area that would help give parties more confidence that document production processes are a worthwhile part of the arbitral process.

Harmonisation would also help to solve the 'double deontology' problem, which can arise during the process of disclosure as it does in respect of witness preparation. For example, the seat of the arbitration may require the attorney to disclose documents that are adverse to their client, even if doing so will place them in violation of national law. Professor Rogers gives an example of a German attorney practising in England who ended up in jail for refusing to disclose client information as required under the UK Proceeds of Crime Act, knowing that making such disclosure would have put him in violation of the German law on confidentiality and subject to disciplinary proceedings in Germany.[55]

55. C.A. Rogers, *Ethics in International Arbitration*, 107 (OUP 2014) (*citing* H. Hellwig, *At the Intersection of Legal Ethics and Globalization: International Conflicts of Law in Lawyer Regulation*, 27 Penn St. Int'l L. Rev. 395, 398–399 (2008)).

### [D] Alleging Misconduct

When in 2014 the Swiss Arbitration Association ('ASA') concluded that 'extremely few complaints' are lodged in international arbitration, it found that the majority of those few that were lodged related not to misconduct as such but rather to 'ethics' in a broad sense: orderly conduct and integrity of arbitral proceedings, admissibility and weighing of evidence, and independence and impartiality of arbitrators.[56] The ASA considered these three strands as all of lesser concern given that arbitral tribunals have wide powers to regulate them

This position, however, does not account for the use of accusations of fraud and dishonesty against opposing counsel as a form of 'guerrilla tactics'. Of course, a serious allegation of fraud is grounds for reporting to the national bar association in which the counsel is regulated.[57] But the threshold is often high. For example, in England, the Solicitors Regulatory Authority ('SRA') will sanction counsel for dishonesty only if the SRA is 'absolutely sure that he or she has been dishonest' on account of 'serious consequences' that flow from such a finding.[58] The other side of the coin is that dishonesty should only be alleged with scarcity, and making such an allegation without good grounds may itself be grounds for sanctions. It is a breach of counsel's ethical obligations in England to allege dishonesty in the absence of cogent evidence of dishonesty, and unless the person against whom it is alleged is given an opportunity to consider and address that evidence.

But not all national rules contain equally stringent tests for alleging and proving dishonesty. This perhaps is the reason why we observe counsel in arbitrations increasingly alleging dishonesty against opposing counsel. Perhaps this is because national rules do not contain any sanctions for frivolous allegations, or perhaps the rules do deal with this, but the improbability of enforcement does not deter such conduct. Using such baseless allegations as a demagogic weapon – because 'all is fair in love and war' – does nothing for the reputation of arbitration. This practice increases the cost of the proceedings and damages the legitimacy of the process. Every time a groundless allegation of misconduct is made, it costs time and money to provide a response and correct the record.[59]

Using such allegations as a means of sowing prejudice should not be permitted, but in the absence of a global standardised code of ethics, should arbitral tribunals take

56. ASA, Statement on the Global Arbitration Ethics Council Discussions (2015), https://www.arbitration-ch.org/en/asa/asa-news/details/983.statement-on-the-global-arbitration-ethics-council-discussions.html?querystart=6l (accessed 1 May 2020); *see also* C. Caher & J. Lim, *Regulation of Counsel and Professional Conduct in International Arbitration*, in International Comparative Legal Guide to: International Arbitration (16th ed. Global Legal Group Ltd 2019), 1–8.
57. A. J van den Berg, *PCA & ICCA, International Commercial Arbitration: Important Contemporary Questions*, 287 (ICCA congress series, no. 11, Kluwer Law International 2003).
58. Solicitors Regulation Authority website, *Suspected Dishonesty*, https://www.sra.org.uk/consumers/problems/fraud-dishonesty/dishonesty-suspected/ (accessed 1 May 2020). *See also Medcalf v. Mardell* [2002] UKHL 27 (*supra* n. 33).
59. D.W. Rivkin, *Ethics in International Arbitration* (9 December 2014), Seoul Arb. Lecture, 22, 23 (2014).

a more active role? Tribunals have an inherent power to police the integrity of proceedings, strengthened by the powers given to them by institutional rules. Tribunals can take an active role in the management of such disputes. Even merely critiquing or admonishing counsel on the record can have a deterrent effect both for the purpose of the present and subsequent proceedings. But tribunals' concerns about taking on the role of police and regulator are understandable.

## §4.07 TOWARDS A COMMON ETHICAL CODE?

The absence of any mandatory international code of conduct that governs arbitral proceedings, its counsel and arbitrators, across the world and that is enforceable against the participants in arbitration allows ethical divergence to sow discontent. Development of a transnational ethics code applicable in arbitration proceedings, along with an enforcement board, would help level the playing field and prevent 'double deontology' as well as problems arising from the existence of the 'ethical vacuum'.

This idea has been proposed on a number of occasions in recent years.[60] But when the Swiss Arbitration Association proposed in 2014 the creation of a Global Arbitration Ethics Counsel to act as the transnational ethics board for arbitration counsel, this proposal was received with mixed reaction and the ASA dropped the proposal in October 2016 on the grounds that the 'time [for a global ethics code] ha[s] not yet come'.[61] Such a global ethics code could arguably give effect to the reasonable expectations of the parties that arbitration will provide a fair and efficient process for the resolution of disputes.

In view of these issues, commentators have offered at least nine possible means of regulating counsel and arbitrator conduct in international arbitration proceedings, and many more have forcefully argued in favour and against each of these options:[62] (i) policing by national bar association(s) under whose jurisdictions advocates are licensed to practice law; (ii) policing by national courts of the seat of arbitration; (iii) policing by national courts where the arbitral award is to be enforced; (iv) policing by

60. *See, e.g.*, R.D. Bishop, *Ethics in International Arbitration*, https://www.arbitration-icca.org/media/0/12763302233510/icca_rio_keynote_speech.pdf (accessed 4 May 2020); and ASA *President's Message, Counsel Ethics in International Arbitration – Could One Take Things a Step Further*, September 2014.
61. ASA, Statement on the Global Arbitration Ethics Council Discussions (2015), https://www.arbitration-ch.org/en/asa/asa-news/details/983.statement-on-the-global-arbitration-ethics-council-discussions.html?querystart=61 (accessed 1 May 2020); *see also* Caher & Lim, *supra* n. 56.
62. *See, e.g.*, C.A. Rogers, *Ethics in International Arbitration* (OUP 2014); Peter Goldsmith QC, Keynote Speech, ICC UK Annual Arbitrators Forum: Ethics in International Arbitration, Conference Materials, 2013; D.W. Rivkin, *Ethics in International Arbitration* (9 December 2014), Seoul Arb. Lecture (2014); S. Schill & C.N. Brower, *Regulating Counsel Conduct Before International Arbitral Tribunals*, in *Making Transnational Law Work in the Global Economy: Essays in Honor of Detlev Vagts* (Cambridge University Press 2010), 488–509; I. Ng, *Rethinking Counsel Ethics in International Arbitration*, Kluwer Arbitration Blog (2019), http://arbitrationblog.kluwerarbitration.com/2019/12/12/rethinking-counsel-ethics-in-international-arbitration/ (accessed 1 May 2020); http://arbitrationblog.kluwerarbitration.com/2016/04/18/who-should-regulate-counsel-conduct-in-international-arbitration/; https://iclg.com/practice-areas/international-arbitration-laws-and-regulations/1-regulation-of-counsel-and-professional-conduct-in-international-arbitration.

arbitral tribunals adjudicating the underlying dispute; (v) policing by arbitral institutions whose rules govern the arbitration; (vi) express standards of conduct incorporated into the parties' agreement; (vii) express standards of conduct set out in the law of the seat of arbitration; (viii) a common standard of conduct agreed upon by counsel; and (ix) an overarching code of conduct for international arbitration common across the sector. It is beyond the scope of this chapter to address the relative merits of each of these options. Until an international consensus emerges, what is most important is the awareness of counsel and arbitrators – who can address these issues head on at the start of the proceedings, and remain attentive to them throughout the proceedings, and attempt to find a common ground to manage such issues and consider sanctions regimes as needed. A proactive approach by counsel and tribunal would help promote fair and even-handed arbitral proceedings.

## §4.08 CONCLUSION

In this chapter, the authors have outlined some of the challenges that arise in the context of arbitration proceedings because of cultural differences. However, despite the differing backgrounds to which users, counsel and arbitrators belong, these participants share objectives which transcend cultural differences – that is of arbitration being 'fair, frugal, fast and foreseeable'.[63]

Given that this is the case, the authors believe there is a common foundation upon which to harness the benefits of cultural diversity in international arbitration. One of the proposed means of doing so is for arbitrators to keep parties' reasonable expectations at the forefront of their considerations while making procedural decisions.

In addition, the authors consider that further discussion about the benefits of a harmonised and enforceable code of conduct in arbitration would be worthwhile.

It has been commented elsewhere that 'we are only now seeing a generation of arbitration practitioners who have grown up on international arbitration'.[64] Perhaps this generation will adopt transnational arbitration culture as its cultural foundation. Until then, it will fall on individual counsel and tribunals to chart the right course through these choppy waters to ensure that the reputation of arbitration is enhanced rather than damaged by cultural differences.

63. Barkett & Paulsson, *supra* n. 3, at 11.
64. F. Singarajah, *Cultural Differences in International Arbitration*, PLC Arbitration Blog, (2020), http://arbitrationblog.practicallaw.com/cultural-differences-in-international-arbitration/ (accessed 30 April 2020).

CHAPTER 5

# The *Belgor* Case: Towards an Extensive Interpretation and Application of Arbitration Agreements

*Anders Reldén & Jacob Frank*

## §5.01 INTRODUCTION

The jurisdiction of an arbitral tribunal only covers issues that fall under the scope of the arbitration agreement. This reflects the consensual nature of the arbitral process. If an arbitration agreement does not cover a specific dispute, the arbitrators have no jurisdiction and a future arbitral award may be set aside or its enforcement may be refused. Therefore it is essential to properly ascertain the scope of an arbitration agreement.

There has long been a debate of whether arbitration agreements should be construed widely or narrowly. There can be no doubt that the current trend in international arbitration is to construe arbitration agreements extensively.[1] Although some jurisdictions apply slightly stricter requirements than would otherwise be the case with respect to the determination of whether an arbitration agreement has been entered into, once such an agreement has been established it is considered that there is no reason for interpreting it narrowly.[2] Favouring a wide interpretation of arbitration clauses avoids the risk of separate proceedings that deal with the same related issues and set of facts. The broad interpretation approach is also typically motivated by an assumption that it is the will of the parties to apply the arbitration agreement to any

1. Born, *International Commercial Arbitration* (The Hague: Kluwer Law International, 2014), 1325 et seq. with extensive references and Redfern & Hunter, *Redfern and Hunter on International Arbitration* (Oxford: Oxford University Press, 2015), 93 et seq.
2. Poudret & Besson, *Comparative Law of International Arbitration* (London: Sweet & Maxell, 2007), 265 et seq.

dispute arising from their commercial relationship. An extensive interpretation would thus correspond to an average and typical *hypothetical* mutual intention of reasonable commercial parties.[3]

Until recently, the international trend had not left its mark in Swedish arbitration law. In *I.H., L. Consulting AB and B.S. v. Kemisten AB and L.M.L.* (NJA 2017 p. 226), the Supreme Court held that:

> An extensive interpretation of an arbitration agreement risks causing a party to be denied the right to have his case tried in court, even though he or she never intended to waive this right. Furthermore, such an application is liable to increase the uncertainty as to what effects an arbitration agreement will have in the future and it may also conflict with the requirement in the Arbitration Act that disputes must concern an identified legal relationship.[4]

When determining the scope of an arbitration agreement under Swedish law, two separate but closely related issues arise.[5] The first is a contract interpretation issue, i.e., the scope shall be determined by interpreting the arbitration agreement. The second issue is a law interpretation issue. Parties cannot refer all their future disputes to arbitration regardless of the basis for such disputes or all disputes arising between the parties during a certain period. The scope of an arbitration agreement is limited by the mandatory requirement in section 1(1) of the Swedish Arbitration Act (SAA) (the Act) that disputes must concern an identified legal relationship (the *identification requirement*). Similar to the arbitrability requirement, the identification requirement is a

3. Born, *supra* n. 1, at 1325 et seq. *See also* e.g., the decision of the House of Lords, 17 Oct. 2007 (*Fiona Trust & Holding & Holding Corporation & Ors 20 v. Yuri Privalov & Ors* 17 sub nom *Premium Nafta Products Ltd. (20th defendant) & Ors v. Fili Shipping Co. Ltd. (14th claimant) & Ors* [2007] UKHL 40), paras 17–18: '*Ordinary businessmen would be surprised at the nice distinctions drawn in the cases and the time taken up by argument in debating whether a particular case falls within one set of words or another very similar set of words. If businessmen go to the trouble of agreeing that their disputes be heard in the courts of a particular country or by a tribunal of their choice they do not expect (at any rate when they are making the contract in the first place) that time and expense will be taken in lengthy argument about the nature of particular causes of action and whether any particular cause of action comes within the meaning of the particular phrase they have chosen in their arbitration clause. [...]. As it seems to us any jurisdiction or arbitration clause in an international commercial contract should be liberally construed.*' and the decision of the Swiss Federal Supreme Court 4A_583/2017 of 1 May 2018, published on 6 Jun. 2018, paras 3.3 and 3.4 (authors' translation): '*The interpretation of an arbitration agreement follows the principles generally applicable to the interpretation of private declarations of intent. The decisive factor is primarily the agreement of the parties' actual will. If such an agreement cannot be determined, the arbitration agreement must be interpreted according to the principle of trust [...] If it is clear that there is a valid arbitration agreement, there is no reason for a restrictive interpretation; rather, it can be assumed that the parties wanted the arbitral tribunal to have comprehensive jurisdiction. [...] In this context, federal court practice assumes that the parties submit their dispute to the arbitral tribunal for assessment as a whole due to a lack of special circumstances and do not want to split it up in such a way that individual questions would have to be submitted to other courts for a decision.*'
4. NJA 2017 p. 226, para. 13. *See also infra* n. 43.
5. The issue of the scope of the arbitration agreement, both *ratione materiae* (i.e., what substantive aspects and disputes are covered by the agreement) and *ratione personae* (i.e., who the parties to the agreement are), is governed by the law applicable to the arbitration agreement. If the place of arbitration is in Sweden, Swedish law will govern the arbitration agreement, unless the parties have (explicitly) agreed otherwise (section 48 of the Act).

statutory validity requirement that restricts the parties' right to submit certain disputes to arbitration.[6] Many other national arbitration laws contain a similar requirement, thus recognizing the need for some degree of precision when parties define the kind of future disputes that they undertake to submit to arbitration. However, it appears that the requirement, in comparison, has had very limited practical importance in these legal systems and there are extremely few reported cases in which an arbitration agreement has been declared invalid for failure comply with this requirement.[7] Although this cannot be used as a pretext for the conclusion that the condition is of no effect, it clearly suggests a broad interpretation being required. The element is also found in the New York Convention.[8]

In what has been described as *'one of the most important arbitration law judgements for years'*,[9] namely *Joint Stock Company Belgorkhimprom v. Koca Inaat Sanayi Ihracat Anonim irketi* (NJA 2019 p. 171, *Belgor*), the Swedish Supreme Court has provided a new precedent regarding the proper determination of the scope of an arbitration agreement, providing for a fairly liberal interpretation not only of the arbitration agreement as such but also of the statutory term 'legal relationship'. In this respect, the precedent brings Swedish arbitration law in line with international arbitration principles. This chapter will address and discuss the precedential value of the judgment and its implications from a practical perspective.

## §5.02 THE *BELGOR* CASE

### [A] Background

The case concerned an arbitral award rendered in a dispute between the Belarussian company Belgor and the Turkish company Koca. In 2011, the parties, as well as a third party,[10] had entered into an agreement under which Koca was to perform certain construction and excavation works in relation to two mining shafts in Turkmenistan

6. The arbitrability requirement, also laid down in section 1(1) of the Act, provides that it is only disputes concerning matters in respect of which the parties *may reach a settlement* that can be referred to one or several arbitrators for resolution under the Act. Disputes which are not amenable to out-of-court settlement are not arbitrable. This means that the limits of arbitrability coincide with the limits of the parties' freedom of contract.
7. Born, *supra* n. 1, at 294 et seq. with extensive references.
8. *See* further section §5.02[B], third bullet point *infra*.
9. Danielsson, *Swedish Arbitration-Related Case Law* in *Stockholm Arbitration Yearbook 2019* (The Netherlands: Kluwer Law International, 2019), 3. However, it should be admitted that this is only partly due to the innovating statements concerning the interpretation and application of arbitration agreements. The Supreme Court also established new precedents in two other respects. One relates to the established presumption that the decision of an arbitral tribunal to deny a request for extension of time should hold, unless the decision appears indefensible. Another precedent was set with respect to the threshold for establishing a procedural irregularity; the Supreme Court clarified that the effect of a procedural error *'should be of some reasonable importance to the challenging party in order to be eligible for challenge'*. These topics will not be discussed further. This article focuses solely on the part of the judgment that deals with the scope determination of arbitration agreements (paras 12–24).
10. The third party, Trust Shakhospectroy (referred to as the 'Executor' in the award), was responsible for technical support and supervision of the Construction Contract.

(the Construction Contract). The Construction Contract contained an arbitration agreement with the following wording:

> Any disputes, disagreements and claims between the Employer and the Contractor emerged because of or in connection with the present Contract or upon violation, termination or invalidity of the present Contract shall be finally settled by arbitration in accordance with the Arbitration Court of the Arbitration Institute of the Stockholm Chamber of Commerce.

Belgor terminated the Construction Contract with effect as of 29 November 2012. The purported reason was that Koca had produced defective works. Following Belgor's termination of the agreement, the parties established a working committee that entered into negotiations on how to determine the parties' respective remaining obligations. On 4 December 2012, in parallel with these negotiations, Belgor requested Koca to perform certain additional works on the shafts (hereinafter 'the Additional Works'). It was common ground between the parties that the Additional Works were performed on the basis of five separate contracts, which did not have arbitration clauses, but which instead stipulated that the parties had the right to refer disputes to the Economic Court in Minsk. The parties ultimately failed to reach a final solution on how to dismantle and terminate their contractual relationship. Against this background, Koca initiated arbitration proceedings and requested that Belgor should be ordered to pay almost USD 11 million for completed works, additional works, machinery and equipment plus interest. Koca further claimed compensation for lost profit in excess of USD 20 million. Belgor, who disputed Koca's requests, requested for its part that Koca should be ordered to pay almost USD 10 million as compensation for defects in the completed works. Moreover, Belgor disputed that the arbitral tribunal had jurisdiction to resolve Koca's claims concerning the Additional Works. According to Belgor, that part of the dispute did not fall under the scope of the arbitration agreement of the Construction Contract.

On 3 April 2015, the arbitral tribunal rendered its award. The tribunal, finding that it had jurisdiction to resolve the claims concerning the Additional Works, partially granted Koca's action against Belgor. The counterclaim submitted by Belgor was rejected in its entirety.

In deciding the issue of jurisdiction, the tribunal held that disputes concerning the Additional Works could not be said to '*arise out of*' the Construction Contract because the Construction Contract did not directly refer to those works.[11] However, in the view of the tribunal, the Additional Works were performed '*in connection with*' the Construction Contract, in particular, '*since the Additional Works were ordered and performed while the parties were still negotiating the consequences of the termination of the construction contract*'.[12] As for the contracts without arbitration clauses (the

11. *Joint Stock Company Belgorkhimprom v. Koca Inaat Sanayi Ihracat Anonim irketi*, SCC Case No. 2013/043, 3 Apr. 2015, para. 81 of the award.
12. *Ibid.*, para. 83 of the award. It may be mentioned that as a matter of Swedish law making fine distinctions in wording between expressions such as 'in connection with', 'in relation to', 'under' and 'arising out of' is considered rather artificial, as commercial parties seldom have contemplated or intended any distinctions between such semantic linguistic differences.

jurisdiction agreement), the tribunal reasoned that they did not exclude jurisdiction for two reasons. First, the tribunal held that the jurisdiction agreement was optional, i.e., it provided the parties with a right but not an obligation to settle disputes in the designated forum. Second, according to the tribunal, it could reasonably be assumed that it had been the intention of the parties to settle all disputes between them in one and the same forum, and that the forum first chosen by them, i.e., arbitration as per the arbitration clause in the Construction Contract, best corresponded to their common intention.[13]

Belgor challenged the award before the Svea Court of Appeal and later the Supreme Court, requesting that the award ought to be wholly or partially set aside *inter alia* on the basis that the tribunal had decided issues not covered by a valid arbitration agreement between the parties.[14] Belgor maintained its position that the Additional Works were not covered by the arbitration agreement of the Construction Contract but instead fell within the scope of the jurisdiction agreement in the separate service agreements that referred to the Economic Court in Minsk. Belgor further contended that the service agreements were not addenda to the Construction Contract but covered other legal relationships than the Construction Contract. Therefore, according to Belgor, the tribunal had lacked jurisdiction over the claims with respect to the Additional Works. Koca's position was that the additional works fell within the scope of the arbitration clause of the Construction Contract.[15] Koca also submitted that as the jurisdiction agreement in the service agreements was optional, it did not exclude the arbitration clause in the Construction Contract.

### [B] The Courts' Determinations

The Court of Appeal began its reasoning by holding that:

> If the challenging party asserts that there exists no valid arbitration agreement that covers the alleged legal relationship, it is for the respondent – Koca in the case at hand – to establish that such an agreement exists.

The Court of Appeal went on to state that as Koca had not presented any detailed account of what the relevant additional works involved or how they were related to the Construction Agreement, the Court of Appeal was not in a position to make a more general assessment of the connection between the Construction Agreement and the Additional Works. However, based on the available information, the court could

13. *Ibid.*, para. 85 of the award.
14. *See* section 34, subsection 1, item 1 of the Act, which provides that an award shall be wholly or partially set aside upon the request of a party if it is not covered by a valid arbitration agreement.
15. It may be mentioned that Koca, in the alternative, before the Court of Appeal argued that the parties had agreed that the additional works were to be covered by the arbitration agreement, either explicitly during the negotiations that took place or by means of Belgor's passivity and implied actions. The Court of Appeal found that Koca had not succeeded in establishing the existence of such separate agreement. The Supreme Court did not address this alternative ground. It is not clear from the judgment whether this was due to Koca withdrawing the assertion or because the Supreme Court did not consider it necessary to rule upon it (given that Koca's first ground was accepted).

conclude *that* there were three parties to the Construction Agreement but only two to the service agreements, *that* the Additional Works were based on several different order placements of which at least one did not have an apparent connection to the Construction Agreement[16] and *that* all orders were placed after Belgor had terminated the Construction Agreement. According to the Court of Appeal, these circumstances implied that the Additional Works were covered by later established, autonomous legal relationships and not by the Construction Agreement. In view of the foregoing, the Court of Appeal found that Koca had not substantiated that the Additional Works were attributable to the legal relationship regulated by the arbitration agreement. The hesitance to expand the scope of the arbitration agreement was based on previous Supreme Court case law, which, as already noted, indicates a restrictive interpretation of arbitration agreements and the term 'legal relationship'.[17] The award was partially set aside.[18]

The Supreme Court reasoned differently and rejected the challenge application. In doing so, the Supreme Court made some innovating statements and outlined the following legal starting points:

- First, the Supreme Court reiterated the basic notion that parties cannot refer all their future disputes to arbitration in an arbitration agreement given the mandatory requirement in section 1(1) of the (SAA) that there must be an 'identified legal relationship'.[19] The underlying rationale of this requirement, the Supreme Court said, is to provide the parties with the ability to foresee the consequences of the arbitration agreement.
- The Supreme Court went on to state that when determining the scope of an arbitration agreement, general principles of Swedish law on contract interpretation apply.[20] However, as the wording of arbitration agreements often is in a standardized form, the Supreme Court concluded that there seldom exist specific circumstances upon which it is possible to determine a specific common intention of the parties. It went on to state that in instances where the

16. The order referred to concerned an order for works regarding construction of installations in connection with a visit by the President of Turkmenistan.
17. The Court of Appeal particularly relied on the following statement, first made in NJA 2010 p. 734, para. 14 (repeated in NJA 2017 p. 226, para. 10): '*The fact that there is a connection between a disputed legal relationship and another legal relationship which is covered by an arbitration agreement can only in exceptional cases and under very special circumstances cause the arbitration agreement to be extended to include the disputed relationship.*'
18. In addition to finding that the arbitral tribunal wrongly had assumed jurisdiction over the claim regarding the Additional Works, the Court of Appeal further found that the arbitral tribunal had committed a procedural error by wrongly assuming that the parties had agreed that interest should commence to accrue on the invoice date. It was undisputed that the awarded compensation for the Additional Works plus interest and other interest amounted to USD 900,875 and USD 1,662,794, i.e., separable parts of compensation awarded in item (i) of the operative part of the award. The relevant compensation was also deemed separable from other parts of the award. Therefore, the arbitral award was only annulled to the extent item (i) of the operative part of the award dealt with the amount USD 2,563,669 (USD 900,875 + USD 1,662,794). The residual part of Belgor's liability under the award (i.e., USD 6,603,733.52 plus litigation costs) thus remained unaffected.
19. *Belgor* para. 12.
20. *Belgor* para. 13.

wording provides for differing interpretations and other relevant interpretation data give no guidance, it is natural to start with the view that the arbitration agreement should fulfil a sensible function and serve as a reasonable set of rules for the parties' respective interests. The assumption, the Supreme Court said, is that parties to a commercial relationship wish to have disputes within the scope of their relationship resolved swiftly and in one cohesive proceeding before one single forum, i.e., an arbitral tribunal appointed by them. The Supreme Court emphasized that a different approach entails the risk of time delays, increased costs and contradicting decisions in matters that are connected.[21]

- The Supreme Court further underlined that when interpreting arbitration agreements and the Act's term 'legal relationship', the principles of the New York Convention should be taken into account. The Supreme Court held that these principles, which serve the purpose of ensuring uniform recognition of arbitration agreements and facilitating the enforcement of arbitral awards, have been taken to justify an extensive interpretation of both the arbitration agreement and the convention's concept of a 'legal relationship' in foreign case law and international jurisprudence.[22]
- The Supreme Court added that the term 'legal relationship' does not only cover those rights and obligations that have been set forth in an original agreement. Subsequent legally relevant circumstances, which alter the content of the agreement, fall within the scope of the term and thereby within the scope of application of an arbitration clause set out in the original agreement.[23]
- Interestingly, having already established a presumption that parties ordinarily do not intend to split disputes that are closely linked between different fora, the Supreme Court also established another presumption. It held that, typically, it is the arbitral tribunal which is best positioned to determine the issue of its own jurisdiction.[24] The starting point for a court is therefore that the arbitral tribunal's interpretation and evaluation of evidence is correct (or, in other words, that its decision should be accepted). Based on this starting point, the Supreme Court held that it is for the party contesting jurisdiction in a challenge proceeding to show that the arbitral tribunal has made an incorrect assessment of the scope of the arbitration agreement.[25]

Having laid down these legal starting points, the Supreme Court made an assessment in casu and found that the contesting party (Belgor) had not invoked any circumstances that constituted grounds for rejecting the arbitration tribunal's assessment of its jurisdiction. Hence, the award was upheld.

21. *Belgor* paras 13 and 18.
22. *Belgor* para. 14. Reference was made to Born, *supra* n. 1, pp. 1317 et seq. and Holtzmann & Neuhaus, *A Guide to the UNCITRAL Model Law on International Commercial Arbitration* (1994) 259.
23. *Belgor* para. 15 (the same statement was made in NJA 2017 p. 226, para. 14).
24. *Belgor* para. 19.
25. *Belgor* para. 20.

## §5.03 DISCUSSION

### [A] The Significance of the Parties' Intentions: Genuine and Hypothetical

The Supreme Court stated that general principles of Swedish contract law on contract interpretation apply when defining the scope of an arbitration agreement. It bears mentioning that according to these principles, the ultimate objective is to determine the common intention of the parties at the time of conclusion of the contract. The rule of *falsa demonstratio non nocet* provides that if a written agreement does not show the common intention, the written text is disregarded.[26] Hence, the starting point for determining the scope of an arbitration agreement is, as with any other commercial agreement, the parties' *genuine* intentions, if such intentions can be established. This state of affairs has not been altered by *Belgor*. Rather, it has been confirmed.[27] In case if it can be proven that the intention of the parties was to limit the jurisdiction of the arbitrators to only some disputes or to certain clearly defined issues, such consensus will override all other circumstances. The same applies if it can be established that one party intended to limit the jurisdiction of the arbitrators to only certain matters and that, at the time of the conclusion, the other party must have been aware of the first party's intention but made no objection.[28]

This being said, once a dispute has arisen, it is often difficult to establish the existence of a common intention and to determine what that common intention may have been. Other objective factors must then be considered. Although due consideration must be given to all relevant circumstances, considerable weight is often given to the wording of the contract (provided that the wording is clear and unambiguous). A party that asserts that the common intention differs from a clear wording faces a heavy burden of proof.[29]

However, it is seldom the case that arbitration agreements are negotiated and agreed against the background of the individual circumstances surrounding the main contract. Rather on the contrary, the arbitration clause in a commercial contract is oftentimes one of the clauses least deliberated (if at all consciously considered by the parties).[30] Typically, even where counsels are involved, either a model clause is used or a prior clause in another contract is copied and pasted. The Supreme Court took notice of these facts when stating that since the wording of arbitration agreements, which often provide for differing interpretations, typically is in a standardized form, there seldom exists specific circumstances upon which it is possible to determine a specific common intention of the parties. It was precisely from that conclusion that the

26. Adlercreutz & Gorton, Avtalsrätt II (Lund, 2010), 58.
27. *See* especially the statement in para. 13 that '*[I]n instances where the wording provides for differing interpretations and other relevant interpretation data give no guidance, it is natural to start with the view that the arbitration agreement should fulfill a sensible function […].*'
28. *See* Lando et al., *Restatement of Nordic Contract Law* (Copenhagen: Djøf Publishing, 2016), § 5-2 with extensive references.
29. Lando et al., *supra* n. 28, at 175.
30. This is why they are often referred to as 'midnight clauses'.

established presumption and default rule emanated; in instances where the wording and other relevant interpretation data give no clear guidance, there is (a rather strong) presumption that commercial parties, as rational business entities, are likely to prefer a dispute resolution mechanism that can deal with all types of claims in a single forum. In practice, this usually means that in cases where the wording of the arbitration agreement allows for two interpretations as to the scope, courts and tribunals will henceforth lean towards the more extensive interpretation. That, in the words of the Supreme Court, allows the arbitration agreement to fulfil a sensible function and serve as a reasonable set of rules for the parties' respective interests.[31]

### [B] The Handling of the Identification Requirement

As explained above, when determining the scope of an arbitration agreement, two separate but closely related issues arise. The first is a contract interpretation issue. The second issue is a law interpretation issue. The scope of an arbitration agreement is limited by the mandatory *identification requirement* that future disputes must concern an identified legal relationship. An arbitration agreement is not valid if the scope is wider than this. In other words, it must be examined whether the scope determination after a proper contract interpretation corresponds to the legal requirement that the legal relationship is identified in the arbitration agreement.

The identification requirement can be interpreted in two different ways.[32] One way of interpretation is that an arbitration clause contained in a main contract is valid to the extent that it relates to the legal relationship that the main contract constitutes and invalid in so far as it relates to other legal relationships, regardless of whether they are related or not. The other is that an arbitration agreement is valid as soon as an identified legal relationship is the subject of the arbitration clause, namely the contract in which the arbitration clause is included. The question of whether the valid arbitration agreement may include related legal relationships would then amount to a question of interpretation and not a question of validity.

31. One issue that arises as a result of the judgment is whether the party relying on the arbitration agreement is required to explicitly introduce and invoke the (*hypothetical* or *reasonable*) common intention of the parties as a factor relevant to the question of the interpretation and scope of the arbitration agreement and thus, ultimately, to the arbitral tribunal's jurisdiction. That depends on whether or not such intention can be regarded as a material circumstance or *legal fact* (Sw. '*rättsfakta*'), or as part of a legal fact. Swedish procedural law makes a distinction between such facts and evidentiary facts (Sw. '*bevisfakta*'). A legal fact is a fact of direct relevance in the sense that a legal consequence (Sw. '*rättsföljd*') is linked to it, whereas an evidentiary fact is a fact of indirect relevance in the sense that its importance lies its evidentiary value in relation to a legal fact. Neither a judge nor an arbitrator is allowed to base his decision on a legal fact not invoked by the parties. Hence, in case an award has been based on a legal fact not invoked by a party, the arbitrators' have exceeded their mandated and the award may be set aside. Following the Supreme Court's judgment, the extensive interpretation principle, based on a reasonable hypothetical common intention, must be considered as a general principle of law. As such, it does not require an invocation of any ultimate fact. The opposite applies to allegations regarding the parties' actual intentions.
32. Heuman, *Har det skett en omsvängning eller omläggning av praxis från restriktiv till extensiv tillämpning av skiljeavtalet?* (SvJT 2019) 534 et seq., at 536.

Another suggested approach has been that the legal relationship that an arbitration agreement should be considered to cover, after a proper contract interpretation, should also be considered as identified in the meaning of section 1(2) of the Act, provided however that the disputed legal relationship had already arisen when the arbitration agreement was concluded.[33] In such case, it will be sufficient with a scope determination based on contract interpretation. The added additional condition is based on the view that it is not possible to identify a legal relationship that did not exist at the time of the conclusion of the arbitration agreement, something which may have special importance in the context of supplementary agreements entered into after the conclusion of the main contract containing the arbitration agreement.[34]

In the authors' view, the Supreme Court's decision in *Belgor* best fits the second interpretation alternative.[35] As will be recalled, the Supreme Court expressly stated that '*the scope of an arbitration agreement is to be determined pursuant to the general principles for contract interpretation*'.[36] The Supreme Court also expressly held that the term 'legal relationship' shall be given a wide interpretation, in accordance with the underlying principles behind the New York Convention. A relaxation of the identification requirement was therefore achieved. If the intention had been to express that the identification requirement would impede a wide contract interpretation based on the assumption that '*parties to a commercial relationship wish to have disputes within the scope of their relationship settled by one single forum*',[37] the Supreme Court would arguably have said so. It did not. The outcome of the case, as well as other statements in the Supreme Court's reasoning, is also consistent with and clearly point in the direction that an expansion of the arbitration agreement may be made to include legal relationships that are closely connected to the legal relationship primarily covered by the arbitration agreement (i.e., the main contract), regardless of whether they existed or not at the time of the conclusion of the arbitration agreement. For instance, the Supreme Court stated that a ground outside the contractual relationship could be deemed to fall inside the applicable scope of the arbitration clause, whereby reference was made to NJA 2007, p. 475.[38] In that case, A and B had entered into an agreement that gave B the right to remove road maintenance substances from a land area belonging to A during a certain period of time. B filed an application with the county administrative board for a permit to continue to remove substances after the said

33. Cf. Lindskog, *Skiljeförfarande* (JUNO, last updated 2018-09-07), section I:0-6.2.2.
34. Lindskog, *supra* n. 33, section I:1-5.1.2 footnote 703 and section I:1-5.1.3. However, Lindskog also argues that the arbitration agreement could be extended to include legal relationships that arise subsequent to the conclusion, but such extension requires evidence that the parties intended the arbitration agreement to apply once the new legal relationship arose (e.g., once a supplementary agreement was entered into). If that is the case, the arbitration agreement can be extended to include the subsequent legal relationship. Cf. in this context Koca's alternative ground and *supra* n. 15.
35. Cf. Heuman, *supra* n. 32, at 538, 546 et seq. and 549 set seq. (although expressing some doubts).
36. *Belgor*, para. 13.
37. *Belgor* paras 13 and 18.
38. *Belgor* para. 17.

period. A brought an action against B claiming compensation. As the basis for its action, A claimed in the first place that the parties were still in a contractual relationship and that B by breaching its duty of loyalty had incurred liability. In the alternative, A argued that there was a contract-like relationship which resulted in liability. Third, A pleaded that the representative of B who had applied for a permit was guilty of fraudulent procedure. The third ground was thus non-contractual in nature. The Supreme Court nevertheless found that the arbitrators had jurisdiction. According to the Supreme Court in *Belgor* '*the non-contractual ground was deemed so closely related to the other grounds for the action that also the former ground was deemed covered by the arbitration clause*'. It is clear that the conduct giving rise to the non-contractual liability – constituting a separate legal relationship – occurred after the conclusion of the arbitration agreement.[39]

It follows that arbitral tribunals and courts should make a contractual analysis in order to determine whether a claim related to a closely connected legal relationship is covered by the arbitration agreement. That is a question of interpretation and not validity.[40]

---

39. *See also infra* n. 44. A different matter is that NJA 2007 p. 475 has been called into question (rightly, in the authors' view) on the basis that the Supreme Court appears to have failed to apply the doctrine of assertion; the claimant itself had alleged that the claim was not based on the main agreement which included the arbitration agreement, which should have been the decisive. In this regard, it may be mentioned that one commentator has argued that the Supreme Court in *Belgor* has abolished the doctrine of assertion (Madsen, *Har varit en udda fågel – HD skrotar påståendedoktrinen inom skiljedomsrätten*, Dagens Juridik 2 Apr. 2019 and 'The Swedish 'Belgor' case and the scope and applicability of arbitral agreements, Tvistlösning inom affärsrätten 21 Feb. 2019, 93 et seq.). The authors strongly disagree. Amongst other things, Madsen finds it remarkable that the Supreme Court in *Belgor* '*did not with a word mention the doctrine of assertion in its decision.*' The reason is, however, simple: the doctrine was of no relevance to the Supreme Court's decision (nor to the arbitral tribunal's award, cf. Schöldström, '*Nej, HD skrotade inte påståendedoktrinen i Belgor-målet – även om det hade varit en välgärning*', Dagens Juridik 16 Apr. 2019). The doctrine of assertion only means that the arbitral tribunal shall not, in case it decides on its jurisdiction in the beginning of the proceedings, assess the existence of the material facts that a claimant claims are covered by a legal relationship within the scope of an arbitration agreement. When deciding on the jurisdiction, the arbitral tribunal shall instead assume that these material facts are present. The effect is that jurisdiction can be established without having to consider and assess the merits of the case. In other words, the opposite party has to accept arbitration even though the material circumstances invoked may not be true or proven. If the claimant's claims are later found to be unproven, the case will be dismissed on the merits rather than rejected for lack of jurisdiction. In addition, and as Madsen himself correctly observes in his article, one starting point for the doctrine of assertion to apply is that the material facts that the claimant references in support of its claim shall fall within the scope of the arbitration agreement, either because it is undisputed or because it has been legally established. That was obviously not the case in *Belgor*.
40. It may be mentioned that the identification requirement does not appear to have obstructed an expansion to related legal relationships as to scope determinations *ratione personae*. Hence, the Supreme Court has in some fairly old judgments declared that an arbitration agreement contained in a contract between the debtor and the creditor is applicable also to the legal relationship between the creditor and the guarantor, i.e., that created by the guarantee (NJA 1896 p. 136 NJA 1916 p. 100 and NJA 1922 p. 135, all confirmed in RH 1985:135; *see also* RH 2003:61).

### [C] The Scope of the Extensive Interpretation Principle

As already mentioned, by its judgment in *Belgor*, the Supreme Court deviated from previous declarations rejecting an extensive interpretation of arbitration agreements. The case has been criticized on the grounds that such previous statements were silently bypassed and for not having stated clearly enough that a reversal in jurisprudence was produced.

As one commentator correctly has observed, the previous statements supporting a restrictive interpretation of arbitration agreements concerned cases where the arbitration agreement had been invoked as a bar to initiated court proceedings. Therefore, the case can be made that it cannot be completely ruled out that the presumption that an arbitration agreement should generally be interpreted expansively is applicable solely in challenge and enforcement proceedings.[41] However, such an approach would not promote legal certainty. The same rules of interpretation should apply regardless of the context and fora in which the issue is being raised. The ultimate consequence would otherwise be that the scope of an arbitration agreement could depend on which party that first succeeds in having the issue of the scope of an arbitration agreement tried by a court or arbitral tribunal.[42] It is arguable (and in fact quite plausible) that the Supreme Court did not intend to create such a legal state of affairs and that the Supreme Court wilfully and knowingly dissociated itself from the previous statements mentioned, with the clear purpose to align the Act with the New York Convention and the principles generally applied in international arbitration.[43]

In this context, it also bears mentioning that the previous Supreme Court cases were all mentioned in the reasoning of *Belgor*, but the statements supporting a restrictive interpretation were not cited. If the Supreme Court had intended that these statements would continue to be guiding and authoritative in court proceedings not preceded by arbitral proceedings, the Supreme Court would arguably have stated so. It did not.[44]

---

41. Heuman, *supra* n. 32, at 549 et seq. Hueman does not take an explicit stand but merely concludes that it is not possible to draw any certain conclusions, although he seems prepared to lean towards the conclusion that the extensive interpretation principle is of general application (*see infra* n. 47).
42. Heuman, *supra* n. 32, at 550.
43. *See* especially paras 13 and 14 of the judgment. It also bears mentioning that the Supreme Court in NJA 2017 p. 226 para. 12 stated by way of an obiter dictum that the fact that there is a connection between a disputed legal relationship and another legal relationship which is covered by an arbitration agreement only in exceptional cases and under very special circumstances can cause the arbitration agreement to be extended to include the disputed relationship, and that such an exceptional case had arisen in NJA 2007 p. 475 (*see supra* n. 29). That reservation, which substantially narrowed down the scope of the judgment in NJA 2007 section 475 from what can be read from the judgment itself, was not repeated (or, in other words, was intentionally left out) in *Belgor* (cf. para. 17). According to the authors, this further supports the conclusion that *Belgor* overturns previous case law. A different matter is whether this reversal will hold (cf. the following footnote).
44. It might be mentioned that four of the five justices that adjudicated the dispute are experienced arbitrators who are regularly appointed in international arbitrations seated in Sweden. Although the composition of the seat in principle should not have any effect on the outcome, it remains to be seen whether the Supreme Court will continue along the chosen path.

To conclude, the important statements relating to the determination of the scope of arbitration agreements are arguably of general application, and the guidance that the Supreme Court gave is relevant regardless of in what type of proceedings the issue arises. This means that Swedish courts should also adopt a liberal construction approach with respect to actions under section 4(a) of the Act (i.e., when faced with a declaratory action with respect to the jurisdiction of the arbitrators), as well as when faced with a jurisdictional objection based on an arbitration agreement.

### [D] The Second Presumption

The Supreme Court also established another, somewhat more controversial, presumption. As will be recalled, the Supreme Court held that, typically, it is the arbitral tribunal which is best positioned to determine the issue of its own jurisdiction. The starting point for a court should therefore be that the arbitral tribunal's interpretation and evaluation of evidence is correct. Based on this starting point, or rather presumption, the Supreme Court established that it is for the party contesting jurisdiction in a challenge proceeding to show that the arbitral tribunal has made an incorrect assessment of the scope of the arbitration agreement. The same line of reasoning was adopted by the Supreme Court in *Kalle Bellander i Stockholm AB v. Plancavergne S.A., Fontane,* NJA 2003 p. 379 (*Kalle Bellander*), to which reference was made.[45] That case concerned the enforcement of a foreign arbitral award.[46]

Exactly what this presumption means is unclear. It relates to the general issue of what effect, if any, that courts should give to arbitrators' jurisdictional rulings, and it effectively provides for a certain standard of review to be applied when courts examine issues regarding the scope of an arbitration agreement. On a principal level, there are two extreme positions that can be taken in this regard. One is that the courts should address the scope of an arbitration agreement only in the most superficial manner and under a very summary (prima facie) standard. An advocate for such approach is Born, who has argued that:

> Disputes over the scope of the arbitration agreement involve a concededly valid arbitration agreement, consensually selecting a neutral tribunal with unchallenged authority to interpret the parties' underlying contract, which is often a key element in disputes over the scope of the arbitration agreement; again, the arbitral tribunal will often include members who are qualified and expert in the law governing the underlying contract, usually also having relevant commercial expertise. It makes very little sense for U.S. (or other) courts to ignore the views of the arbitrators regarding the scope of the arbitration agreement in these circumstances.[47]

45. That judgment has been the subject of severe criticism by Lindskog, *see* Lindskog, *supra* n. 33, section 54:5.1.3.
46. *See also* NJA 2009 not N 9.
47. Born, *supra* n. 1, at 1199 et seq.; cf 3298: '*The scope of a tribunal's authority is necessarily intertwined with substantive decisions about the meaning of the parties' underlying contract, which the parties have committed to the arbitrators' determination, and the tribunal's resolution of these issues should be accorded substantial deference.*'

The other extreme position is that the appropriate court should make a full and de novo enquiry as to scope issues, without taking any account of the reasoning of the arbitral tribunal. This approach can be considered to be most consistent with the fact that the judicial *ex post* control in challenge and enforcement proceedings, after all, is a *remedial* function intended to constitute a procedural safeguard. The procedural safeguard lies in the very fact that a full review is made.[48] To use a metaphor, there is a danger in shielding the arbitrators' jurisdictional assessment from independent judicial scrutiny as it would leave 'the foxes in charge of guarding the chicken coop'.

The judicial practice on matters relating to what deference that should be given to the arbitrators' decision on their competence varies between jurisdictions. There appears to be support for both extreme positions and everything in between.[49]

There is an argument that the judicial reviewability of an arbitral tribunal's determination on the scope of its own jurisdiction should differ depending upon whether the court is concerned with challenge of a Swedish award or enforcement of a foreign award. The reason would be that in cases of enforcement of a foreign award, foreign law normally governs the arbitration agreement. That was also the situation in *Kalle Bellander*. The Supreme Court expressly took into account that:

> In the present case, it should also be borne in mind that French law governs the question of whether a valid arbitration agreement has been entered into. Against this background [...] there is reason to assume in the enforcement proceeding that the interpretation and evaluation of evidence made by the arbitral tribunal based on the material it had available is correct.[50]

When foreign law is applicable to the arbitration agreement, it appears reasonable that a Swedish court as a starting point respects the assessment made by a tribunal consisting of internationally active arbitrators. Such tribunal may even be considered better equipped to try the issue of its own jurisdiction in the given situation.[51] Conversely, in challenge proceedings, Swedish law typically governs the arbitration agreement (which was also the case in *Belgor*).[52] That means that Swedish law determines issues such as allocation of the burden of proof, applicable evidentiary requirements, substantive principles of interpretation and validity requirements.[53] It has, on good grounds, been questioned if not Swedish courts should have at least as good (or perhaps even better) a position as an arbitral tribunal to assess issues as to the scope of the arbitration agreement when Swedish law applies to the arbitration agreement.[54] This is true not least in cases where the arbitral tribunal consists of

48. Lindskog, *supra* n. 33, section 54:5.1.3.
49. *See* Born, *supra* n. 1, at 3296 et seq. (annulment) and 3547 et seq. (enforcement).
50. *Kalle Bellander*, at p. 383.
51. Heuman, *Bevisbördan för skiljeavtal och tolkningsresonemang som grund för skiljebundenhet*, JT 2011/12, 663. For a different opinion, *see* Lindskog, *supra* n. 33, section 54:5.1.3.
52. If the place of arbitration is in Sweden, Swedish law will govern the arbitration agreement, unless the parties have agreed otherwise, *supra* n. 5.
53. Specifically the arbitrability and identification requirements.
54. Heuman, *supra* n. 32, at 534 et seq., at 549, and Schöldström, *Har Belgor förändrat prövningen av en skiljenämnds behörighet och handläggningsfel?* (JT 2019) 243 et seq., at 245.

foreign arbitrators with little or no experience of Swedish law.[55] There is also a convincing argument that the Supreme Court, as a precedential body, should take the lead over the development of the law and not yield to the various assessments made by arbitral tribunals to the different issues that can arise when determining the scope of an arbitration agreement under Swedish law.[56] Importantly, when challenge proceedings concern the question of whether an arbitration agreement extends to a particular dispute, it must be expected that the award already contains statements on this issue. If the claimant in the challenge proceedings has not made a jurisdictional objection during the arbitral proceedings, a challenge action will be pointless as that party will be deemed to have waived its right to rely on such ground for challenge.[57]

One may also consider instances where the two presumptions established by the Supreme Court in *Belgor* operate in different directions. The practical example is that the arbitral tribunal has applied a restrictive interpretation to the arbitration agreement. In a subsequent challenge proceeding, the court must then assume that the tribunal has made a proper assessment by its restrictive interpretation, but at the same time the court should consider the first presumption rule favouring an extensive interpretation. In such case, there would be support for both a restrictive and an extensive interpretation.[58] It is somewhat unclear as how such a situation should be resolved. One way of dealing with this issue could be that the second presumption should not be considered applicable in cases where the arbitral tribunal has erroneously applied a restrictive interpretation approach, in contradiction with the first presumption established in *Belgor*. It is only when the tribunal has applied a broad interpretation to the scope of arbitration agreements based on the presumption that the parties desire a single dispute resolution mechanism before one adjudicatory body for all disputes relating to their agreement that the second presumption comes into play. Such an approach would also make it easier to accept that the starting point for courts should be that the arbitral tribunal's assessment is correct. A relatively broad 'pro-arbitration' rule of interpretation based on the assumption that the parties wish for an all-encompassing jurisdiction of the arbitral tribunal corresponds to international standards and does not require in-depth knowledge of Swedish case law (anymore). On the other hand, the outer limits of the identification requirement should normally be a matter for courts to decide independently of the arbitrators' own jurisdictional findings.

To summarize, it is clear that the second presumption entails that an arbitral tribunal's decision on its own jurisdiction is to be given some degree of judicial deference, but it still leaves the ultimate decision as to scope issues to the Swedish

55. In the arbitration proceedings between Belgor and Koca, only the chairperson was a Swedish lawyer. The parties had not invoked any Supreme Court case law and the tribunal made no reference to such case law in its determination on the scope of the arbitration agreement.
56. Heuman, *supra* n. 51, at 663.
57. *See* section 34(2) of the Act, which provides that a party forfeits its right to rely upon a ground for challenge which, through participation in the proceedings without objection, or in any other manner, the party may be deemed to have waived. However, examples might be conceivable, in which a party does not realize that the arbitrators have gone beyond the scope of the arbitration agreement until after an award has been rendered.
58. Heuman, *supra* n. 32, at 548.

courts. However, given the great importance that the second presumption arguably will have for arbitral proceedings seated in Sweden, one must hope that the Supreme Court will soon clarify the second presumption's closer meaning and that it will make more distinct how careful and meticulous the courts' judicial scrutiny should be.[59] It would also be useful if the Supreme Court gives its view on whether a distinction should be made between challenge and enforcement proceedings (or, rather, whether a differentiation is required depending upon the law governing the arbitration agreement).

It is clear, however, (at least to the authors) that the Supreme Court limited the second presumption to arbitral determinations of scope issues *rationae materiae* under an unquestionably valid agreement to arbitrate.[60] Hence, from the judgment follows no presumption that an arbitral tribunal's determination on scope issues *rationae personae* is correct.[61]

Conversely, it is somewhat unclear to what extent the established presumption will be considered applicable in proceedings under the new section 2(2) of the Act (which provides that if the arbitral tribunal renders an interim decision affirming its jurisdiction, a party may appeal against the decision to a Court of Appeals within a thirty-day period). In the authors' view, if a presumption of the kind in question is to apply in challenge proceedings, there is no reason why it should not apply in proceedings under section 2(2) of the Act.

### [E] The Burden of Proof

The second presumption led the Supreme Court to conclude that it is for the party contesting jurisdiction in a challenge proceeding '*to show*' (Sw. *visa*) that the arbitral tribunal has made an incorrect assessment of the scope of the arbitration agreement. One commentator has argued that the Supreme Court did not place a burden of proof on the party contesting jurisdiction (i.e., the claimant in challenge proceedings) by this statement, *inter alia*, on the basis that the tribunal's assessment can hardly be

59. One possible source of inspiration could be the standard of review that is applied in retrospect with regard to the arbitral tribunal's determinations on competition law issues. Here, the review is aimed at whether the arbitral tribunal's conclusions are based on an acceptable legal analysis, rather than whether these conclusions correspond to those of the court. As long as the conclusions of the arbitral tribunal are reasonably motivated and fall within the scope of what could reasonably be concluded from competition case law and jurisprudence, the award will be not be declared invalid (*see Systembolaget Aktiebolag v. The Absolut Company Aktiebolag*, NJA 2018 p. 323, para. 16). This means that a court, in order to be in a position to determine whether an arbitration award should be deemed invalid due to peremptory competition law provisions, must undertake a certain - but not full - review of the merits of the arbitral tribunal's decision on the competition law issues. Also, this review relates solely to the tribunal's legal reasoning, and is not aimed at re-evaluating the tribunal's evidential findings, unless particular reasons exist to do so (*ibid.*, para. 17).
60. This as opposed to NJA 2003 p. 379, where the issue was whether a valid agreement had been entered into. *See also infra* n. 62.
61. Naturally, the same is true for determinations on arbitrability issues.

considered as an issue in the fact that can be proven right or wrong.[62] The authors agree with this proposition and submit that it holds especially true as regards the arbitral tribunal's interpretation of the arbitration agreement, which is clearly an issue of law and which cannot be treated as a factual circumstance subject to proof. In this context, it also bears mentioning that the Swedish word '*visa*' can be used in many different meanings and does not necessarily have to address issues of evidence.

The better understanding is probably that it is up to the claimant in the challenge proceedings to put forth compelling arguments explaining why the arbitrators' earlier consideration of the matter should not be accepted. Rather than *proving* that the tribunal made an incorrect assessment, it is a matter of *convincing* a court that the tribunal's evaluation of evidence is clearly erroneous or that it made a too far-reaching interpretation of the scope of the arbitration agreement. Importantly, under Swedish law, an arbitral tribunal is obliged to apply the fundamental principle that it is the party alleging that an arbitration agreement has been formed and who wishes to invoke the arbitration agreement in his own favour that has the burden of proving the facts and circumstances from which the arbitral tribunal should draw the conclusion that a valid arbitration agreement has been formed.[63] The burden of proof in the arbitral proceedings is in principle the same when it comes to determining whether the scope of an existing arbitration agreement extends to a particular dispute.[64]

62. Schöldström, *supra* n. 54, at 245 et seq. However, in the authors view, a rule that would provide that it be up to the claimant in challenge proceedings to show (prove) that the arbitral tribunal has made an incorrect assessment of the scope of the arbitration agreement would not be incompatible with the fundamental principle that the burden of proof of the existence of an arbitration agreement is on the party relying upon the agreement. These are separate issues. It could very well be that the burden of proof for the existence of an arbitration agreement stays on the party asserting its existence, while the allocation of the burden of proof shifts when it comes to determining whether the scope of an existing (proven) arbitration agreement extends to a particular dispute in challenge proceedings. The Supreme Court's statement is explicitly limited to the arbitral tribunal's determination *of the scope of the arbitration agreement*, once established. The basic principle that the burden of proof *of the existence of an arbitration agreement* is on the party relying upon the agreement thus remains unaffected.
63. Lindskog, *supra* n. 33, section I:0-2.1.3 footnote 37, Heuman, *Skiljemannarätt*, 1999, pp. 49, 55, 59, 235 et seq. and 591 et seq. and Heuman, *supra* n. 51, at 650 and 653.
64. However, since the Supreme Court in *Belgor* has adopted an expansive interpretation principle and rather strong presumption as to the scope of the arbitration agreement that favours the party invoking the arbitration agreement to its advantage, the burden of proof in this context has become less relevant. The established strong presumption that commercial parties want all their disputes to be resolved in a single proceeding (rather than in multiple proceedings in different forums) will often play a decisive role in determining the scope. As the reasoning typically will be based on an average and *hypothetical* mutual intention of reasonable commercial parties (save where there is clear evidence and interpretation data suggesting that the parties intended to limit the scope), the party relying on the arbitration agreement will in effect escape a burden of proof. The interpretation will thus be based on normative considerations when the factual circumstances invoked in support of a certain common intention are not deemed conclusive (refer to the matter of principle Heuman, *supra* n. 51, at 664 et seq.).

## §5.04 CONCLUDING REMARKS

By its judgment in *Belgor*, the Supreme Court has adapted Swedish arbitration law to the international developments discussed above by applying a broad interpretation to the scope of arbitration agreements and at the same time relaxing the statutory identification requirement. The presumption is mandated by a reasonable assumption that parties to arbitration agreements typically, as rational business entities, wish for a single dispute resolution mechanism before one adjudicatory body for all disputes relating to their agreement rather than multiple proceedings that entail increased costs, delays and great risks of inconsistent results in matters that are connected. A presumption of this kind has long been applied in most developed national arbitration regimes and by international arbitral tribunals.

A few difficulties of application remain to be solved with respect to the second presumption, which is somewhat more controversial and requires clarification. When state courts lend state power to enforce an arbitral award, there must arguably be some kind of independent examination of the scope the arbitration agreement, from which the tribunal draws its power to render a binding award at first hand. It remains to be seen how the judgment will be received in the arbitration community. It seems likely, and indeed one must hope, that *Belgor* will not be the last word on this very important topic.

CHAPTER 6

# Expedited Arbitration Rules for Investment Disputes: ICSID Amendment Process and UNCITRAL Working Group II

*Crina Baltag*

In 1993, Lord Mustill referred to international arbitration as being 'by definition, fast-track' and he added, '[t]hat was why the parties chose it as their method of resolving disputes'.[1] However, Lord Mustill also noted, '[this] has changed in the last forty years [with] the creation of the new, slow-track arbitration which is the kind of arbitration which is the subject of almost everything written and spoken on the subject'.

With arbitration becoming increasingly costly and lengthy, stakeholders[2] have started to address these issues and propose suitable mechanisms for reinstating

1. Michael Mustill, *Comments on Fast-Track Arbitration*, Journal of International Arbitration, Volume 10, Issue 4 (1993), pp. 121–125, p. 122.
2. Peter Morton, *Can a World Exist Where Expedited Arbitration Becomes the Default Procedure?*, Arbitration International, Volume 26, Issue 1 (2010), pp. 103–114, p. 105, suggestively emphasizing that the delay in the arbitration proceedings is the result of the actions of all stakeholders involved:

   - Tribunal availability: 'The first date all three members of the tribunal are available for a one week hearing in the relevant window is in 18 months time'.
   - Counsel availability: 'I have four other cases coming to trial in autumn next year and we need to fit things in around that, so these dates are actually good for us'.
   - Expansive disclosure process: 'We need time to do a thorough trawl for all conceivably relevant documents, both hard copy and electronic, and we want to allow plenty of time to obtain disclosure from our opponents'.
   - Expansive witness evidence: 'We have 10 witnesses and we will need time to sit down with each of them and run through details of their involvement with the documents, after which we will need to prepare a detailed witness statement for them – all of that is going to take many months'.
   - Witness availability: 'Of our 10 witnesses, three are abroad, four have since left the company and it will take time to arrange a convenient time to meet with them and get

arbitration as an efficient mechanism for resolving commercial disputes.[3] Two notable arbitration rules are still to implement expedited arbitration proceeding: the United Nations Commission on International Trade Law (UNCITRAL) Arbitration Rules and the International Centre for Settlement of Investment Disputes (ICSID) Arbitration Rules.

At the fifty-first session of the UNCITRAL in 2018, it was agreed that Working Group II would take up issues relating to expedited arbitration.[4] The work of Working Group II is aimed 'at improving the efficiency of the arbitral proceedings, which would result in reduction of costs and duration of the proceedings',[5] and expedited arbitration, 'as a streamlined and simplified procedure with shortened time frame' could ensure this efficiency goal.[6]

At the same time, the ICSID Arbitration Rules Amendment Process, now at the 4th Working Paper published in February 2020, is advancing a set of expedited arbitration rules for ICSID investment arbitration proceedings. This is in line with the overall amendment process of the ICSID Arbitration Rules, and, in particular, with the efforts of reducing the duration of the arbitration proceedings, where possible. The UNCITRAL Working Group III on Investor-State Dispute Settlement (ISDS) Reform is also addressing concerns with costs and duration of investment disputes as ongoing concerns with the ISDS system, in addition to the outcome of the arbitration proceedings – inconsistency in arbitral decisions and the lack of predictability of such outcome –, and the arbitrators appointed in the investment arbitration cases.[7]

This chapter undertakes a brief review of the feasibility of expedited arbitration for investment disputes, given their peculiarities and complexity, noting that, at this

them to agree their statements and we understand that the first time all 10 are available is well into next year'.

- Dilatory tactics and their accommodation by the tribunal: 'Our opponents are looking to string things out to suit their purposes and the tribunal is unfortunately letting them get away with it'.

3. *See* Giacomo Marchisio, *Recent Solutions to Old Problems: A Look at the Expedited Procedure under the Newly Revised ICC Rules of Arbitration*, ICC Dispute Resolution Bulletin, Issue 1 (2017), pp. 76–81, p. 77.
4. UNCITRAL, *Settlement of Commercial Disputes. Draft Provisions on Expedited Arbitration. Note by the Secretariat*, A/CN.9/WG.II/WP.212, para. 1.
   For a discussion regarding the terminology used – 'expedited', 'fast-track', 'accelerated', *see* Yas Banifatemi, *Expedited Proceedings in International Arbitration*, in Laurent Lévy and Michael Polkinghorne (eds), *Expedited Procedures in International Arbitration*, Dossiers of the ICC Institute of World Business Law, vol. 16 (Kluwer Law International, 2017), pp. 9–33, pp. 9–10.
5. UNCITRAL, *Report of Working Group II (Dispute Settlement) on the Work of Its Sixty-Ninth Session (New York, 4–8 February 2019)*, A/CN.9/969, para. 13.
6. UNCITRAL, *Report of Working Group II (Dispute Settlement) on the Work of Its Sixty-Ninth Session (New York, 4–8 February 2019)*, A/CN.9/969, para. 14.
7. The UNCITRAL Working Group III began its works in November 2017 and was entrusted with a broad mandate to: (a) first, identify and consider concerns regarding investor-State dispute settlement; (b) second, consider whether reform was desirable in the light of any identified concerns; and (c) third, if the Working Group were to conclude that reform was desirable, develop any relevant solutions to be recommended to the Commission. UNCITRAL, *Report of the U.N. Commission on International Trade Law 50th Session (3-21 July 2017)*, U.N. Doc. A/72/17 (2017), para. 244.

time, this is still work in progress.[8] This is done with reference to the ICSID Amendment Process, as well as to the work of UNCITRAL Working Group II, although the Group is still to decide on whether the proposed expedited rules would apply to other types of arbitration proceedings than commercial ones.[9] Before advancing to these core issues, the chapter will first take a look at expedited arbitration provisions in institutional arbitration and identify some key unsettled issues, which are either likely to emerge or are already addressed in the UNCITRAL and ICSID discussions.

## §6.01 OVERVIEW OF THE CURRENT EXPEDITED ARBITRATION PROVISIONS

In 2015, the White & Case – Queen Mary Arbitration Survey discussed the benefits of expedited arbitration proceedings.[10] Ninety-two per cent of the participants favoured the inclusion of simplified arbitration proceedings in institutional arbitration rules, 59% as an opt-in mechanism and 33% as a mandatory provision, based on a certain value of the claim.[11] On this latter aspect, while a significant number of respondents (40%) suggested the amount of USD 1 million as the yardstick for the application of simplified/expedited proceedings, the follow-up interviews revealed that the value of a claim does not necessarily reflect the complexity of a dispute and due attention must be paid to what parties consider to be fit for an expedited resolution of the dispute.[12]

The first institutions to provide for expedited arbitration proceedings were World Intellectual Property Organization (WIPO), in 1994, followed by China International Economic and Trade Arbitration (CIETAC), later in 1994, and The Arbitration Institute of the Stockholm Chamber of Commerce (SCC), in 1995.[13] In 2002, the International Court of Arbitration of the International Chamber of Commerce (ICC) set up a task force for exploring the ways in which time and costs in arbitration of small claims could be reduced.[14] The 2017 ICC Arbitration Rules currently provide for expedited

8. References in this paper are made available to documents on or before 12 Apr. 2020.
9. UNCITRAL, *Report of Working Group II (Dispute Settlement) on the Work of Its Seventieth Session (Vienna, 23–27 September 2019)*, A/CN.9/1003, paras 14–15.
10. White & Case and Queen Mary University of London, School of International Arbitration; *2015 International Arbitration Survey: Improvements and Innovations in International Arbitration*, available at http://www.arbitration.qmul.ac.uk/media/arbitration/docs/2015_International_Arbitration_Survey.pdf, last visited 8 Apr. 2020.
11. *2015 International Arbitration Survey: Improvements and Innovations in International Arbitration*, p. 26.
12. *2015 International Arbitration Survey: Improvements and Innovations in International Arbitration*, p. 26.
13. For an overview of the key provisions of the 2017 SCC Rules for Expedited Arbitration, *see* Anja Havedal Ipp, *Expedited Arbitration at the SCC: One Year with the 2017 Rules*, Kluwer Arbitration Blog, 2 Apr. 2018, available at http://arbitrationblog.kluwerarbitration.com/2018/04/02/expedited-arbitration-scc-one-year-2017-rules-2/, last visited 10 Apr. 2020.
14. ICC, *Guidelines for Arbitrating Small Claims under the ICC Rules of Arbitration*, ICC International Court of Arbitration Bulletin, Volume 14, Issue 1 (2003), pp. 29–35. *See also*, ICC, *Controlling Time and Costs in Arbitration*, 2007, available at https://iccwbo.org/content/uploads/sites/3/2018/03/icc-arbitration-commission-report-on-techniques-for-controlling-time-and-costs-in-arbitration-english-version.pdf, last visited 11 Apr. 2020.

proceedings under Article 30 and Appendix VI.[15] The 2016 Singapore International Arbitration Centre (SIAC) Arbitration Rules include specific provisions on expedited arbitration in Rule 5, while the 2018 Hong Kong International Arbitration Centre (HKIAC) Arbitration Rules regulate expedited arbitration in Article 42. The London Court of International Arbitration (LCIA) does not provide for expedited arbitration, but it does advance, in Article 9 of the LCIA Arbitration Rules, the expedited formation of the arbitral tribunal in case of exceptional emergency. Further, the LCIA Arbitration Rules give broad discretion to the arbitral tribunal, in particular under Article 14.4, which empowers the arbitral tribunal to expedite the proceedings if the circumstances of the case so require.[16]

Most expedited arbitration provisions allow parties to opt-in to such procedure, based on their consent, while few, including the ICC, provide for the automatic application of the expedited arbitration when certain criteria are met. It is common to see fallback provisions also included in the rules, referring to the circumstances in which expedited proceedings are no longer required, and the proceedings will follow the normal route. There is a general preference for a sole arbitrator, rather than a three-member arbitral tribunal (Article 17 of the 2017 SCC Rules for Expedited Arbitration; and even when the parties have agreed on a three-member tribunal, such as Article 2(1) of Appendix VI of the ICC Arbitration Rules); procedural timetable are adjusted to the expedited nature of the arbitration (in ICC proceedings, no Terms of Reference; in SCC proceedings, the case management conference to be scheduled in seven days as of the referral of the case to the arbitral tribunal (Article 29(4) of the 2017 SCC Rules for Expedited Arbitration)); limitation of exchange of submissions to one or maximum two rounds (Article 45(9) of the VIAC Arbitration Rules, etc.); frontloading of the case is provided (Article 6 of the SCC Expedited Rules provide that the request for arbitration constitutes the statement of claims); the procedure follows without a hearing (Article 33(1) of the 2017 SCC Rules for Expedited Arbitration); short deadlines, including for issuing the arbitral award, are advanced (in ICC arbitrations, given the scrutiny of the award, the deadline is shorter, although the scrutiny process is also shorter);[17] and the possibility to issue non-reasoned arbitral awards is also provided for (Article 42(1) of the 2017 SCC Rules for Expedited Arbitration).

Available statistics seem to confirm that expedited proceedings are a useful addition to institutional arbitration. In 2017, SCC had 36% of its cases under the expedited rules; between 2010 and 2017, SIAC had 341 applications for expedited

15. As explained, the interest in adopting specific expedited arbitration rules was triggered by the high number of claims below USD 2 million. *See* José Ricardo Feris, *The 2017 ICC Rules of Arbitration and the New ICC Expedited Procedure Provisions: A View from Inside the Institution*, ICC Dispute Resolution Bulletin, Issue 1 (2017), pp. 63–75, p. 65.
16. For examples of 'fast-track' arbitrations before the institutionalization of expedited arbitration, *see* Yas Banifatemi, *Expedited Proceedings in International Arbitration*, pp. 10–11.
17. ICC, *ICC Note to Parties and Arbitral Tribunals on the Conduct of the Arbitration under the ICC Rules of Arbitration*, in force 1 Jan. 2019, para. 135:

> If the Expedited Procedure Provisions apply, any draft award submitted to the Court will be scrutinised as soon as possible, and in any event no later than two to three weeks of receipt by the Secretariat.

proceedings, out of which 186 were accepted; in 2019, HKIAC had received 21 applications for the expedited procedure and had granted 15. As of 1 April 2019, 70 cases have been, or are being, conducted under the ICC expedited procedure provisions.

There are, however, controversial issues in expedited arbitration that are still subject to debate, as also emerges from the UNCITRAL Working Group II discussions. For example, whether the parties should consent to expedited arbitration (opt-in mechanism) or automatically be directed to expedited arbitration (opt-out mechanism with fallback provisions, when the expedited procedure is no longer suited to the case) when the criteria are met. This particular aspect is relevant not only from the perspective of consent – party autonomy as the cornerstone of arbitration – but also with regard to the criteria to be applied for an automatic application of the expedited arbitration rules. For instance, the amount in dispute is not the only element defining the complexity of a dispute. Further, a cut-off value is a controversial issue which may be misused by the parties. For the latter concern, the ICC, for instance, provides that the arbitral tribunal may take into account whether, by artificially inflating its claims, a party has prevented the Expedited Procedure Provisions from applying.[18] Both ICSID and UNCITRAL advance consent (i.e., opt-in mechanism) as the only criteria for the application of the expedited arbitration rules.

A further matter relates to the composition of the arbitral tribunal, and in particular, cases when the parties have agreed to a three-member arbitral tribunal, but the expedited arbitration rules provide for a sole arbitrator (Article 2(1) of Appendix VI of the ICC Arbitration Rules; Rule 5.2(b) of SIAC Arbitration Rules). On this point, the Singapore High Court in 2015 in *AQZ v. ARA*, under 2010 SIAC Arbitration Rules, upheld the sole arbitrator's award even in the presence of the parties' express provision to refer the dispute to a three-arbitrator tribunal.[19] The court concluded 'that the arbitral proceedings were conducted in accordance with the parties' agreement'.[20] Following this decision, the 2016 SIAC Arbitration Rules expressly included in Rule 5.3 that '[b]y agreeing to arbitration under these Rules, the parties agree that, where arbitral proceedings are conducted in accordance with the Expedited Procedure under this Rule 5, the rules and procedures set forth in Rule 5.2 shall apply even in cases where the arbitration agreement contains contrary terms'. This has been recently confirmed by Singapore International Commercial Court in *BXS v. BXT*.[21] The court highlighted that, by agreeing to the 2016 SIAC Arbitration Rules, the parties also agreed

18. ICC, *Note to Parties and Arbitral Tribunals*, para. 104.
19. *AQZ v. ARA* [2015] SGHC 49. *See* further, Gary Born and Jonathan Lim, *AQZ v ARA: Singapore High Court Upholds Award Made under SIAC Expedited Procedure*, Kluwer Arbitration Blog, 9 Mar. 2015.
20. *AQZ v. ARA*, para. 135. *See also*, José Ricardo Feris, *The 2017 ICC Rules of Arbitration and the New ICC Expedited Procedure Provisions: A View from Inside the Institution*, p. 65, explaining that the 2017 ICC Arbitration Rules have two general principles characterizing the expedited proceedings. One of them, in Art. 30 of the 2017 ICC Arbitration Rules, provides that the parties agree that the expedited procedure provisions shall prevail over any contrary term in the arbitration agreement. As such, parties cannot depart from the essential features of the expedited arbitration.
21. *BXS v. BXT* [2019] SGHC(I)10.

to Rules 5.2 and 5.3 of the SIAC Rules, which include the fact that a dispute shall be heard by a sole arbitrator, rather than by a three-member tribunal.[22] Therefore, the court concluded, 'the fact that the arbitration was heard by a sole arbitrator under the Expedited Procedure did not contravene the parties' arbitration agreement'.[23] Both draft UNCITRAL Expedited Arbitration Provisions and the proposed ICSID Arbitration Rules give preference to the consent of the parties, and, in the absence of such agreement, provide for the sole-arbitrator tribunal as the default option.

A last issue[24] refers to the relationship between due process and expedited proceedings. In the discussions in the Working Group II, it was explained that arbitrators are often concerned that the award would be challenged on the basis that the tribunal has failed to give the opportunity to the parties to be heard, the so-called due process paranoia.[25] As explained in the context of the Working Group II, as 'the notions of due process and fairness were stressed as important elements of international arbitration that should not be overlooked in streamlining the arbitration procedure',[26] UNCITRAL is working to prepare 'expedited arbitration provisions ... to balance on the one hand, the efficiency of the arbitral proceedings and on the other, the rights of the parties to due process and to fair treatment'.[27]

The issue of due process in the context of expedited arbitration proceedings was addressed by the Svea Court of Appeal in 2012. In Case No. T-6238-10, the Court had to decide whether the fact that in the expedited arbitral proceedings under the SCC Rules the sole arbitrator decided not to hold a hearing to hear the witnesses' testimony constituted a breach of Swedish public policy.[28] Considering that Article 27(1) of the applicable 2010 SCC Rules for Expedited Arbitrations provided that '[a] hearing shall be held if requested by a party and if deemed necessary by the Arbitrator', the Court concluded that the decision not to hold a hearing did not contradict the rules applicable to the proceedings.[29] In *China Machine v. Jaguar,* where the parties had consented to expedited ICC arbitration proceedings, Singapore High Court emphasized that expedited proceedings do not trump arbitral tribunal's 'responsibility to ensure due

22. *BXS v. BXT*, para. 12.
23. *BXS v. BXT*, para. 12.
24. For arbitrators, another concern might be the lower fees in expedited arbitration proceedings. *See*, for example, in ICC expedited proceedings, fees lower than the general scales (*see* 2017 ICC Arbitration Rules, Appendix III: Arbitration Costs and Fees).
25. *See also*, White and Case and School of International Arbitration, Queen Mary University of London, *2018 International Arbitration Survey: The Evolution of International Arbitration*, available at http://www.arbitration.qmul.ac.uk/media/arbitration/docs/2018-International-Arbitration-Survey---The-Evolution-of-International-Arbitration-(2).PDF, last visited 9 Apr. 2020, p. 27.
26. UNCITRAL, *Report of Working Group II (Dispute Settlement) on the Work of Its Sixty-Ninth Session (New York, 4–8 February 2019)*, A/CN.9/969, para. 23.
27. UNCITRAL, *Settlement of Commercial Disputes. Draft Provisions on Expedited Arbitration. Note by the Secretariat*, A/CN.9/WG.II/WP.212.
28. Case No. T 6238-10, Judgment of the Svea Court of Appeal, 24 Feb. 2012, p. 6.
29. Case No. T 6238-10, p. 9.

process'.[30] However, the Court continued, 'the Tribunal had to do so within the strictures that the parties had placed it in, principally the constraint of time'.[31]

On the particular issue of due process, Working Group II emphasized that '[t]he limited number of case law where due process in the context of expedited arbitration was mentioned indicates that, in their scrutiny of awards, enforcement courts have sought to strike a balance between, on the one hand, the arbitrators' powers and discretion in implementing expedited procedure and giving effect to the policy of time and cost efficiency and, on the other hand, the requirements of due process and fairness'.[32]

## §6.02 INVESTMENT ARBITRATION AND THE SUITABILITY OF EXPEDITED PROCEEDINGS

Arbitrating investment disputes has its peculiarities stemming out of the nature of the dispute, as well as from the parties involved,[33] which become relevant when assessing the feasibility of implementing expedited arbitration provisions. State party involvement is the main element which should be factored in, with a view of the complexity of State apparatus, complex internal organization, approvals and authorizations to be

30. *China Machine New Energy Corporation v. Jaguar Energy Guatemala LLC and AEI Guatemala Jaguar Ltd* [2018] SGHC 101, para. 127.
31. *China Machine v. Jaguar,* para. 129.
32. UNCITRAL, *Settlement of Commercial Disputes. Draft Provisions on Expedited Arbitration. Note by the Secretariat,* A/CN.9/WG.II/WP.209, para. 12.
33. *See* Karl-Heinz Böckstiegel, *Commercial and Investment Arbitration: How Different Are They Today? The Lalive Lecture 2012,* Arbitration International, Volume 28, Issue 4 (2012), pp. 577–590, explaining the difference between commercial and investment disputes – not always a straightforward distinction:

> Distinguishing between commercial and investment arbitration may sometimes already be difficult or misleading. Quite often disputes concern a contract between a corporation created by a foreign investor in a state on one side and on the other side a state enterprise. Such a contract will contain what one would consider a 'normal' arbitration clause referring to an institution of commercial arbitration. However, a closer look shows that it is really an investment dispute. A recent example from my own practice is our ICC award of last December between daughter companies of Exxon Mobil and PDVSA in Venezuela which was published immediately. I might add that in that case, we had a scenario which is also found frequently nowadays, namely that the investor starts additionally a parallel BIT arbitration to be on the safe side (p 578).

Anthea Roberts explains that the 'growing divergence between commercial and investment arbitration … is occurring due to differences in the fields' substantive law and professional communities.' (Anthea Roberts, *Divergence Between Investment and Commercial Arbitration,* Annual Meeting of the American Society of International Law 2012, American Society of International Law, New York, United States, pp. 297–300).

*See also,* Stephan Wittich, *The Limits of Party Autonomy in Investment Arbitration,* in Christina Knahr, Christian Koller, Walter Rechberger and August Reinisch (eds), *Investment and Commercial Arbitration: Similarities and Divergences* (Eleven International Publishing, 2010), pp. 47–71.

cleared before any decision.[34] The 'involvement of States, even if represented ... by a law firm, tend to make the proceeding more formal' and also translate in 'longer periods for submitting their memorials and evidence, because the decision process between counsel and the various state agencies involved may be more complex and time consuming'.[35]

Further, investment arbitration proceedings raise specific issues, such as the public interest in the underlying dispute, in particular when the alleged breach of State's obligations towards investor concerns its legislative and executive decisions or the conduct of its judiciary.[36] The nature of the disputes and the public interest thereof also raises issues of transparency of investment arbitration,[37] usually reflected in the additional time added to the procedural milestones and to the proceedings, in general.[38] As explained by Professor Böckstiegel, 'regarding confidentiality and transparency, we have what is probably the most striking difference between commercial

34. *See* Carolyn B. Lamm, et al., *Users' Perspectives on Challenges Facing the Institutions in a Changing World,* ICSID Review-Foreign Investment Law Journal, Volume 24, Issue 1 (Spring 2009), pp. 23–35, p. 26:

> Given the unique nature of sovereign parties, respondent-States generally need more time to prepare pleadings than private parties. Public policy implications require intra-government coordination of various agencies, often with divergent interests.

*See* other consequences deriving from State participation in the proceedings, such as resource constraints and problems with evidentiary gathering: Adam Raviv, *Achieving a Faster ICSID,* pp. 710 et seq.

This is not limited to investment disputes; it must be equally considered in commercial disputes when State and State entities are involved. *See,* for example, the 2012 *ICC Report on State, State entities and arbitration,* which refers to certain practices of the ICC when it comes to arbitrations involving States, such as the appointment of a three-member arbitral tribunal (paras 62–64), as well as elements to be taken into consideration by States, such as transparency of arbitral proceedings (para. 21). Further on ICC practice on investment treaty arbitration cases, *see* Andrea Carlevaris and Joel Dahlquist Cullborg, *Investment Treaty Arbitration at ICC,* ICC Dispute Resolution Bulletin, Issue 1 (2017), pp. 25–31.

35. Karl-Heinz Böckstiegel, *Commercial and Investment Arbitration: How Different Are They Today? The Lalive Lecture 2012,* p. 585. *See also* the statement of Chile with respect to the amendment of the ICSID Arbitration Rules and the inclusion of expedited proceedings: 'la apropiada defensa del Estado requiere tiempo y la coordinación de más de una entidad, además de los asesores externos. Por lo tanto, la inclusión de este capítulo es una preocupación para nuestro país.' (ICSID, *Compendium of State and Public Comments on WP #3,* 27 Feb. 2020, p. 47).
36. *See also* participation of *amici curiae* (non-disputing parties): ICSID Arbitration Rules, Rule 37(2); SCC Arbitration Rules, Art. 3 of Appendix III. Investment Treaty Disputes; NAFTA Free Trade Commission on Non-disputing Party Participation of 7 Oct. 2003.
37. *See* increased transparency obligation in arbitration proceedings further implemented in the past years with the new generation of IIAs – *see* CETA Art. 8.36 – and the adoption of the UNCITRAL Transparency Rules.
38. *See,* for example, *Gabriel Resources Ltd. and Gabriel Resources (Jersey) v. Romania,* ICSID Case No. ARB/15/31, under Canada-Romania BIT, in force 23 Nov. 2011, and UK-Romania BIT, in force 10 Jan. 1996, whereas the Canadian BIT, in Annex C contains transparency obligations. The burden on the costs and duration of the proceedings are reflected in the 27 Procedural Orders issued by the arbitral tribunal.

and investment arbitration'.[39] However, while there might be 'good reasons for the increased transparency, ... it does not make the procedure more efficient'.[40]

Further, the consent to arbitrate investment disputes is usually the result of the offer of the host State to arbitrate under an international investment agreement (IIA), followed by the acceptance of the offer by the investor by submitting the dispute to arbitration.[41] As such, a separate agreement to opt for expedited proceedings might be difficult to obtain after the dispute arises, in particular in consideration of the host State's presence in the arbitration. This is confirmed by the fact that the settlement rate in investment disputes is very low,[42] which raises the question of whether such agreement is attainable at all.

A discussion about the characteristics of investment arbitration and expedited proceedings, in particular, the aim being the increased efficiency of the proceedings by reducing the duration and costs thereof, can only be properly addressed with reference to the work of the UNCITRAL Working Group III on ISDS Reform. Among the three categories of concerns with ISDS identified by the Working Group III are the costs and duration of ISDS.[43] Regarding duration, concerns are directed at the following stages of the arbitration process: '(i) the appointment/composition of the tribunal, (ii) disclosure, discovery or document production and (iii) the issuance of the award (the period between the final hearing and the rendering of the award including deliberations when drafting the award)'.[44] No doubt, as also confirmed in the discussions in the Working Group III, costs and duration are interrelated issues, with lengthy proceedings resulting in higher costs.[45] Statistics show that the average length of ICSID arbitration cases between 2015 and 2017 was three years and seven months from the constitution of the tribunal to the arbitral award.[46] However, when discussing the length of investment arbitration proceedings and suggesting that their duration is a concern, this cannot be

39. Karl-Heinz Böckstiegel, *Commercial and Investment Arbitration: How Different Are They Today? The Lalive Lecture 2012*, p. 587.
40. Karl-Heinz Böckstiegel, *Commercial and Investment Arbitration: How Different Are They Today? The Lalive Lecture 2012*, p. 587.
41. *See*, in general, Jan Paulsson, *Arbitration Without Privity*, ICSID Review – Foreign Investment Law Journal, Volume 10, Issue 2 (1995), pp. 232–257.
42. *See* National University of Singapore, *Survey on Obstacles to Settlement of Investor-State Disputes*, Centre for International Law Working Paper 18/01, 2018, pp. 11 et seq.
43. UNCITRAL, *Report of Working Group III (Investor-State Dispute Settlement Reform) on the Work of Its Thirty-Fourth Session (Vienna, 27 November–1 December 2017)*, A/CN.9/930/Rev.1, paras 35–78.
44. UNCITRAL, *Possible Reform of Investor-State Dispute Settlement (ISDS) – Cost and Duration. Note by the Secretariat*, A/CN.9/WG.III/WP.153, para. 25.
45. UNCITRAL, *Report of Working Group III (Investor-State Dispute Settlement Reform) on the Work of Its Thirty-Fourth Session (Vienna, 27 November–1 December 2017)*, A/CN.9/930/Rev.1, para. 38; UNCITRAL, *Possible Reform of Investor-State Dispute Settlement (ISDS) – Cost and Duration. Note by the Secretariat*, A/CN.9/WG.III/WP.153, para. 27.
46. ICSID, Working Paper #1, Schedule 9: Addressing Time and Cost in ICSID Arbitration, para. 3. As metaphorically put by a scholar, '[i]nvestment arbitration is not for the impatient.' (Adam Raviv, *Achieving a Faster ICSID*, in Jean E. Kalicki and Anna Joubin-Bret (eds), *Reshaping the Investor-State Dispute Settlement System. Journeys for the 21st Century* (Brill. Nijhoff, 2015) pp. 653–717, p. 653.

done in the abstract, but with reference to a 'suitable comparator'.[47] What may appear to be a lengthy proceeding in one dispute, might be perfectly reasonable in another. Short proceedings should not be automatically labelled as better proceedings.

The Working Group III discussions are useful exercise in this sense, as they try to identify the reasons why proceedings might have variable durations. This can be explained by the dispute itself: the complexity of the dispute requiring 'extensive volume of evidence'.[48] Or by the behaviour of the parties and their counsel: States generally take longer in preparing their representation in the proceedings and submitting their evidence and defences, 'as they may need to coordinate among a number of authorities'.[49] Or by the composition of the arbitral tribunal and the conduct of the proceedings: the constitution of the arbitral tribunal and the lack of a proactive case management are listed as the main sources of delay in the conduct of investment arbitration proceedings.[50] Among the possible measures to address the concerns about the duration of ISDS proceedings, the UNCITRAL Working Group III suggested various possible measures, including: (a) stricter timelines to address lengthy durations; (b) improved management of the proceedings, including the requirement of submission of memorial in full detail and the use of modern technologies etc.[51] It is interesting to point out here that the 2018 School of International Arbitration and White & Case International Arbitration indicates that lengthy proceedings are not confined to ISDS, but respondents consider this a problem of arbitration in general.[52]

## §6.03 ICSID AMENDMENT PROCESS AND UNCITRAL WORKING GROUP II

While the mandate of the Working Group II is focused 'preliminarily on international commercial arbitration', still the relevance of the proposed rules on investment and other types of arbitration is reserved for the later stage of the discussions.[53] This cautious approach is understandable and recognized as such by the Working Group II, given the parallel work of the UNCITRAL Working Group III in ISDS reform,[54] and that

47. UNCITRAL, *Possible Reform of Investor-State Dispute Settlement (ISDS) – Cost and Duration. Note by the Secretariat*, A/CN.9/WG.III/WP.153, para. 66. *See* further discussion on the length of WTO and ICJ cases, UNCITRAL, *Possible Reform of Investor-State Dispute Settlement (ISDS) – Cost and Duration. Note by the Secretariat*, A/CN.9/WG.III/WP.153, paras 67–75.
48. UNCITRAL, *Possible Reform of Investor-State Dispute Settlement (ISDS) – Cost and Duration. Note by the Secretariat*, A/CN.9/WG.III/WP.153, para. 79.
49. UNCITRAL, *Possible Reform of Investor-State Dispute Settlement (ISDS) – Cost and Duration. Note by the Secretariat*, A/CN.9/WG.III/WP.153, para. 83.
50. UNCITRAL, *Possible Reform of Investor-State Dispute Settlement (ISDS) – Cost and Duration. Note by the Secretariat*, A/CN.9/WG.III/WP.153, paras 87–91.
51. UNCITRAL, *Possible Reform of Investor-State Dispute Settlement (ISDS) – Cost and Duration. Note by the Secretariat*, A/CN.9/WG.III/WP.153, para. 101.
52. White & Case and School of International Arbitration, Queen Mary University of London, *2018 International Arbitration Survey: The Evolution of International Arbitration*, p. 31.
53. UNCITRAL, *Report of Working Group II (Dispute Settlement) on the Work of Its Seventieth Session (Vienna, 23–27 September 2019)*, A/CN.9/1003, paras 14–15.
54. For the work of the UNCITRAL Working Group III, *see*, https://uncitral.un.org/en/working_groups/3/investor-state, last visited 8 Apr. 2020.

certain issues might overlap.[55] This would become relevant in particular with regard to the application of the UNCITRAL Rules on Transparency in Treaty-Based Investor-State Arbitration. If the expedited rules would be presented as an appendix to the UNCITRAL Arbitration Rules, then the UNCITRAL Rules on Transparency would apply to the expedited proceedings, unless expressly excluded by the parties.[56]

The ICSID Arbitration Rules Amendment Process[57] commenced in 2018 is presented with the purpose of achieving the following objectives: (i) continued modernization of ICSID procedure; (ii) simplification of the rules; (iii) reducing time and cost; (iv) going green, by reducing the paper burden of proceedings will further reduce time and cost and respect environmental concerns.[58] On reducing the duration of the ICSID arbitration proceedings, the proposed amendments address the constitution of the arbitral tribunals,[59] provide for a general obligation for parties and arbitrators to conduct the proceedings in an expeditious manner,[60] incorporate more flexibility in the organization of hearings and witness examination,[61] and introduce expedited arbitration provisions.[62] Working Paper #1 of the ICSID Amendment Process explains that the purpose of the proposed expedited arbitration provisions is to reduce the length of three main phases of the ICSID arbitrations, which have long durations: (i) the establishment of the arbitral tribunal; (ii) written procedures; (iii) rendering the arbitral award.[63] By implementing the expedited procedure, the arbitration proceedings could conclude within 470–530 days after the date of registration of the request for arbitration.[64] Compared to 49 months, the average duration of an arbitration

55. UNCITRAL, *Report of Working Group II (Dispute Settlement) on the Work of Its Seventieth Session (Vienna, 23–27 September 2019)*, A/CN.9/1003, para. 15:

> it was pointed out that if the work would eventually result in revisions of the UNCITRAL Arbitration Rules (the 'Rules'), caution should be taken as the Rules were generic in nature, with wide application, including in investment and State-to-State arbitration. It was reiterated that the Working Group should not seek to address the specific aspects of expedited proceedings in the context of investment arbitration, as Working Group III (Investor-State Dispute Settlement Reform) was currently tasked with considering the reform of investor-State dispute settlement. It was clarified that the Working Group could seek guidance from the Commission when addressing issues, which might overlap with the work of Working Group III.

*See also*, UNCITRAL, *Report of Working Group II (Dispute Settlement) on the Work of Its Seventy-First Session (New York, 3–7 February 2020)*, A/CN.9/1010, paras 16–18; UNCITRAL, *Settlement of Commercial Disputes. Draft Provisions on Expedited Arbitration. Note by the Secretariat*, A/CN.9/WG.II/WP.212, paras 7–10.

56. UNCITRAL, *Report of Working Group II (Dispute Settlement) on the Work of Its Seventy-First Session (New York, 3–7 February 2020)*, A/CN.9/1010, para. 18.
57. *See* the process at https://icsid.worldbank.org/en/amendments, last visited 11 Apr. 2020.
58. ICSID, *Working Paper #1. Proposals for Amendment of the ICSID Rules*, 2 Aug. 2018, para. 5.
59. ICSID, *Working Paper #4. Proposals for Amendment of the ICSID Rules*, February 2020, Rules 18 et seq.
60. ICSID, *Working Paper #4*, Rule 3.
61. ICSID, *Working Paper #4*, Rules 32 and 38.
62. ICSID, *Working Paper #4*, Rules 75–86.
63. ICSID, *Working Paper #1*, para. 657.
64. ICSID, *Working Paper #1*, para. 655.

procedure,[65] the proposal of expedited proceedings appears to substantially contribute to addressing the concern with the length of the arbitration proceedings and 'endeavour to strike a balance between an expedited procedure ... and a realistic schedule for investment disputes given their special characteristics'.[66] Nevertheless, expedited arbitration will continue to be an arbitration under the ICSID Convention and, therefore, 'the framework and mandatory provisions of the Convention apply'.[67]

The proposed ICSID provisions provide for an opt-in model for expedited arbitration, meaning that an agreement is needed in addition to the agreement to arbitrate.[68] Draft ICSID Arbitration Rule 75(1) provides that:

> The parties to an arbitration conducted under the Convention may consent at any time to expedite the arbitration in accordance with this Chapter ('expedited arbitration') by jointly notifying the Secretary-General in writing of their consent.[69]

Reference to the expedited arbitration may be contained in the arbitration agreement, if there is a contract between the parties, or in the State's offer to arbitrate, be it in an IIA or in the domestic legislation of the host State.[70]

The current draft Expedited Arbitration Provisions of the UNCITRAL Working Group II also advances consent as the exclusive criterion for the application of the provisions. It was considered that an express consent will guarantee that awareness of the parties as to the application of the provisions, with the consequences deriving from this, as well as making it possible 'to introduce more stringent rules therein, without raising concerns about due process and the enforceability of the eventual award'.[71]

Both ICSID and UNCITRAL draft expedited arbitration provisions preserve the option to opt out of the rules when certain conditions are met. Proposed Rule 86 of the ICSID Arbitration Rules provides for the situations for exiting the expedited arbitration which include (i) the joint notification by the parties; (ii) upon request of a party, allowing the arbitral tribunal to decide that an arbitration no longer be expedited, based on the complexity of the issues, the stage of the proceedings and all other relevant circumstances. Similarly, Draft Provision 1 of the UNCITRAL Working Group II Expedited Arbitration Provisions provides that (i) the parties may decide to exit the expedited proceedings, and that (ii) in exceptional circumstances, a party may request

65. ICSID, *Working Paper #1*, para. 586:

> The latest available numbers based on all ICSID arbitration proceedings which concluded with an Award during the past 15 years demonstrate that the average duration from registration of the case until the rendering of the Award was approximately 49 months.

66. ICSID, *Working Paper #1*, para. 662.
67. ICSID, *Working Paper #1*, para. 673.
68. *See* comments from the ICSID Contracting States, confirming the preference for express consent for expedited arbitration: ICSID, *Compendium of State and Public Comments on WP #3*, 27 Feb. 2020, pp. 47–48.
69. ICSID, *Working Paper #4. Proposals for Amendment of the ICSID Rules*, February 2020, p. 74.
70. The consent to expedited arbitration shall not apply in case of resubmission of the dispute, including after annulment (proposed Rule 86).
71. UNCITRAL, *Report of Working Group II (Dispute Settlement) on the Work of Its Seventy-First Session (New York, 3–7 February 2020)*, A/CN.9/1010, para. 21.

the arbitral tribunal to determine that the expedited arbitration provisions shall not apply to the arbitration, in which case, consideration should be given to the overall circumstances of the case, including the amount in dispute, the urgency of the resolution of the dispute and the proportionality of the amount in dispute to the estimated cost of arbitration.[72]

Proposed ICSID Arbitration Rule 76 gives the parties the option to proceed with a sole arbitrator or with a three-member arbitral tribunal. In Working Paper #1, ICSID highlighted that '[t]ypically, a proceeding conducted by a Sole Arbitrator is more expeditious than a proceeding with several arbitrators'. This position is also reflected in proposed Rule 76(3), which provides for the sole-arbitrator tribunal as the default if the parties fail to agree on either option.[73] Draft Expedited Arbitration Provisions of the UNCITRAL Working Group II currently provide, in Provision 3, that there shall be one arbitrator, unless otherwise agreed by the parties.[74] Sole-arbitrator tribunals are, indeed, associated with lower costs and speedier proceedings, as also reflected in the new generation of international investment agreements, such as the EU-Canada Comprehensive Economic and Trade Agreement (CETA), which provides for the sole-arbitrator rule when the investor is a small or medium-sized enterprise or the compensation or damages claimed are relatively low.[75]

Rules 80 and 81 of the proposed ICSID Arbitration Rules provide for a procedural timetable of the expedited proceedings. Bifurcation of the proceedings is not allowed under the expedited provisions or is the objection that a claim manifestly lacks legal merit under current ICSID Arbitration Rule 41(5). Rule 81(1)(g) advances that the hearing in expedited ICSID arbitrations shall be held within sixty days as of the filing of the last submission, that is nine months after the first session.[76] Unlike other

72. UNCITRAL, *Settlement of Commercial Disputes. Draft Provisions on Expedited Arbitration. Note by the Secretariat*, A/CN.9/WG.II/WP.212/Add. 1, p. 2.
73. This is also in line with Art. 37(2)(b) of the ICSID Convention.
74. UNCITRAL, *Settlement of Commercial Disputes. Draft Provisions on Expedited Arbitration. Note by the Secretariat*, A/CN.9/WG.II/WP.212/Add. 1, p. 2. For the UNCITRAL Working Group II Expedited Arbitration Provisions, an additional discussion in the context of the constitution of the arbitral tribunal concerns the appointing authority. UNCITRAL, *Report of Working Group II (Dispute Settlement) on the Work of Its Seventy-First Session (New York, 3–7 February 2020)*, A/CN.9/1010 offers interesting insight into this debate, with majority favouring the Secretary-General of the Permanent Court of Arbitration for designating the appointing authority (para. 76).
75. Article 8.23.5 of EU-Canada Comprehensive Economic and Trade Agreement (signed 30 Oct. 2016):

> The investor may, when submitting its claim, propose that a sole Member of the Tribunal should hear the claim. The respondent shall give sympathetic consideration to that request, in particular if the investor is a small or medium-sized enterprise or the compensation or damages claimed are relatively low.

76. On the effects of bifurcation on the timeline of ICSID arbitrations, *see* Lucy Greenwood, *Revisiting Bifurcation and Efficiency in International Arbitration Proceedings*, Journal of International Arbitration, Volume 36, Issue 4 (2019), pp. 421–430; Adam Raviv, *Achieving a Faster ICSID*, pp. 687 et seq.

    But see the concern expressed by some ICSID Contracting States that this removes important defence tools for States: ICSID, *Compendium of State and Public Comments on WP #3*, 27 Feb. 2020, p. 47.

institutional rules, as shown above, the proposed expedited provisions of the ICSID Arbitration Rules keep the presumption of a need for oral hearings. The UNCITRAL Working Group II draft provisions currently provide for different options to be considered in the context of holding an oral hearing: some States have expressed the view that the arbitral tribunal should be obliged to hold a hearing, in order to provide the parties with the opportunity to be heard,[77] while others favour the discretion of the arbitral tribunal whether to hold a hearing, given the accelerated nature of expedited arbitration.[78] Further, under Rule 81 of the proposed ICSID Arbitration Rules, written submissions are limited to two rounds of submissions, with an additional limitation in the second round, on the number of pages submitted – 100 pages. Similarly, interpretation, revision and annulment of arbitral awards rendered in ICSID expedited proceedings have adjusted time limits, in the light of the expedited nature of the proceedings. The UNCITRAL Working Group II Expedited Arbitration Provisions are still to define the timeframes of the arbitration, but there is a general preference for the draft rules to include a time frame for rendering the arbitral award.[79]

## §6.04 CONCLUDING REMARKS

Expedited arbitration proceedings for investment disputes could be a response to the concerns with duration and costs, as highlighted by both UNCITRAL Working Groups II and III, as well as by ICSID. However, one must also pay due attention to solutions which are available at the pre-arbitration stage as well as possibly addressing the length and, consequently, the costs of the arbitration, including by way of drafting the arbitration agreement or effectively making use of the procedural mechanisms in the underlying IIA, such as the cooling-off periods.

The main concern with the feasibility of expedited proceedings for investment disputes is the condensed timeframe. Comments from ICSID Contracting States to the amendments of the ICSID Arbitration Rules appear to confirm, first, that States do require more time for preparing their submissions, and, second, that this reality might have a serious impact on the feasibility of effective expedited proceedings. The comment from the Slovak Republic in the context of the ICSID Arbitration Rules Amendment Process summarizes this concern: 'This tool might be effective for claimants. Nevertheless, respondents, being states may face lack of time for preparing submissions'.[80] This tension between allowing realistic and sufficient time to the

77. UNCITRAL, *Report of Working Group II (Dispute Settlement) on the Work of Its Seventy-First Session (New York, 3–7 February 2020)*, A/CN.9/1010, para. 108.
78. UNCITRAL, *Report of Working Group II (Dispute Settlement) on the Work of Its Seventy-First session (New York, 3–7 February 2020)*, A/CN.9/1010, para. 109.
79. UNCITRAL, *Report of Working Group II (Dispute Settlement) on the Work of Its Seventy-First Session (New York, 3–7 February 2020)*, A/CN.9/1010, para. 92.
80. ICSID, *Rule Amendment Project – Member State & Public Comments on Working Paper # 1 of 3 August 2018*, p. 395. *See also* the comment made by Israel: 'We suggest to reconsider whether this timeline provided in this rule (and for the entire procedure) is feasible, especially on the part of states.' (ICSID, *Rule Amendment Project – Member State & Public Comments on Working Paper # 1 of 3 August 2018*, p. 402).

parties in these complex investment disputes and ensuring the efficiency of the arbitration proceedings is also emphasized in one of the ICSID Working Papers:

> Electing an EA [Expedited Arbitration] necessarily means parties and counsel have to make certain compromises. First, parties and counsel must be prepared to limit the length of submissions and the number of separate procedural applications they bring (e.g., requests for provisional measures and production of documents). Practice has shown that many arbitrations are delayed due to the high number of procedural applications made by the parties during the proceeding. By definition, an arbitration cannot be expedited if there are numerous disputes as to refusals to produce documents, special procedures, and the like. As a result, the approach of counsel will be vital to making the EA effective.[81]

Further, both as a perceived benefit and as a concern, one should consider that expedited arbitration provisions might trigger an increase in small value investment arbitration claims, as well as the increased access of small- and medium-size investors to this dispute resolution mechanism.[82]

Ending on a positive note, expedited arbitration proceedings for investment disputes would potentially address the legitimacy of the ISDS and the confidence in the system and the institutions involved in the process. To this end, the words of Judge Holtzmann in 1995 are still valid:

> When discussing this subject in London ten years ago, I spoke of the sloth and the dinosaur, cautioning that we must not allow arbitration to be as slow as the sloth or as cumbersome – and therefore as obsolete – as the dinosaur. Reassessing the situation today, I suggest that while all international arbitrations may have not yet developed the swiftness of the gazelle, some progress has been made toward curing the slothfulness of arbitrations and averting the fate of the dinosaur.
>
> Perhaps the most significant development in this regard has been an increasing recognition by the arbitration community – users, practitioners and arbitrators – that there is a pressing need to improve the efficiency of arbitral proceedings.[83]

81. ICSID, *Working Paper #1*, para. 663.
82. *See* Corporate Counsel International Arbitration Group (CCIAG), *Submission by the CCIAG to UNCITRAL Working Group III*, 18 Dec. 2019, para. 75. *See also* comments from ICSID Contracting Parties on the amendments of the ICSID Arbitration Rules: 'The expedited procedure would in many cases be of great use to SMEs, while at the same time it could bring significant efficiency to ISDS, thus benefiting the respondent State as well.' (Portugal, 21 Dec. 2018, comment to Working Paper #1, ICSID, *Rule Amendment Project – Member State & Public Comments on Working Paper # 1 of 3 August 2018*, p. 392).
83. Howard M. Holtzmann, *Streamlining Arbitral Proceedings: Some Techniques of the Iran-United States Claims Tribunal*, Arbitration International, Volume 11, Issue 1 (1995), pp. 39–50, p. 39.

CHAPTER 7

# COVID-19 and the Embracing of Technology: A 'New Normal' for International Arbitration

*Matthew Saunders*

## §7.01 INTRODUCTION

The signs of the Black Death pandemic of the fourteenth century can still be seen across Europe, in the surviving names of long-abandoned medieval villages and religious institutions. The death rate in England and across much of Europe was thought to be between 40% and 60% of the population; every facet of life continued to be impacted by the event for many decades. The disruptive economic impact on the availability of labour was profound, with many historians arguing that the changed balance of power between employer and labourer accelerated the end of feudal societal structures. This encouraged greater mobility of labour and higher wages and contributed to the notion of organised labour that underpins much social and economic change in post-medieval Europe.

Comparisons between the closing decades of the fourteenth century and COVID-19 of the third decade of the twenty-first century are clearly not the work of international arbitration lawyers. However, one parallel that can be drawn, even now before the full repercussions can be known, is the extent of the disruptive effect on working practices across Europe. The effective ban on international travel and the move to 'working from home' has been almost universal.

Few senior international arbitration lawyers are without 'gold card' frequent flyer status on at least one major airline and, not infrequently, hotel chains too. It has been suggested – largely with a 'straight face' – that the first and business class lounges at London's Heathrow Airport are one of the prime spots for international arbitrator 'networking'. While movements such as the 'Green Pledge' (now the Campaign for

Greener Arbitrations) have highlighted the environmental impact of avoidable travel, for many practitioners – and certainly many tribunal members – the default position has always been a preference for 'in person' hearings. Usually held at the seat of arbitration, in a city chosen as 'neutral' by parties who are not based there, and attended by witnesses, experts and advocates for very often several weeks. The costs of such an exercise are unsurprisingly high, but incurring them has – in the authors' experience – seldom been seen as avoidable, and very seldom been subject to meaningful scrutiny when legal costs come to be awarded. In essence, it has for many years been accepted that extensive travel to facilitate 'in person' meetings is an unavoidable – even desirable – element of the practice of international arbitration.

It is of course the case that use has increasingly been made of video technology. Reliable technology has been available for a decade, and cheap reliable technology for five years or so (Apple's 'FaceTime' product was first launched in 2010). Its use in international arbitration has however largely been limited to situations where a witness was unable to participate in person, or where the relative cost and inconvenience of travel as against the significance of their evidence was such that use of videoconferencing was considered acceptable. Approaches have varied between international arbitration centres and indeed legal cultures – with least adoption being on the part of those cultures where cross-examination of witnesses is 'most sacrosanct'. (In the authors' experience, practice in Scandinavia has been relatively accommodating but in London greatly less so.)

## §7.02 IMPACT OF COVID-19

COVID-19 changed all that. The government-mandated 'lockdowns', aimed at slowing the virus' spread, introduced an effective prohibition on international travel and non-essential domestic travel, as well as closure of offices and many factories. The impact on economic activity of lockdowns has been dramatic; for example, in the UK, the Bank of England forecast the largest single drop in economic activity since 1706 (when poor harvests combined with the economic impact of a war with France saw a 15% drop in economic output).[1]

By the end of March 2020, tens of millions of office workers were working from home, making extensive use of remote working technology. Chief among the tools utilised have been videoconferencing tools such as Zoom, Google Hangouts, GoToMeeting, Microsoft Teams and BlueJeans. Allowing for occasional impromptu appearances by family pets and young children, experiences have been positive, at least gauged by the impact on the share price of Zoom which was approximately USD 68.8 at the start of 2020 but had risen to USD 166.75 as of 15 May 2020.[2]

1. The Guardian, *War and the Weather: What Caused the Huge Economic Slump of 1706?*, https://www.theguardian.com/business/2020/may/07/what-caused-the-economic-slump-of-1706-#maincontent (accessed 28 May 2020).
2. Zoom Video Communication Inc's website, *Stock Quote & Chart*, https://investors.zoom.us/stock-information/stock-quote-chart (accessed 18 May 2020).

The legal sector has been no different, with extensive adoption of videoconferencing, including rapid application to mediations and hearings. Commercial operators of arbitration hearing centres have moved swiftly to offer online hearing options and 'hybrid' offers of partial online hearings. Many of those who were previously sceptical of extensive use of videoconferencing have had little alternative but to embrace it. Whether those who believe that cross-examination of witnesses can only ever be conducted when 'you can see the whites of their eyes' want it or not, the technology 'genie' is now 'out of the bottle'. The question now is whether arbitral institutions – and the international community more widely – will seize and build upon the opportunities that this disrupting event has offered.

The devastating societal and economic impact of COVID-19 is undeniable. However, there are positives that can be found in this new way of working, not least the environmental impact, the savings in terms of cost and efficiency, and the potential to make international arbitration more accessible to those who lack the resource to properly engage in the process. In this chapter we look at those positives, and what needs to be done to ensure that we build on them going forward into a post-COVID-19 era.

## §7.03 WHAT THE ARBITRATION COMMUNITY CAN LEARN FROM THE COVID-19 PANDEMIC

Arbitration has, on various occasions, been hailed as an efficient and economical means of dispute resolution. While such factors have been lauded by its promoters, widespread criticism has been levied at the international arbitration community for failing to manage costs effectively and adopting the delay-inducing practices, such as extensive document production, that national courts are now moving away from. Costs of arbitration are now consistently rated as the '*worst characteristic*' of arbitration, followed closely by a lack of speed.[3]

Institutions have taken the lead in seeking to bring about change by amending arbitral rules to introduce procedures such as for summary dismissal of claims[4] and have also published guidance on how technology may be used to save time and costs in arbitration.[5]

Although a majority (61%) of arbitration users are of the view that '*increased efficiency, including through technology*' is the factor that is most likely to have a significant impact on the future evolution of international arbitration,[6] use of technology in the conduct of arbitration has remained limited, not least due to lack of familiarity.[7] It has been suggested that such lack of familiarity is due to the high cost of

3. Queen Mary University of London, *2018 International Arbitration Survey* ('*2018 Survey*'), pp. 7–8.
4. *See*, e.g., SIAC Arbitration Rules, Rule 29 (2016).
5. *See*, e.g., ICC Commission Report, *Information Technology in International Arbitration*, International Chamber of Commerce (ICC, 2017).
6. 2018 Survey, p. 29.
7. 2018 Survey, p. 32.

technology which is still relatively new[8] (although a dispassionate analysis might well suggest that such arguments ceased to have currency a good few years ago). However, the COVID-related experience has clearly demonstrated not only that technology exists that can make the arbitral process more efficient, but also that the technology is affordable (and in some cases free).

Experience of compulsory 'working from home' has had an obvious effect on familiarity with conferencing technology. There are also other technology tools that could have a particular effect on access to 'know how' that has historically been the preserve of 'insiders' practising in the major international arbitration centres. We look at these below.

### [A] Choosing the Right Arbitrator

Experienced arbitration practitioners know very well that one of the most important decisions they ever take is whom to nominate as arbitrator in a dispute. Much effort is typically expended on sourcing views and information from colleagues and contacts as to relevant characteristics of a potential appointee. For all its significance, the most used sources of information for choosing an arbitrator have been demonstrated to be word of mouth and internal colleagues.[9] Historically, tech-based harnessing and analysis of data have played little role.

The 'resource gap' is one dimension of the justice gap and refers to the deterrent effect that costs of legal services have on the pursuit of legal solutions.[10] A further example of this gap would appear to exist where parties without the ability to sound out experienced colleagues and 'ask around' need to take decisions as to whom they will appoint. Technology is ideally placed to bridge this 'resource gap' and ensure a more level playing field.

Arbitrator Intelligence and Global Arbitration Review's Arbitrator Research Tool are two platforms that collect information about arbitrator decision-making on issues such as case management, document production, interim relief etc. Such information is eagerly sought by parties seeking to appoint arbitrators as it provides them with insight as to the course that may be taken by a potential arbitrator.[11] The online nature of such resources means that they are accessible globally and do not require pre-existing knowledge of a potential arbitrator's preferences as to approach or access to individuals with such knowledge. (The cynic would observe that where significant subscriptions need to be paid to access the databases, one form of exclusion is simply swapped for another.)

The real excitement perhaps lies in getting into the 'real meat of the matter' and deploying trend analysis and 'big data' tools to predict how an arbitrator might

8. 2018 Survey, p. 32.
9. 2018 Survey, p. 20.
10. Sundaresh Menon, *Technology and the Changing Face of Justice*, in Maxi Scherer (ed.), Journal of International Arbitration (© Kluwer Law International; Kluwer Law International 2020, Volume 37 Issue 2) pp. 167–190.
11. 2018 Survey, p. 21.

approach substantive legal decisions. Users of international arbitration have certainly indicated that they would like more information about how a prospective arbitrator has previously dealt with substantive issues and whether an arbitrator is likely to adopt a 'black letter' or a more commercial approach.[12] Such information could be available in the near future through analysis of awards which are increasingly publicly available and might perhaps go further by analysing a prospective arbitrator's digital profile to uncover unconscious bias. This is likely to give rise to an increasingly lively debate as to the ethics of such approaches.

### [B] Improving Efficiency in Document Production

Nothing provokes heated debate along the civil law/common law divide in international arbitration quite like the issue of document production. Its utility may be debated, but the degree to which it can add to the costs of a dispute is beyond debate.

Properly applied, advances in information technology and machine learning can make the processes of collection, review and production of electronic documents more efficient and cost effective. The IBA Arb40 Subcommittee's guide to Technology Resources for Arbitration Practitioners lists currently available technological advances that can be used to augment or assist an international arbitration.[13]

Software applications can be used with document review platforms to further assist document collection, review and production. As regards document collection, software can assist with the review of documents in unstructured data formats (such as chats, MMS and SMS messages) by grouping the messages into a coherent format that can be read sequentially. Software can also help visualise data by, for example, providing a bird's-eye view of the flow and volume of email or email timelines. As regards document production, auto-redaction tools can reduce the time needed for the linear review of documents containing privileged and sensitive information. Technology such as continuous active learning and predictive coding can also assist in the actual review of documents by categorising and coding large volumes of documents in a shorter period of time.

These technologies that improve efficiency in document production have been in existence for some time. However, the extent to which they are routinely adopted in international arbitration remains limited. Now that COVID-related travel restrictions have made it impossible for clients and lawyers physically to visit client offices to collect documents for the purposes of review, increasing reliance has necessarily been placed on technology to bridge the physical gap. Even cases with relatively small populations of documents for review and production now require the use of electronic review platforms if teams working remotely are to function effectively.

The variety of document management and review technologies available highlights once again the 'resource gap' in international arbitration. In order to avoid an 'arms race' in the adoption and application of review technology, the development and

12. 2018 Survey, pp. 21–22.
13. IBA, *Technology Resources for Arbitration Practitioners*, https://www.ibanet.org/technology-resources-for-arbitration-practitioners.aspx (accessed 16 April 2020).

promulgation of 'industry standards' with up-to-date procedural protocols is needed. With the exception of the Chartered Institute of Arbitrators' Protocol for E-Disclosure in International Arbitration, there remains little available.

### [C] Increase in Virtual Hearings

Arbitral institutions have long recognised that certain disputes can be resolved perfectly satisfactorily without a hearing, especially those within a particular trade or profession. Although documents-only arbitration has been commonplace in commodity and trade disputes, it has not been widely adopted in commercial disputes more broadly. In the absence of an agreement between the parties, the default position remains that parties are entitled to have an oral hearing. For example:

(1) Article 19.1 of the LCIA Arbitration Rules 2014 provides that '[a]*ny party has the right to a hearing before the Arbitral Tribunal on the parties' dispute at any appropriate stage of the arbitration (as decided by the Arbitral Tribunal), unless the parties have agreed in writing upon a documents-only arbitration*'.
(2) Article 32.1 of the SCC Arbitration Rules 2017 states that '[a] *hearing shall be held if requested by a party, or if the Arbitral Tribunal deems it appropriate*'.
(3) Article 25.6 of the ICC Arbitration Rules 2017 gives the arbitral tribunal discretion to '*decide the case solely on the documents submitted by the parties unless any of the parties requests a hearing*'.

The importance that parties have historically placed on a hearing, and the satisfaction they derive from having ventilated their case in front of an arbitral tribunal, makes it unlikely that the frequency of documents-only arbitrations will greatly increase in the foreseeable future. However, the success of videoconferencing technologies in working from home is certain to expedite the transition to virtual hearings in circumstances where, pre-COVID, 78% of users had never or rarely utilised '*virtual hearing rooms*' yet 66% took the view that '*virtual hearing rooms*' are a form of technology that is worth using more.[14] In so far as COVID-related travel restrictions mean that physical hearings cannot proceed, then conducting virtual hearings will, in any event, amount to 'making a virtue out of necessity'.

'Virtual hearings' also further contribute to bridging the 'justice gap' that can exist in dispute resolution. The burden on parties to converge physically and temporally for the purposes of a hearing ('physical gap') has been cited as the second dimension of the justice gap.[15] By removing this requirement and the significant travel and accommodation cost that accompany it (the world's major arbitral venues are among the most expensive cities to stay in), virtual hearings can further democratise

14. 2018 Survey, p. 32.
15. Sundaresh Menon, *Technology and the Changing Face of Justice*, in Maxi Scherer (ed.), Journal of International Arbitration (© Kluwer Law International; Kluwer Law International 2020, Volume 37 Issue 2) pp. 167–190.

arbitration. International arbitration, unconstrained by the requirements of transparency that dictate court hearings to be open to the public, should be a leader in this area.

### [D] Videoconferencing in Arbitration

Arbitral institutions have long recognised the importance of virtual hearings and have incorporated provisions in their arbitral rules allowing for the use of technology for such hearings. For example:

(1) Article 24(4) of the ICC Arbitration Rules 2017 allows the arbitral tribunal to conduct case management conferences through videoconference, even in the absence of agreement between the parties. Appendix IV to the ICC Rules sets out case management techniques that include '[u]*sing telephone or video conferencing for procedural and other hearings where attendance in person is not essential*'.
(2) Article 19.2 of the LCIA Arbitration Rules 2014 vests the arbitral tribunal with the '*fullest authority* [...] *to establish the conduct of a hearing, including its date, form, content, procedure, time-limits and geographical place. As to form, a hearing may take place by video or telephone conference or in person (or a combination of all three)*'.
(3) Article 28(2) of the SCC Arbitration Rules 2017 allows the case management conference to be conducted '*in person or by any other means*' which would naturally include a videoconference.

Although institutional rules provide expressly for the use of videoconferencing for case management conferences and procedural hearings, the COVID-19 pandemic has shown a general lack of such clarity in the rules for a merits hearing which, as explained in the next section, may be exploited by unwilling parties who may contend that the absence of specific permission for virtual hearings must mean that they are impermissible, absent the full consent of all parties.

Reduced costs and increased efficiency are not the only benefits of virtual hearings. Eliminating international air travel also benefits the environment and conforms with the Campaign for Greener Arbitrations which requires that arbitrators suggest, and counsel consider '*that witnesses or experts give evidence through video-conferencing facilities, rather than attend hearings in person*'.[16]

There are a number of videoconferencing technologies already available that have been usefully applied in arbitration. The ICC has licensed access to Microsoft Teams, VidyoCloud and Skype for Business, and ICC technical support is available

16. Greenwood Arbitration, *The Campaign For Greener Arbitrations Guiding Principles*, https://www.greenwoodarbitration.com/greenpledge (accessed 24 April 2020).

remotely to assist tribunals with using such platforms.[17] Other platforms include Zoom, BlueJeans and Cisco TelePresence.[18]

A key historical justification for limiting the use of virtual hearings has been the belief in common law jurisdictions that there is no substitute for a physical cross-examination of a witness and the keen insight into the truthfulness of the testimony it allegedly provides. This perception, coupled with common law arbitrators coming from the (relatively) tech-unfriendly worlds of the judiciary or the bar, has resulted in the use of videoconferencing being limited to circumstances where specific conditions, such as incapacity to travel, inhibit attendance in person.

Even in the common law world there has been considerable debate on the importance of being able to assess a witness' demeanour by requiring their physical attendance. In *Hanaro Shipping v. Cofftea Trading* [2015] EWHC 4293 (Comm), the High Court of England and Wales rejected an argument that there was a procedural imbalance between one party's witnesses giving evidence in person while the counterparty's witnesses gave evidence only by videoconference. The judge held as follows:[19]

> [...] Finally I should say in relation to the video link Mr Buckingham suggested that there would be an imbalance between witnesses who have to give evidence by video link and witnesses who give evidence in person. I am not persuaded that there is such a risk. Perhaps in the early days of video link when the quality of the video link was poor and it was a novelty, perhaps that might have been said, but these days I do not consider that that can be said.

By contrast, in *Jiangsu Shagang Group Co Ltd v. Loki Owning Company Ltd* [2018] EWHC 330 (Comm), the Court set aside an award of USD 68 million in damages observing that the tribunal had not appropriately assessed the credibility of one of the key witnesses. That witness did not speak English and gave evidence by an unreliable video link which may have led the tribunal to its conclusion as to the witness' credibility. The case highlights the fact that where videoconferencing technologies are used, then infrastructure of a minimum quality threshold must be deployed.

The High Court of England and Wales also made observations about the importance of a good video link in *PEC Ltd v. Asia Golden Rice Company Ltd* [2014] EWHC 1583 (Comm):

> 34. [...] However, it is less clear whether anyone other than Mr Narang gave approval: Mr Mirchandani's evidence about this was not assisted because the video-link to India broke down while he was being cross-examined about this. I conclude on balance that Mr Mirchandani probably did not give approval in advance ... .

17. ICC Guidance Note on Possible Measures Aimed at Mitigating the Effects of the COVID-19 Pandemic (9 April 2020).
18. IBA, *Technology Resources for Arbitration Practitioners Audio and Videoconferencing*, https://www.ibanet.org/technology-resources-for-arbitration-av.aspx (accessed 20 April 2020).
19. *Hanaro Shipping v. Cofftea Trading* [2015] EWHC 4293 (Comm), para. 16.

It will be readily noted that much has changed since this decision in terms of availability of reliable technology. Where sufficiently advanced technology is available, a virtual hearing has been found to be as effective as a physical one, with one arbitrator noting:

> The fact we were conducting a virtual hearing was almost forgotten as the matter got underway. Hearing oral argument was no different really from physical hearings. Much is said about how conducting cross examination of a witness over video-link is more difficult or less effective than in person. That might be true in the past with slow video feeds or where there is a poor quality connection but in our modern age, and based on listening to 6 witnesses over video-link in this case, and counsel for one party conducting the proceedings entirely by video-link, I think that concern needs reassessing. I would have no hesitation conducting more hearings in this format.[20]

## §7.04 PRACTICAL ISSUES IN USING TECHNOLOGY

The overwhelming response of the arbitral community to COVID-19 has been 'business as usual'. In addition to driving the technical evolution of international arbitration, this focus on maintaining hearing arrangements in the event physical hearings cannot proceed has also highlighted issues of consent and availability of relevant protocols.

### [A] Prior Consent to a Virtual Hearing: Preference or Prerequisite?

Can a tribunal issue directions for the hearing to be conducted virtually, despite one party's refusal to consent to a fully or partially virtual hearing? If the tribunal does issue such directions, is an arbitral award more susceptible to challenge? The rules of many institutions sadly lack clarity on this issue.

A notable exception is Article 19.2 of the 2014 LCIA Rules which gives the tribunal '*the fullest authority under the Arbitration Agreement to establish the conduct of a hearing, including its date, form* [...]. *As to form, a hearing may take place by video or telephone conference or in person (or a combination of all three)* [...]'.

The ICC Guidance Note on Possible Measures Aimed at Mitigating the Effects of the COVID-19 Pandemic notes that where a tribunal decides to proceed with a virtual hearing without party agreement, or over party objection, an issue may arise as regards the enforceability of the award in circumstances where Article 25(2) of the 2017 ICC Rules (which provides that the tribunal '*shall hear the parties together in person if any of them so requests*') is construed as referring to a physical hearing. The Guidance Note, relying upon the French language version of the ICC Rules, suggests that such language refers to the parties having an opportunity for a live, adversarial exchange and does not preclude a virtual hearing. It has been suggested that at the time many institutional

20. GAR, *Covid-19: Participants in SIAC Case Share Success of Virtual Hearing*, https://globalarbitrationreview.com/article/1225832/covid-19-participants-in-siac-case-share-success-of-virtual-hearing, (accessed 4 May 2020).

rules were drafted, virtual merits hearings were not addressed simply because the technology was not available. Thus, it is not that they were excluded, merely not expressly contemplated by the rule-makers. This lacuna has resulted in requiring institutions, tribunals and practitioners to interpret the rules in a manner consistent with modern practice and technology that accommodates virtual merits hearings notwithstanding the absence of any express reference. Many might say that utilitarian and purposive interpretation represents simple common sense, but this lack of clarity in rules inevitably enables the counterargument to be run and creates potential problems for those wishing to progress arbitrations but having to deal with objections to a virtual hearing.

Even if institutional rules lack specificity on the issue of whether parties can expressly be obliged to conduct a virtual hearing, the institutional rules and curial laws do typically provide tribunals with wide powers as to the conduct of hearings which can be argued implicitly to accommodate virtual hearings partially or fully. For example, section 34 of the English Arbitration Act, 1996 states that it shall be for the tribunal to decide '*all procedural and evidential matters*', which include where the proceedings are to be held.[21] While it is arguable that the discretion to determine where the hearing is to be held would include the discretion to decide whether a hearing is to be held through videoconference, there remains the risk that a court or tribunal may construe party consent to a virtual hearing as a prerequisite in such circumstances.

There is clearly a risk in the wake of a COVID-19 necessitated virtual hearing (whether fully or partially) that a recalcitrant party will seek to challenge an award on the basis that the virtual hearing was conducted without its consent, or that the virtual hearing somehow prevented it from presenting its case. Any supervisory court handling such a challenge would be well served by adopting an effects-based approach aimed at determining whether a virtual hearing has in fact had the effect of preventing a party from presenting its case (whether due to poor IT infrastructure or other reasons). The fact that either the relevant party or its counsel lacked the willingness to adapt to video technology should not carry weight.

At least in the UK, from a court litigation perspective, the position has been clear that the emergency regulations enacted as a consequence of the pandemic actively contemplate hearings continuing on a virtual basis. In *Re One Blackfriars Ltd, Hyde v. Nygate* [2020] EWHC 845(Ch), the judge held that sections 53–56 and Schedule 25 of the Coronavirus Act 2020, in making express provision for online trials, gave a strong indication that the Government expected the work of the civil courts to continue: '*The message is that as many hearings as possible should continue and they should do so remotely as long as that can be done safely.*' There is no reason why the same approach should not be adopted to arbitral hearings, unless the parties had expressly reserved the right to a physical hearing in their arbitration agreement. Those arbitral institutions whose rules do not clearly permit virtual hearings should rectify the position rapidly.

21. This power is subject to the right of the parties to agree any matter. *See* s. 34(1) of the Arbitration Act, 1996.

### [B] Early Engagement on Issues of Technology

By engaging at an early stage with parties on issues relating to the use of technology (particularly in the context of a virtual hearing), arbitral tribunals can effectively ensure a level playing field and mitigate the risk of bona fide challenges to an award on the basis of breach of natural justice or due process arising from the use of technology. Such early engagement should address issues such as: (a) the technologies to be used and their availability to the parties; (b) responsibility for ensuring that the technologies function as intended; and (c) the tribunal's discretion in adapting the agreed-upon procedure to ensure equality of arms.

Practical Law has developed a draft procedural order for videoconference arbitration hearings[22] that addresses some of these issues and requires:

(1) all parties attending the hearing including counsel, arbitrators, parties and witnesses to have high-speed broadband sufficient to support the platform being used;
(2) a secondary method of connecting to the platform (such as telephone); and
(3) arbitrators and counsel to conduct a test session of the platform which will include a mock direct and cross-examination of the hearing.

Tribunals may also rely upon institutional guidance such as the Seoul Protocol on Video Conferencing in International Arbitration (*Seoul Protocol*)[23] published earlier this year which is intended to serve as best practice for conducting videoconferences in international arbitration. It sets out principles dealing with examination of witnesses generally (including requiring parties to ensure that the technological requirements are met[24] and giving the tribunal discretion to terminate the videoconference if it is '*so unsatisfactory that it is unfair to either Party to continue*'),[25] technical requirements,[26] test conferencing and audio backup,[27] interpretation[28] and other preparatory arrangements.[29]

The importance of engaging on such issues was noted by the High Court of England and Wales in *Re One Blackfriars Ltd, Hyde v. Nygate* [2020] EWHC 845(Ch) in the context of an application seeking to adjourn a trial on account of the pandemic and objecting to a virtual trial on account of technological challenges. The Court held as follows:

22. The draft procedural order can be accessed at: http://protect-eu.mimecast.com/s/4BXjClO xBcgkDwYUDWHoV (accessed 4 May 2020).
23. The Seoul Protocol can be downloaded from: http://www.kcabinternational.or.kr/user/Board /comm_notice.do?BD_NO = 172&CURRENT_MENU_CODE = MENU0015&TOP_MENU_CODE = MENU0014, (accessed 4 May 2020).
24. Seoul Protocol, Art. 1.1.
25. Seoul Protocol, Art. 1.7.
26. Seoul Protocol, Art. 5.
27. Seoul Protocol, Art. 6.
28. Seoul Protocol, Art. 7.
29. Seoul Protocol, Art. 9.

> I am not satisfied, however, that the technological challenges which no doubt will be presented are so great as to make it appropriate to adjourn now. In my judgment, co-operation and planning is essential if a remote trial in this case is going to be possible, and that is why I have ordered the parties to co-operate in seeking potential remote trial platforms and document handling systems. In light of the comments by Birss J cited above I would expect any proposed system to subject to robust testing from as many of the locations from which participants are likely to be giving evidence (or making submissions) not only to ensure adequate video and audio quality but to ensure that documents can be displayed quickly. In particular, careful attention must be paid to the Internet bandwidth available at the locations from which witnesses intend to give evidence.[30]

Additionally, tribunals must be cognisant of factors unique to their case that may necessitate a particular approach. For example: (a) where a majority of witnesses are providing evidence by videoconference it may be advisable for all witnesses to follow the same process even if some could attend in person; (b) is witness conferencing involved and are there any special arrangements – such as ensuring experts' meetings can take place remotely; (c) whether administration of the virtual hearing should be outsourced to a third party to ensure independence in the control of the technology (and the availability of independent technicians to sort out problems).

### [C] Data Security and Confidentiality

Hacking and other cybersecurity breaches are not unknown in international arbitration. In 2015, during the course of the arbitration between China and the Philippines in relation to territory in the South China Sea, the websites of the Permanent Court of Arbitration, Philippines' Department of Justice and the law firm representing the Philippines were hacked.[31]

While the probability of such security breaches in private commercial arbitrations may be less than in the state arena, the increased use of technology, including significant use of domestic broadband connections, does increase the likelihood of such breaches. Infamously, Zoom has been the subject of much criticism when it was discovered that anyone with access to the video link for the conference could view the videoconference – and interrupt it with inappropriate material.[32]

Institutional rules do not typically address issues of cybersecurity and 'industry standards' of specific application to international arbitration are yet to emerge. Some limited guidance is found in the Seoul Protocol which requires cross-border connections to be safeguarded to prevent unlawful interception,[33] applies limits to the number

30. *Re One Blackfriars Ltd, Hyde v. Nygate* [2020] EWHC 845(Ch), para. 50.
31. Thomson Reuters, Practical Law Arbitration Blog, *Addressing Emerging Cyber Risks: Reflections on the ICCA Cybersecurity Protocol for International Arbitration*, http://arbitrationblog.practicallaw.com/addressing-emerging-cyber-risks-reflections-on-the-icca-cybersecurity-protocol-for-international-arbitration/ (accessed 4 May 2020).
32. The Guardian, *Singapore Bans Teachers Using Zoom after Hackers Post Obscene Images on Screens*; https://www.theguardian.com/world/2020/apr/11/singapore-bans-teachers-using-zoom-after-hackers-post-obscene-images-on-screens (accessed 28 May 2020).
33. Seoul Protocol, Art. 2.1(c).

of observers present during the videoconference to only necessary individuals, and requires the tribunal to verify the identity of the individuals present.[34] It also prohibits any recording of the videoconference without the permission of the tribunal.[35]

The 2020 ICCA-NYC Bar-CPR Cybersecurity Protocol for International Arbitration (*Cybersecurity Protocol*) provides a framework to determine reasonable information security measures that can be applied in an arbitration. The Cybersecurity Protocol comprises fourteen principles but does not supersede any applicable law, arbitration rules or other binding obligations[36] that may deal with the same issues. In determining '*reasonable cybersecurity measures*' the Cybersecurity Protocol requires the parties and the tribunal to consider, among others, the risk profile of the arbitration by taking into account prescribed factors, existing information security practices and infrastructure, and proportionality of any measures relative to the size, value and risk profile of the dispute.[37] By avoiding a one-size-fits-all approach the Cybersecurity Protocol allows parties and the tribunals to make bespoke arrangements, taking into consideration the risks and impact of any cybersecurity breaches, that would ensure that arbitration remains an efficient and cost-effective process.

The coming months will likely see further progress, with law firms in a number of arbitral centres cooperating in the establishment of criteria for common electronic platforms for arbitral hearings.

### [D] Other Points of Practical Importance

Draft procedural orders such as that prepared by Practical Law operate as a checklist to ensure 'no surprises' at the virtual hearing. In addition, early consideration should be given to myriad issues that are more complex when not all parties are in the same room. These include:

(1) *Translation:* In an entirely virtual hearing (i.e., where none of the witness, translator, counsel or tribunal are physically together), simultaneous or real-time translation may be problematic as parties, counsel and arbitrators are required to listen to multiple audio streams. The position can be simplified by using technology that would give the option of allowing individuals to only listen to the interpreter's audio feed. Technologies such as Zoom allow the host to assign to participants the role of 'interpreters'. Such participants will see a different interface, intended to make switching channels easier. Alternatively, consecutive translation can be used in much the same manner as it would be at a physical hearing albeit without the interpreter being physically present in the same room as the witness. It will remain important that the interpreters have the ability to see the witness, given the importance for them in appreciating 'non-verbal' elements of an individual's communication.

34. Seoul Protocol, Art. 3.1.
35. Seoul Protocol, Art. 8.1.
36. Cybersecurity Protocol, Principle 4.
37. Cybersecurity Protocol, Principle 6.

(2) *Witness coaching:* The absence of a physical hearing means the tribunal has limited control over who is in the room with the witness. The Seoul Protocol deals with this risk by requiring the videoconferencing system to show a reasonable part of the interior of the room in which the witness is located[38] while also requiring the tribunal to verify the identity of each individual present.[39] Alternatively, parties could be asked to use a camera (or cameras) that show the entire room or the witness could simply be asked to rotate their laptop camera to show the whole room. Tribunals will need to be prepared to be robust in allaying concerns that witnesses might be utilising a 'phone a friend' approach to dealing with questions on cross-examination.

(3) *Sitting hours:* In a cross-border dispute with various time zones, some or all parties may be forced to sit at unsociable hours, which may adversely impact a party's ability to present its case (although arguably the issues are really not so different from those imposed by jet lag and the fatigue associated with long-distance travel with which international arbitration practitioners will be well aware).

(4) *Change in advocacy styles:* The nature of oral and written advocacy would also need to be adjusted to account for a virtual hearing. In relation to the former, it is potentially easier to judge the tribunal's reaction to arguments and respond to their questions in a physical hearing which may render oral advocacy more dynamic and allow for lengthier oral submissions. Capturing and holding the tribunal's attention in a virtual setting is likely to be more difficult. Interaction between tribunal members in a fully virtual hearing where the tribunal is not together in one place may also be restricted. One practical result of this challenge is likely to be a greater reliance on written memorials and submissions, and use of documents such as skeleton arguments that may give greater structure to oral submissions. It could be argued that this would be no bad thing in any event and that anything which serves to focus an advocate's attention on the important points, and encourages preparedness and forethought, is to be encouraged.

(5) *Changes in tribunal dynamics*: Many presiding arbitrators go to great lengths to ensure that their tribunals have a functioning dynamic, that arbitrators have every opportunity to engage with each other and to operate effectively as a collective, rather than three individuals. However, not all do so. Without the opportunity to 'gel' over dinner, coffee or however else, there is a risk that the influence of a presiding arbitrator increases and that of party nominees diminishes. Given the fundamental role of party influence over tribunal composition and functioning, this is a real challenge. It may be a greater challenge where tribunal members do not already have significant experience of the dynamics of videoconferencing, e.g., through law firm meetings or social Zoom calls. That said, this is likely to become less of a problem given the increasing familiarity with videoconferencing generally post-lockdown.

38. Seoul Protocol, Art. 1.2.
39. Seoul Protocol, Art. 3.1.

This is however an area where some degree of 'awareness raising' on the part of arbitral institutions may pay dividends.

## §7.05 CONCLUSION

Throughout history, pandemics have changed the way society operates. By accelerating the adoption of flexible working (ironically, through mandating its use in a most inflexible fashion), the measures passed by governments globally in order to limit the transmission of COVID-19 provide a real opportunity for the international arbitration community to do things differently and to adopt ways of working that limit the need for the 'circus' of international arbitration hearings in London, Paris or Stockholm at vast expense to users. The potential benefits are not just as to cost, environment and overall efficiency but, more fundamentally, may go to narrowing the perceived 'justice gap' and encouraging the adoption of international arbitration as a process that is fair and accessible to users wherever they may be located, and however deep their pockets may be.

There is no 'silver lining' to the health emergency that COVID-19 has occasioned, but there are benefits that can come from having to do things differently. None of the technology that has been widely adopted was new, but attitudes to its utilisation are widely changed. The international arbitration community has an opportunity to adopt changed ways of working. It should be seized.

# CHAPTER 8
# Emergency Arbitration: A Maturing and Evolving Procedure

*Eva Storskrubb*

## §8.01 THE CONTEXT OF INTERIM RELIEF IN ARBITRATION

Interim relief and the possibility of recourse to proceedings for interim relief is an important aspect of commercial dispute resolution. In cases concerning, for example, industrial action, intellectual property, rights to ownership of, for example, shares, bank guarantees or other security under a contract, or simply the right to payment under a contract, and many more varied circumstances, interim relief can be crucial to preserve assets against dissipation or otherwise safeguard a factual or legal situation in anticipation of a final ruling on the merits. The main and traditional purpose of interim relief is to ensure that enforcement of rights remains possible once a final ruling on the merits is rendered. Thus, interim relief is classically considered to have a conservatory and protective nature and not intended to formally resolve a dispute. However, the purpose has been strategically broadened in many jurisdictions to encompass also a wider pallet of aims and parties also use interim relief strategically for many reasons. These broader aims can for example include to secure evidence or to achieve a de facto summary resolution of the dispute.[1] The critical importance for the parties of interim relief, as well as the strategic power it entails, coupled with the inherently provisional nature of the relief renders it potent but also open to abuse. Thus, it is important that the procedural rules and judicial practices support a well-balanced approach to interim relief, including necessary safeguards.[2]

1. Westberg, *Det provisoriska rättsskyddet i tvistemål: Bok I*, 66–69 and 75–77 (Juristförlaget i Lund 2004).
2. *Ibid.*, 129–139, *see* further in an EU context, E. Storskrubb and G. Cuniberti, 'Provisional Relief', in B. Hess S. Law and P. Ortolani (eds) *Luxembourg Report on European Procedural Law, Volume 1: Impediments of National Procedural Law to the Free Movement of Judgments* (Beck Hart 2018).

In an arbitration context, the power of arbitral tribunals to order interim measures has been highly controversial.[3] It was historically not possible to obtain interim relief from the arbitral tribunal, in particular not before an arbitral tribunal had been constituted under the relevant arbitration rules and framework, which can take several months.[4] Therefore, it was common for parties that had agreed to arbitrate their dispute, to have to seek interim relief from domestic courts. Consequently, the means of urgent interim relief in the domestic courts of the relevant jurisdictions and whether such relief is available also in support of claims that are to be resolved in arbitration, so-called concurrent authority, is an important practical factor to consider for parties finding it necessary to seek interim relief.[5] Depending on the jurisdictions concerned, one significant difference between interim relief granted by arbitral tribunals and that awarded by courts can be the latter's clear enforceability, including coercive powers and the means to force execution against assets.[6] Another main practical difference is that the availability of ex parte interim relief, which is traditionally not available in arbitration.[7] Nevertheless, for various reasons and in different scenarios, the parties may not consider that interim relief sought from domestic courts is a feasible way forward even when it is available. In addition, the concurrent authority, albeit well recognized, is an exception to the principle of arbitral exclusivity and judicial non-interference in arbitration.[8] Commentators have even noted that to the extent a dispute is settled or the main arbitral proceedings are not instituted after court-ordered interim relief, the national court can be held to have played a central role in ending or deciding

3. Croft et al., *A Guide to UNCITRAL Arbitration Rules*, 268 (CUP 2013).
4. *Ibid.*, 269 and Born, *International Arbitration: Law and Practice*, 210, 212 and 217 (Kluwer Law International 2nd ed. 2015). Note that in some jurisdictions it remains the exclusive prerogative of domestic courts to provide interim relief and arbitral tribunals are prohibited from doing so.
5. Born, *supra* note 4, 219–226, notably in some jurisdictions national law limits the concurrent authority of courts, e.g., the English Arbitration Act under which it is only possible for a court to grant interim relief under specific circumstances if the arbitral tribunal is unavailable. Another example is courts that are not able to grant interim relief in support of foreign arbitration. *See also* P. Cavalieros and J. Kim, *Emergency Arbitrators Versus the Courts: From Concurrent Jurisdiction to Practical Considerations*, 35 Journal of International Arbitration 257, 285–286 (2018), on concurrent jurisdiction with respect to emergency arbitration ('EA') specifically.
6. Born, *supra* note 4, 217–219, some jurisdictions and the UNCITRAL Model Law of 2006 provide also for enforcement of tribunal awarded interim relief. However, there is considerable uncertainty as to international enforcement under the New York Convention. *See* further Cavalieros and Kim, *supra* note 5, 287–297, and G. Hanessian and E.A. Dosman, *Songs of Innocence and Experience: Ten Years of Emergency Arbitration*, 27 American Review of International Arbitration 229–235 (2016), concerning specifically the issue of enforceability of EA interim relief in various jurisdictions. The position in Sweden is negative towards enforcement, *see inter alia* P. Shaughnessy, 'Interim Measures' in U. Franke et al. (eds), *Arbitration in Sweden: A Practitioner's Guide*, 106–108 (Kluwer Law International 2013) and Heuman, *Skiljemannarätt* 346 (Nordstedts Juridik 2010).
7. Most domestic laws and institutional rules explicitly or explicitly exclude ex parte interim relief in arbitration. However, the 2006 version of the UNCITRAL Model Law Art. 17(B) provides for preliminary ex parte orders that are not enforceable, which entail that the effectiveness of the rule is questioned, *see* Born, *supra* note 4, 216–217. In addition, some institutional rules exceptionally provide for ex parte interim relief, *see* SCAI Rules 26(3). *See* further Hanessian and Dosman, *supra* note 6, 222–223, in the EA context.
8. Born, *supra* note 4, 219.

the case. That may be considered to undermine the parties' choice of dispute resolution method, i.e., arbitration.[9]

It is against the above-mentioned backdrop that emergency arbitration (EA) rules have been implemented by arbitration institutes since 2006, with the International Centre for Dispute Resolution (ICDR) being credited for first implementing such rules, and in the decade since then we have gone from considering EA rules an innovation to holding them to be the norm.[10] As a few examples, the Arbitration Institute of the Stockholm Chamber of Commerce (SCC) included EA in its rules in 2010, whereas the Court of Arbitration of the International Chamber of Commerce (ICC) did so in 2012.[11] The availability of EA rules is considered to support the autonomy and efficacy of arbitration.[12] An emergency arbitrator is a sole arbitrator appointed by the arbitration institute to render a decision upon an application for emergency interim relief before the arbitral tribunal itself has been constituted. The EA rules differ between arbitration institutes, for example, some of them allow an emergency arbitrator to be appointed even before the request for arbitration has been filed.[13] However, the idea is to enable a highly expedited procedure in the arbitration framework for obtaining interim relief that precedes the constitution of the arbitral tribunal. The emergency arbitrator's powers cease upon the constitution of the arbitral tribunal and, if ordered, the interim relief will have no formally binding effect on the subsequently appointed arbitral tribunal.[14]

In 2019, the Arbitration Commission of the ICC published a report on EA proceedings under the ICC Rules of Arbitration (the 'ICC EA Report').[15] The report is based on eighty EA cases during 2012–2018. Thus, it covers a significant number of cases. The ICC is not the first international arbitration institute to publish information of this sort. For example, the SCC and the Swiss Chambers' Arbitration Institute (SCAI) have published regular case overviews since enacting specific rules on EA.[16] Recently

9. Hanessian and Dosman, *supra* note 6, 215.
10. *Ibid.*, 216–218 provide a brief historic overview of the development of EA including all the central international arbitration institutes.
11. *Ibid.*, 217, for a list of multiple arbitration institutes. *See* further I. Knoll-Tudor, 'The Arbitrator and the Arbitration Procedure, Emergency Arbitration: Evidence and Practice from Seven Arbitral Institutions', in C. Klausegger et al. (eds), *Austrian Yearbook on International Arbitration*, 250–252 (Manz'sche Verlags- und Universitätsbuchhandlung 2019), for an overview of the adoption of EA rules by seven institutes and a table of their EA case load.
12. *See* P. Shaughnessy, 'The Emergency Arbitrator', in P. Shaughnessy and S. Tung (eds), *The Powers and Duties of an Arbitrator: Liber Amicorum Pierre A. Karrer*, 340 (Kluwer Law International 2017).
13. In such rules there is often a deadline within which the request for arbitration concerning the main proceedings must be filed, *see inter alia* the ICC Rules, Appendix V Arts 1(6) and 2(1), and the SCC Rules, Appendix II Art. 1(1) and Art. 9(iii)–(iv). *See* further Cavalieros and Kim, *supra* note 5, 280, on the timing of the EA application.
14. *See inter alia* Hanessian and Dosman, *supra* note 6, 219–221.
15. https://iccwbo.org/publication/emergency-arbitrator-proceedings-icc-arbitration-and-adr-commission-report/ (accessed 27 Mar. 2020).
16. Prior SCC Reports can be found here https://sccinstitute.com/media/194250/ea-practice-note-emergency-arbitrator-decisions-rendered-2015-2016.pdf: A. Havedal Ipp, *Practice Note 2015-2016*; L. Knapp, *Practice Note 2014* and J. Lundstedt, *Practice Note 2010-2013*. The most recent report for the Swiss Chambers can be found here https://www.swissarbitration.org/files/620/Emergency%20Proceedings%20Article/SCAI%202020%20Report%20on%20Emergency%20

the SCC reported on the first full decade of its EA cases.[17] Other international arbitration institutes also provide some case studies or limited EA information.[18] This entails that we now have a considerable body of information relating to how EA is applied in practice from tribunals seated in many jurisdictions.

The purpose of this chapter is to reflect on and critically assess EA as a maturing and evolving tool of international arbitration. For this purpose, one of the main themes dealt with in the ICC EA Report is analysed below, namely the requisites for granting emergency relief (section §8.02). As noted above, the need for EA rules has not arisen in a void but relates to the existence of urgent interim relief in courts and whether such relief is effective and available also in the support of claims that are to be resolved in arbitration. It is notable that in the Queen Mary International Arbitration Survey of 2015, 93% of respondents were in favour of arbitration institutes implementing EA rules.[19] Thus, there appears to be a wide acceptance of such a tool and a desire to have such an option available. Notwithstanding, 46% of the respondents still preferred to seek interim relief from domestic courts (with 29% stating a preference for EA and 26% being undecided).[20] These figures might slightly have changed today with the increasing use of and familiarity with EA procedures among the users of arbitration. However, the overall results of the survey demonstrate both a pendulum and a dichotomy between the use of these two, in many cases concurrent, means of obtaining interim relief. For strategic reasons, including time and costs, flexibility and availability, as well as the need for ex parte relief and formal execution, one of these means may be more relevant to pursue in a particular case.[21] Therefore, when analysing the evolution of EA, it may be useful to compare it to certain aspects of interim relief awarded by courts and also be aware of potential parallel developments of harmonization of interim relief in international litigation (section §8.03). Finally, some conclusions will be drawn on the future of EA reflecting upon the strengths and weaknesses of EA as a tool of international arbitration (section §8.04).

---

Relief%20under%20the%20Swiss%20Rules_Final_20200228.pdf, SCAI, *Emergency Relief under the Swiss Rules (Art 43) – An Overview after 8 Years of Practice* (2020). (All accessed 27 Mar. 2020).

17. The most recent SCC information can be found here https://sccinstitute.com/about-the-scc/news/2020/emergency-arbitration-at-the-scc-a-decade-in-review/?link_id = q2juacYCwgOh (accessed 19 Apr. 2020).
18. *See inter alia* information of the London Court of International Arbitration (LCIA) at https://www.lcia.org/adr-services/lcia-notes-on-emergency-procedures.aspx and statistics of Singapore International Arbitration Center ('SIAC') https://siac.org.sg/2014-11-03-13-33-43/facts-figures/statistics (both accessed 27 Mar. 2020). Further information can be found in the doctrine based on interviews with institutes, *inter alia* Hanessian and Dosman, *supra* note 6, 225–227.
19. The Queen Mary International Arbitration Survey 2015, *Improvements and Innovations in International Arbitration*, 29, available at http://www.arbitration.qmul.ac.uk/media/arbitration/docs/2015_International_Arbitration_Survey.pdf (accessed 27 Mar. 2020).
20. *Ibid.*, 27.
21. Cavalieros and Kim, *supra* note 5, 293–300.

## §8.02 THE REQUISITES FOR GRANTING EMERGENCY INTERIM RELIEF

### [A] Background

Most rules of arbitral institutes do not elaborate upon the types of available emergency relief or on the scope of and conditions for granting interim relief.[22] The ICC Rules merely note that EA proceedings concern 'urgent interim or conservatory measures that cannot await the constitution of an arbitral tribunal ...',[23] whereas the general rules on conservatory and interim measures state that 'the arbitral tribunal may, at the request of a party, order any interim or conservatory measure it deems appropriate'.[24] The SCC Rules explicitly state the same for EA proceeding, holding that the emergency arbitrator has the power to upon request 'grant any interim measures it deems appropriate'.[25] This is also the case under the ICDR, Hong Kong International Arbitration Centre (HKIAC), and Singapore International Arbitration Centre (SIAC) rules, which only refer to the urgent need or necessary relief.[26] In addition, although many modern arbitration acts today confirm that arbitrators are empowered to grant interim relief, traditionally they remain silent on the types of measures and on the requisites or substantive standard for granting interim relief.[27] As an example, section 25(3) of the Swedish Arbitration Act merely sets out that: 'Unless the parties have agreed otherwise, the arbitrators may, at the request of a party, decide that, during the proceedings, the opposing party must undertake a certain interim measure to secure the claim which is to be adjudicated by the arbitrators.'[28]

This lack of substantiation of the scope and conditions for interim relief may of course be a conscious choice of arbitral institutions and legislators not to limit explicitly or overregulate the powers of arbitral tribunals, i.e., to adopt a 'minimalist approach' that enables wide discretion for the arbitral tribunal.[29] Another explanation from a legislator's perspective may be that, because interim arbitral relief is not considered enforceable in that specific jurisdiction, there is less risk in granting flexibility to the arbitral tribunal and, concurrently, little need to specifically regulate its scope and

22. Hanessian and Dosman, *supra* note 6, 227, note that there are exceptions such as the Australian Centre for International Commercial Arbitration (ACICA) rules.
23. ICC Rules Art. 29.
24. ICC Rules Art. 28.
25. Appendix I to the SCC Rules 2017 Art. 1(2) referring to Art. 37(1) of the SCC Rules 2017.
26. Hanessian and Dosman, *supra* note 6, 227.
27. Blackaby and Partasides, *Redfern & Hunter on International Arbitration*, 315 (Kluwer Law International 6th ed. 2015).
28. An interesting question raised in the doctrine is whether this general provision on the arbitral tribunal's power to grant interim measures 'during the proceedings' can also be held to empower an emergency arbitrator that is appointed before the main arbitral proceedings are even instituted. If the answer is negative the basis of that empowerment would merely lie in the parties' arbitration agreement referring to institute rules that provide for EA proceedings. *See* P. Shaughnessy, *Pre-arbitral Urgent Relief: The New SCC Emergency Arbitrator Rules*, 27 Journal of International Arbitration 337, 355–357 (2010). *See also* Born, *International Arbitration: Cases and Materials*, 882–883 (Kluwer Law International 2015) who raises the question '... is an "emergency arbitrator" really an arbitrator?'.
29. Shaughnessy *supra* note 6, 108–109.

conditions.[30] However, it may also be the case that legislators, in general, have not found it necessary to regulate interim relief ordered by arbitral tribunals as this has historically not been perceived as a common occurrence. Historically, such relief was generally not at all available, alternatively not available before the arbitral tribunal was actually constituted.[31] A request for interim relief is often prompted by urgency. Interim relief is often sought before – or when – the main proceedings are instituted. Parties have traditionally had no other choice than to turn to the courts for interim relief where they could not await the constitution of the arbitral tribunal.

However, the availability of EA rules that enable interim relief to be awarded *before* the constitution of the arbitral tribunal and even *before* the filing of a request for arbitration, has increased in the past decade and the number of EA proceedings have increased.[32] The lack of rules on interim relief in the arbitral setting may be perceived as a potential void. From a procedural perspective, it is common that there are specific rules (based on statute or developed in case law) for the scope and conditions for interim relief in domestic civil proceedings. To the extent that the institute rules and the *lex arbitri* are silent on the issue, the question also arises as to the legal basis for the parties' submissions on and the arbitral tribunal's analysis of these issues. One approach can potentially be to draw inspiration from the above-mentioned domestic procedural rules. However, that is not considered by many commentators to be a suitable approach for arbitration. Particularly in the context of international arbitration, many commentators argue that domestic procedural rules of the seat should not play a significant role.[33]

At the international arbitration level, both the UNCITRAL Model Law and the UNCITRAL Arbitration Rules in their reformed versions, from 2006 and 2010 respectively, provide a comprehensive set of rules for interim relief. The intention behind the reforms was specifically to provide a full framework for interim relief in arbitration in order to provide legal certainty and guidance.[34] Both sets of rules provide the same conditions for interim relief in Articles 17(A)(1) and 26(3):[35]

(a) Harm not adequately reparable by an award of damages is likely to result if the measure is not ordered, and such harm substantially outweighs the harm that is likely to result to the party against whom the measure is directed if the measure is granted; and
(b) There is a reasonable possibility that the requesting party will succeed on the merits of the claim. [...].

In addition, both instruments also provide a definition of the scope of the relief in Articles 17(2) and 26(2) according to which an arbitral tribunal can order a party to:

30. Lindskog, *Skiljeförfarande*, 689 (Nordstedts 2012).
31. Born, *supra* note 4, 210, 212 and 217.
32. *See inter alia* Knoll-Tudor, *supra* note 11, 251–253 for a compilation of statistics on EA proceedings.
33. *See inter alia* Shaughnessy, *supra* note 6, 109, and C. Boog, 'The Laws Governing Interim Measures in International Arbitration' in F. Ferrari and S. Kröll (eds), *Conflict of Laws in International Arbitration*, 409, 426–428 (Sellier 2010).
34. Paulsson and Petrochilos, *UNCITRAL Arbitration*, 217–218 (Kluwer Law International 2017).
35. Available at https://uncitral.un.org/en/texts/arbitration (accessed 27 Mar. 2020).

(a) Maintain or restore the status quo pending determination of the dispute;
(b) Take action that would prevent, or refrain from taking action that is likely to cause, current or imminent harm or prejudice to the arbitral process itself;
(c) Provide a means of preserving assets out of which a subsequent award may be satisfied; or
(d) Preserve evidence that may be relevant and material to the resolution of the dispute.

Both deal with interim relief ordered by an arbitral tribunal and do not expressly address the possibility of an emergency arbitrator that may order the same relief. Notably, what we call EA proceedings as defined above are not to be confused with the preliminary orders that arbitral tribunals can grant ex parte in the UNCITRAL Model Law provisions on interim relief.[36]

In some UNCITRAL Model Law jurisdictions, the provisions on interim relief form part of the *lex arbitri*.[37] However, the soft law impact of the UNCITRAL Model Law and UNCITRAL Arbitration Rules is arguably more far-reaching. Both instruments are the result of extensive collaborative work and negotiations under the auspices of the UNCITRAL framework. In addition, they deal with interim relief in a comprehensive manner. Therefore, the provisions on interim relief in both instruments are often taken to represent arbitral practice on interim relief.[38] In addition, commentators refer to them as a codification that represents general principles that are 'universally accepted' on interim relief in arbitration.[39] One commentator specifically observed that they constitute an amalgam drawn from the evolution of interim relief practice in the context of investor-state arbitration.[40] However, they are also understood to originate from commonly accepted standards for interim relief in domestic courts.[41] Further, it has also been noted that the definition of scope of interim relief has been approached with caution as the drafters have aimed to achieve a solution that leaves enough room for co-existing national understandings of interim relief.[42] Hence, it is perceived as customary for both parties and emergency arbitrators to draw inspiration and guidance from them in EA practice.[43] One of the issues that will be analysed further below based on the ICC EA Report is whether this perception is carried through in practice and

36. *See supra* note 7. Notably the UNCITRAL Model Law but not the UNCITRAL Arbitration Rules, provides the arbitral tribunal with the power to grant a preliminary order on interim relief ex parte, UNCITRAL Model Law Art. 17(B). *See* Paulsson and Petrochilos, *supra* note 34, 232–234, for a discussion why the same provision was not included in the UNCITRAL Arbitration. The issue of ex parte interim relief in arbitration is still a fiercely controversial issue, *see* Binder, *International Commercial Arbitration and Mediation in UNCITRAL Model Law Jurisdictions*, 297–300 (Kluwer Law International 4th ed. 2019) and H. van Houtte, *Ten Reasons Against a Proposal for Ex Parte Interim Measures of Protection in Arbitration*, 20 Arbitration International 85 (2004).
37. Boog, *supra* note 33, 428.
38. Blackaby and Partasides, *supra* note 27, 315.
39. Paulsson and Petrochilos, *supra* note 34, 218.
40. M.J. Goldstein, *A Glance into History for the Emergency Arbitrator*, 40 Fordham International Law Journal 779 (2017).
41. Binder, *supra* note 36, 293–296.
42. *Ibid.*, 292.
43. *See inter alia* Knoll-Tudor, *supra* note 11, 263, and K-Y. Kim and B. Satish, 'Legal Criteria for Granting Interim Relief in Emergency Arbitrator Proceedings: Where Are We Now and Where

whether there is indeed a universal standard with respect to the scope of and conditions for interim relief.

### [B] The ICC EA Report and Other Practice

#### *[1] General Issues*

Statistics show that EA rules of multiple arbitration institutes are being used and that emergency arbitrators are providing recourse to parties. Many arbitration institutes provide statistics on EA applications, and this information is updated regularly. Commentators have also reviewed the statistics; generally, it appears as if EA interim relief has been awarded under many institutional rules in slightly above or below half of the applications.[44] Similar figures also emerge from the information of 2020 on the first ten years of application of the SCC EA Rules. During this period, interim relief was awarded in 45% of the cases.[45] In the ICC EA Reports, the percentage is lower, of the eighty cases reviewed interim relief was awarded in twenty-three cases, i.e., in 29% of the cases. However, based on a closer breakdown of the report, the following emerges. Only seventy-two of the applications progressed to an assessment (in eight cases the application was withdrawn, in three of these cases based on a settlement). However, due to various preliminary issues, including applications being dismissed for lack of jurisdiction or other so-called threshold issues, an emergency arbitrator actually reviewed the merits of the EA application in only fifty-six of the eighty cases reviewed in the report. Of these cases that proceeded to a full review of the merits of the application, the relief applied for was granted wholly or in part in twenty-three cases, i.e., in 41% of the cases.[46]

Further, the ICC EA Report deals with a number of issues that have arisen in practice that it calls 'threshold issues' including applicability, admissibility and jurisdiction. Such issues include whether the ICC EA rules were applicable temporally, whether the ICC EA rules could be applied when the parties had agreed to another pre-arbitral procedure, whether concurrent application for interim relief to a court could affect the jurisdiction of the emergency arbitrator and other jurisdictional arguments of various kinds.[47] In addition, the report raises the interesting issue of the law applicable to the threshold issues.[48] Such issues may be considered to be requisites for EA interim relief as they can impact whether an application will be successful and they often concern preliminary procedural matters based on which an application can be dismissed. Some of the EA reports of other arbitration institutes also demonstrate

---

Do We Go From Here?' in N. Kaplan and M.J. Moser (eds), *Jurisdiction, Admissibility and Choice of Law in International Arbitration: Liber Amicorum Michael Pryles*, 178 (Kluwer Law International 2018).

44. Hanessian and Dosman, *supra* note 6, 225–226. *See also* Knoll-Tudor, *supra* note 11, 252.
45. SCC, *supra* note 17.
46. ICC EA Report, *supra* note 15.
47. *Ibid.*, 10–17.
48. *Ibid.*, 16. *See also* Goldstein, *supra* note 40, 780–785, regarding the adjacent issue of the prima facie standard for review of jurisdiction.

that such preliminary issues have arisen.[49] 'Threshold issues' will not be further dealt with in this contribution. The focus in the following will rather be on what the ICC EA Report calls 'substantive standards', i.e., the specific conditions for granting interim relief.

However, the test of urgency, which is a relevant factor in the substantive standards, as will be developed below, can also be considered relevant as a threshold issue. As noted above, the construct of EA rules is such that the relief can only be applied for until the arbitral tribunal is constituted. It is perhaps inherent also in the name itself, 'EA', that there is an urgency in the relief sought. Hence, the ethos underlying the purpose of EA relief is that it cannot await the constitution of an arbitral tribunal.[50] This is explicitly mentioned in the ICC Rules that refer to 'urgent interim or conservatory measures that cannot await the constitution of an arbitral tribunal ...'.[51] Thus, the ICC EA practice shows that some arbitrators apply this criterion as a separate or distinct from urgency as applicable to the substantive conditions for interim relief. In other cases the emergency arbitrator applied the 'cannot wait' test together with a broader urgency assessment.[52] The report also states that it may not, in the end, lead to a different result, whether 'cannot wait' is assessed separately. However, if an emergency arbitrator chooses to not grant the relief because the 'cannot wait' test is not fulfilled, there may, depending on the circumstances, be more flexibility for the applicant to argue for interim relief from the arbitral tribunal once constituted.[53]

### *[2] The Conditions Applied*

According to the ICC EA Report, the conditions for interim relief applied by the emergency arbitrators included (i) likelihood of success of the merits (*fumus bonus iuris*); (ii) danger of delay including risk of irreparable harm (*periculum in mora*); (iii) urgency (as noted above some independently and some as part of or in connection with danger of delay); and (iv) balance of equities (proportionality). In addition, some emergency arbitrators also referred to or considered the principles of (v) not aggravating the dispute and (vi) not prejudging the merits of the case.[54] Not all of the emergency arbitrators applied all the conditions, but the two first conditions were much more commonly applied than the others.[55] In addition, emergency arbitrators can of course choose to apply the conditions in any order practicable, which naturally entails that if an application is dismissed for lack of fulfilling one condition, the other relevant conditions may not have been assessed. The conditions mentioned in the ICC EA Report, to a significant degree, mirror the practice that has emerged in the SCC EA

49. SCAI, *supra* note 16, 1, and Havedal Ipp, *supra* note 16, 15.
50. *Ibid.*, 2.
51. Article 29.
52. ICC EA Report, *supra* note 15, 13–14.
53. *Ibid.*, 14.
54. *Ibid.*, 24–28. Note that ICC EA Report list the conditions in a different order.
55. *Ibid.* Likelihood of success (31 of 80 cases); danger in delay (40 of 80 cases); balance of equities (16 of 80 cases); no prejudgment of the merits (19 of 80 cases); and risk of aggravation (12 of 80 cases).

cases. In the latest practice note of the SCC, it is noted that a set of factors have crystalized as the commonly acceptable prerequisites (after jurisdiction) including: (i) chance of success on the merits, (ii) urgency, (iii) irreparable harm, and (iv) proportionality.[56] In the latest report of the SCAI, the first three criteria mentioned above for the ICC and the SCC are also noted as the three criteria consistently applied. In the words of the report the criteria are: (i) whether the applicant has a prima facie case on the merits, (ii) whether urgency justifies the requested measures, and (iii) whether there is a risk of irreparable harm or substantial harm.[57]

In addition, commentators reviewing cases of a number of arbitration institutes, including ICDR and SIAC, note that practice shows that emergency arbitrators had considered factors that fall in the three broad categories elaborated in the UNCITRAL Model Law; i.e., (i) the adequacy of the case on the merits (prima facie case, likelihood of success), (ii) the nature of the potential harm (grave, serious, irreparable), and (iii) the balance of harms (proportionality).[58] Thus, very broadly speaking, one can perhaps say that some form of harmonized categories of potential conditions can be derived from practice. However, from the above, it also emerges that there are also potentially slight differences in the approach. For example, in the note of the SCAI, the condition of balancing of equities (proportionality) is not mentioned. In the ICC EA Report it is alleged that this is a common law principle.[59] Whether or not one agrees with that comparative law characterization of the source of the condition, this difference between the institutional reports highlights that furthering a perception of a harmonized categories does not perhaps give the full picture. In addition, there are various ways of formulating the conditions. The slightly different terminology used may merely be different ways of formulating the same condition. But it may also indicate nuances in the understanding of how the conditions should be interpreted. Therefore, one needs to look further into both what basis emergency arbitrators have used for identifying the conditions and how the conditions have been interpreted (sections §8.02[B][3] and §8.02[B][4] below).

Two further factors relevant to the prerequisites in the ICC EA Report should be mentioned before further analysing the conditions, starting with the provision of security. The ICC Rules, as some other institutional EA rules, explicitly provide that emergency arbitrators can subject an interim relief order to posting security.[60] According to the report, there were only two cases in which some form of security was ordered.[61] Thus, one can state that this opportunity has so far rarely been used by emergency arbitrators. The lack of cases in which security has been ordered appears to be supported by information from other arbitration institutes.[62] Second, the type of interim relief has varied, which entails that many different kinds of interim relief have

56. Havedal Ipp, *supra* note 16, 17.
57. SCAI, *supra* note 16, 2.
58. Hanessian and Dosman, *supra* note 6, 228.
59. ICC EA Report, *supra* note 15, 27.
60. ICC Rules, Art. 28, and Appendix V, Art. 6(7). *See also inter alia* SCC Rules, Art. 37(2) and Appendix II, Art. 1(2).
61. ICC EA Report, *supra* note 15, 28.
62. *Ibid.*, 29.

been sought and awarded. These include among anti-suit injunctions (also anti-arbitration injunctions), asset preservation, orders prohibiting action or demanding certain performance, orders concerning corporate body appointments or meetings, and measures concerning bank guarantees.[63]

### *[3] The Legal Basis for the Conditions*

According to the ICC EA Report, emergency arbitrators have overall showed a preference to avoid taking guidance from the applicable domestic law when assessing the conditions for interim relief and have instead chosen an approach propagated by commentators to look at international arbitration standards.[64] Commentators claim that this approach is more aligned to the expectation of the parties in international arbitration and likely to result in broadly uniform and predictable results.[65] According to the ICC EA Report, emergency arbitrators have in forty-nine cases been willing to apply conditions 'developed in connection with the granting of interim measures by arbitral tribunals'.[66] It is difficult to determine which these might be. Possible candidates include: the UNCITRAL conditions in its Model Law and Arbitration Rules, the practice developed and reported for interim relief in investor-state arbitration cases, or the practice developed and reported in the context of the EA under the ICC rules, or other institutional rules during the past decade. One can assume that there may be variations in the sources actually used by emergency arbitrators when seeking to identify an international standard.[67] The report further notes that emergency arbitrators have referred to 'common principles of law' and 'international sources'.[68] Such statements are also generic and unspecific, and they may signal de facto harmonization where multiple international sources mentioned above are consulted and taken as a form of guidance. However, due to the generic nature, it is hard to establish. In the case at hand it would naturally be useful for the parties to have more specific information. The report also notes as a recommendation that an early discussion on the standard or conditions to be applied by the emergency arbitrator with the parties is to be encouraged.[69]

Notwithstanding the general preference to avoid applying domestic law mentioned above, according to the report, emergency arbitrators have in a significant number of the cases also considered the *lex arbitri* or the *lex causae* when assessing an EA application.[70] In one case the emergency arbitrator considered mandatory law of the *lex arbitri*, and in a number of other cases the emergency arbitrators stated that they should be guided by the *lex arbitri*. However, if the *lex arbitri* is silent on the

63. *Ibid.*
64. *Ibid.*, 23.
65. *See inter alia* Shaughnessy, *supra* note 6 and Boog, *supra* note 33.
66. ICC EA Report, *supra* note 15, 23. Similar results emerge for under the SCC EA Rules, *see* Ragnwaldh, Andersson and Salinas, *A Guide to the SCC Arbitration Rules* 181 (Kluwer 2019).
67. Boog, *supra* note 33, 444.
68. ICC EA Report, *supra* note 15, 23.
69. *Ibid.*
70. *Ibid.*

conditions, the emergency arbitrators have found themselves free to resort to international sources.[71]

The same pattern is confirmed by the SCC Reports. In two cases, the emergency arbitrator explicitly referred to provisions on interim relief in the Swedish Code of Judicial Procedure.[72] In another case, the emergency arbitrator referred to lacking coercive powers under Swedish law as the *lex arbitri* to order compulsion under threat of a fine ('*vite*' in Swedish),[73] and in a further case the emergency arbitrator referred to Swedish principles in holding that interim relief should not amount to advance enforcement of the award and must be a reversible measure.[74] Thus, the reference to domestic law has been made both with respect to the conditions for interim relief as well as the interim relief as such. However, according to the latest SCC Report, in most cases, the emergency arbitrators refer to the broad discretion given under the SCC Rules and the *lex arbitri*, and thus take into account and respect the *lex arbitri*, but due to its silence then proceed to use internationally established standards including the UNCITRAL Model Law and the practice established in prior EA cases in order to set out the conditions for interim relief.[75]

#### *[4] The Interpretation of the Conditions*

Based on the ICC EA Report and all the available institutional reports on case practice it is not possible to fully analyse fully how the conditions have been interpreted. Confidentiality has permitted the reports to include only very brief summaries of the cases. The reports do not reveal the full reasoning and assessments of the emergency arbitrators. However, what one can distil from the ICC EA Report is that there is a no uniform application of the conditions. For example, in relation to urgency it is explicitly noted that the interpretation and scope of the condition was far from uniform in the cases reviewed.[76] In addition, with respect to the two other central and most applied conditions, likelihood of success on the merits (*fumus bonus iuris*) and danger of delay including risk of irreparable harm (*periculum in mora*), there are variances in practice.

First, in relation to likelihood of success on the merits, it is noted in the ICC EA Report that many emergency arbitrators require that the applicant must establish a prima facie case. However, this does not in itself clarify what level of probability of success on the merits that emergency arbitrators demand. Emergency arbitrators have sometimes under the SCC Rules understood this criterion to mean a mere showing that the elements of a claim are present, whereas most emergency arbitrators set a higher bar requiring the applicant to show a reasonable possibility of success. Under the ICDR Rules the test is according to the report often framed as a good prospect of success,

71. *Ibid.*
72. Lundstedt, *supra* note 16, 2 and Knapp *supra* note 16, 4.
73. Lundstedt, *supra* note 16, 24.
74. Havedal Ipp, *supra* note 16, 14.
75. *Ibid.*, 6, 10, 11, 13, 16 and 17. *See* further Ragnwaldh, Andersson and Salinas, *supra* note 66.
76. ICC EA Report, *supra* note 15, 24.

which is potentially an even slightly higher bar.[77] Commentators have also noted the multitude of ways in which emergency arbitrators can frame the condition as well as set the bar for the level of probability of success, indicating some leeway in the exercise of arbitrators' discretion.[78] The same commentators identify two levels of standard for the condition, the higher standard of 'reasonable possibility of success on the merits' and a lower standard of 'prima facie protectable interest' or 'possible that the applicant will succeed on the merits'.[79] They further argue for applying a lower standard due to the special nature of EA proceedings compared to process for applying for interim relief before an arbitral tribunal, including the very short time frames in EA proceedings and the fact that the parties will often not be able to marshal full evidence before the emergency arbitrator.[80] In addition, they raise the concern noted as a separate principle in the ICC EA Report, namely the risk that the EA proceedings are considered to prejudge or prejudice the applicant's case in the full arbitration.[81]

Another commentator also warns the emergency arbitrators against applying their own domestic understanding of the conditions as framed in, for example, in the UNCITRAL Model Law. He argues that there is no automatic common understanding of the conditions such as likelihood of success and that the emergency arbitrator must give them 'texture' and 'content'.[82] The same conditions may be used in many legal cultures for domestic interim relief but differently appreciated and developed in domestic case law and practice. Thus, in order to avoid the risk of emergency arbitrator giving the condition a domestic interpretation, he posits that an increased understanding of the international historic reference points for the conditions is necessary.[83] The practice developed in investor-state arbitration as well as the *travaux préparatoires* of the UNCITRAL Working Group that prepared the 2006 Reform specifically on interim relief are included in the suggested reference points.[84] Interestingly he notes that with respect to the condition of likelihood of success on the merits there is the biggest difference between the traditional common law standard and the international arbitration standard. He argues that in the international arbitration context, there was a conscious retreat from the common law standard often requiring a substantial likelihood of success on the merits to a lower standard now found in the UNCITRAL Model Law and Arbitration Rules, i.e., a reasonable possibility of success on the merits.[85] He finally agrees with the commentators referring to the special nature of the EA proceeding and the need for the EA proceedings not to prejudge the merits of the case. Thus, he also advocates for a potentially even lower interpretation of standard for the condition likelihood of success in the EA context.[86]

77. *Ibid.*, 25.
78. Kim and Satish, *supra* note 43, 181.
79. *Ibid.*, 181–182.
80. *Ibid.*, 187–189.
81. *Ibid.*, 183 and 189.
82. Goldstein, *supra* note 40, 780.
83. *Ibid.*, 780.
84. *Ibid.*, 794.
85. *Ibid.*, 793–795.
86. *Ibid.*, 796.

With respect to the second condition of danger of delay, including the risk of irreparable harm, the ICC EA Report notes that there is a lack of consensus and even ongoing debate on the level of harm necessary to satisfy the condition. The report further notes that in many domestic jurisdictions the level of harm typically entails showing that it cannot be compensated by a damages award. However, in the international arbitration context a slightly lower standard of harm is also commonly applied, that entails showing serious or grave harm, albeit possible to compensate monetarily.[87] In all of the forty cases reviewed in which the condition was applied it is not clear which level of harm was applied. However, in just over half of the cases, twenty-one, the emergency arbitrator did not apply a literal meaning of irreparable harm but rather referred to serious and substantial harm.[88] In the first SCC EA Report it was noted that emergency arbitrators applied a rather strict test with respect to urgency and irreparable harm.[89] In addition, in the conclusions of the most recent SCC Report it is also noted that where the harm can be compensated by damages most emergency arbitrators under the SCC Rules have found the application unwarranted.[90] Thus, the overall practice under the SCC Rules appears to apply a standard slightly stricter than noted in the majority of the ICC cases.

Commentators have also with respect to the risk of harm condition found that there is a considerable variance in practice, both with respect to the standard and the burden of proof.[91] One commentator even asks whether we should be surprised or distressed that there is no common understanding.[92] However, he also finds that the history of its development in investor-state arbitrations and the drafting history of the UNCITRAL Model Law show that the condition is applied in a more flexible manner than a traditional and restrictive common law application of the condition. Thus, serious and grave harm can be used as the standard rather than demanding that it be literally irreparable.[93] In particular, the commentator also refers to *travaux préparatoires* of the UNCITRAL Working Group on arbitration that the intention behind the wording 'harm not adequately reparable by an award on damages' was to provide more flexibility because 'irreparable harm' could present a too high threshold.[94] Finally, other commentators propose that in addition to using the condition of substantial harm, emergency arbitrators could use ordering security as a tool to offset, for example, lack of evidence of full harm and also to calibrate the relative hardship faced by the parties when interim relief is ordered.[95]

87. ICC EA Report, *supra* note 15, 25.
88. *Ibid.*, 26.
89. Lundstedt, *supra* note 16, 25.
90. Havedal Ipp, *supra* note 16, 18.
91. Kim and Satish, *supra* note 43, 183–186.
92. Goldstein, *supra* note 40, 785.
93. *Ibid.*, 785–793. *See also* Hanessian and Dosman, *supra* note 6, 229.
94. *Ibid.*, 791.
95. Kim and Satish, *supra* note 43, 189–190.

### [C] Conclusion

The perception that it is customary for emergency arbitrators to draw inspiration and guidance from international sources and soft law in the form of the UNCITRAL framework is carried through in EA practice. There appears to be a broad acceptance that these sources can be used as guidance in the event that there are no more specific conditions elaborated in the relevant *lex arbitri* or institutional rules. There seems to be a broad and common understanding of which conditions to apply, at least when it comes to the two conditions of likelihood of success on the merits (*fumus bonus iuris*) and danger of delay including risk of irreparable harm (*periculum in mora*). Further, to the extent that there are no mandatory or other obstacles in the *lex arbitri* there also appears to be a common understanding of the broad discretion of emergency arbitrators in relation to the scope of interim relief and the measures that can be ordered. However, there is no universal application and interpretations of the conditions. Practice shows that there is a variance in the application of the most commonly applied requisites regardless of the institutional context of the relevant EA procedure. Regardless of the fact that emergency arbitrators want to adhere to an international standard it is perhaps not always clear what that standard is, and emergency arbitrators may invariably be affected by their own legal cultures.

Thus, there is a reason for both parties and emergency arbitrators to be aware of these divergences and nuances in the application of the requisites. As noted in the ICC EA Report, it would be useful for the parties that emergency arbitrators are transparent in how they will apply the conditions at an early stage of the process. In addition, if a deeper uniformity is to be achieved in the interpretation of the main requisites for EA interim relief, it is imperative that the arbitration institutes continue to publish reports on the practice and that a dialogue on the requisites is continued in the doctrine and other relevant fora in the arbitration community.

## §8.03 A COMPARATIVE LENS

### [A] Introduction

As confirmed above there appears to be a broad consensus that emergency arbitrators should and de facto do look to international sources for guidance on the interpretation of the requisites for interim relief to the extent that the *lex arbitri* is silent. Hence, there appears to be a broad common understanding that domestic procedural law regarding interim relief rendered in courts should not be a primary source of guidance.[96] Indeed, even domestic courts that have had to review EA interim relief have recognized that the broad discretion of the emergency arbitrator and that the emergency arbitrator may apply standards different from domestic courts.[97] The purpose of this chapter is not to challenge or criticize that premise. However, we cannot entirely exclude underlying

96. Boog, *supra* note 33, 426–430.
97. Hanessian and Dosman, *supra* note 6, 229–230.

legal cultural perceptions that may inform emergency arbitrators' understanding of the prerequisites and how to interpret them, even unconsciously. In order to avoid that emergency arbitrators do so, it is important to have a clear awareness of both the domestic perspective and the broader international standard. A commentator referred to above was able to conduct such an analysis from a common law perspective.[98] Thus, it is arguably useful to also present other domestic perspectives in order to further such a comparative exercise also outside the common law domain. In addition, in order to develop EA proceedings as a tool of international arbitration, development and discourse in other international contexts of interim relief can perhaps be used as a comparative inspiration or benchmark. In this section the Swedish domestic perspective on interim relief is briefly outlined. In addition, recent European cross-border developments with respect to interim relief are briefly presented.

### [B] A Domestic Example

According to Chapter 15 of the Swedish Code of Judicial Procedure,[99] an application for an interim relief can be granted if the applicant shows probable cause that it has a claim against another party that is or can form the basis of judicial proceedings or be determined by another similar procedure (condition of probable cause), and if it is reasonable to suspect that the opposing party, by carrying on a certain activity, by performing or refraining from performing a certain act, or by other conduct, will hinder or render more difficult the exercise or realization of the applicant's right or substantially reduce the value of that right (condition of risk of sabotage).[100] Risk of sabotage means that the applicant must show that the risk is objectively determinable, impending and that the opposing party's action is imminent or ongoing.[101] Although the condition refers to a risk of future sabotage, a measure that has been taken earlier by the opposing party will most likely affect the assessment.[102] Another condition in section 15(6) of the Code of Judicial Procedure is that the applicant must deposit security up-front with the court for the loss that the opposing party may suffer. This requirement should be applied in view of section 3(22) of the Enforcement Code, which states that the applicant has a strict liability for all the damages that the opposing party suffers due to the enforcement, including economic loss.[103] Hence, the size of the security deposit is of importance when the court assesses whether to grant an application for an interim relief or not.

98. Goldstein, *supra* note 40.
99. An unofficial translation to English is available here https://www.government.se/49e41c/contentassets/a1be9e99a5c64d1bb93a96ce5d517e9c/the-swedish-code-of-judicial-procedure-ds-1998_65.pdf (accessed 19 Apr. 2020).
100. Section 15(1-3) of the Swedish Code of Judicial Procedure (1942:740).
101. Westberg, *supra* note 1, Book 3, 39 and 89. *See also* Ekelöf et al, *Rättegång tredje häftet*, 26-31 (Nordsteds juridik, 8th ed., 2018).
102. *Ibid.*, 256.
103. *Ibid.*, Book 4, 219–221 and 226–247.

Even though it is not explicitly stated in Chapter 15 of the Code of Judicial Procedure, another requisite that needs to be considered is the proportionality principle. This entails that there must be a balance between the aimed result of the interim measure and the negative effects that come with it, and a court can reject an application if interim relief would lead to disproportionate damage in comparison to the reasons for awarding it.[104] The Swedish Supreme Court has held that the proportionality principle can overlap the assessment of the other requirements.[105] The proportionality principle is of special importance when a security deposit does not fully protect the opposing party for its potential loss.[106]

Chapter 15 section 5 of the Code of Judicial Procedure provides that no application may be granted unless the opposing party has been given the opportunity to respond. However, if the applicant can show that such a delay places its claim at risk (condition of imminent danger), the court may immediately, without the hearing of the opposing party (ex parte), impose a measure to remain effective until otherwise ordered. The Swedish Supreme Court has stated that imminent danger can be regarded as a requirement of a qualified risk of sabotage, where the degree of urgency applies especially. There must be a significant reason for the court to grant relief without hearing the opposing party, for example, if it is to be feared that notice of the application will trigger the opposing party to immediately take a sabotage measure.[107] If interim relief has been granted without the hearing of the opposing party, the court must, when the opposing party has been served and submitted its comments, immediately reconsider if the interim measure should stand or be reversed.[108]

### [C] European Developments

There have been several recent and interesting developments at an international level in Europe concerning interim relief. Since 2017, the European Account Preservation Oder Regulation[109] (the 'Regulation') has been applicable and offers successful applicants in local domestic courts in the European Union (EU) the possibility to attach bank accounts in other EU Member States, i.e., it constitutes the first uniform and directly enforceable cross-border interim measure in the EU.[110] Under the Regulation an applicant creditor can obtain a European Account Preservation Order (EAPO) which prevents the subsequent enforcement of the creditor's claim from being jeopardized through the transfer or withdrawal of funds up to the amount specified in the EAPO which are held by the debtor or on his behalf in a bank account maintained in a

104. *Ibid.*, Book 4, 191–334, and Swedish Supreme Court case NJA 1993 page 182. *See also* Ekelöf, *supra* note 101, 31-32.
105. Swedish Supreme Court case NJA 2018 page 189.
106. Westberg, *supra* note 1, Book 4, 270.
107. Swedish Supreme Court case NJA 2005 section 29.
108. Ekelöf, *supra* note 101, 23-24. *See also* Swedish Chancellor of Justice case JK 1983:23.
109. Regulation (EU) No. 655/2014 establishing a European Account Preservation Order procedure to facilitate cross-border debt recovery in civil and commercial matters [2014] OJ L 189/59.
110. The Regulation is applicable in all EU Member States except the UK and Denmark.

Member State.[111] The possibility to apply for an EAPO is available to the creditor as an alternative to interim relief under domestic law.[112] In order to obtain an EAPO the applicant must show: (i) an urgent need for a protective measure because there is a real risk that, without such a measure, the subsequent enforcement of the creditor's claim against the debtor will be impeded or made substantially more difficult, and (ii) that it is likely to succeed on the substance of its claim.[113] In the recitals to the Regulation is it noted that the conditions for issuing an EAPO should strike an appropriate balance between the interest of the creditor in obtaining interim relief and the interest of the debtor in preventing abuse of the interim relief.[114] In addition, where ex parte interim relief is applied for specific safeguards are stipulated in order to prevent abuse and protect the debtor's rights. The safeguards include the possibility of requiring the creditor to provide security and a rule on the creditor's liability for any damage caused to the debtor by the EAPO.[115]

A major study on domestic procedures in the EU complied for the EU Commission also included provisional relief within its scope. The results of the study demonstrate among other that most Member States apply the two conditions for interim relief, urgent threat of impairment (*periculum in mora*) and the existence of a claim (*fumus bonus iuris*).[116] In addition, some EU Member States also have other conditions including the balancing of the parties' risks (proportionality). With respect to interpretation of the conditions the interesting result of the study concerns the applicant's duty to substantiate prima facie its claim on the merits. Here, the study showed a clear variance in the standard applied. In some EU Member States a prima facie plausible existence of the right whose protection is sought is deemed sufficient, while other Member States adhere to a higher standard including 'a good arguable case'.[117]

The research project of the European Law Institute (ELI) and UNIDROIT on European Rules of Civil Procedure that commenced in 2014 is due to be published soon.[118] The project is a soft law project to create model civil procedural rules for Europe and has already raised debate on the potential further harmonization of civil procedure in the EU and interest among the EU institutions.[119] The rules include a section on provisional and protective measures that have drawn inspiration from the

---

111. Regulation, *supra* note 109, Art. 1.
112. *Ibid.*, Arts 1 and 16.
113. *Ibid.*, Art. 7.
114. *Ibid.*, Recital 14.
115. *Ibid.*, Recitals 17–19, Arts 12 and 13.
116. Storskrubb and Cuniberti, *supra* note 2. The Report is also available at https://op.europa.eu/en/publication-detail/-/publication/531ef49a-9768-11e7-b92d-01aa75ed71a1/language-en (accessed 19 Apr. 2020) *see* Chapter 3 Provisional Measures, 232–233.
117. *Ibid.*
118. *See* project information at https://www.europeanlawinstitute.eu/projects-publications/current-projects-feasibility-studies-and-other-activities/current-projects/civil-procedure/ and https://www.unidroit.org/work-in-progress/transnational-civil-procedure (both accessed 17 May 2020) for available public reports regarding the process of the project. *See also* J. Soarbji, 'The ELI-UNIDROIT Project: An Introduction and an English Perspective' in A. Nylund and M. Strandberg (eds), *Civil Procedure and Harmonisation of Law*, 36–46 (Intersentia 2019).
119. *See* E. Storskrubb, 'EU Civil Justice at the Harmonisation Crossroads', in A. Nylund and M. Strandberg (eds), *Civil Procedure and Harmonisation of Law*, 28–32 (Intersentia 2019).

ALI UNIDROIT Principles of Transnational Civil Procedure[120] of 2006 and from a multitude of comparative sources in a European context. The section on provisional and protective measures includes a general part with provisions that apply to all types of measures and a special part with separate rules for different types of interim relief. This chapter is not the place to present the rules. However, they will include specific conditions for different types of interim relief as well as an overall principle of proportionality. As an example of the specific conditions, an applicant for asset preservation must show: (i) a good chance of succeeding on the substantive merits, and (ii) that it is likely that, without such an order, enforcement of a final judgment against the respondent will be impossible or exceedingly difficult.[121]

### [D] Comparative Reflexions

There are a number of reflexions that arise from the brief and non-exhaustive presentations above on the approach under Swedish law and European law developments with respect to interim relief in comparison to what we have learnt about the arbitration practice in an EA context. Only a few will be touched upon here. First, what appears to be a difference is how the condition *periculum in mora*, danger in delay, is framed and applied in practice. As we have seen, the UNCITRAL framework of the Model Law and the Arbitration Rules frame this as, 'harm not adequately reparable by an award of damages' and many emergency arbitrators in both ICC and SCC EA practice have interpreted this condition in a strict or literal manner. However, commentators referred to above have argued that this is in most cases an impossible standard to meet in a commercial case, and that this was not the intention behind the condition as elaborated in the UNCITRAL framework. Rather it has been argued that serious and grave harm is a more appropriate standard rather than demanding that harm be literally irreparable.

In both the Swedish and the EU provisions mentioned above, the condition is worded in an arguably alternative manner and the focus of the application, the condition is also perhaps slightly different. In the Swedish context the condition is called risk of sabotage and the focus is on conduct that will hinder or render more difficult the exercise or realization of the applicant's right or substantially reduce the value of that right. Under the Regulation the condition is framed as 'a real risk that enforcement of the creditor's claim against the debtor will be impeded or made substantially more difficult'. Although the underlying purpose of the condition is the same, due to the way it is framed the focus appears different. It is easy to consider that the manner in which the applicant provides proof that the condition is fulfilled may be very different depending on that focus. The purpose here is not to argue that the

120. https://www.unidroit.org/instruments/transnational-civil-procedure (accessed 7 May 2020).
121. The author has participated in the project and been involved in two of its Working Groups and has access to the unpublished draft of the project, at the time of writing publication forthcoming in 2020.

international arbitration provisions or EA practice should entirely change its focus. However, the different way of framing the same condition may be instructive to further the understanding of the aim underlying the condition and be useful in the continued dialogue on EA practice.

The second reflection is that the possibility to require the applicant to provide security is so rarely used in the EA practice. According to the ICC EA Report security has been required only in two cases. However, commentators referred to above, suggest that emergency arbitrators could use ordering security more often as a tool to offset, for example, lack of evidence of full harm and to calibrate also the relative hardship faced by the parties when interim relief is ordered. In contrast, to post security is central requisite for an applicant for interim relief in Swedish courts, and also considered a central safeguard under the Regulation. A further observation is that the balance of equities (proportionality) condition has been applied in relatively few cases according to the ICC EA Report, albeit that can be considered to be reflected in the UNCITRAL rules that require that the 'harm substantially outweighs the harm that is likely to result to the party against whom the measure is directed if the measure is granted'. The reason for it not having been applied so often may be that it is in many cases applied as a final condition when all the other conditions have been met. However, it may be remembered that the Swedish Supreme Court has held that the proportionality principle can overlap the assessment of the other requirements as noted above. Similarly, in the ELI and UNIDROIT project the principle of proportionality is placed in the general part of the rules on provisional measures, as a general principle to be applied in all cases. The purpose here is not to argue that the EA practice has been lacking in this respect. However, it may be useful and instructive to highlight the potential of both the possibility of ordering security as a safeguard and the use of the balance of equities condition for emergency arbitrators to enable them to calibrate their actions in granting or dismissing EA applications.

## §8.04 FUTURE PERSPECTIVE FOR A MATURING AND EVOLVING PROCEDURE

The reports on EA practice by the arbitration institutes, such as the very insightful ICC EA Report that has been the inspiration and starting point for the chapter, demonstrate that it is a maturing and evolving procedure. There are certainly issues that still remain debated and may hamper its usefulness in certain cases such as lacking enforceability and ex parte procedures.[122] However, the reports also show that EA proceedings are being used and are providing needed redress for many parties in international arbitration. This chapter has attempted to examine more closely what EA practice tells us about the requisites for interim relief. In particular, to examine whether emergency arbitrators use international standards as guidance and whether a universal standard has emerged with respect to the scope of and conditions for interim relief. The results of the analysis above are that there is a broad consensus for using international

122. *See supra* note 6–7 and 36.

standard as guidance, but there is no universal application in the interpretation of that guidance. The variance in the EA practice shows that there is a need for further comparative understanding and dialogue on the requisites. This chapter is a contribution thereto.

CHAPTER 9

# The Right to a Public Hearing in Arbitration in Light of ECtHR Judgments

*Daria Kozlowska-Rautiainen*[*]

## §9.01 INTRODUCTION

On 2 October 2018, the European Court of Human Rights (ECtHR) issued a decision in *Mutu and Pechstein*[1] (hereinafter referred to as '*Pechstein*') in which it found, *inter alia*, that the German speed skater Claudia Pechstein had the right to a public hearing based on Article 6(1) of the European Convention on Human Rights (ECHR)[2] in relation to an arbitration before the Court of Arbitration for Sport (CAS).

The CAS arbitration was based on an arbitration agreement signed by Pechstein during her registration for the 2009 World Speed Skating Championships.[3] The rules of the CAS applicable at the time provided that a hearing is private unless both parties agree otherwise.[4] Yet, Pechstein explicitly requested for a public hearing. When the request was not fulfilled and the award rendered after a hearing held in camera,

* This chapter has been written within the framework of the Employment Arbitration Research Network. Particular thanks are due to Erik Sinander and other members and persons affiliated with the Research Network for their comments and support.

1. *Mutu and Pechstein v. Switzerland*, Nos 40575/10 and 67474/10 (ECtHR 2 Oct. 2018). Pechstein's application was joined with an application by a Romanian football player Adrian Mutu, who also complained about a violation of the Art. 6(1) ECHR by Switzerland, but with regard to the lack of independence and impartiality of the tribunal in his CAS arbitration.
2. Article 6(1) of the ECHR provides as follows: 'In the determination of his civil rights and obligations or of any criminal charge against him, everyone is entitled to a fair and public hearing within a reasonable time by an independent and impartial tribunal established by law. ...'.
3. *Pechstein v. DESG and ISU*, KRZ 6/15, 2 (BGH 7 Jun. 2016), English translation available on https://www.tas-cas.org/fileadmin/user_upload/Pechstein___ISU_translation_ENG_final.pdf (accessed 15 Jun. 2020).
4. Rule R57 CAS Code C. Special Provisions Applicable to the Appeal Arbitration Procedure, which has been changed after the decision of the ECtHR in *Pechstein*.

Pechstein applied to set aside the CAS award in the Swiss Federal Supreme Court. After an unsuccessful challenge of the CAS award, Pechstein then filed an application to the ECtHR against Switzerland on the basis of a violation of Article 6(1) ECHR.

According to the ECtHR case law, the right to a public hearing as enshrined in Article 6(1) ECHR is waived in a voluntary arbitration, but applies in a compulsory arbitration.[5] With regard to Pechstein, the ECtHR found that, even though the arbitration was not de jure compulsory, it was nonetheless 'compulsory' to her, because her only choice was either to enter into the arbitration agreement or to be unable to compete and earn a living.[6] Consequently, according to the ECtHR, Pechstein had not waived the right to a public hearing.[7]

What should an arbitral tribunal do when faced with a unilateral request for a public hearing? Is the privacy of arbitration threatened? Can the ruling regarding Pechstein be relevant beyond sports arbitration? Or can the arbitration community disregard the possible applicability of Article 6(1) ECHR to arbitrations not involving athletes?

In this chapter I argue that the reasoning presented by the ECtHR in *Pechstein* could in certain specific circumstances be applied also beyond sports arbitrations, e.g., to employment or consumer arbitration, or even to commercial arbitration. However, in my view, the effect of the decision should not be exaggerated.

What is important in this context is to acknowledge the need for sensitivity towards the potential application of Article 6(1) ECHR to arbitration even where the arbitration is not de jure compulsory. A party's request for a public hearing should not be disregarded without conducting an analysis or providing reasons which could exempt the otherwise possibly applicable right to a public hearing.

The aim of this chapter is to analyse the issue of applicability, relevance and fulfilment of the right to a public hearing in arbitration in order to dispel some of the uncertainty that can derive from the decision in *Pechstein*.

This chapter is addressed primarily to arbitrators, and secondarily to arbitration users, court judges and academics. It adds a new perspective regarding the specific issue of the right to a public hearing to the already existing discussion on the broader theme of human rights and arbitration.[8] The right to a public hearing in investment

5. *Mutu and Pechstein, supra* n. 1, at 95–96. *See also Bramelid and Malmström v. Sweden,* Nos 8588/79 and 8589/79, 30 (Report of the Commission 12 Dec. 1983) where the ECtHR provided 'normally Article 6 poses no problem where arbitration is entered into voluntarily', and *Tabbane v. Switzerland (dec.),* No. 41069/12, 29 (ECtHR 1 Mar. 2016), where the ECtHR provided that the applicant freely waived the protections enshrined in Art. 6(1) ECHR as he entered into the arbitration agreement freely. If an arbitration is compulsory, the protections are not effectively waived. *See Suda v. Czech Republic,* No. 1643/06 (ECtHR 28 Oct. 2010).
6. In French – the original language of the decision, the word used is *forcé. Mutu and Pechstein, supra* n. 1, at 115.
7. *Mutu and Pechstein, supra* n. 1, at 147.
8. *See,* e.g., M.V. Benedettelli, *The European Convention on Human Rights and Arbitration: The EU Law Perspective,* 463–518, in Ferrari (ed.) The Impact of EU Law on International Commercial Arbitration (Juris Publishing 2017); S. Besson, *Arbitration and Human Rights,* ASA Bulletin, Vol. 24, Issue 3, 395–416 (September 2006); R. Briner and F. von Schlabrendorff, *Article 6 of the European Convention on Human Rights and Its Bearing upon International Arbitration,* 89–109, in R. Briner, L.Y. Fortier, K.P. Berger & J. Bredow (eds) Law of international business and dispute

arbitration is not discussed in this chapter and neither is the issue of the validity of arbitration agreements.

After providing background information regarding *Pechstein* and other relevant recent developments (*see* §9.02), I consider three main questions:

(1) *When is the right to a public hearing enshrined in Article 6(1) ECHR applicable in arbitration and when is it waived based on the jurisprudence of the ECtHR?* (*see* §9.03)

First, the general exceptions to the applicability of Article 6(1) ECHR are considered. Then, the focus shifts to an analysis of the conditions for the waiver of the right to the public hearing: the waiver being free, unequivocal and lawful, the waiver being accompanied by appropriate guarantees, and the tribunal being established by law. If any of the above conditions are not fulfilled, the rights deriving from Article 6(1) ECHR apply.[9]

(2) *What is the relevance of the ruling of the ECtHR in Pechstein for arbitration?* (*see* §9.04)

In this section, I first show that a de facto compulsory arbitration could be found beyond the very specific circumstances of *Pechstein* and that the impact goes beyond sports arbitration. I then explain why arbitrators should take into account rulings of the ECtHR. Finally, I consider the importance of privacy in arbitration in order to help examine the risk of organizing a public hearing in arbitration.

(3) *How does one go about fulfilling the right to a public hearing in arbitration?* (*see* §9.05)

As the final question I consider the practical challenges an arbitrator could face when organizing a public hearing in an arbitration.

## §9.02 THE PECHSTEIN SAGA AND RECENT DEVELOPMENTS

Before commencing the analysis, it is pertinent to provide some background information about *Pechstein* as well as to mention some other relevant recent developments.

*Pechstein* is more appropriately referred to as the Pechstein saga, as cases were brought to courts not only in Switzerland but also in Germany. The divergent decisions of the national courts and the ECtHR emphasize the controversy surrounding the question that is at the centre of this chapter.

---

settlement in the 21st century, Liber Amicorum Karl-Heinz Böckstiegel (Carl Heymanns Verlag 2001); A. Jaksic, *Arbitration and Human Rights* (Peter Lang 2002); J.C. Landrove, *European Convention on Human Rights' Impact on Consensual Arbitration An état des lieux of Strasbourg Case-Law and of a Problematic Swiss Law Feature*, 73–101, in Besson, Hottelier and Werro (eds) Human Rights at the Center (Schulthess 2006).

9. The aim is not to provide an exhaustive analysis of the above issues as this would be impossible to achieve in a short article. Instead, the objective is to shed light on this topic, to provide guidance regarding possible interpretation of future borderline cases, and to provoke discussion.

### [A] The Pechstein Saga

Claudia Pechstein – a German five-time Olympic gold medalist in speed skating – entered into an arbitration agreement with the International Skating Union (ISU) when signing a registration form for the World Speed Skating Championships that took place in 2009 in Norway.[10]

Following the anti-doping blood tests performed during the 2009 Championships, the ISU filed a complaint to its Disciplinary Commission against Pechstein.[11] The Disciplinary Commission imposed a two-year-long ban on Pechstein for illegal doping and took away the medal she won in the 2009 Championships.[12] Based on the arbitration agreement, Pechstein appealed the decision to the CAS. After holding a hearing in camera, despite Pechstein's request for a public hearing, the arbitral tribunal confirmed the ban.[13] Pechstein challenged the CAS award before the Swiss Federal Supreme Court, *inter alia*, on the ground that she was not afforded a public hearing. The challenge was dismissed.[14] With regard to Article 6(1) of the ECHR, the Swiss Federal Supreme Court found that the provision was invoked incorrectly because it is not applicable to voluntary arbitration.[15]

Pechstein also started proceedings before German courts against the ISU and the German Speedskating Union with which she was affiliated, i.e., Deutsche Eisschnelllauf-Gemeinschaft (DESG). After her claim was dismissed in the Regional Court in Munich, Pechstein appealed to the Higher Regional Court of Munich, which found that the arbitration agreement was invalid due to the abuse of market position by the ISU and that, because the arbitration agreement constituted a violation of anti-trust law, the recognition of the CAS award constituted a violation of public policy.[16] However, the German Federal Court of Justice, after balancing the rights and interests of the parties,[17] disagreed with the finding of Higher Regional Court of Munich that the ISU abused its dominant position. Moreover, the German Federal Court of Justice did not find a violation of Article 6(1) of the ECHR and stated that Pechstein was party to voluntary arbitration.[18]

---

10. *Pechstein v. DESG and ISU*, BGH 7 Jun. 2016, *supra* n. 3, at 2. For an in-depth comment on this case *see* B. Ehle and I. Guaia, *Bundesgerichtshof, Az. KZR 6/15, Pechstein v. International Skating Union (ISU), 7 June 2016*, 415–427, in Duval and Rigozzi (eds) Yearbook of International Sports Arbitration 2016 (Springer 2016).
11. *Mutu and Pechstein*, *supra* n. 1, at 19.
12. *Pechstein v. DESG and ISU*, BGH 7 Jun. 2016, *supra* n. 3, at 3.
13. *Mutu and Pechstein*, *supra* n. 1, at 20–21.
14. *Pechstein v. ISU and DESG*, 4A_612/2009 (TF 10 Feb. 2010). Subsequent motion for revision has also been rejected. *See* 4A_144/2010 (TF 28 Sep. 2010).
15. *Ibid.*, at 4.1.
16. *Pechstein v. DESG and ISU*, U 1110/14 (OLG Munich 15 Jan. 2015) and *Pechstein v. DESG and ISU*, BGH 7 Jun. 2016, *supra* n. 3, at 10.
17. *See*, e.g., *Pechstein v. DESG and ISU*, BGH 7 Jun. 2016, *supra* n. 3, at 57–61.
18. The BGH stated as follows: '… the jurisdiction of ordinary courts may be excluded in arbitration agreements if the arbitration agreement has been entered into voluntarily, is lawful and clearly worded, if further the arbitration procedure has been designed in accordance with the guarantees given in Art. 6 ECHR and if the arbitral awards can be set aside by a court of law in case of procedural errors … these requirements have been fulfilled. According to the case law of the European Court of Human Rights, the fact that the Plaintiff is obliged, to be able to exercise her

On 11 November 2010 Pechstein filed an application to the ECtHR against Switzerland.[19] Her application was joined with an application by a Romanian football player Adrian Mutu,[20] who had also complained against a violation of Article 6(1) ECHR by Switzerland, but with regard to a CAS tribunal lacking independence and impartiality.

With regard to Pechstein, the ECtHR found that based on the circumstances of the case Pechstein was a party to compulsory arbitration and, hence, that she had not waived the protections provided in Article 6(1) of the Convention.[21] The ECtHR, therefore, reached a different conclusion to those of the Swiss Federal Supreme Court and the German Federal Court of Justice. This finding underlines the controversy regarding the question of whether a party to an arbitration that is not de jure mandatory can have a right to a public hearing on the basis of Article 6(1) ECHR.

### [B] Recent Developments That Followed the Decision in *Pechstein*

In the recent judgment in the case of *Ali Riza and others v. Turkey* from 28 January 2020, the ECtHR was faced with similar questions to those in *Pechstein*. The ECtHR reiterated the principles spelled out in *Pechstein*, including *inter alia* that, where an arbitration is compulsory, the safeguards of Article 6.1 have to be provided.[22]

Following the decision in *Pechstein*, CAS has amended Rule 57 of its Code which provided that a hearing is held in private unless both parties agree otherwise. The rule was supplemented with the following text:

> At the request of a physical person who is party to the proceedings, a public hearing should be held if the matter is of a disciplinary nature. Such request may however be denied in the interest of morals, public order, national security, where the interests of minors or the protection of the private life of the parties so require, where publicity would prejudice the interests of justice, where the proceedings are exclusively related to questions of law or where a hearing held in first instance was already public.[23]

Finally, on 15 November 2019, a public hearing was held for the second time in the history of CAS in the case of a Chinese swimmer Sun Yang.[24] The practical solutions

profession, to sign the registration form imposed by the Second Defendant does not mean that the arbitration agreement has not been voluntarily signed and therefore infringes the Convention ...' *Ibid.*, at 65.

19. *Mutu and Pechstein*, *supra* n. 1, at 1.
20. *Ibid.*, at 8.
21. *Ibid.*, at 115.
22. *Ali Riza and others v. Turkey*, Nos 30226/10, 17880/11, 17887/11, 17891/11 and 5506/16, 175–177, 181 (ECtHR 28 Jan. 2020).
23. *See* CAS Code C. Special Provisions Applicable to the Appeal Arbitration Procedure, R57 https://www.tas-cas.org/en/arbitration/code-procedural-rules.html (accessed 15 Jun. 2020).
24. The first one being a hearing in a case of an Irish swimmer Michelle Smith de Bruin in 1999. *See* the information provided by the CAS itself in the release regarding Yang's hearing https://www.tas-cas.org/fileadmin/user_upload/CAS_Media_Release_6148_Hearing_15.11.19.pdf (accessed 15 Jun. 2020). Although, in this case both parties agreed to have a public hearing, it is my contention that Pechstein's quest for a public hearing in the CAS arbitration in one way or another paved the way to the public hearing in Sun Yang's arbitration.

regarding the organization of a public hearing are relevant for the third question considered in this chapter, i.e., how to fulfil the right to a public hearing in arbitration.

## §9.03 LIMITATIONS AND CONDITIONS FOR WAIVER OF THE RIGHT TO A PUBLIC HEARING ENSHRINED IN ARTICLE 6(1) ECHR

This section sheds light on the question of when the ECtHR could consider if a party has a right to a public hearing. The discussion commences with Article 6(1) ECHR and its limitations and then the attention turns to the conditions under which the right to a public hearing can be waived in arbitration.[25] As part of the latter analysis, I first consider the question of when a waiver is made freely. I then discuss the issue of an unequivocal and lawful waiver. I conclude by considering what guarantees might have to be given for the waiver to be effective and when a tribunal is considered to be established by law.

### [A] Article 6(1) ECHR and Its Limitations

Article 6(1) of the ECHR, which contains the right to a public hearing, has been described as an 'omnibus provision'[26] and 'a pithy epitome of what constitutes a fair administration of justice'.[27] According to paragraph 1 of Article 6:

> In the determination of his civil rights and obligations or of any criminal charge against him, everyone is entitled to a fair and *public hearing* within a reasonable time by an independent and impartial tribunal established by law. ... (author's emphasis)

From the perspective of the ECHR, a public hearing provides an element of public scrutiny intended to protect a party from administration of justice taking place behind closed doors. As such, a public hearing is an important element of the right to a fair trial, which is enshrined in Article 6(1). This in turn helps to achieve the goal of Article 6(1), which is a fair hearing.[28]

---

25. In Pechstein's case it was lack of free waiver, but there could be also other conditions of waiver which when unfulfilled that could result in Art. 6(1) being applicable to arbitration.
26. B. Rainey, E. Wicks and C. Ovey, *The European Convention on Human Rights*, 274 (Oxford University Press 2017).
27. N. Mole and C. Harby, *The Right to a Fair Trial: A Guide to the Implementation of Article 6 of the European Convention on Human Rights, Human Rights Handbooks, No. 3* (Council of Europe Publishing, 2006).
28. *See*, e.g., *Pretto and others v. Italy*, No. 7984/77 (ECtHR 8 Dec. 1983); *Malhous v. the Czech Republic*, No. 33071/96, 55-56 (ECtHR 12 Jul. 2001); *B and P v. UK*, Nos 36337/97 and 35974/97, 36 (ECtHR 24 Apr. 2001); *Ramos Nunes De Carvalho e Sá v. Portugal*, No. 55391/13 (ECtHR 21 Jun. 2016). *See also* Guide to Art. 6 of the Convention, 72 (CoE, ECHR 2019) https://www.echr.coe.int/Documents/Guide_Art_6_ENG.pdf (accessed 15 Jun. 2020); K. Reid, *A Practitioner's Guide to the European Convention on Human Rights*, 226 (Sweet and Maxwell 2012); Rainey et al., *supra* n. 26, at 300.

However, the right to a public hearing is not absolute. Article 6(1) enumerates the following limitations of the right:

> the press and public may be excluded from all or part of the trial in the interests of morals, public order or national security in a democratic society, where the interests of juveniles or the protection of the private life of the parties so require, or to the extent strictly necessary in the opinion of the court in special circumstances where publicity would prejudice the interests of justice.

Moreover, the ECtHR has found in some cases that holding no hearing at all is permissible. A case can be decided on documentary evidence and written submissions where, e.g., (i) no facts are contested,[29] (ii) the dispute is not complex,[30] (iii) the dispute is of a technical nature,[31] or (iv) the dispute concerns an unambiguous question of law.[32]

According to the case law of the ECtHR, the parties waive some protections of Article 6(1) ECHR when they enter into an arbitration agreement,[33] but the waiver has to be given in a *free, lawful and unequivocal* manner.[34] Moreover, with regard to some rights, 'minimum guarantees commensurate to its importance' have to be provided for the waiver to be effective.[35] The waiver of the right to a public hearing in arbitration is considered uncontroversial.[36] This part of the rights protected in Article 6(1) ECHR can be considered to conflict with the privacy of arbitral proceedings.[37] As noted in *Nordström-Janzon and Nordström-Lehtinen v. Netherlands*:

> In some respects – in particular as regards publicity – it is clear that arbitral proceedings are often not even intended to be in conformity with Article 6. ...[38]

The sections below provide an analysis of the conditions that are required for the waiver of Article 6(1) rights in arbitration, and in particular for the waiver of the right to a public hearing.

29. *See*, e.g., *Döry v. Sweden*, No. 28394/95, 37 (ECtHR 12 Nov. 2002); *Saccoccia v. Austria*, No. 69917/01, 73 (ECtHR 5 Jul. 2007) and *Speil v. Austria*, No. 42057/98, 29 (ECtHR 5 Sep. 2002).
30. *See*, e.g., *Speil*, *supra* n. 29, at 29.
31. *See*, e.g., *Döry*, *supra* n. 29, at 41–43.
32. *See*, e.g., *Allan Jacobsson v. Sweden* (No. 2), No. 16970/90, 49 (ECtHR 19 Feb. 1998).
33. *Albert and Le Compte v. Belgium*, Nos 7288/75 and 7496/76 (ECtHR 10 Feb. 1983). Some protections like the right to submit claims to an adjudicator, be it an arbitral tribunal or a national court cannot be waived. *See*, e.g., Landrove, *supra* n. 8, at 78–79. For more on the topic *see also* Benedettelli, *supra* n. 8, at 508–510.
34. *Mutu and Pechstein*, *supra* n. 1, at 96, relying on cases of *Eiffage S.A. and Others v. Switzerland*, No. 1742/05 (ECtHR 15 Sep. 2009); *Suda*, *supra* n. 5; *R. v. Switzerland*, No. 10881/84 (Commission decision of 4 Mar. 1987), *Suovaniemi and others v. Finland*, No. 31737/96 (ECtHR 23 Feb. 1999) and *Tabbane*, *supra* n. 5, at 25–27.
35. *Mutu and Pechstein*, *supra* n. 1, where para. 96 is essentially a copy of para. 27 from the decision in *Tabbane*, *supra* n. 5.
36. *See*, e.g., Briner and von Schlabrendorff, *supra* n. 8, at 98 and Benedettelli, *supra* n. 8, at 509.
37. More on the importance of privacy in arbitration under §9.04[C].
38. *Nordström-Janzon and Nordström-Lehtinen v. Netherlands*, No. 28101/95 (ECtHR 27 Nov. 1996).

### [B] Free Waiver

A waiver is considered to be made freely when a party voluntarily enters into an arbitration agreement.[39] As the ECtHR reasoned in *Tabbane v. Switzerland*, the applicant freely waived the protections enshrined in Article 6(1) of the Convention as he entered freely into the arbitration agreement, not acting under duress:

> On the contrary, by exercising his contractual freedom, he signed an arbitration agreement with the Colgate company containing an arbitration clause to resolve disputes that could arise between them ... In concluding this arbitration agreement, the claimant expressly and freely renounced the possibility of submitting disputes potentially arising in the future to an ordinary court, which would have offered all the guarantees of Article 6 of the Convention. There is no indication that the applicant acted under duress in signing the arbitration agreement.[40]

According to the above, it could be concluded that a waiver is given freely when a party enters into an arbitration agreement based on contractual freedom and not under duress.

In *Pechstein*, the ECtHR expressly drew a distinction between voluntary arbitration and compulsory arbitration. When the arbitration is voluntary, the waiver is considered to be given freely. The ECtHR found this to be the case with regard to the first applicant - Mutu. On the subject of arbitration that is compulsory by law, however, the ECtHR stated that:

> [i]f arbitration is compulsory, in the sense of being required by law, the parties have no option but to refer their dispute to an arbitral tribunal, which must afford the safeguards secured by Article 6 § 1 of the Convention.[41]

The ECtHR then argued that arbitration can also be deemed to be compulsory, even though it is not compulsory under the law, if the circumstances of the case nevertheless oblige a party to arbitrate:

> even though it had not been imposed by law but by the ISU [International Skating Union] regulations, the acceptance of CAS [Court of Arbitration for Sport] jurisdiction by the second applicant [Pechstein] must be regarded as 'compulsory' arbitration within the meaning of its case-law (contrast Tabbane ...). The arbitration proceedings therefore had to afford the safeguards secured by Article 6 § 1 of the Convention.[42]

To differentiate this arbitration from arbitration mandated by law, I refer to this type of arbitration, as de facto *compulsory arbitration*.[43]

The distinction between de jure compulsory arbitration and de facto compulsory arbitration is useful because, while it is not difficult to determine when an arbitration

39. *See*, e.g., *Tabbane*, *supra* n. 5, at 29. *See also Bramelid and Malmström*, *supra* n. 5, at 30.
40. *Tabbane*, *supra* n. 5, at 29 (own translation from French).
41. *Mutu and Pechstein*, *supra* n. 1, at 95.
42. *Ibid.*, at 115.
43. For instance, Besson used the term *forced*, probably borrowed from the French *forcé* to make the distinction. *See* Besson, *supra* n. 8, at 398–399. However, in the Mutu and Pechstein decision, the ECtHR used the term *forcé* to refer to both de jure and de facto compulsory arbitration. *See*

is de jure compulsory (i.e., compulsory by law), determining when an arbitration is de facto compulsory (i.e., compulsory in fact) is not as easy. For example, as stated above, the Swiss Federal Supreme Court and the German Federal Court of Justice came to a different conclusion than the ECtHR on this very issue in the circumstances that applied to Pechstein.

A distinction also needs to be made between arbitration agreements that are entered into under duress and de facto compulsory arbitration. The common factor between arbitration agreements entered into under duress and de facto compulsory arbitration is that the party in question has no choice but to enter into the arbitration agreement. However, the difference is that in the case of duress there is an unlawful threat[44] and the arbitration agreement would be unenforceable.[45] In de facto compulsory arbitration, however, the party is not unlawfully threatened.

I will proceed to discuss the reasoning of the ECtHR in *Pechstein*, in which Mutu was found to be party to voluntary arbitration whereas Pechstein was found to be party to compulsory arbitration.

### *[1] Cases of Mutu and Pechstein*

*Pechstein* (formally referred to as the *Mutu and Pechstein* case) comprised of two applications regarding the violation of Article 6(1) ECHR by Switzerland - that of Romanian football player Adrian Mutu and that of German speed skater Claudia Pechstein. The first applicant in the case - the Romanian football player Adrian Mutu - complained about the violation of Article 6(1) ECHR by Switzerland on the basis that the Swiss Federal Supreme Court did not annul the CAS award against him on grounds of a lack of independence and impartiality of the tribunal.[46] Mutu did not complain about the lack of a public hearing, but his case is relevant because he argued that the CAS arbitration was compulsory for him and hence that the protections from Article 6(1) ECHR - in his case to an independent and impartial tribunal - applied.

The ECtHR found that Mutu entered into the arbitration agreement voluntarily and that he had waived the rights deriving from Article 6(1) ECHR freely. The main reason for this conclusion was that, based on the applicable regulations for football players at the time, Mutu had the option of going to court in case of a dispute with his football club, and hence he was not obliged to go to arbitration. According to Article 42 of the 5 July 2001 FIFA (fr: Fédération Internationale de Football Association, en: International Federation of Association Football) Regulations for the Status and Transfer of Players (2001 FIFA Regulations) the arbitration was to be established

*Mutu and Pechstein*, *supra* n. 1, at 95 and 115 (original, French language version). Therefore, I have decided to follow the term de facto compulsory used previously by, e.g., Benedettelli. *See* Benedettelli, *supra* n. 8, at 507.

44. G. Born, *International Commercial Arbitration*, 812 (2nd ed., Kluwer Law International 2014).
45. *Ibid. See*, e.g., Art. II(3) of the New York Convention on the Recognition and Enforcement of Foreign Arbitral Awards 1958.
46. Mutu's case is further discussed under §9.03[C].

'[w]ithout prejudice to the right of any player or club to seek redress before a civil court in disputes between clubs and players ...'.[47]

The above would have sufficed to establish that Mutu freely waived rights enshrined under Article 6(1), but the ECtHR also considered the circumstances of the case more generally. It started by stating that a player, even a famous one, is a weaker party in negotiations with a football club. However, the ECtHR went on to note that Mutu did not show that all players in his club were forced to enter into an arbitration agreement, nor did he show that he tried finding employment with a different club or that a different club refused to hire him because he did not want to be bound by an arbitration agreement. Neither did Mutu show that he was not able to rely on the above-mentioned Article 42 and bring the case to court.

The ECtHR concluded that Mutu was not party to compulsory arbitration, because he did not show that:

> he was faced with a binary choice between accepting the arbitration clause and earning his living by practising his sport at professional level, on the one hand, or not accepting it and completely abandoning the idea of competing at that level, on the other. The Court thus finds no reason to suggest that 'compulsory' arbitration is at issue in the first applicant's [Mutu's] case.[48]

How, then, was the situation of Pechstein different? The main difference was that there were no regulations in place which would have provided her with the option to go to a national court. But why was the arbitration in her case compulsory? In assessing whether Pechstein's waiver was free, the ECtHR took into account the decision of the Swiss Federal Supreme Court which admitted that where a sports federation provides for arbitration in its regulations, the athletes have the choice either to agree to arbitration or to practice sports at a non-professional level.[49] The ECtHR also noted that the ISU has been suspected by the European Commission of holding a dominant position. [50] In order to take part in the competitions organized by the ISU, athletes were obliged to accept the applicable ISU rules that provided for CAS arbitration in case of a dispute.

The ECtHR differentiated Pechstein's case from those where a party would have a choice between entering into an agreement with one party or another.[51] It concluded that:

> the only choice in the second applicant's case was between accepting the arbitration clause and thus earning her living by practising her sport professionally, or not accepting it and being obliged to refrain completely from earning a living from her sport at that level.

47. *See* the 2001 FIFA Regulations under https://resources.fifa.com/image/upload/fifa-rstp-2001.pdf?cloudid=maqzja40s2b90xdxik0k (accessed 15 Jun. 2020).
48. *Mutu and Pechstein*, *supra* n. 1, at 120.
49. *Ibid.*, at 111.
50. *Ibid.*, at 112. Interestingly, the German Federal Court of Justice admitted that ISU had a dominant position, but found that it did not abuse its position with regard to Pechstein's case. *See Pechstein v. DESG and ISU*, BGH 7 Jun. 2016, *supra* n. 3.
51. As was the case in *Tabbane*, *supra* n. 5, *Eiffage*, *supra* n. 34.

> Having regard to the restriction that non-acceptance of the arbitration clause would have entailed for her professional life, it cannot be asserted that she had accepted that clause freely and unequivocally.[52]

In its decision, the ECtHR therefore found that Article 6(1) applied, i.e., Pechstein had the right to a public hearing because the arbitration was de facto compulsory and none of the exceptions to the right was met.[53]

In its subsequent decision in *Ali Riza and others v. Turkey*, the ECtHR reiterated the principles spelled out in *Pechstein*, including *inter alia* that where an arbitration is deemed to be compulsory, the safeguards from Article 6(1) ECHR have to be provided.[54]

### [C] Unequivocal Waiver

The mere existence of an arbitration agreement that has been freely entered into does not suffice in order to ensure that the waiver is unequivocal (i.e., unambiguous). The ruling in *Suovaniemi and others v. Finland* sheds light on what is meant by an unequivocal waiver.

In *Suovaniemi* the ECtHR found that the waiver was unequivocal, because the applicants 'had not sought the withdrawal, during the arbitral proceedings, of the arbitrator whose independence and impartiality they were challenging'.[55] In the arbitration, Suovaniemi and others first raised an issue of potential partiality of the arbitrator that they appointed, but after the arbitrator assured them that he had no tasks that would compromise his impartiality and offered to resign, the party explicitly approved the arbitrator. When later in the proceedings a letter was allegedly found that could call into question the impartiality of the arbitrator, Suovaniemi and others did not raise this issue. Instead, they only brought up the concerns about the independence and impartiality of the arbitrator after they lost the arbitration proceedings and moved to challenge the award in a Finnish court.

Similarly, in *Pechstein*, the ECtHR found that Mutu's waiver was given freely, but that Mutu did not unequivocally waive his right to challenge the independence and impartiality of the arbitrators.[56] The circumstances of the case can be summarized as

52. *Mutu and Pechstein*, *supra* n. 1, at 113–114.
53. *Ibid.*, at 181–182.
54. In this case, Ali Riza and Serkan Akal, complained that the members of the Arbitration Committee lacked independence and impartiality and additionally Akal's application concerned three other alleged violations of Art. 6(1), one of which was lack of a hearing. The arbitration proceedings before the Arbitration Committee were compulsory. And this issue was not contested. It would have been very interesting to read the decision regarding this complaint, but the ECtHR found that the members of the Arbitration Committee lacked the required independence and impartiality and hence, the other complaints do not need to be examined. *See Ali Riza*, *supra* n. 22, at 175–177, 226. *Ali Riza v. Switzerland* No. 74989/11 regarding a breach of Art. 6(1) is pending before the ECtHR.
55. *Suovaniemi*, *supra* n. 34.
56. However, *see* the Dissenting Opinion putting into question the possibility of the waiver not being unequivocal, but being free. The dissenting judges argued that: '[i]t is difficult to conceive, however, that an individual could waive his right to an independent and impartial tribunal and yet still have benefit of a "fair hearing" within the meaning of Article 6§1 of the Convention'.

follows. Mutu tested positive for cocaine which led to his employer - Chelsea FC - terminating his employment. On 20 April 2005 a Football Association Premier League Appeals Committee (FAPLAC) decided that Mutu unilaterally breached his employment contract within the meaning of the 2001 FIFA Regulations.[57] Mutu appealed against this decision to the CAS and a tribunal presided by Dirk-Reiner Martens upheld the decision of the FAPLAC.

Thereafter, the FIFA Dispute Resolution Chamber (DRC) ordered Mutu to pay compensation to Chelsea based on the breach established by the FAPLAC, and upheld by the CAS tribunal. Mutu then appealed this decision to the CAS. In the further CAS arbitration Chelsea appointed Dirk-Reiner Martens as a party-appointed arbitrator. Mutu unsuccessfully challenged this appointment. Mutu's appeal from the DRC decision was dismissed by the CAS tribunal consisting of, the arbitrator appointed by Mutu, the challenged arbitrator appointed by Chelsea and the presiding arbitrator Luigi Fumagalli. Mutu then challenged the award in the Swiss Federal Supreme Court on the basis of lack of independence and impartiality of Martens as well as the presiding arbitrator whose law firm Mutu suspected to have represented Chelsea FC's owner. On 10 June 2010 the Swiss Federal Supreme Court rejected the challenge.[58]

The difference between the case of Suovaniemi and that of Mutu was that Mutu brought a challenge against the arbitrator during the arbitral proceedings. As a result, despite the waiver being established freely, it was not found to be unequivocal in Mutu's case.[59] Consequently, the safeguards provided under Article 6(1) ECHR should have been provided.

With regard to Pechstein, the Court found that '[h]aving regard to the restriction that non-acceptance of the arbitration clause would have entailed for her professional life, it cannot be asserted that she had accepted that clause freely and unequivocally'.[60] It seems that the compulsory character of the arbitration was seen by the Court as resulting in the waiver being neither free nor unequivocal. It should be noted that Pechstein explicitly requested a public hearing in front of the CAS tribunal and was not afforded one.[61]

What, then, would the ECtHR have decided if Pechstein had had an option to go to a court but freely chose to go to arbitration? Let us consider a situation where the remainder of the facts of the case are same, i.e., Pechstein requested a public hearing and was not afforded it, and the Swiss Federal Supreme Court dismissed her appeal. The decisions regarding Mutu and Suovaniemi and others concern impartiality and independence of the arbitrators. Is there a difference between the right to an independent and impartial tribunal and the right to a public hearing? Could the ECtHR consider that a party who has voluntarily entered into an arbitration agreement, i.e., waived the right freely, still has the right to a public hearing?

Joint Partly Dissenting, Partly Concurring Opinion of Judges Kelle and Serhides in *Mutu and Pechstein, supra* n. 1, at 26 and 27.

57. Articles 21–23 of the 5 Jul. 2001 FIFA Regulations for the Status and Transfer of Players.
58. *Mutu v. Chelsea FC Ltd.* 4A_458/2009 (TF 10 Jun. 2010).
59. *Mutu and Pechstein, supra* n. 1, at 15 and 122.
60. *Ibid.*, at 114.
61. *Ibid.*, at 181.

I believe that the decision of the Court in *Suovaniemi and others v. Finland* can be the key to this question. The Court stressed that there is a difference between the various rights protected by Article 6(1) of the ECHR and held that the right to a public hearing was less crucial than the right to an impartial and independent tribunal. The Court also emphasized the private character of arbitration as being one of the main features legitimizing arbitration. It stated the following:

> Waiver may be permissible with regard to certain rights but not with regard to certain others. A distinction may have to be made even between different rights guaranteed by Article 6. Thus, in the light of the case-law it is clear that the right to a public hearing can be validly waived even in court proceedings ... The same applies, a fortiori, to arbitration proceedings, one of the very purposes of which is often to avoid publicity. On the other hand, the question whether the fundamental right to an impartial judge can be waived at all, was left open in the *Pfeifer and Plankl v. Austria* case, as in any case in the circumstances of that case there was no unequivocal waiver.[62]

The Dissenting Opinion in *Pechstein* is also revealing with regard to the views of the judges concerning the hierarchy of the rights protected by Article 6(1) of the Convention. Judges Keller and Serghides argued that:

> it is conceivable that a procedure could be fair even in the absence of a public hearing or even where the parties did not have access to all the documents. It is difficult to conceive, however, that an individual could waive his right to an independent and impartial tribunal and yet still have the benefit of a 'fair hearing' within the meaning of Article 6 § 1 of the Convention.[63]

It is my contention that, in the above hypothetical scenario, if the ECtHR found that Pechstein waived her rights freely, the waiver of the right to a public hearing would also be considered unequivocal.

### [D] Lawful Waiver

The waiver should also be lawful.[64] The ECtHR does not provide extensive guidance regarding this condition for waiver. In the context of arbitration, it could be argued that an arbitration agreement that would not be enforceable in the first place should not be considered as resulting in a lawful waiver. For instance, arbitration agreements entered into under duress,[65] by fraud, by a party who does not have legal capacity, or with regard to matters that are non-arbitrable should not be considered as lawfully waiving protections under the ECHR.

62. *Suovaniemi, supra* n. 34.
63. Joint Partly Dissenting, Partly Concurring Opinion of Judges Keller and Serghides in *Mutu and Pechstein, supra* n. 1, at 27.
64. *Mutu and Pechstein, supra* n. 1, at 96.
65. *See*, e.g., *Tabbane, supra* n. 5, at 29.

According to Article 35(1) ECHR, matters with regard to which the national remedies have not been exhausted are inadmissible.[66] Considering that a party can apply to the ECtHR only after the national remedies have been exhausted, cases where the waiver was unlawful should - in principle - not even be decided by the ECtHR. A national court should already have found, e.g., an arbitration agreement entered into under duress or by a party without legal capacity to be invalid, and a national court should already have set aside the arbitral award based on such an agreement.

#### *[1] Lawful Waiver Should Not Be Confused with the Requirement of a Waiver to Be Permissible*

In the older decisions, the ECtHR referred to the requirement that the waiver must be deemed to be permissible. In the recent decisions, the ECtHR refers to the criterion of lawfulness. It can be questioned whether permissibility and lawfulness are used by the ECtHR as synonyms.

In *Plankl v. Austria* the Court stated that the waiver has to be first, *permissible* and second, given in an unequivocal manner. As provided above, in the *Suovaniemi and others v. Finland* judgment, the Court provided that the '[w]aiver may be permissible with regard to certain rights but not with regard to certain others'.[67] The Court decided in this case that the applicant's waiver of the right to an impartial tribunal was considered to be unequivocal and it could be validly made in so far as domestic law afforded sufficient protection, i.e., the waiver was considered permissible. The requirement for the waiver to be *permissible* seems to have been understood in a different way than the requirement of a lawful waiver.

### [E] Appropriate Guarantees

The Court has indicated in its case law that it is not enough that the waiver is given freely, unequivocally and lawfully, but that certain rights require *guarantees that are commensurate to the importance of that waiver*.[68] A court will assess which rights require guarantees and what guarantees are appropriate with regard to the individual circumstances of each case. Hence, it is difficult to provide a general answer to those questions.

In the *Pfeifer and Plankl v. Austria* decision from 1992, the Court stated that the rights that require guarantees for the waiver to be effective are the procedural rights.[69] In *Tabbane v. Switzerland*, the Court provided that the guarantees commensurate to the waiver of the right to appeal an arbitral award were that Tabbane was able to select an arbitrator, that the procedure was governed by Swiss law, that the Federal Court

66. *See also* Practical Guide on Admissibility Criteria, 22 (CoE, ECHR 2019) https://www.echr.coe.int/Documents/Admissibility_guide_ENG.pdf (accessed 25 Mar. 2020).
67. *Ibid.*
68. *See Tabbane, supra* n. 5, *Pfeifer and Plankl v. Austria*, No. 10802/84 (ECtHR 25 Feb. 1992), *Suovaniemi, supra* n. 34, *Mutu and Pechstein, supra* n. 1.
69. *See Pfeifer and Plankl, supra* n. 68, at 37.

heard Tabbane's arguments and took into account relevant facts and provisions, and that the decision was reasoned and did not appear arbitrary.[70]

In *Suovaniemi and others v. Finland*, the Court considered the guarantees commensurate to the importance of the waiver and emphasized that the 'relevant Finnish legislation does not appear arbitrary or unreasonable ..., the applicants were represented by counsel'.[71]

The above cases refer to the decision being reasoned, the legislation not being arbitrary or unreasonable, and the party being represented by counsel.

The following view of the ECtHR expressed *inter alia* in *Pechstein* is also of importance: '[a]rbitration clauses, which have undeniable advantages for the individual concerned as well as for the administration of justice, do not in principle offend against the Convention'.[72]

Thus, from the point of view of the ECHR, voluntary arbitration is allowed in principle. Modern arbitration acts provide sufficient protections to the parties, including the right of a party to present its case, the right to an independent and impartial tribunal, the right to choose an arbitrator or have an arbitrator chosen for the party, and the right to challenge the award before a national court.

### [F] Tribunal Established by Law

One additional important requirement under Article 6(1) of the ECHR is that the tribunal must be established by law.[73] This does not mean that each arbitral tribunal must be established by legislation, but that it should be established 'in accordance with the will of the legislature'.[74]

In *Pechstein*, the ECtHR found that CAS had the appearance of a tribunal established by law.[75] The dissenting opinion in the case questions this view and points out that a deeper analysis should have been provided.[76]

### [G] Concluding Remarks

The above analysis of the limitations of the right to a public hearing and the conditions for the waiver of the right to a public hearing in arbitration shows that this issue does not only revolve around the question of whether an arbitration is compulsory or voluntary. It is a much more complex matter and it is important – especially for

70. Tabbane, *supra* n. 5. *See also* Information Note on the Court's case-law, No. 194, 22 Mar. 2016 https://www.echr.coe.int/Documents/CLIN_2016_03_194_ENG.pdf (accessed 15 Jun. 2020).
71. *Suovaniemi, supra* n. 34.
72. *Mutu and Pechstein, supra* n. 1, at 94 referring to *Tabbane, supra* n. 5, at 25.
73. *See*, e.g., *Mutu and Pechstein, supra* n. 1, at 138.
74. *Ibid.*, at 138.
75. *Ibid.*, at 149.
76. Joint Partly Dissenting, Partly Concurring Opinion of Judges Keller and Serghides in *Mutu and Pechstein, supra* n. 1, at 21–22. A more extensive discussion on this question has been since then conducted in *Ali Riza and Others v. Turkey. See Ali Riza, supra* n. 22, at 194–195 and 201–204.

arbitrators – to know all the conditions for waiver and the limitations to the rights protected by Article 6(1) ECHR.

## §9.04 POTENTIAL RELEVANCE OF *PECHSTEIN* BEYOND SPORTS ARBITRATION

In this section I aim to answer the question of the relevance and potential future impact of the decision of the ECtHR in *Pechstein* for arbitration, beyond the context of CAS and sports arbitration. To consider the potential relevance of *Pechstein* on arbitration I will focus on three questions: (1) in what circumstances can one be a party to a de facto compulsory arbitration? (2) why should the arbitration community care about the decisions of the ECtHR? and (3) how important is privacy in arbitration?

### [A] De Facto Compulsory Arbitration Beyond the Pechstein Example

The circumstances in which Pechstein entered into the arbitration agreement were quite special. With regard to Pechstein the ECtHR stated that she had a binary choice of either 'accepting the arbitration clause and thus earning her living by practising her sport professionally, or not accepting it and being obliged to refrain completely from earning a living from her sport at that level'.[77] The criterion here was not the level of earnings, but rather the right to practice her profession – which was competing on a professional level and not, e.g., working for ice skating shows or coaching.

The case has already had an impact on CAS arbitration, since Rule 57 of the CAS Code now provides that a public hearing should be held at a request of a party. The provision is not limited solely to compulsory arbitrations. However, it is very narrow in scope, referring only to physical parties and the disciplinary nature of the dispute and additionally limiting it by adding express exceptions, most of which are also provided in Article 6(1) of the ECHR.

In 2006 Besson argued as follows:

> Article 6 (1) is fully applicable to compulsory arbitration, that is to say arbitration imposed on the parties by law ... This principle is only apparently clear because the boundaries of compulsory arbitration may be uncertain in some cases. Typically, in sports-related disputes, arbitration is normally not imposed by law, but it is very often imposed on the athletes by their Federation or by the International Olympic Committee. It is not 'compulsory' but 'forced' arbitration. In his recent book, Antonio Rigozzi has submitted that arbitration remains valid and desirable to resolve sports-related disputes, but that the procedural guarantees, notably the independence and impartiality of the arbitral tribunal, should be subject to strict standards. I find that this approach is sensible and is to be approved.[78]

Is Pechstein's case only relevant to athletes? For what other parties could an arbitration be de facto compulsory? As one author has pointed out, an arbitration

77. *Mutu and Pechstein*, *supra* n. 1, at 113.
78. Besson, *supra* n. 8, at 398–399.

agreement could be considered to be de facto forced on a weaker party, such as an employee, consumer, or financial investor, but the same author subsequently challenges this view by arguing that modern arbitration legislation provides guarantees equivalent to those of the national courts and that arbitration with weaker parties only creates an issue when the stronger party abuses its power.[79]

Laws protect weaker parties: for instance, (a) by removing certain cases from the scope of arbitrable disputes; (b) by requiring that terms of contracts with consumers are individually negotiated, as required by Article 3(1) of the Directive on Unfair Terms in Consumer Contracts; and (c) in the Nordic context, by allowing an unreasonable term to be set aside, as provided in Article 36(1) of both the Swedish and Finnish Contract Acts. Finally, there are also protections against abuse of dominant position that could come into play. It is not the goal of this chapter to discuss the above protections in relation to the enforceability of the arbitration agreement, but they are nevertheless relevant to the question of whether a public hearing might be required. As part of the Council of Europe system the ECHR has forty-seven contracting states, including Russia. The reach of the ECHR goes far beyond the European Union and hence, the analysis of protections of weaker parties in all the contracting states does not fit into the scope of this chapter. Therefore, the below sections consider hypothetical scenarios where the enforceability of the arbitration agreement is not at issue, but the question is solely of whether a party has the right to a public hearing.

One group of persons that could potentially be in a situation comparable to Pechstein are highly specialized workers who can only be employed by a limited number of entities and where those entities all require that an arbitration agreement is included in the employment contract.[80] For example, if universities in the whole country required arbitration agreements, then for an academic who is focused on a specialized and national issue this could lead in the eyes of the ECtHR to a de facto compulsory arbitration for that individual. According to the argumentation of the ECtHR in *Pechstein*, the party should have no other choice for earning in its profession. It is quite a strict test, but not the strictest. The ECtHR did not consider Pechstein's possibility to earn a living outside of her profession. Therefore, an argument that a highly specialized employee could have changed careers should not be persuasive in determination of whether an arbitration is de facto compulsory.

Arbitration could be considered to be de facto compulsory for parties who entered into agreements for the sales of goods or services that are essential for them and are provided by limited entities who all require an arbitration clause in the contract. Those goods could be prosthetics, hearing aids and other goods or services influencing the quality of life.

79. *See* Benedettelli, *supra* n. 8, at 506–508. For more on the issue of arbitration with weaker parties *see*, e.g., Tilman Niedermaier, *Arbitration Agreements Between Parties of Unequal Bargaining Power: Balancing Exerciseson Either Side of the Atlantic*, 1 ZDAR, 12–21 (2014).

80. A presentation on the influence of the Pechstein case on Swedish employment arbitration titled: *Reasonable arbitration clauses in employment contracts – Does the Pechstein case have any impact for employment arbitration in Sweden?* was held by Erik Sinander within the framework of the Employment Arbitration Research Network at the Stockholm Centre for Commercial Law in Stockholm on 13 Nov. 2019 (unpublished).

A de facto compulsory arbitration could potentially also be found to exist between business parties. In *Pechstein* the ECtHR recalled *Eiffage*, where the party was not party to a compulsory arbitration, because it could have chosen another business partner. The ECtHR stated:

> it is difficult to believe that the company Eiffage, which is very active in the sector of civil engineering but also in that of private housing, would be obliged to accept arbitration clauses in order to exist as a construction company. For a company of that kind, a decision to renounce one or more public procurement contracts comprising an arbitration clause could have repercussions in terms of its turnover but probably not in terms of its capacity to thrive in the construction business.[81]

What if a company does not have a choice and can either enter into an arbitration agreement or be forced to cease its operations? This could be the case for a company whose business relies on having access to a rare type of goods that only one supplier delivers, or to facilities such as harbours, airports, or railways. If the entity that controls the rare goods or facilities requires an arbitration agreement in its contracts, then this could potentially be considered as a de facto compulsory arbitration for the other party.

Based on the argumentation presented in *Pechstein*, the ECtHR could find not only athletes and other specialized employees, but in very specific circumstances also certain consumers, or even parties in commercial arbitrations to be in a de facto compulsory arbitration. For an arbitration to be considered compulsory, it is not enough for the choice to be a 'Hobson's choice', i.e., *a take it or leave it* situation,[82] where it is nevertheless possible to go to another place and get employment or the necessary goods or services. For instance, in case of employment arbitration, it should not suffice that one of many potential employers required an arbitration clause in the employment contract, if there were other potential employers that did not have this requirement. A party should have *no other choice* but to enter into an arbitration agreement in order to work in its profession, get the essential goods or keep its business operating.

### *[1] The Need for a Public Hearing*

The ECtHR did not simply end its analysis upon establishing that the arbitration in *Pechstein* was de facto compulsory. The ECtHR went on to list circumstances which emphasized the need for a public hearing in this particular case. The ECtHR added that:

> the questions arising in the impugned proceedings – as to whether it was justified for the second applicant to have been penalised for doping, and for the resolution

81. *Mutu and Pechstein*, *supra* n. 1, at 107.

82. On the *take it or leave it* arbitration agreements and their validity in sports arbitration *see*, e.g., A. Rigozzi and F. Robert-Tissot *'Consent' in Sports Arbitration: Its multiple Aspects. Lessons from the Canas Decision, in Particular with Regard to Interim Measures*, 59–94, in Elliot Geisinger and Elena Trabaldo – de Mestral, ASA Special Series No. 41 'Sports Arbitration: A Coach for Other Players?' (Juris Net LLC 2015).

> of which the CAS heard testimony from numerous experts – *rendered it necessary to hold a hearing under public scrutiny.*[83] (emphasis added)

Furthermore, the following circumstances were also noted as supporting the need for a public hearing in *Pechstein*:

- The sanction imposed (a two-year ban from competing) 'carried a degree of stigma'.[84]
- The sanction 'was likely to adversely affect her professional honour and reputation'.[85]
- The Swiss Federal Court noted that, considering the role of CAS in sports arbitration, holding a public hearing would have been 'desirable'.[86]

A question arises as to whether these circumstances were decisive – for example, would the ECtHR have taken a different decision if the dispute was simply a matter of damages and did not affect the party's reputation? In principle, the answer should be in the negative.

Based on the ECtHR case law, where an arbitration is compulsory, the right to a public hearing[87] should be afforded, unless any of the exceptions apply. However, it is my contention that based on the argumentation by the ECtHR in *Pechstein*, one could argue that providing reasons for a refusal of a party's request for a public hearing is likely to make a difference in the subsequent examination of the issue by a national court or the ECtHR.

In a hypothetical case of a potentially de facto compulsory arbitration with, e.g., a highly specialized employee there could be no need for a public hearing. Moreover, it is important to return to the cases where the ECtHR found that no hearing was necessary, as, e.g., (i) no facts were contested,[88] (ii) the dispute was not complex,[89] (iii) the dispute was of technical nature,[90] or (iv) the dispute concerned an unambiguous question of law.[91] *A fortiori*, where a hearing is not necessary, a public hearing is not necessary either.

### [B] Why Should Arbitrators Be Concerned with a Ruling of the ECtHR?

What is the relevance of the decision of the ECtHR for arbitration? Should an arbitral tribunal care about the decision in *Pechstein*?

According to the *principle of the fourth instance*, the ECtHR is not a next instance of the national courts.[92] Therefore, the ECtHR does not overturn the judgment of the

83. *Mutu and Pechstein, supra* n. 1, at 182.
84. *Ibid.*
85. *Ibid.*
86. *Ibid.*, at 178 and 182
87. Among the other protections of Art. 6(1) ECHR.
88. *See*, e.g., *Döry, supra* n. 29, at 37; *Saccoccia, supra* n. 29 at 73, and *Speil, supra* n. 29, at 29.
89. *See*, e.g., *Speil, supra* n. 29, at 29.
90. *See*, e.g., *Döry, supra* n. 29, at 41–43.
91. *See*, e.g., *Allan Jacobsson, supra* n. 32, at 49.
92. Rainey et al., *supra* n. 26, at 275.

national court or the arbitral award.[93] The role of the ECtHR is to assess whether the state's legislation or the protections given by the state or the state bodies in the particular proceedings fulfil the aims of, e.g., Article 6 ECHR. This subsidiary and supervisory role of the ECtHR was emphasized by the ECtHR in *Pechstein*.[94] It is the role of the forty-seven contracting states to 'ensure that the fundamental rights and freedoms enshrined therein are respected and protected on a domestic level'.[95]

As follows from the above, a state can be responsible under the ECHR, e.g., when its legislation offends against the rights of the Convention or the state did not provide protections it should have provided.[96] Courts in the contracting states are, therefore, bound by the ECHR in, e.g., proceedings regarding setting aside or enforcement of arbitral awards.[97]

In *Pechstein*, the ECtHR found that Switzerland had breached the ECHR, as the Swiss Federal Supreme Court failed to set aside the CAS award on the basis of a lack of a public hearing as requested by Pechstein. Therefore, in order to avoid the ECtHR finding a contracting state to be in violation of the ECHR, the national courts in the applicable jurisdictions should set an award aside, or refuse to enforce an award, in circumstances where there is the right to a public hearing which has not been fulfilled.

The vague category of de facto compulsory arbitration brings uncertainty to an area where certainty is a pivotal feature - i.e., enforceability of arbitral awards. Essentially it could be said that the decision of the ECtHR adds to an unclear scope of cases an additional ground - based on Article 6(1) ECHR - for challenging and resisting enforcement of arbitral awards in the contracting states of the ECHR.

Does the above mean that in the efforts to render an enforceable award, the tribunal should organize a public hearing every time a party requests it, where the circumstances of the case even to the smallest extent suggest that the arbitration could de facto be compulsory? The answer is not straightforward.

In the previous section the discussion was centred around the ECtHR perspective - the right to a public hearing and the interests it protects as well as around the unclear line between party autonomy and the human rights guarantees, i.e., the waiver of the rights in arbitration. It is now time to consider the arbitral tribunal's perspective.

When faced with a request for a public hearing in a rare borderline case, the arbitral tribunal would have to choose between either (a) organizing a public hearing in a possibly voluntary arbitration, likely going against arbitration rules providing for a private hearing, which would mean not respecting the parties' agreement on the procedure, or (b) denying a public hearing in a potentially compulsory arbitration - both of which options could risk the enforceability of the award. In order to weigh the above risks, it is important to consider the significance of privacy in arbitration.

93. *Ibid.*
94. *Mutu and Pechstein*, *supra* n. 1, at 70.
95. *Ibid.*, at 66–67.
96. *Ibid.* Applications can be brought against contracting states, public officials or bodies for which the state may be responsible, in other words where alleged violation can be attributed to the state. *See*, e.g., Practical Guide on Admissibility Criteria, *supra* n. 66, at 47.
97. *See*, e.g., Landrove, *supra* n. 8, at 99 referring to Swiss courts.

### [C] Importance of Privacy in Arbitration

Privacy is one of the key features, or the hallmarks, of arbitration, as Born puts it.[98] It is said to aim at not only protecting confidential information from third parties but also preventing third parties from intervening in the administration of justice.[99] Privacy refers to keeping third parties out of the hearing room and confidentiality has to do with information that requires protection.[100]

Unlike confidentiality, the principle of privacy of the hearing in arbitration has been considered rather uncontroversial. Most of the modern arbitration rules provide for the privacy of the arbitral hearing.[101] For instance, the UNCITRAL Arbitration Rules provide in Article 28(3) that hearings are held in camera unless the parties agree otherwise. The Arbitration Rules of the Arbitration Institute of the Stockholm Chamber of Commerce (SCC Rules) provide the same in Article 32(3) and the Arbitration Rules of the London Court of International Arbitration (LCIA Rules) are similar, but they explicitly require the parties' agreement to be in writing.[102] The Arbitration Rules of the International Chamber of Commerce International Court of Arbitration (ICC Rules) require not only parties' agreement, but also tribunal's approval, to open the door to the hearing room for persons that are not involved in the proceedings.[103]

Arbitration laws are often silent on the issue of privacy.[104] The United Nations Commission on International Trade Law Model Law on International Commercial Arbitration (UNCITRAL Model Law), the Swiss, US and Swedish arbitration laws are all silent regarding this question. What is then the basis of privacy? The argument of protecting confidential information shared in the arbitration, as raised by Born, is not very persuasive, because privacy does not equal confidentiality. The reason should rather be traced back to what arbitration is: 'a private and consensual system of dispute resolution',[105] the private nature of arbitration, and the fact that arbitration is an out-of-court dispute resolution method.

In their treatise on arbitration, Lew, Mistelis and Kröll noted the following about the privacy of arbitration, as opposed to the public nature of the courts:

> Just as national courts are public, arbitration is generally private. In the same way as every contract between parties is a private matter between them, so too the arbitration agreement is private between the parties. Accordingly, when a dispute arises it is to be resolved in the private dispute resolution system agreed between the parties, subject to certain safeguards.[106]

98. Born, *supra* n. 44, at 2235, *see also Ibid.*, at 89–90.
99. *Ibid.*, at 2781–2782.
100. I. Smeureanu, *Confidentiality in International Commercial Arbitration*, International Arbitration Law Library, Volume 22, 4–5 (Kluwer Law International 2011).
101. Born, *supra* n. 44, at 2811.
102. Article 19.4 of the LCIA Arbitration Rules.
103. *See* Art. 26.3 *in fine* of the ICC Arbitration Rules.
104. Born, *supra* n. 44, at 2811–2812.
105. N. Blackaby and C. Partasides et al., *Redfern and Hunter on International Arbitration*, 2 (Oxford University Press 2015).
106. J. Lew, L. Mistelis and S. Kröll, *Comparative International Commercial Arbitration*, 4 (Kluwer Law International 2003).

The above reflects the argumentation in *Oxford Shipping Co. Ltd v. Nippon Yusen Kaisha*where the English High Court stated that:

> [t]he concept of private arbitration derives simply from the fact that the parties have agreed to submit to arbitration particular disputes arising between them and only between them. It is implicit in this that strangers shall be excluded from the hearing. ...[107]

In the Swedish context, despite the lack of an explicit provision on the privacy of the hearing, it is considered clear that arbitration hearings are private.[108] In *Bulbank*, the Supreme Court of Sweden provided that '[f]rom the private nature of arbitration proceedings follows that third parties do not have the right to be present at the proceedings or access written documents of the file'.[109]

The Supreme Court further provided that:

> [a] general starting point for deciding the confidentiality issue is that arbitration proceedings are based on an agreement. (Arbitration proceedings prescribed by law are ignored herein.) It follows from this that arbitration proceedings are of a private nature, which is not changed by the fact that certain aspects thereof are regulated by law.[110]

From the above, it can be argued that the Supreme Court of Sweden connects the private nature of arbitration to the arbitration agreement. *A contrario*, in relation to arbitrations mandated by law, privacy should not be assumed in the same way. This is in line with the ECtHR case law, considering that in compulsory arbitration the protections of Article 6(1) ECHR are not waived.[111]

Privacy is not only based on the arbitration agreement; privacy can also be seen as legitimizing the agreement. The Swedish Labour Court has found an arbitration clause in an employment contract of a personal assistant to be fair according to section 36 of the Contract Act for the very reason of privacy of arbitral proceedings.[112] The Labour Court stated that the reasonableness has to be assessed by considering the circumstances of the case. Here, the Association of Healthcare Providers and the Swedish Municipal Workers' Association had decided when drafting the standard-form employment contract that disputes should be settled by arbitration and not in court in order to prevent circumstances of a personal nature from becoming public.[113]

---

107. *Oxford Shipping Co. Ltd v. Nippon Yusen Kaisha* [1984] QBD (Comm) 2 Lloyd's Rep 373, 378 (26 Jun. 1984).
108. *See*, e.g., Bo G.H. Nilsson and B. Rundblom Andersson *Fundamental Principles of International Arbitration in Sweden*, 6, in Franke et al. (eds) International Arbitration in Sweden: A Practitioner's Guide (Wolters Kluwer 2013).
109. *Bulgarian Foreign Trade Bank Ltd (Bulbank) v. A.I. Trade Finance Inc*, T 1881-99/ NJA 2000 section 538, 6 (HD 27 Oct. 2000) English translation available on https://www.arbitration.sccinstitute.com/views/pages/getfile.ashx?portalId = 89&docId = 1083535&propId = 1578 (accessed 15 Jun. 2020).
110. *Bulbank, supra* n. 109.
111. *Mutu and Pechstein, supra* n. 1, at 95. *See also Suovaniemi, supra* n. 34, *Suda, supra* n. 5, at 49.
112. As noted by Sinander in his presentation, *supra* n. 80. *AD 2018 no. 30*, A 99/17 (AD 16 May 2018).
113. *AD 2018 no. 30*, at 10 (own translation).

The Labour Court further emphasized that whether sensitive information is disclosed or not in the particular proceedings does not influence the assessment of the reasonableness of the arbitration clause.[114] Hence, it could be concluded that according to the Swedish Labour Court, privacy of arbitration is important on an abstract level, not merely to protect sensitive information in the particular proceedings.

Also, the ECtHR recognizes the importance of privacy of the hearing in arbitration. In its decision from 1999 in *Suovaniemi*, where the ECtHR stated that:

> in the light of the case-law it is clear that the right to a public hearing can be validly waived even in court proceedings. ... The same applies, a fortiori, to arbitration proceedings, one of the very purposes of which is often to avoid publicity.[115]

Here, the privacy of arbitration is raised to a level of being one of the main characteristics that motivates the parties' choice of this dispute resolution method.

Based on the above, it could be argued that privacy in arbitration is derived from the private nature of arbitration and is such an important feature that it can even legitimize the choice of arbitration as a dispute resolution method. In voluntary arbitration it is a legitimate expectation that a hearing is private. The right to a private hearing becomes part of parties' agreement where arbitration rules providing for the privacy of the hearing are chosen to govern the arbitration.

In *Pechstein*, the ECtHR stated that Pechstein could *at best* had hoped for an *indirect* application of Article 6(1) ECHR, when she gave consent to CAS jurisdiction.[116] The ECtHR has decided to 'thus proceed from the assumption ... that acceptance of the arbitration clause could constitute a waiver of all or part of the Article 6 § 1 safeguards'.[117]

In case of a compulsory arbitration the parties should not have the same expectations regarding the privacy of the hearing.[118] This is not controversial with regard to de jure compulsory arbitration, as in such an arbitration, the parties are well aware that their arbitration is mandated by law.

An example of compulsory arbitration can be seen in respect of redemption of minority shares disputes under the Finnish Companies Act. In this type of proceeding many aspects are public. The names of the arbitrators are announced publicly, a trustee is appointed by a national court and that appointment is made public, and importantly, the award is registered in the trade register. Despite the hearing not being public as a starting point, the Finnish legislation provides a number of protections that are not available in voluntary commercial arbitrations. It could be argued that the protections provided by law suffice to guarantee the rights enshrined in Article 6(1) ECHR.

From the point of view of legal certainty, it seems problematic to simply equate de facto compulsory arbitration with de jure compulsory arbitration. In case of de jure compulsory arbitration, it is clear that the arbitration is not voluntary, and privacy should not be assumed. However, it might not be clear whether an arbitration is de

114. *Ibid.*, at 11.
115. *Suovaniemi, supra* n. 34.
116. *Mutu and Pechstein, supra* n. 1, at 102.
117. *Ibid.*, at 103.
118. *Ibid.*, at 95. *See also Suovaniemi, supra* n. 34, *Suda, supra* n. 5, at 49 and *Bulbank, supra* n. 109.

facto compulsory. One could say that with regards to athletes and CAS arbitration, there is some level of certainty achieved, partly due to the change in the CAS Rules providing explicitly for a possibility of a public hearing in matters of disciplinary nature. However, with regards to other specialized employees and, in some specific circumstances, consumers and companies, the situation is less evident. Therefore, when examining whether a party has a right to request for a public hearing unilaterally, the *starting point* for such determination should be an assumption that the arbitration is voluntary and the hearing is private.

### [D] Concluding Remarks

What is the potential relevance of the recent ECtHR decisions for arbitration? For the parties to CAS arbitrations the relevance is manifested in the change of the CAS Rules providing a possibility of a public hearing in a narrow scope of cases. Even though the amended provision limits the right to request for a hearing unilaterally to physical persons in disciplinary matters,[119] a public hearing in CAS arbitration is a possibility.

What about cases other than sports arbitration? As discussed in the first part of this section, in principle the argumentation from *Pechstein* could apply to disputes with employees,[120] consumers or even companies. However, the determination that an arbitration is de facto compulsory is case specific and the threshold is high. A decision to organize a public hearing based on a unilateral request should not be taken lightly considering the importance of the privacy of arbitral proceedings. Allowing the public to attend a hearing in an arbitration which is not compulsory could potentially risk the enforceability of the arbitral award.

## §9.05 FULFILLING THE RIGHT TO A PUBLIC HEARING IN ARBITRATION

Despite the narrow scope of cases where a tribunal would decide that a public hearing should be organized, it is pertinent to examine how one goes about organizing the public hearing. Issues include: where to announce the hearing, where to hold it, how to allow the public in - in person or through a broadcast, how to protect the confidential information and avoid abuses, who bears the cost of all of that, etc. Those are only some of the questions that one should consider in the post-Pechstein era.

Two recent developments aid in answering the above questions. The first one is the already-mentioned public hearing organized in a CAS arbitration concerning a disciplinary case brought by the World Anti-Doping Agency against a Chinese swimmer Sun Yang and Fédération Internationale de Natation. This was only the second

119. *See* Rule R57 CAS Code C. Special Provisions Applicable to the Appeal Arbitration Procedure.
120. As argued by Sinander, *supra* n. 80.

public hearing in the history of CAS and it was organized on 15 November 2019, twenty years after the first one.[121] In this case, both parties asked for the public hearing.

The second development is more of a theoretical character. In December 2019, an organization called the Center for International Legal Cooperation released the Hague Rules on Business and Human Rights Arbitration (Hague Rules). This soft law aims to be 'a set of procedures for the arbitration of disputes related to the human rights impacts of business activities'[122] Even though the Hague Rules are still very new and time will show if they are going to be used in practice, they are of interest in the following discussion, because they provide that as a rule the hearing will be public, subject to exceptions. The solutions provided in the Hague Rules regarding organization of a public hearing are also considered below.

### [A] Announcement

Simply opening the door to the hearing room does not make the hearing public. The public should be duly notified of the hearing. In one case, the ECtHR considered a hearing not to fulfil the requirement of being public when it was held in prison and the public was not adequately notified of the hearing and of access to the hearing.[123]

How does one inform the public about the hearing? In institutional arbitrations, the announcement could be given on the institution's webpage. Would this be enough? To some extent one could argue that such an announcement would not be sufficient, because if it was not known that a dispute existed in the first place, the interested persons would not search for an announcement on that institution's website. In the context of international commercial arbitration, various aspects make it questionable whether an announcement in itself would be sufficient, including (a) the large number of institutions, (b) the fact that there are ad hoc arbitrations, and (c) the lack of one leading information channel.

When should the announcement be made? The Hague Rules prescribe that the tribunal should provide the public with the information about the date, time and place of the hearing sufficiently in advance. In the case of the hearing of Sun Yang, the media release was given one month before the hearing.[124]

### [B] Public Access

Announcing the time and place of the hearing might not be enough, if the hearing is held in a remote place and the cost of attending the hearing creates an obstacle for the interested persons to attend the hearing. In an international arbitration, the hearing

121. *See* the information provided by the CAS itself in the release regarding Yang's hearing https://www.tas-cas.org/fileadmin/user_upload/CAS_Media_Release_6148_Hearing_15.11.19.pdf (accessed 15 Jun. 2020).
122. Preamble to the Hague Rules on Business and Human Rights Arbitration.
123. *Riepan v. Austria*, No. 35115/97 (ECtHR 14 Feb. 2001).
124. The release can be found, e.g., here https://cdn.swimswam.com/wp-content/uploads/2019/10/CAS_Media_Release_6148_Hearing_15.11.19.pdf (accessed 15 Jun. 2020).

may often be said to be in a remote place for at least some of the interested persons. However, from the point of view of Article 6(1) of the ECHR, the right to a public hearing is a human right of the party to the dispute, rather than the right of the interested person to get access to the hearing. Giving an opportunity for the hearing to be publicly scrutinized should be deemed to be sufficient in this context, even if not all interested members of the public will in practice be able to attend.

Apart from, or even instead of, providing access in person to the hearing, a live broadcast could be organized. In the hearing in the Sun Yang case, previously registered persons had access to a public viewing area. The hearing was also broadcasted in a live stream and the links to the video recordings of the hearing were available online.[125] Although this chapter focuses on commercial arbitration, it is also worth mentioning that the International Center for Settlement of Investment Disputes, which has already gained experience in organizing public hearings, broadcasts such hearings in a separate room which is open to the public, or if parties so agree, online.[126] The Permanent Court of Arbitration (PCA) has also organized public access to the hearings in some cases through video broadcasting. For instance, in *The Renco Group, Inc. v. Republic of Peru* and *The Renco Group, Inc. & Doe Run Resources, Corp. v. Republic of Peru & Activos Mineros, S.A.C.* where the PCA acts as registry, a public hearing regarding preliminary objections and bifurcation was held in the form of a video conference which was streamed live on 12 and 13 June 2020.[127]

The Hague Rules provide the tribunal with broad powers to arrange the hearing so that the access of the public is facilitated in an appropriate way.[128] The commentary to the Hague Rules gives examples of video and other technological solutions that could allow the public to gain access to the hearing.

Does it suffice that the public is given access to the hearing, or should it also get access to the evidence referred to at the hearing: the written witness statements, expert reports, documents? What about parties' written submissions? The scope of the information that should be made public is not obvious.

The Hague Rules approach this question broadly. According to the transparency objectives enshrined in the Hague Rules, the key documents in arbitration proceedings are to be made public. This covers not only the parties' briefs and the tribunal's decisions and awards but also expert reports and witness statements.[129] The tribunal is

125. The hearing is available in parts under the following links https://vimeo.com/373204016; https://vimeo.com/373351335; https://vimeo.com/373377323; https://vimeo.com/373416320. (accessed 15 Jun. 2020).
126. *See* Access to the proceedings explained on https://icsid.worldbank.org/en/Pages/process/Oral-Procedure-Convention-Arbitration.aspx (accessed 15 Jun. 2020).
127. *See* the announcement regarding the public hearing on https://pca-cpa.org/en/news/pca-case-no-2019-46-47-public-hearing-on-bifurcation-and-preliminary-objections/ (accessed 28 Sep. 2020). Regarding earlier practice, see a press release regarding a public hearing in *Professor Christian Doutremepuich and Antoine Doutremepuich (France) v. The Republic of Mauritius* held at the Peace Palace, The Hague on 12 and 13 Jun. 2019 and streamed live on https://pcacases.com/web/sendAttach/2639 (accessed 28 Sep. 2020).
128. Article 41.3 of the Hague Rules.
129. *See* Art. 40.1 of the Hague Rules. Exhibits and other documents not covered in Art. 40.1 could be published on tribunal's own initiative or a request of any party (Art. 40.2).

to send the documents to the repository which will make them available to the public.[130]

The above approach of the Hague Rules is very far reaching. However, from the point of view of the right to a public hearing as provided in Article 6(1), such a wide scope of transparency is not necessary.

### [C] Protection of Confidential Information

During a public hearing it can be challenging to protect confidential information from being disclosed. When the access to the hearing is provided in person and the access requires registration, one could have some control over the information being revealed during the hearing. A video recording could be edited before providing it to the broader public.

For instance, the ECtHR has considered that a hearing held at a military base, where the public had to sign in order to attend it, constituted a public hearing.[131] The restriction of access was legitimized by the security requirements.

The uncertainty about the protection of confidential information during a public hearing can influence case strategy, choice of arguments, evidence used, etc., which in turn can influence party's due process rights negatively.

### [D] Costs

Transparency is expensive. The costs could include: a bigger hearing room, public announcements, broadcasting, translation, costs connected to the protection of confidential information to name a few. Who should bear the cost of the hearing being public? Should it be the party who requests the hearing to be public, the stronger party, the losing party, or should some of the costs be borne by the institution or even by the state where the arbitration is seated?

In the Sun Yang arbitration, both parties requested the hearing to be public. The award in the Sun Yang case does not distinguish the costs of the public hearing. However, under the CAS Code, the costs of the arbitration (including arbitrators' fees and costs) are borne by the CAS[132] and own costs of representation, witnesses, translation are carried by the parties.[133] Hence, the costs of a public hearing are split between the CAS and the parties.

In a compulsory arbitration, it could be assumed that there is often an imbalance between the parties. It would seem unreasonable and would limit the opportunity to rely on the right to a public hearing if it was the party requesting the hearing to be public who would have to bear the costs of the public nature of the hearing. In some arbitrations with weaker parties, the stronger party might need to bear the costs of the arbitration for the arbitration agreement not be considered unreasonable or incapable

130. Article 40.3 of the Hague Rules.
131. *Hood v. UK*, No. 27267/95, 120 (ECtHR 28 May 1998).
132. Rule 65.2 of the CAS Code.
133. Rule 65.3 of the CAS Code.

of being performed.[134] Hence, potentially, the stronger party would also need to cover the costs of a public hearing. The question of who bears the costs of a public hearing needs to be answered from case to case, taking into consideration specific circumstances of each arbitration.

### [E] Concluding Remarks

Arbitration is based on the principle of privacy of the proceedings. Hence, organizing a public hearing may pose practical challenges. There is a myriad of questions that an arbitral tribunal should be ready to answer, including for instance: how to provide the access of the public to the hearing? What information should be made public and how to protect confidential information? And last but not least who will pay for all the additional costs connected with organizing a public hearing?

## §9.06 CONCLUSIONS

The right to a public hearing can be applicable to arbitration when some of the conditions for waiver are not fulfilled or when limitations to the right to a public hearing, or the right to a hearing in general, apply in a case. The condition for waiver that raises the most controversy in the context of this chapter is that the waiver is to be given freely. It is this requirement that influences whether an arbitration is voluntary or compulsory.

With regard to Pechstein, the ECtHR found that the arbitration was de facto compulsory for Pechstein as her choice was only between entering into the arbitration agreement and not earning a living in her profession, i.e., competing in speed-skating.

De facto compulsory arbitration could potentially be found not only in the context of sports and employment arbitration but also in some rare instances of consumer or even commercial arbitration. Whether an arbitration is de facto compulsory needs to be established based on the circumstances of each case and the threshold for the determination should be high. The test applied in *Pechstein* was much stricter than just a 'take it or leave it' choice. If a party could find comparable employment somewhere else or if a party could find a different business partner than the one that required entering into an arbitration agreement, the arbitration should not be considered compulsory.

Where an arbitral tribunal determines that the right to a public hearing applies, organizing public access to the hearing in an arbitration, especially in an ad hoc arbitration, can cause practical difficulties. The arbitral tribunal will need to consider, *inter alia*, where to hold the hearing, where to announce it, who pays for it what exactly should be made public, and how to protect confidential information.

However, where the compulsory character of an arbitration is not clear, it is difficult to argue that the tribunal should organize a public hearing based on a

134. *See* Niedermaier, *supra* n. 79, 18–19 (2014) referring to the judgment of the German Federal Court of Justice, III ZR 33/00 (BGH 14 Sep. 2000).

unilateral request of a party. Considering the importance of privacy of the hearing in arbitration, erring on the side of a public hearing potentially puts the award at risk.

In the efforts to render an enforceable award, the arbitral tribunal should be sensitive to the possibility of Article 6(1) ECHR applying to the arbitration at hand. When denying the request of a party for a public hearing in a borderline case, it is advisable that the tribunal gives reasons for its decision taking into consideration the circumstances of the case, the conditions for waiver, as well as limitations to the right to a public hearing under Article 6(1) ECHR.

It is important that arbitral tribunals are aware of the potential applicability of the right to a public hearing enshrined in Article 6(1) ECHR to arbitrations that are de facto compulsory. However, providing the right in practice is not without challenges, including: (1) the complexity of the conditions for waiver of the right to a public hearing, (2) the vagueness of the category of de facto compulsory arbitration and its exceptional character, (3) privacy being an important principle of arbitration, and (4) practical issues with organizing public hearings.

CHAPTER 10

# Fast Track Arbitration in the Nordics: Where Do We Go from Here?

*Ola Ø. Nisja*

## §10.01 INTRODUCTION

All the Nordic countries have their own well-established arbitral institutions. The SCC,[1] DIA,[2] FAI[3] and OCC[4] all offer fast track arbitration, as do many commonly used institutes outside the Nordics,[5] such as the ICC,[6] SIAC,[7] CIETAC,[8] SCAI[9] and DIS.[10] UNCITRAL's Working Group II has since its 69th session in February 2019 had

1. Arbitration Institute of the Stockholm Chamber of Commerce, cf. 2017 Rules for Expedited Arbitration, in force from 1 Jan. 2017.
2. The Danish Institute of Arbitration, cf. DIA Rules of Simplified Arbitration, in force from 1 May 2013.
3. The Arbitration Institute of the Finland Chamber of Commerce, cf. the 2020 FAI Expedited Arbitration Rules, in force from 1 Jan. 2020.
4. The Arbitration and Dispute Resolution institute of the Oslo Chamber of Commerce, cf. 2017 Arbitration and Fast-track Arbitration Rules Chapter VII, in force from 1 Jan. 2017.
5. Somewhat surprisingly, The Nordic Arbitration Centre of the Iceland Chamber of Commerce (NAC) does not offer a fast track system. From the international scene, neither does the London Court of International Arbitration (LCIA).
6. International Chamber of Commerce, cf. ICC Arbitration Rules Art. 30 and its Appendix VI ('Expedited Procedure Provisions'), in force from 1 Mar. 2017.
7. Singapore International Arbitration Centre, cf. SIAC Arbitration Rules 6th ed. section 5, in force from 1 Aug. 2016.
8. China International Economic and Trade Arbitration Commission, cf. CIETAC Arbitration Rules Chapter 6 ('Summary Procedure'), in force from 1 Jan. 2015.
9. Swiss Chambers' Arbitration Institution (SCAI), cf. Swiss Rules of International Arbitration Art. 42 ('Expedited Procedure'), in force from 1 Jun. 2012.
10. The German Arbitration Institute (DIS), cf. DIS Arbitration Rules Annex IV in force from 1 Mar. 2018.

expedited arbitration as one of its main topics for discussion.[11] The Nordic Offshore and Maritime Arbitration Association (NOMA) is working on its own rules on fast track arbitration. Bespoke fast track rules are readily available and provide robust, cost-effective alternatives to full-scale arbitration. Still, the use of fast track arbitration continues to be rather limited in the Nordics, generally speaking.

This chapter seeks to explore what characterizes fast track arbitration in the Nordics, why we need fast track arbitration and attempts to explain why fast track arbitration is not used more frequently. Finally, some thoughts are given as to what may make this – in the author's view – often highly adequate form of dispute resolution more recognized and thus more used.

## §10.02 FAST TRACK ARBITRATION IN THE NORDICS

### [A] General

'Fast track' (the OCC), 'expedited' (the SCC and FAI) or 'simplified' (the DIA) are all names on types of arbitration processes aimed at obtaining awards quicker and at a lower cost than through ordinary (full-scale) arbitration. This form of arbitration – when used – is typically chosen for lower value or less complicated disputes.

By way of example, the OCC states as follows in the Preface of its 2017 Rules:

> A simplified form of arbitration is Fast-track Arbitration, a method which is fast, more efficient and less costly.

The move towards an increased focus on fast track arbitration must be seen in conjunction with a general requirement for greater efficiency in arbitration, be it national or international, ad hoc or institutional. It is no longer necessarily the case that international arbitration is slow and costly compared to other ways of obtaining a final and enforceable decision from a third party. This is partly because parties (with assistance from their counsel) adopt more sophisticated approaches to arbitration. The institutions themselves have also modernized in many aspects, and to a much larger degree now require greater efficiency from parties and arbitrators than just ten to fifteen years ago.

Three specific characteristics shall be visited below: (1) the use of a sole arbitrator, (2) the appointment process and (3) specific adaptions with regards to the process in order to reduce time expenditure and cost.

### [B] The Use of a Sole Arbitrator

Fast track regimes normally operate with *a sole arbitrator*. In many jurisdictions, the fall back rule is that unless the parties have agreed otherwise, three arbitrators should

11. *See* https://uncitral.un.org/en/working_groups/2/arbitration. The papers prepared by the Working Group contain a number of interesting discussions.

be appointed.[12] For smaller value and less complicated disputes, there is normally no need to have three arbitrators in order to ensure a correct decision. It will in such cases often be difficult to defend the costs of a three-arbitrator panel. Having three persons agree on an award (and procedural decisions) as opposed to one person making the decisions will also regularly imply more time passing with the exchange of drafts and discussions among the tribunal members.

### [C] The Appointment Process

Since the goal with fast track arbitration is to offer a more efficient system than normal full-scale arbitration as it is practised throughout the Nordic countries, the sole arbitrator must be *expediently appointed by the institution* either where it is the institution who appoints the sole arbitrator at the outset or where the parties have the opportunity to agree but fails do to so within a given deadline.

Although the appointed sole arbitrator may be challenged due to lack of impartiality, independence or otherwise as the relevant institutional rules and the applicable procedural law sets out, the appointment processes chosen in the fast track regimes will in my experience regularly go much swifter than if the parties for instance first shall try to agree on a panel, and failing to do so need to have the institution make the appointment in whole or in part.[13] Some party autonomy or at least flexibility can thus arguably be said to be lost; however, less time is used – normally also reduced cost to external counsel typically handling such processes. Party autonomy can in any case arguably be said to have been respected since it is the parties themselves who have chosen a system for resolving their disputes which involves fast track arbitration.

For disputes that especially fit for fast track proceedings (smaller and less complex), this balance should be acceptable provided that one can trust that the institutions will do an adequate job finding the right arbitrator prior to appointment, which the users in my experience can trust when it comes to the Nordic institutions.

### [D] Specific Adaptions with Regards to the Process in Order to Save Time and Cost

A final characteristic is that the rules in the different manners have regulation in order to decrease time and cost spent in the period after appointment and until award compared to full-scale processes, for instance, that the *time available for the tribunal to issue its award* is shorter, that the *time allowed for an oral hearing* (if any) and not least the *number and length of the pleadings*, as well as limitations relating to *what evidence should be presented.*

A number of such adaptions can of course be accommodated for by the parties and the tribunal in a full-scale arbitration in a Procedural Order No. 1 or similar procedural documents set out typically after having conducted a Case Management

12. An example is the Norwegian Arbitration Act 2004 section 12 second sentence.
13. As would for instance be the situation under the OCC, cf. the OCC Rules Art. 8.

Conference. However, in my experience, this is often easier said than done since the parties may not necessarily be so inclined to agree at this point in the dispute, and that the tribunal in these situations may be less inclined to set out, for instance, an aggressive schedule for pleadings and timing for an oral hearing that at least one party communicates that it does not want in order to ensure due process (or rather accommodate for due process paranoia). The potential for conducting full-scale arbitrations in a more efficient manner is in my experience thus not a strong argument against choosing fast track arbitration for smaller disputes.

## §10.03 THE NEED FOR FAST TRACK ARBITRATION

In my mind at least, there can be little doubt that there is a need for quicker and more cost-effective arbitration processes than what one normally sees in a full-scale arbitration for a rather huge number of cases. I also firmly believe that fast track arbitration is the best solution when it comes to smaller value and less complicated disputes. Thus, there is, in my view, a clear need for fast track arbitration, and it should be used more frequently.

One can however take on an even broader perspective. There is in my view a need for the legal community – also in the Nordics – to adopt a more dynamic and modern approach to dispute resolution. Too many disputes within the domestic court systems proceed through several layers of courts (more often than not the possibility to appeal is used to its full extent in my experience) and full-scale arbitrations are embarked upon, without sufficient consideration being given to the most *appropriate* way of resolving the dispute. Many disputes neither require nor deserve full-scale procedures. Too few cases are negotiated to settlement, mediated or resolved by other means such as early neutral evaluation or minitrials. And too few cases are resolved through fast track arbitration (which, as opposed to the other means just mentioned, also has the clear benefit of providing a binding and enforceable third party decision).

Choosing fast track arbitration usually involves obtaining a final award more quickly, with reduced legal costs (counsel, experts and arbitrators). As demonstrated under section §10.02, the process is simpler, or in more positive terms: leaner. The case can, in my view, be made that legal processes in the Nordics are in general often leaner, more straightforward and efficient than in many jurisdictions outside the Nordics. Thus, one could say that fast track arbitration encompasses a somewhat Nordic spirit where we try not to make things more complicated than they need to be. Fast track arbitration is indeed well-suited to handle a large number of the disputes which today go to full-scale arbitration and domestic courts in a more appropriate manner. With a leaner process, the internal resources used by the parties can also be reduced significantly. In my experience such internal resources can often be a bigger cost than counsel and tribunals.

Certainly a case can be made, as discussed both above and reverted to below, that there is a price to be paid by choosing fast track arbitration since the risk of wrong decisions may increase as the level of thoroughness and detail inevitably decreases.

First of all, this risk needs to be balanced against the importance of the dispute. In commercial disputes, the importance and complexity will often – but not always – reflect the value. For lower value disputes, it can thus often be accepted – and it is in accordance with many domestic court systems to accept – that simpler procedures are employed. When it comes to fast track arbitration this risk is also significantly reduced by the usually ample opportunities to make a case for a more thorough process if that proves to the appropriate way of resolving the dispute. Fast track arbitration is not a quick and dirty process, but a more efficient and lean way of resolving disputes which do not need or deserve a full-scale arbitration. A good fast track arbitration system strikes the balance between due process and efficiency.

My conclusion is that there is a true need for fast track arbitration, and that this need is not covered by other forms of dispute resolution.

## §10.04 USE OF FAST TRACK ARBITRATION IN THE NORDICS

Using the reported case load from the SCC, DIA, FAI and OCC, Marie Nesvik has summarized the use of fast track arbitration in the Nordics.[14] Taking the four major general institutions and the reported numbers over the last three years,[15] approximately 15 % of the handled cases were handled under a fast track procedure. However, when removing the SCC with its average of almost 33 %, the portion of fast track arbitrations at the remaining three institutions is reduced to less than 8 %. It would be interesting to see an analysis of why we see such a difference. SCC has obviously done something right. The following comment from Anja Havedal Ipp relating to fast track arbitration at the SCC is worth noting:

> In agreeing to arbitrate under the [SCC] Expedited Rules, arbitration users are aware of the limited scope of the procedure; in a sense, they are agreeing to resolve their disputes in the same spirit as the merchants in Redfern & Hunter's historical retrospect on arbitration. Perhaps this procedural simplicity is precisely what has made expedited arbitration an increasingly attractive dispute resolution method.[16]

Again using Norway as an example, where the vast proportion of arbitration cases still are ad hoc, the percentage of arbitrations being conducted on a fast track basis is insignificant. The Norwegian Arbitration Act 2004 has as its default rule that three arbitrators shall be appointed.[17] Thus, unless the parties agree otherwise (often challenging when a dispute has arisen), the matter will be decided by three arbitrators, which certainly involves a higher cost than with a sole arbitrator. For a number of

14. Marie Nesvik, *Fast Track Arbitration: Efficiency vs. Due Process*, Norwegian Arbitration Day, 2020. An article based on the speech will be published in a Norwegian Arbitration Day, 2020 edition of *MarIus*.
15. For the FAI, SCC and DIA, Nesvik used 2016–2018, and for the OCC she used 2019. The percentages above are calculated based on the statistics presented by Nesvik.
16. Anja Havedal Ipp, *Expedited Arbitration at the SCC: One Year with the 2017 Rules*, available at the Kluwer Arbitration Blog.
17. Norwegian Arbitration Act 2004 section 12. This is in contrast to, for example, Art. 12(2) of the ICC Rules, which starts from the premise that, where the parties have not agreed upon the number of arbitrators, the ICC Court shall appoint a sole arbitrator.

typical cases where there is an arbitration clause in the contract, the costs of external counsel and arbitrators are likely to exceed the amount in dispute. Although such disputes will concern minor amounts in terms of international arbitration, few Nordic companies will be happy to abandon claims of hundreds of thousands of NOK, or even a million or two, due to disproportionally high legal costs. Opting for fast track arbitration with a sole arbitrator will thus significantly reduce one part of the costs, and with the simplified process it is of course also the purpose to reduce costs to external counsel. In my experience, also the latter is regularly the case. Knowing that far from all disputes are high value, it is difficult to find good reasons for not using fast track arbitration more.

## §10.05 EXPLAINING THE LIMITED USAGE

### [A] General

If one asks why we do not see more fast track arbitration, one may get all sorts of responses from lawyers. Some may refer to an alleged lack of due process (*see* section §10.03 above). Others may argue that certain players in the legal community see full-scale arbitration as a good line of business, and that fast track arbitration normally will entail less work for such players and thus they may lack the necessary inclination to advice their clients to include fast track regimes in the contract. For my part, I have too much faith in the legal market to accept the latter reasoning, at least for the clear majority of advisors and decision makers.

In this section I will rather raise some other potential explanations: First I will discuss whether the regulatory frameworks (the institutional rules) are sufficient (section §10.05[B]) and whether the potential upside presented above is too limited (section §10.05[C]). Then I raise the question as to whether we lack the right arbitrators (section §10.05[D]). Finally, I will present what in my opinion is the main reason why we do not see more fast track arbitration – lack of knowledge (section §10.05[E]), and finally the quick fix: adaption of arbitration clauses (section §10.05[F]).

### [B] Are the Regulatory Frameworks (The Institutional Rules) Sufficient?

Arbitration institutions always work on their rules in order to adapt and optimize. This is also the case for the fast track rules adopted by the four major Nordic institutions. However, in general, the institutional rules on fast track arbitration in the Nordics are well written and in my experience work adequately. The different rules all have their pros and cons, as do all such rules, but I fail to see that a perceived insufficiency in relation to the arbitral rules contributes to the lack of fast track arbitration cases in any significant way. That is not to say that the rules cannot be further enhanced, *see* section §10.06 below.

### [C] Is the Potential Upside Too Limited?

A more relevant question is what the parties win by accepting to have certain or all disputes handled under the fast track regimes. Indeed, it is not that uncommon for fast track arbitrations to be converted to full-scale procedures, where necessary or appropriate. As the number of disclosure requests increases, along with the potential procedural orders, the pleadings expand, and the volume of evidence grows, parties may from time to time be struck by a (perhaps irrational, but all the same real) fear of the process becoming too simplistic for a dispute which – as in so many cases – turns out to be wider in ambit than was initially envisaged.

The solution opted for in these situations will often be to try to persuade the other party to convert to full-scale proceedings. Although reaching consensus on such issues between the parties may be difficult once a dispute has arisen, such conversion is not necessarily controversial. Why not? The other side has been struck by the same fear.

Whether or not the tribunal is bound by such a joint request from the parties, or has the competence to accept a request from just one party, will depend on the interpretation of the institutional rules and the applicable procedural law. In the situation described, the tribunal – which may at this point have caught on a mild due process paranoia related to how the matter has evolved – will in my experience often be inclined to accept such conversion or accept adaptations to the process provided that this is not contrary to the institutional rules and applicable procedural law, notwithstanding the fact that this will regularly increase cost and time expenditure.

There can however be no question that with a well-administered fast track arbitration – where the key often will be to *keep* the case on the fast track – the award will be issued faster and at a significantly reduced cost, the latter particularly being ensured by the tribunal regularly being constituted by a sole arbitrator and with clear limitations on the number and scope of pleadings. Thus, the upside is there, and if it no longer is – there is normally potential to make adaptations and in some cases even convert to full scale. In my view, a lack of potential upside cannot explain why we do not see more fast track arbitration cases in the Nordics.

### [D] Do We Lack the Right Arbitrators?

The arbitral community in the Nordics is still rather small. Although the pool of candidates for appointment is increasing, more work needs to be carried out to ensure that a new generation of arbitrators is properly educated and trained. Some frequently used arbitrators may also benefit from training on how to conduct a fast track arbitration process – a great and practical topic for many of the arbitration seminars being organized in the Nordics these days. Competence and experience should be shared. More focus and higher degree of knowledge will bring us a good step further.

This being said, there is a massive talent pool of potential arbitrators available, and a dispute resolution community continuously recruiting new talent with able and willing younger lawyers with a keen interest in arbitration. Thus, a lack of right arbitrators – had it been a true problem at all – would only need to be temporary.

### [E] Lack of Knowledge of the Alternative (and More Adequate) Route

Having discussed a number of views that could have been - but is not - sufficient to adequately explain and substantiate the still limited use of fast track arbitration we can turn to what in my view is the main reason why we do not see more fast track arbitration cases: lack of knowledge and understanding of the adequacy of fast track arbitration.

The parties and counsel regularly working with institutional arbitration, particularly international arbitration, have for years been acquainted with fast track arbitration as a concept. However, beyond the sometimes narrow confines of the arbitral community itself, there is still a need to hear more about fast track arbitration and learn more of the advantages in order to increase use. Very often it is not the same lawyers (or client representatives) who work with disputes and who draft the dispute resolution clauses in bespoke contracts.

At a first glance, this may appear to be a simplistic explanation. However, given the premises that a number of disputes do not need or deserve handling through full-scale arbitration and that fast track arbitration is a proper and sound form of dispute resolution which entails both less time consumed and lower cost, there really is no other valid reason. This is also my personal experience: When fast track arbitration is explained to clients and lawyers outside the disputes sphere, the result is often implementation of layered clauses in future contracts.

### [F] Fast Track Arbitration Needs to Be Included in the Dispute Resolution Clauses

Although it happens from time to time, it is generally being too optimistic to hope that parties in dispute will agree on using fast track arbitration, where the arbitration clause envisages a conventional, full-scale procedure. In practice, if we are to increase the number of cases being handled under the fast track regimes, that option should be set out in the dispute resolution clause in the contract. If arbitration clauses routinely gave parties the option to adopt expedited procedures, those procedures could be more widely used. However, the best and clearly most effective solution is in my view to use layered clauses, where certain disputes are channelled into a fast track, i.e., that the parties are not just reminded of the option, but agree that certain disputes should be handled under a fast track regime when entering into the contract.

The OCC model clause can be used as an example a straightforward layered clause:

> Any dispute, controversy or claim arising out of or in connection with this contract, or the breach, termination or invalidity thereof, shall be finally settled by arbitration in accordance with the Rules of the Arbitration and Dispute Resolution Institute of the Oslo Chamber of Commerce in force at any time.
>
> The rules for fast-track arbitration shall apply where the amount in dispute does not exceed NOK [...]. The amount in dispute includes the claims made in the

request for arbitration and any counterclaims made in the response to the request for arbitration.

Where the threshold should be set can be discussed, but EUR 500,000 can easily be justified,[18] in many contracts even higher. If such multi-layered clauses are included in contracts, more cases will of course go to fast track arbitration and thus be resolved using less time and money. This will again create more fast track practice and certainly increase knowledge – a positive spiral for parties to arbitration processes and the legal community.

## §10.06 LOOK TO SWEDEN AND BEYOND: THE NORDICS

Fast track arbitration is Nordic in its essence. It is quick (as are the Nordic courts), less costly (as are often legal costs in the Nordics) and unbureaucratic – as the Nordic countries are when compared to many other countries. Thus, there is, in my view, potential for the Nordics being front runners internationally when it comes to fast track arbitration.

We are living in a very exciting time for arbitration. From having been something of a gentlemen's club with numerous esoteric unwritten rules arbitration – both international and domestic – arbitration has undergone a significant process of modernization over the past few years. There is much more transparency, much more diversity and all in all higher quality today. Processes and institutions that used to be considered slow and old fashioned are now leading the way as dynamic and forward-thinking players in the legal market.

At the same time, costs to resolve a dispute continue to increase, be it counsel, arbitrators, experts or venue. The parties – at least one of them – will eventually pick up the bill. Parties to arbitration processes have required and will continue to require the legal community to adopt proactive measures in order to reduce costs and time spent. Fast track arbitrations for the relatively smaller cases is a very good response: Fast track the disputes which neither need nor deserve a full-scale arbitration.

One way to further increase knowledge and quality of fast track arbitration could be for the Nordic institutions to develop fast track arbitration together. This could entail more innovation, more practice and more research on what works and what does not in a fast track process. The result does not need to be (and probably will not be) uniform the rules across the Nordics. The differences in the procedural law of the Nordic countries cannot be overcome by the four institutions alone. A uniform Nordic arbitration code is not likely in the near future. Furthermore, a joint set of rules may reduce the flexibility, and thus a main edge, of the individual institutions who know their domestic markets well and need to be able to differentiate their services and adapt swiftly in order to stay attractive as dispute resolution centres.

This is not to say that there is no room for more cooperation in order to improve the arbitration products offered. Cooperation between the Nordic institutions should,

18. By way of example, the ICC Expedited Procedure Provisions apply if the amount in dispute does not exceed USD 2 million.

in my view, rather be through establishing fora for exchange of experience and knowledge through workshops and seminars. A joint fast track arbitration forum or workshop where members of the Nordic arbitration community are invited would be a good start. We also need more research on fast track arbitration, and here the leading research centres have an important part to play.

CHAPTER 11

# Recent Finnish Supreme Court Case Law in the Arbitration Landscape

*Kirsi Kannaste & Laura Tuure*[*]

## §11.01 INTRODUCTION

This chapter is intended to provide the international readership of the Stockholm Arbitration Yearbook insight into the recent Finnish Supreme Court judgments related to arbitration. The three judgments discussed below have clarified what constitutes sufficient grounds for setting arbitral awards aside under Finnish law. The judgments address due process (the *Due Process* case, KKO 2018:48), the binding effect of arbitration agreements vis-à-vis third parties as guarantors (the *Guarantor* case, KKO 2019:111) as well as the relationship between arbitration, bankruptcy and property law (the *Bankruptcy Estate* case, KKO 2019:64). As the judgments involve issues that are likely to arise in many jurisdictions, the authors hope that even non-Finnish readers will benefit from the observations below. Lastly, the chapter also provides a brief update on the possible revision of the Finnish Arbitration Act (1992/967, the 'FAA').

## §11.02 FINDING A BALANCE BETWEEN A PARTY'S RIGHT TO PRESENT ITS CASE AND ARBITRATOR'S CONDUCT OF PROCEEDINGS: THE DUE PROCESS CASE (KKO 2018:48)

### [A] Introduction

The first of the Finnish Supreme Court's judgments to be discussed was rendered on 26 June 2018[1] and provides useful guidance on finding the balance between parties' right

* The authors would like to extend their thanks to associate trainee Malviina Linninen for her background research for the article.

1. *The Due Process Case*, decision No. KKO:2018:48, Case No. S2017/54 (KKO 26 June 2018).

to present their cases and arbitrators' right to conduct the proceedings. The question was whether the respondent was provided sufficient opportunity to present his case[2] when the arbitrator had ignored his observations on the amount of damages because they were not made until the closing statement. An insufficient opportunity to present one's case constitutes a ground for setting the award aside under section 41 of the FAA. The Supreme Court found that the arbitrator's procedural decision not to observe the respondent's arguments made in the closing statement had not violated the respondent's right to be heard or his right to sufficiently present his case. Consequently, the action for setting the award aside was rejected.

### [B] Background and the Lower Court Judgments

A had worked as the CEO of a Finnish and an Estonian company. Pursuant to A's executive employment contract, disputes arising out of the contract were to be resolved in arbitration in accordance with the arbitration rules of the Arbitration Institute of the Finland Chamber of Commerce (the FAI). The Finnish and Estonian companies had transferred all their claims to their principal owner E Group Plc (hereinafter, 'E') with the result that E and A became the parties to the arbitration clause.

In the arbitration E claimed damages from A arguing that A as CEO had made unlawful decisions regarding travel expenses, additional benefits and their processing in the accounts of the Finnish company, due to which the company had been ordered to pay tax increases, additional taxes and late payment penalties. During the arbitration, A opposed the claim in his written reply without submitting any specific grounds concerning the amount of the claim. However, later in his written closing statement, submitted after the hearing, A argued that the amount of the claim included payments for which he was not liable while at the same time accepting liability for the bulk of the monetary amount of the claim. In making the final award, the arbitral tribunal did not observe A's arguments presented in his closing statement concerning the amount of the damages because it was presented only after the hearing. The arbitral tribunal ordered A to pay the entire amount claimed by E.

A initiated setting aside proceedings in the Helsinki District Court on the ground that he had not been given a sufficient opportunity to present his case since the arbitral tribunal had not considered his submission concerning the amount of the claimed damages presented to the tribunal only after the hearing in a post-hearing brief (written closing statement). The District Court, however, found that A had had a sufficient opportunity to present his views on both the grounds and amount of the damages during the proceedings, but he had not availed himself of this opportunity before his closing statement. Furthermore, the District Court noted that the parties had effectively

2. Article V(1)(b) of the New York Convention provides that recognition and enforcement of the award may be refused if 'a party was otherwise unable to present its case'. The wording in s. 24.1 of the Swedish Arbitration Act (SFS 1999:116) provides that 'The arbitrators shall afford the parties, to the extent necessary, an opportunity to present their respective cases in writing or orally.' Similarly, the Arbitration Rules of the Arbitration Institute of the Stockholm Chamber of Commerce (2017, the 'SCC Rules'), Art. 23.2.

agreed on preclusion preventing new arguments being made in the written closing statements. If A's arguments concerning the alleged amount of damages made in his written closing statement had been admitted by the arbitral tribunal, E would have also had to have been reserved an opportunity to present counter-arguments and possible evidence which would have led to a delay from the originally agreed procedural plan.

The Court of Appeal likewise dismissed A's claim by stating that a clear procedural timetable had been established to secure the expediency of the proceedings. While (contrary to the District Court) the Court of Appeal considered that the arbitrator had not issued a completely unambiguous preclusion order, it also concluded that it ought to have been clear to the parties on the basis of the procedural timetable that the claims and their grounds were to be presented before the set date and that they would risk not being considered by the tribunal should they be presented after the set date without a weighty reason. Since A had not put forward any acceptable reason for not objecting to the amount of the damages before his closing statement, the Court of Appeal held that A had been given a sufficient opportunity to present its case.

### [C] The Judgment of the Supreme Court

The Supreme Court dismissed A's claims and confirmed the conclusion of the Court of Appeal. While section 41 of the FAA provides that an arbitral award may be set aside if the arbitral tribunal fails to give a party a sufficient opportunity to present its case, the Supreme Court noted that the preparatory legislative works state that it is sufficient that a party is *given* an opportunity to be heard – if that opportunity is not used, the arbitrators are not prevented from deciding on the matter. Furthermore, by referring to precedent KKO 2008:77,[3] the Supreme Court noted that the applicability of arbitration for the settlement of commercial disputes depends to a large extent on the binding nature and enforceability of the arbitration award. For that reason, the grounds on which the validity of awards can be disputed have both in domestic and in international regulation been sought to be restricted so that only clear formal errors and relatively gross procedural errors may result in the nullity or the setting aside of an award.

The Supreme Court also stated that according to section 25(2) of the FAA, either party may amend or supplement its claims and their grounds during the arbitral proceedings unless the proceedings would thereby be unduly delayed, but that this provision only applies if the parties have not agreed otherwise. As arbitration is largely based on party autonomy, and the procedural provisions of the FAA are mostly non-mandatory, if the parties have not agreed otherwise, the authority to decide is left to the arbitrators on the basis of section 23 of the FAA.[4] According to section 23 of the

3. *Polar Electro v. Werfen Australia*, Decision No. KKO:2008:77, Case No. S2006/716 (KKO 2 July 2008).
4. In this regard, s. 23 of the FAA essentially corresponds with Art. 19 of the Model Law.

FAA, when deciding on the procedure, the arbitrators need to observe the other provisions of the FAA and take into account the requirements of equal treatment of the parties and the expediency of the procedure. This means finding a balance between those provisions and the mandatory section 22 of the FAA, i.e., the requirement of providing the parties with a sufficient opportunity to present their cases – a general procedural principle of due process that cannot be dispensed with. If compromised, the violation of the principle forms grounds for setting the award aside pursuant to section 41 of the FAA.

In this particular case, the Supreme Court noted (similar to the Court of Appeal) that the procedural timetable that the parties had agreed on did not constitute such a preclusion order that would have expressly restricted the parties' right to present new arguments after the set date. According to the Supreme Court, such restriction would have required a clear preclusion order issued by the arbitrator and accepted by the parties. In the absence of a clear preclusion order, it is for the arbitral tribunal to evaluate on a case-by-case basis whether deciding on the matter would be unduly delayed should a party's procedural motion be accepted – such as A supplementing his grounds for the dismissal of part of the claims. According to the Supreme Court, the arbitrators have wide discretion in this regard, with the principles of equal treatment of the parties, the parties' right to present their case and procedural expediency defining the outlines of such discretion. Importantly, the Supreme Court noted that it is not a sufficient ground to set aside an award if the court hearing the case had evaluated the excessiveness of the delay differently from the arbitral tribunal. Instead, the bar for setting aside an arbitral award must be set to a level where the party's right to be heard has been infringed so that, as a consequence, the party has been denied a sufficient opportunity to present its case.

Continuing on the merits of this particular case, the Supreme Court found that A had not altered its claims during the arbitration, but he had, however, supplemented his grounds for dismissal in his closing statement. Since E had already in its statement of claim presented the claim to which A's observations related, the Supreme Court reasoned that A could have made the allegations about the amount of the claim already in the written phase before the hearing. Since A had not availed himself of this opportunity before his closing statement or presented any reason for such conduct, and since the established process timetable sought to structure the procedure so that the disputed issues would be identified already in the written phase, the Supreme Court concluded that A was able to anticipate that any submissions made at a later stage would risk not being considered. For the above reasons, the Supreme Court held that the arbitral tribunal's procedural decision was not to be considered unpredictable or surprising and that A's opportunity to present his case had not been undermined in a way to constitute a reason for setting the award aside under the FAA.

### [D] Analysis: Confirmation of Arbitrators' Margin of Discretion in Making Procedural Decisions

The Supreme Court's judgment in *Due Process* provides useful guidance to arbitrators in cases where the seat leads to the application of the FAA on the procedural issues.[5] It establishes that arbitrators indeed have wide discretion in balancing procedural decisions between the right to be heard, expediency of the proceedings and equal treatment of the parties – it is insufficient that as a result of an *ex post* assessment of the arbitral tribunal's procedural decision the competent court would view the delay to the proceedings differently from the tribunal, as long as the court finds that in making the procedural decision the party's opportunity to present its case was not denied. Therefore, the Supreme Court confirmed that it is up to the arbitrators to determine the excessiveness of the delay that would be caused if the action was allowed,[6] thus also allowing room for a procedural judgment rule, i.e., 'a court will not second-guess an arbitrator's exercise of his procedural judgment, if his decision is based on a bona fide assessment of the case and is reasonable under the circumstances'.[7]

The Supreme Court's reluctance to revisit the arbitral tribunal's procedural decision and the Court's recognition of the tribunal's discretion in making such decisions set a relatively high threshold for finding that a party was not given sufficient opportunity to present its case. The said approach can be seen to follow the position taken by the Supreme Court already previously in its landmark judgment KKO 2008:77, where the foothold of arbitrators' wide margin of discretion was confirmed. In that judgment, the Supreme Court found that the party's right to sufficiently present its case was not violated although the arbitral tribunal had based its decision on section 36 of the Finnish Contracts Act (the equivalent being section 36 of the Swedish Contracts Act) without specifically providing the parties with an opportunity to argue on the applicability of section 36 of the Contracts Act.[8] Together these judgments can be viewed to provide the arbitrators with a rather spacious safe harbour for making procedural decisions.

---

5. Better knowledge of the actual impact of robust case management decisions on the enforceability of arbitral awards in the particular judicial system(s) where the arbitration is either seated or the award is likely to be sought to be enforced has been introduced as one solution to fighting due process paranoia. *See* Remy Gerbay, *Due Process Paranoia* (Kluwer Arbitration Blog, 6 June 2016).
6. This is also a prerequisite for rightfully limiting the parties' right to amend or supplement their claims under s. 25(2) of the FAA.
7. *See* Klaus Peter Berger & J. Ole Jensen, *Due Process Paranoia and the Procedural Judgment Rule: A Safe Harbor for Procedural Management Decisions by International Arbitrators*, XIV(54) Rev. Bras. Arb. 73, 76 (2017).
8. Case KKO 2008:77 would in itself merit a full-length article and, indeed, it has spurred several commentaries. *See, e.g.*, Jan Waselius & Tanja Jussila, *Does the Adversarial Principle Prevail in Arbitration? – An Analysis of Case KKO 2008:77* (Juridiska Föreningens Tidskrift, 2011/4–5 p. 712). In this article, however, suffice it to say that together the two judgments have been seen to express a pro-arbitration attitude. *See* Mika Hemmo: *Tarpeellinen asianajotilaisuus, prekluusio ja oikeus suulliseen käsittelyyn – välimiesten harkintavallasta uuden kotimaisen oikeuskäytännön valossa* (Liikejuridiikka 2018/3 p. 42).

However, the users of arbitration need not to worry that the safe harbour would lead to their right to be heard being trodden on. In light of the factual background of the case, the procedural decision reached by the arbitrator perhaps cannot be described – at least from a Finnish and a Swedish perspective – as a particularly gutsy or surprising one but rather as a necessary means to prevent the proceedings from unnecessarily stretching and wadding. After all, A had been provided the right to present his case throughout the proceedings and decided not to present certain specific arguments before his closing statement without an acceptable reason.[9] While 'an instinct to protect the parties' due process rights is a vital part of any successful arbitrator's DNA',[10] the restriction of not allowing the respondent's arguments is likely to have been based on the arbitrator's comfort of knowing that the opportunity to present those arguments had been available to the respondent ever since he had received the statement of claim. Therefore, the judgment also confirms a certain requirement of active advocacy for the parties as well, meaning that they will need to actively and effectively make use of the means available to them to present their case.

The flipside of the Supreme Court's judgment is of course that it does not establish when the delay to the proceedings would have been acceptable, and the respondent's submission should have been accepted. (This of course was also not the issue to be resolved in the case.) This is particularly so since the Supreme Court did not base its decision on the (ambiguous) preclusion order having shaped the parties' reasonable expectations, as did the District Court and the Court of Appeal, but on the arbitrator's margin of discretion to assess whether excess delay to the proceedings would be caused by allowing A's late arguments and to balance such delay against A's right to be heard. In other words, the Supreme Court did not confront the issue regarding the existence of a valid preclusion order but instead considered the case as an issue of a party's right to present its case. Under such reasoning, the procedural timetable had only an indirect impact on the arbitrator's mandate to conduct the proceedings (and also meant that the arbitral tribunal's procedural decision not to observe A's arguments presented in his closing statement could not have been regarded as surprising by A).[11]

9. While the Swedish Supreme Court's recent judgment in *Belgor* (*Joint Stock Company Belgorkhimprom v. Koca Insaat Sanayi Ihracat Anonim Sirketi*, NJA 2019 p. 171, Case No. T- 5437-17 (NJA 20 March 2019), para. 41) did not concern a preclusion order or the right to submit supplementary rebuttal arguments in the closing statement but a respondent's right to submit an expert report to the arbitral tribunal, the requirement of an acceptable reason by the respondent having not availed itself of the right in accordance with the procedural timetable was also mentioned by the Swedish Supreme Court in its reasoning as to why the denial of the respondent's right did not constitute a denial of the party's right to present its case. Similarly, *CicloMulsion AG v. NeuroVive Pharmaceutical AB*, NJA 2019 p. 382, Case No. T796-18 (NJA 30 April 2019), para. 12.

10. Klaus Peter Berger & J. Ole Jensen, *Due Process Paranoia and the Procedural Judgment Rule: A Safe Harbor for Procedural Management Decisions by International Arbitrators*, XIV(54) Rev. Bras. Arb. 73, 76 (2017).

11. Certain case commentaries have pointed out that the Supreme Court should have specifically commented upon preclusion. Under Finnish law, party autonomy of course extends to preclusion, thus allowing the parties to freely agree on any kind of preclusion rules. The FAI Arbitration Rules (not applicable to the case at the time) also include a specific mandate to arbitrators to order preclusion (Art. 35 of the FAI Arbitration Rules in force as of 1 January 2020 and Art. 33.3 of the FAI Arbitration Rules in force as of 1 June 2013). However, the approach

However, as is well known, due process paranoia rests on a belief that domestic courts will have a stricter understanding of due process than arbitrators.[12] While the apprehensions regarding the possible unenforceability of the award belong to normal risk-awareness and guarantee a fair and one-time procedure for the parties, an unfounded and ill-suited extension of the parties' procedural rights is no longer based on the arbitrators' pursuit for a just outcome but rather on their fear of rendering an unenforceable award. The Supreme Court's judgment is therefore a necessary confirmation that under Finnish law only a denial of the party's opportunity to present its case will amount to such an infringement that the award is to be set aside.[13] The Supreme Court therefore expressed support for arbitrators' margin of discretion in reaching procedural management decisions.

## §11.03 AN ARBITRATION AGREEMENT IN A PRINCIPAL LOAN AGREEMENT AND ITS BINDING EFFECT VIS-À-VIS GUARANTORS: THE *GUARANTOR* CASE (KKO 2019:111)

### [A] Introduction

In *Guarantor*[14] from 19 December 2019, the Supreme Court found that an arbitration clause included in a loan agreement bound not only the debtor but also the company that had guaranteed the debtor's loan.[15] The action for setting the award aside on the basis of the arbitral tribunal having exceeded its mandate by resolving a question concerning the rights of a guarantor, i.e., a third party to the loan agreement was dismissed by the Supreme Court.

chosen by the Supreme Court nonetheless touches upon the same elements as the tribunal would have had to consider even if an ambiguous preclusion order had been in place: the requirements of equal treatment of the parties, the expediency of the procedure and the parties' opportunity to present their case.

12. Michael Polkinghorne & Benjamin Ainsley Gill, *Due Process Paranoia: Need We Be Cruel to Be Kind?* 34(6) J. Int'l Arb. 935, 938 (2017). In the 2015 survey by Queen Mary University of London and White & Case due process paranoia was defined as 'a perceived reluctance by tribunals to act decisively in certain situations for fear of the award being challenged on the basis of a party not having had the chance to present its case fully'. *See* Queen Mary University of London & White & Case: *2015 International Arbitration Survey: Improvements and Innovations in International Arbitration*, 2.
13. *See* the *Due Process Case*, para. 19.
14. Decision No. KKO:2019:111, Case No. S2018/745 (KKO 19 December 2019).
15. On a general level, the basic principle in Finland is that arbitration agreement is binding on the civil law universal successors of the parties to the arbitration agreement. Also in singular succession situations usually the one who acquires the right under the main agreement will be bound by the arbitration clause. However, the prerequisite is that the successor was aware or should have known about the arbitration agreement at the time of the succession. Möller Gustaf, *Välimiesmenettelyn perusteet* (Helsinki: Lakimiesliiton Kustannus, 1997), 21–22.

### [B] Background

As a legal background to the international reader, there is no specific provision under Finnish law as to the binding effect of an arbitration agreement other than towards a private guarantor, i.e., a natural person giving a guarantee.[16] Regarding private guarantors, section 37 of the Act on Guarantees and Third-Party Pledges (361/1999) explicitly provides that a private guarantor shall not be bound by an agreement, concluded before the dispute, to the extent that disputes concerning the guarantee are to be submitted to arbitration.[17]

As for the factual background of the case, company A had provided funding to companies active in developing countries. B was an Indian company that manufactured concrete elements for the construction industry and C an Indian real estate company. B and C belonged to the same group of companies owned by the Y family. XY acted as the CEO of both B and C.

A and B had signed a loan agreement in 2009 which contained an arbitration clause to the effect that disputes arising out of and relating to the loan agreement were to be finally settled in arbitration in accordance with the FAI Arbitration Rules by a sole arbitrator. The loan agreement was subsequently amended three times by separate amendment agreements in 2009 and 2012. All of the amendment agreements contained a dispute resolution clause that referred to the arbitration clause in the loan agreement.

Later in 2009, after the loan agreement had been executed, C became a guarantor for payment (as for its own debt) for B's debt to A. The dispute resolution clause in the guarantee undertaking provided that A was entitled to bring disputes arising out of the guarantee undertaking before Helsinki District Court as the first instance. However, in the third amendment agreement between A and B, C agreed that it would accept the amendment agreement and the amended amount of the loan under that agreement.

The CEO XY signed the loan agreement on behalf of B, and the guarantee undertaking and the third amendment agreement on behalf of C. All these three engagements determined Finnish law as the applicable law however specifically excluding the application of the Act on Guarantees and Third-Party Pledges to the guarantee undertaking.

A initiated arbitration proceedings against B and C jointly for the repayment of the loan under the loan agreement and the amendment agreements. C contested the arbitral tribunal's jurisdiction among others on the ground that no arbitration agreement had been entered into between C and A, and that any claims based on the

16. Pursuant to the Act on Guarantees and Third-Party Pledges (361/1999), the definition of private guarantor does not, however, cover a person who at the time of giving the is the managing director, a member of the board, the supervisory board or another comparable body, a general partner or a founder in the debtor corporation or foundation, or a parent corporation, nor a person who holds, directly or indirectly, at least one third of the shares or votes of a company, or has a comparable holding or control in another corporation.
17. Pursuant to the preparatory works of the Act (Government Bill 189/1998 vp, 72–73), neither does an arbitration clause concluded in the main agreement bind the private guarantor even if he has known about the clause and the guarantee has for example been included in the main agreement.

guarantee undertaking should be settled in the Helsinki District Court as provided in the guarantee undertaking.

The arbitral tribunal found that it had jurisdiction to resolve the matter by stating that C had become bound by the arbitration agreement because it was aware of the arbitration clause in the loan agreement when it undertook to guarantee the loan. In the final award rendered in 2015, the tribunal obliged B and C jointly to pay A the capital amount of the amended loan agreement with claimed interest.

C initiated court proceedings to set aside the award pursuant to section 41(1) of the FAA by arguing that the arbitral tribunal had exceeded its authority. Both the District Court and the Court of Appeal rejected C's action.

### [C] The Judgment of the Supreme Court

The question before the Supreme Court was whether the arbitral tribunal had exceeded its authority when it had decided the matter also in respect of guarantor C on the basis of the arbitration clause included in the loan agreement.

Previous Finnish case law establishes that a guarantor can invoke an arbitration agreement against the creditor concluded between the debtor and the creditor and, on the other hand, that an arbitration agreement in the principal loan agreement does not prevent claims being pursued against the guarantor in general courts where the guarantee does not include an arbitration agreement.[18] Also among Finnish legal scholars unanimity prevails as to the guarantor's ability to invoke an arbitration clause in the principal loan agreement at least when the guarantor knew or should have known about the arbitration clause when agreeing to guarantee the loan.[19] However, the question of whether a creditor can invoke an arbitration agreement in the principal loan agreement against the guarantor has not been the subject of previous case law. In this respect the views among Finnish legal scholars also vary. Some commentators are of the opinion that the guarantor should specifically accept to be bound by the arbitration agreement whereas some have argued that the creditor could invoke the arbitration agreement also where the guarantor knew or should have known about the arbitration agreement before agreeing to the guarantee.[20] Overall, however, the question of the binding effect of arbitration agreements in principal loan agreements in respect of non-private guarantors is unresolved in Finland.

The Supreme Court stated that the rule concerning private guarantors cannot be taken as a starting point for non-private guarantors because their need for protection may essentially deviate from that of private guarantors.[21] As for non-private guarantors, the general rule to be extracted from the Supreme Court judgment is however rather brief. According to the Court, the circumstances under which companies can

18. KKO 1930 II 555; KKO 1939 II 424; KKO 1953 II 103; KKO 1933 I 58; KKO 1936 II 507.
19. Möller, *supra* n. 15, 24–25.
20. No unanimity on this question can, however, be said to prevail. Möller, *supra* n. 15, 25.
21. The preparatory works for the Act on Guarantees and Third-Party Pledges (HE 189/1998 vp, 72) provide that private guarantors are in need of protection as they cannot be assumed to be familiar with arbitration and related costs.

undertake to guarantee other companies' loans can vary significantly. Therefore, the Supreme Court concluded that the assessment of the binding effect of an arbitration agreement in the principal loan agreement vis-à-vis the guarantor must be made case by case. Elements to be taken into account in such assessments include guidance available from previous case law,[22] the specific characteristics of arbitration, practical needs as well as the protection of the guarantor.

In this particular case, the Supreme Court stated that C was not a party to the loan agreement containing the arbitration clause, and the arbitration clause had not been expressly referred to in the guarantee undertaking. Further, according to the Supreme Court, the wording of the guarantee or the fact that C had agreed to the amended amount of the loan in the third amendment agreement did not as such mean that C had expressly agreed to be bound by the arbitration agreement. In addition, the guarantee had a specific dispute resolution clause. Therefore, according to the court, no far-reaching conclusions could be made regarding C's intention to be bound by the arbitration clause.

Regardless of the above, the Supreme Court then went on to summarise the particular circumstances of the case that led the Court to consider that C nonetheless was bound by the arbitration agreement. Those included the following: (i) the guarantee undertaking was issued in such a way that it concerned solely the amended loan agreement; (ii) the loan agreement, the amendment agreements and the guarantee undertaking were parts of the overall arrangement between the companies concerning the principal loan; (iii) no particular arguments to protect C in its capacity as the guarantor had been made; and (iv) the interpretation according to which C should be bound by the arbitration agreement could be supported by the practical need to concentrate the resolution of commercial disputes concerning the same overall arrangement to one dispute resolution method. On the above grounds the Supreme Court found that since A's claim concerned the repayment of debt under the principal loan agreement and the amended loan agreements, which C had agreed to guarantee as if it were its own debt, and since the dispute between A and B was to be finally settled in arbitration, the arbitrator had not exceeded its authority when it had found to have jurisdiction also in respect of C.

### [D] Analysis: The Need for Case-Specific Assessment Remains

The most obvious takeaway of the judgment is that although in this case the guarantor was found to be bound by the arbitration agreement, the judgment does not provide overarching generally applicable rules as to the binding effect of arbitration agreements in loan agreements extending to guarantors. The case-by-case assessment rule therefore provides little clarification to standard practice in Finland.

22. The Supreme Court's judgment in the *Guarantor Case* includes a summary of precedents KKO 1990:106, KKO 1992:155, KKO 2007:18 and KKO 2013:84 that may be relevant as guidance when considering whether the creditor is entitled to invoke an arbitration agreement in the principal loan agreement against the guarantor. It is not possible, however, to summarise those cases within the confines of this article.

In this particular case, there were specific circumstances that justified the conclusion in respect of C: the loan agreement and the guarantee undertaking were signed by the same person XY and, therefore, the guarantor C had become aware of the arbitration clause in the loan agreement. Furthermore, the guarantee undertaking specifically excluded the application of the Act on Guarantees and Third-Party Pledges, and although it included a specific dispute resolution clause, it was not an exclusive one. The dispute resolution clause in the guarantee undertaking also indicated that C had accepted the possibility of litigation in Finland and, therefore, according to the Supreme Court, the binding effect of the arbitration agreement could not be regarded as surprising for C.[23]

There are, however, certain statements in the judgment that extend beyond the circumstances of the particular case. First of all, the Supreme Court stated that the provisions in the Act on Guarantees and Third-Party Pledges concerning private guarantors do not as such serve as the basis of assessment in respect of non-private guarantors and, thus, recognising the different level of protection required by these two types of guarantors, the possibility to extend arbitration agreements to non-private third-party guarantors was unlocked. Moreover, the lack of certainty regarding the guarantor's intent to be bound by the arbitration agreement did not prevent the Supreme Court from reaching a conclusion that, given the overall circumstances of the case, C was indeed regarded to be bound by the arbitration agreement.

In addition, the Supreme Court attached particular weight to the need for arbitration to produce final and binding awards (which in turn requires that the grounds for setting aside awards are restricted), as well as to the practical need of concentrating all disputes relating to the same commercial arrangement to be resolved within one dispute resolution method. To this end, the Supreme Court repeated familiar wording from its previous case law by stating that only clear formal errors specified in the FAA and relatively gross procedural errors may cause the nullity or the setting aside of an award. As to claims concerning excess of mandate, the Supreme Court stated that the arbitral tribunal can be seen to have exceeded its authority for example when it has settled a dispute which is not governed by a valid arbitration agreement between the parties.[24]

What unfortunately still remains unresolved, however, is under which circumstances a non-private guarantor is not bound by an arbitration clause in the loan agreement. Is there a requirement that the guarantor was aware or should have known about the arbitration agreement before issuing the guarantee? In addition, rules regarding bankruptcy or third-party protection under property law may of course

23. In this regard, the reasoning of the Supreme Court is perhaps not the most ideal one. After all, for an Indian company with little understanding of the Finnish legal system, agreeing to litigate in Finland does not automatically mean that the company had perceived that the guarantee could also be settled in arbitration in Finland but it could have also consciously selected different dispute resolution mechanisms in the loan agreement and the guarantee undertaking. However, taking into account the overall specific circumstances of the case, the interpretation of the Supreme Court is very sensible.

24. *Polar Electro v. Wer;ren Australia*, Decision No. KKO:2008:77, Case No. S2006/716 (KKO 2 July 2008).

further cause the inapplicability of the arbitration agreement. Some more light is shed on the question of the binding subjective scope of arbitral agreements in the field of bankruptcy and property law in the Supreme Court judgment detailed below.

## §11.04 ARBITRATION, BANKRUPTCY, PLEDGE AGREEMENTS AND THIRD PARTY PROTECTION: THE *BANKRUPTCY ESTATE* CASE (KKO 2019:64)

### [A] Introduction

The Finnish Supreme Court's judgment in *Bankruptcy Estate*[25] rendered on 18 July 2019 concerns an arbitration agreement contained in a pledge agreement and its binding effect vis-à-vis the pledgor's creditors. The Supreme Court was presented with the question of whether, in view of the fundamental premise that an arbitration agreement is only binding on the parties to the arbitration agreement, the arbitral tribunal had exceeded its authority by resolving a question concerning the rights of third parties.[26]

### [B] Legal Framework

*Bankruptcy Estate* concerns questions pertaining to the perfection of pledge as well as the binding effect of a pledge agreement in bankruptcy. To this end, before introducing the facts of the case, some background information on Finnish law may be helpful to the international reader.

Compared to the other Nordic jurisdictions, the Finnish Bankruptcy Act (120/2004), comprehensively reformed in 2004, can be characterised by the high level of autonomy provided to creditors and the strength of the position of secured creditors.[27] Insolvency laws in Finland are largely mandatory and, therefore, the debtor cannot effectively agree, for example, to weaken the legal position of creditors or limit the right of succession of the bankruptcy estate to enter into contractual relationships instead of the debtor.[28] As a rule, agreements not concerning receivables subject to bankruptcy remain valid even after the bankruptcy. Thus, an arbitration agreement

25. Decision No. KKO:2019:64, Case No. S2017/675 (KKO 18 July 2019).
26. In addition, a subsequent question raised before the Court was whether a decision on the costs of arbitration can be set aside on the grounds of partially setting aside the award. While the question in itself is an interesting one, may it suffice to state within the confines of this article that the Supreme Court found that as the tribunal's award on costs did not specify the allocation of costs as to the claims decided by the tribunal and, therefore, it was not possible to determine the costs relating to the claims regarding which the tribunal was found to have exceeded its mandate, the tribunal's decision on costs was also to be set aside in its entirety.
27. Risto Koulu, *Konkurssioikeus*, in Risto Koulu, Heidi Lindfors & Johanna Niemi (eds), *Insolvenssioikeus* (Helsinki: WSOYpro 2004, Sanoma Pro, Alma Talent Oy 2017), 17.
28. Risto Koulu, *Johdatus insolvenssioikeuteen*, in Risto Koulu, Heidi Lindfors & Johanna Niemi (eds), *Insolvenssioikeus* (Helsinki: Alma Talent Oy 2017), 128–129; *The Social Insurance Institution of Finland v. Bankruptcy Estate of A*, Decision No. KKO:2016:100, Case No. S2015/236 (KKO 18 December 2016).

made before the bankruptcy binds the bankruptcy estate in disputes initiated after the bankruptcy and falling within the ambit of the arbitration agreement.[29] However, principles protecting third parties may restrict the validity of agreements in bankruptcy. If the dispute concerns a question that the debtor could not have agreed on with binding effect on its creditors before the bankruptcy, arbitration agreements concerning such questions are also not binding on the bankruptcy estate.[30]

As for pledge law, the principle of publicity is one of the overriding principles in Finland. A pledge agreement has legal effects only *inter partes* until perfection requirements are duly fulfilled.[31] The effectiveness of a pledge and the priority of the creditor created by the pledge in bankruptcy require, as a rule, that the pledge has been duly perfected. A pledge of receivables is created by a pledge agreement that must be perfected by a notice to the debtor.[32] A pledge agreement has no specific formal requirements, but in the notice the debtor must explicitly be required to make payments to the pledgee.[33] Since there are no formal requirements for pledge agreements, pursuant to section 2 of the FAA which states that any dispute in a civil or commercial matter which can be settled by agreement between the parties may be referred to arbitration, disputes regarding or arising out of pledge agreements can in principle be referred to arbitration. However, as above, mandatory provisions can restrict the binding scope of such agreements.

### [C] The Judgment of the Supreme Court

#### *[1] Background and the Arbitral Process*

Finnish entities A Ltd and B Ltd had entered into a pledge agreement over certain receivables in 2011. The pledge agreement contained an arbitration clause submitting all disputes arising out of the agreement to arbitration, the applicable law being Finnish law. The pledgor A was declared bankrupt in 2012. In 2013, B initiated arbitration against the bankruptcy estate of A relying on the arbitration clause in the pledge agreement.

B requested the arbitral tribunal to confirm, among other things, that the pledge had been duly perfected in accordance with Finnish law (claim 1.2) and that the pledge agreement and the pledge were in force and bound the bankruptcy estate (claim 1.7). The bankruptcy estate in turn requested the arbitral tribunal to dismiss the claim due to the tribunal's lack of jurisdiction. It contended that B's claims were preliminary questions to recovery to the bankruptcy estate, belonging to the exclusive jurisdiction of general courts.

29. KKO 1952 I 1; The preparatory works for the reform of the bankruptcy legislation (HE 26/2003 vp), 50, 130.
30. Möller, *supra* n. 15, 23.
31. Janne Kaisto, *Puhdas esinevastuu ja panttioikeuden yleiset opit (Die reine dringliche Haftung und die allgemeinen Lehren des Pfandrechts)*, Defensor Legis 5/2005 1005, 1009 (2005).
32. *See*, e.g., Jarmo Tuomisto, *Saatavan panttaus* (Helsinki: Talentum, 2015), 53.
33. *See*, e.g., *Cooperative Bank Y v. Bankruptcy Estate of A*, Decision No. KKO 2005:131, Case No. S2003/335 (KKO 13 December 2005).

In a voting decision, the arbitral tribunal granted B's claims. The arbitral tribunal found that the bankruptcy estate was bound by the arbitration agreement.[34] It considered that as far as the matter did not concern actual recovery to the bankruptcy estate, which pertained to the exclusive jurisdiction of general courts, the tribunal had the jurisdiction to resolve the validity, force and binding effect of the pledge agreement, as well as to review the evidence and legal facts concerning the interpretation of the pledge and the pledge agreement. However, the tribunal noted that it did not have jurisdiction to determine whether the pledge had been duly perfected (claim 1.2). Further, the tribunal noted that it did not have jurisdiction to determine whether the pledge was binding if the action was to be reversed in cases of recovery to the bankruptcy estate (claim 1.7), nor had this been requested by B.[35] In 2014, the tribunal rendered the final award where it confirmed B's claims and obliged the bankruptcy estate to cover B's legal costs and the costs of the arbitration.

### *[2] The Lower Court Judgments*

The bankruptcy estate sought to set aside the award in the Helsinki District Court on the basis that the tribunal had exceeded its authority (section 41(1)(1) of the FAA) when deciding on B's claims 1.2 and 1.7.

The Helsinki District Court found that it followed from the mandatory provisions of the Bankruptcy Act that an arbitration agreement concluded before bankruptcy did not bind the bankruptcy estate to the extent the dispute concerned the perfection of the pledge, which the debtor could not have agreed upon with a binding effect towards its creditors. By confirming that the pledge had been duly perfected, the arbitral tribunal had simultaneously also confirmed the binding effect of the pledge vis-à-vis bankruptcy creditors. Thus, the District Court set aside the arbitral award in respect of claims 1.2 and 1.7.

The Helsinki Court of Appeal upheld the District Court's judgment by reasoning that the perfection of the pledge and its binding effect towards third parties were questions that A did not have the authority to agree on in a manner binding the bankruptcy estate and A's creditors. Therefore, the arbitration agreement was also not binding on A's bankruptcy estate in these respects and the tribunal had in the same respects also exceeded its authority.

34. The decision was made by a majority vote. One of the three arbitrators voted in dissent and held that the bankruptcy estate was not bound by the arbitration agreement in relation to a dispute concerning the perfection of the pledge.
35. The dissenting arbitrator considered that claims 1.2 and 1.7 concerned the rights of third parties i.e., the rights of other bankruptcy creditors. The perfection of the pledge was a condition for the pledge to be binding towards third parties. As the bankruptcy estate had not accepted the arbitration agreement concluded by A or itself entered into a new arbitration agreement, the arbitration agreement did not bind the bankruptcy estate in relation to a dispute concerning the perfection of the pledge. Thus, it was a question of the scope of the arbitration agreement, but not of the exclusive jurisdiction of a general court over disputes involving perfection of a pledge.

#### *[3] The Judgment of the Supreme Court*

The question before the Supreme Court was whether the arbitration agreement was binding on the bankruptcy estate in relation to B's claims 1.2 and 1.7 and whether the arbitrators had exceeded their authority in resolving these claims.

The Supreme Court stated that, as in Sweden, it is established in Finland that a bankruptcy estate is not bound by an arbitration agreement made by the debtor in cases of recovery to a bankruptcy estate when the matter concerns the creditors' legal remedy to reverse an action regarding the debtor's property.[36]

Furthermore, the court stated that it has been established that principles protecting third parties mean that agreements cannot be made to the detriment of third parties regarding their rights in rem. Therefore, as the debtor cannot determine the in rem protection of a right based on an agreement, correspondingly, a bankruptcy estate cannot be bound by an arbitration clause regarding such protection.

Consequently, the Supreme Court noted that the tribunal had confirmed that the pledge had been duly perfected before the company was declared bankrupt (claim 1.2) and thereby the tribunal had not only confirmed the contractual obligations of the parties but gone beyond that, in essence confirming a direct effect on A's bankruptcy creditors who were not parties to the pledge agreement or the arbitration agreement.

In addition, according to the Supreme Court, also the confirmation by the tribunal of the validity of the pledge and the pledge agreement vis-à-vis the bankruptcy estate (claim 1.7) meant that the award had confirmed the pledge had been duly perfected. Therefore, the effects of the award were not restricted to resolving questions regarding the pledge agreement *inter partes*.

The Supreme Court therefore concluded that because A could not have agreed with B on the binding effect of the pledge vis-à-vis A's future bankruptcy creditors or on the fulfilment of the prerequisites for the pledge to obtain in rem protection in bankruptcy, there was no valid arbitration agreement in this respect and the bankruptcy estate was therefore not bound by the arbitration agreement concerning B's claims 1.2 and 1.7. Consequently, the arbitral tribunal had exceeded its authority and, as stipulated in section 41(1)(1) of the FAA, the award was to be set aside respectively.

### [D] Analysis: Binding Scope of Arbitration Agreements

The Supreme Court's judgment addresses the question of the mandate of an arbitral tribunal: the Supreme Court found that the arbitrators had exceeded their jurisdiction within the meaning of section 41(1) of the FAA when they had resolved questions that were not matters capable of being agreed on by the debtor with a binding effect on the bankruptcy estate and, thereby, resolved questions in respect of which there was no valid arbitration agreement. As stated above, it is also noteworthy that the Supreme

36. *Five Seasons Fritidsaktiebolags konkursbo (bankruptcy estate) v. Five Seasons Försäljningsaktiebolag*, NJA 1993 p. 641, Case No. Ö240-92 (NJA 26 November 1993); *Svenska Kredit*, NJA 2003 p. 3, Case No. Ö3504-01 (NJA 2 January 2003); Lars Welamson & Mikael Mellqvist, *Konkurs: och annan insolvensrätt* (Stockholm: Wolters Kluwer, 2017), 163.

Court's judgment does not concern arbitrability. In fact, the arbitrability provision (section 2) of the FAA is not even mentioned in the judgment.[37]

As freedom of contract is a fundamental rule in the Finnish judicial system, also disputes that may be settled by agreement may, as a rule, be validly resolved through arbitration.[38] Thus, also insolvency and property law related disputes, such as the validity of a pledge agreement and other *inter partes* aspects, are in principle *arbitrable,* i.e., capable for settlement by arbitration. However, arbitrability is a separate question of the binding subjective scope of the arbitration agreement. Therefore, the dispute could as such be arbitrable but, to the extent that the dispute involves the determination of a third-party right, e.g., when it concerns perfection of a pledge, the parties to the arbitration agreement are not capable of agreeing on the binding effect of the pledge *ultra partes*, rendering the matter beyond the scope of the arbitration agreement and therefore also beyond the jurisdiction of the tribunal.[39]

Whether an arbitration agreement shall remain valid vis-à-vis the bankruptcy estate is ultimately defined by the nature of the disputed issue itself. Indeed, as the Supreme Court confirmed, if the matter does not touch solely on the obligations *inter partes* but instead concerns an issue that the debtor could not have agreed on before the bankruptcy with a binding effect towards the bankruptcy estate, the bankruptcy estate is not bound by the arbitration agreement.[40] It was specifically confirmed in the judgment that third-party rights' protection in rem, i.e., the validity of the right in rem (such as a pledge) in relation to third parties to their detriment, is an issue of this kind. Therefore, the Supreme Court's decision preserved the protected position of bankruptcy creditors.

A similar approach has been taken in Sweden. As is well known, in the Swedish system a bankruptcy estate is bound by an arbitration agreement entered into by the debtor company with respect to contractual rights succeeded to by the bankruptcy estate.[41] On the other hand, a bankruptcy estate is not bound by an arbitration agreement where the dispute concerns an issue over which the debtor company could not have had a right of disposition, such as whether a particular claim enjoys protection in rem in a future bankruptcy of the debtor company.[42]

37. Section 2 of the FAA provides that any dispute in a civil or commercial matter which can be settled by agreement between the parties may be referred for final decision to be made by one or more arbitrators. In cases where an arbitral tribunal would have resolved a non-arbitrable question, the award would be invalid under s. 40(1) of the FAA.
38. In Sweden *see*, e.g., *Five Seasons Fritidsaktiebolags konkursbo (bankruptcy estate) v. Five Seasons Försäljningsaktiebolag*, NJA 1993 p. 641, Case No. Ö240-92 (NJA 26 November 1993).
39. Tuomas Hupli, *Välimiesmenettely konkurssissa ja yrityssaneerauksessa*, Defensor Legis 3/2015, pp. 437 and 444.
40. The position is similar to that taken in Sweden. *See*, e.g., Torgny Håstad, *Något om skiljedomsavtals verkan mot tredje man, Process och exekution: vänbok till Robert Boman* (Uppsala: Iustus Förlag, 1990), 180.
41. *See*, e.g., Lars Heuman, *Skiljemannarätt* (Stockholm: Norstedts Juridik AB 1999), 102; Stefan Lindskog, *Skiljeförfarande – En kommentar* (Stockholm: Norstedts juridik, 2012), 224–225; Anders Relden & Ola Nilsson, *Chapter 3 The Arbitration Agreement*, in Ulf Franke, Annette Magnusson, et al. (eds), *International Arbitration in Sweden: A Practitioner's Guide* (Alphen aan den Rijn: Kluwer Law International, 2013), 75.
42. In *Five Seasons Fritidsaktiebolags konkursbo (bankruptcy estate) v. Five Seasons Försäljningsaktiebolag*, NJA 1993 p. 641, Case No. Ö240-92 (NJA 26 November 1993), the Swedish Supreme

## §11.05 CONCLUDING REMARKS

Finland is in a strong position to serve as a place for international arbitration especially due to its political neutrality, geographical location, respect for the rule of law, freedom from corruption, and well-functioning regulatory and operational setting. As for the regulatory setting, the FAA was enacted in 1992 (and there have been five minor amendments since). Although the almost 30-year-old Act has worked well in practice, there have been initiatives for revision particularly in order to align the Finnish arbitration regulation with the UNCITRAL Model Law. In 2019, the Finnish Ministry of Justice launched a reform project, at the initiative of the Finland Chamber of Commerce, in order to determine the needs for revision under the current Act. The reform project is, however, still in the early stages.

One of the most notable distinctive features of the FAA that has generated calls for revision is the possibility to challenge an arbitral award on two separate legal grounds: (i) that the arbitral award is invalid (section 40) and (ii) that the arbitral award should be set aside (section 41). Section 40 of the Act provides that the court may declare an arbitral award invalid if, among others, the matter resolved by arbitration is non-arbitrable or if the award is in conflict with *ordre public*. Section 40 does not include any time limit for filing the action for annulment. Pursuant to section 41, a court may set aside an arbitral award upon the request of a party within three months of the date on which the party received a copy of the award, when certain conditions are met. These include, among others: (i) arbitrators exceeding their mandate, (ii) challenges on the arbitrators' impartiality and independence and (iii) the arbitrators' failure to give a party a sufficient opportunity to present its case.

Both sections 40 and 41 have remained unrevised since the enactment of the FAA in 1992, and the elimination of the invalidity provision (section 40) has been the focus of the revision discussion, in particular because the contents of the section have been criticised for being inconsistent with both the UNCITRAL Model Law and the general idea of effective business dispute resolution. Especially the absence of a time limit for filing an action for annulment of the arbitral award is seen as undermining the finality of arbitral awards.[43] However, this internationally rare distinction between the invalidity and annulment of an arbitral award is similar to the Swedish legislation, where the division was upheld as a result of the recent 2019 revision of the Swedish Act. In this context it should also be noted that under the UNCITRAL Model Law the grounds for setting aside an award can be invoked as grounds for refusal of recognition and enforcement of an arbitral award even after the time limit for filing an action for setting aside the award has expired. Thus, as far as the grounds for invalidity are concerned, the difference between Finnish law and the Model Law is more apparent than real.

Court confirmed that a bankruptcy estate was not bound by an arbitration agreement where the dispute concerned unlawful distribution of assets since the parties to the arbitration agreement, i.e., the debtor and its contracting party, could not have entered into an agreement regarding distribution of assets with binding effect towards the bankruptcy estate and its creditors.

43. Heidi Merikalla-Teir, *Finland Takes Important Steps to Increase Its Attractiveness as a Venue for International Arbitration: Launch of the Revision Process of the Finnish Arbitration Act Announced* (Kluwer Arbitration Blog, 17 May 2019).

With regard to parties from foreign countries, it would probably be appropriate to provide that the current grounds for invalidity would instead form such grounds for refusal of recognition and enforcement. Those grounds can be validly invoked even when the time limit for filing an action for setting aside the award has expired.

During 2014–2019, twelve applications for annulling an award were brought before the Finnish Courts of Appeal or the Supreme Court.[44] In two cases, the award was annulled in full, and in one case the award was annulled in part. The roughly estimated average length of the annulment proceedings in which the judgment was rendered during 2014–2019 was two years nine months from the date the proceedings were initiated in a district court until the date of the final judgment. As is also portrayed by the recent judgments, the Finnish courts recognise the integrity of arbitration by avoiding unnecessary interference in decisions rendered by arbitral tribunals, and can thus be said to be generally arbitration friendly.

While there are no official statistics on the number of arbitral awards challenged in Finland, following the international trend, the number could also be on the rise in Finland. In order for arbitration to maintain its reputation as an effective and final method of solving disputes, the finality of an arbitral award must be able to be determined by the court without undue delay which, as stated above, is also one of the key priorities in the discussions about the reform of the FAA.[45] Indeed, in the discussion concerning the Finnish legal reform, it has been deemed desirable to simplify and shorten the setting aside proceedings of an arbitral award by centralising the actions in one court, changing over to a discretionary appeal model and reducing the time limit for raising the claim from three months to two months. Eventually, in particular, the speed and the costs of the arbitration proceedings depend on the finality of the arbitral award. The other proposed changes to the Act include derogating from the written form requirement for arbitration agreements and adding provisions on granting interim measures by the arbitral tribunal.

As is apparent from the above, the number of challenges to arbitral awards in Finland does not as such merit the revision of the FAA. However, improvements such as reducing the time limit for setting the award aside from three to two months, as in the recent Swedish Arbitration Act reform, would also be a welcome change in Finland. Furthermore, the causality requirement introduced in Sweden in respect of setting aside an arbitral award, i.e., the requirement that the arbitrators not only exceeded their mandate, but that they did so '*in a manner that probably influenced the outcome*' of the case, could also be a thinkable reform in Finland. After all, the 'relatively gross procedural errors' requirement expressed in the Supreme Court's judgments commented on above implies the same requirement of causality.

44. The first instance for hearing annulment cases is the District Court level. There is no publicly available database on the number of annulment cases overall, and the above number of cases is based on queries made to the courts. Out of the twelve cases, nine cases were decided finally by the Courts of Appeal and three cases by the Supreme Court.
45. *See* Merikalla-Teir, *supra* n. 43.

A revision of the FAA is anticipated and would support the development of arbitration in Finland. In the meantime, the recent Supreme Court judgments demonstrate that the Finnish courts understand and support the values and principles of arbitration.

## SOURCES

### Literature

Berger, Klaus Peter & Jensen, J. Ole, *Due Process Paranoia and the Procedural Judgment Rule: A Safe Harbor for Procedural Management Decisions by International Arbitrators*, XIV(54) Rev. Bras. Arb. 73 (2017).

Gerbay, Remy, *Due Process Paranoia* (Kluwer Arbitration Blog, 6 June 2016).

Hemmo, Mika, *Tarpeellinen asianajotilaisuus, prekluusio ja oikeus suulliseen käsittelyyn – välimiesten harkintavallasta uuden kotimaisen oikeuskäytännön valossa* (Liikejuridiikka 2018/3 p. 42).

Heuman, Lars, *Skiljemannarätt* (Stockholm: Norstedts Juridik AB 1999).

Hupli, Tuomas, *Välimiesmenettely konkurssissa ja* yrityssaneerauksessa, Defensor Legis 3/2015.

Håstad, Torgny, *Något om skiljedomsavtals verkan mot tredje man, Process och exekution: vänbok till Robert Boman* (Uppsala: Iustus Förlag, 1990).

Kaisto, Janne, *Puhdas esinevastuu ja panttioikeuden yleiset opit (Die reine dringliche Haftung und die allgemeinen Lehren des Pfandrechts)*, Defensor Legis 5/2005 1005 (2005).

Koulu, Risto, *Johdatus insolvenssioikeuteen*, in Koulu, Risto, Lindfors, Heidi & Niemi, Johanna (eds), *Insolvenssioikeus* (Helsinki: Alma Talent Oy, 2017).

Koulu, Risto, *Konkurssioikeus*, in Koulu, Risto, Lindfors, Heidi & Niemi, Johanna (eds), *Insolvenssioikeus* (Helsinki: Alma Talent Oy, 2017).

Koulu, Risto, *KKO:n ratkaisut kommentein 2018:I: KKO 2018:48 Prekluusio välimiesmenettelyssä* (Helsinki: Talentum Fokus, 2018).

Lindskog, Stefan, *Skiljeförfarande – En kommentar* (Stockholm: Norstedts juridik, 2012).

Merikalla-Teir, Heidi, *Finland Takes Important Steps to Increase its Attractiveness as a Venue for International Arbitration: Launch of the Revision Process of the Finnish Arbitration Act Announced* (Kluwer Arbitration Blog, 17 May 2019).

Möller, Gustaf, *Välimiesmenettelyn perusteet* (Helsinki: Lakimiesliiton Kustannus, 1997).

Ovaska, Risto, *Välimiesmenettely – kansallinen ja kansainvälinen riidanratkaisukeino* (Helsinki: Edita, 2007).

Polkinghorne, Michael & Gill, Benjamin Ainsley, *Due Process Paranoia: Need We Be Cruel to Be Kind?* 34(6) J. Int'l Arb 935 (2017).

Relden, Anders & Nilsson, Ola, *Chapter 3 The Arbitration Agreement*, in Franke, Ulf, Magnusson, Annette, et al. (eds), *International Arbitration in Sweden: A Practitioner's Guide* (Alphen aan den Rijn: Kluwer Law International, 2013).

Tuomisto, Jarmo, *Saatavan panttaus* (Helsinki: Talentum, 2015).

Waselius, Jan & Jussila, Tanja: *Does the Adversarial Principle Prevail in Arbitration?: An Analysis of Case KKO 2008:77* (Juridiska Föreningens Tidskrift, 2011/4–5 p. 712).

Welamson, Lars & Mellqvist, Mikael, *Konkurs: och annan insolvensrätt* (Stockholm: Wolters Kluwer, 2017).

Queen Mary University of London & White & Case: *2015 International Arbitration Survey: Improvements and Innovations in International Arbitration.*

**Case Law**

*Bankruptcy Estate case*, Decision No. KKO:2019:64, Case No. S2017/675 (KKO 18 July 2019).

*CicloMulsion AG v. NeuroVive Pharmaceutical AB*, NJA 2019 p. 382, Case No. T796-18 (NJA 30 April 2019).

*Cooperative Bank Y v. Bankruptcy Estate of A*, Decision No. KKO 2005:131, Case No. S2003/335 (KKO 13 December 2005).

*The Guarantor Case*, Decision No. KKO:2019:111, Case No. S2018/745 (KKO 19 December 2019).

*The Due Process Case*, Decision No. KKO:2018:48, Case No. S2017/54 (KKO 26 June 2018).

*Five Seasons Fritidsaktiebolags konkursbo (bankruptcy estate) v. Five Seasons Försäljningsaktiebolag*, NJA 1993 p. 641, Case No. Ö240-92 (NJA 26 November 1993).

*Joint Stock Company Belgorkhimprom v. Koca Insaat Sanayi Ihracat Anonim Sirketi*, NJA 2019 p. 171, Case No. T- 5437-17 (NJA 20 March 2019).

*Polar Electro v. Werfren Australia*, Decision No. KKO:2008:77, Case No. S2006/716 (KKO 2 July 2008).

*Svenska Kredit*, NJA 2003 p. 3, Case No. Ö3504-01 (NJA 2 January 2003).

*The Social Insurance Institution of Finland v. Bankruptcy Estate of A*, Decision No. KKO:2016:100, Case No. S2015/236 (KKO 18 December 2016).

*Rakentaja-yhtymä Anselm Autio v. Komljakoff*, Decision No. KKO 1930 II 555, Case No. 3672. (KKO 6 November 1930).

*Määttänen v. Sakkola Municipality*, Decision No. KKO 1933 I 58 (28 August 1933).

*Salomaa v. O.Y. Laatuvilja*, Decision No. KKO 1936 II 507, Case No. 442 RD 1936 (KKO 17 November 1936).

*Korpilahden Osuuskauppa r.l. v. Niemi*, Decision No. KKO 1939 II 424, Case No. 675/286 VD 1939 (KKO 22 September 1939).

*Kivinen v. Ristola and Lämpö-Linko Oy*, Decision No. KKO 1952 I 1 (KKO 8 January 1952).

*Järvelin v. Järvelin*, Decision No. KKO 1953 II 103 (KKO 16 September 1953).

## LEGAL SOURCES

Arbitration Rules of the Finland Chamber of Commerce in force as of 2020.
Arbitration Rules of the Finland Chamber of Commerce in force as of 2013.
Arbitration Rules of the Arbitration Institute of the Stockholm Chamber of Commerce (2017).
Act on Guarantees and Third-Party Pledges (361/1999).
Bankruptcy Act (120/2004).
Finnish Arbitration Act (1992/967).
Preparatory works for the reform of the bankruptcy legislation (HE 26/2003 vp).
Preparatory works for the Act on Guarantees and Third-Party Pledges (HE 189/1998 vp).
Swedish Arbitration Act (SFS 1999:116).
UNCITRAL Model Law on International Commercial Arbitration of 1985.

CHAPTER 12

# Court Control on Arbitral Awards: Public Policy, Uniform Application of EU Law and Arbitrability

*Giuditta Cordero-Moss*

## §12.01 INTRODUCTION

Arbitration is increasingly criticized in the public debate.[1] Among the criticism being raised is that arbitration does not ensure an accurate application of the law.

The need to ensure an accurate application of European Union (EU) law led the Court of Justice of the European Union (CJEU), in the famous *Achmea* case,[2] to exclude the arbitrability of investment disputes between EU Member States. Thus, for *investment* arbitration, the CJEU denied arbitrability of disputes relating to EU law.

Also in *commercial* arbitration, various national courts have excluded the arbitrability of disputes that require an accurate application of EU law, notably in the field of commercial agency. The CJEU in *Achmea* seemed, to the contrary, to accept that commercial arbitral tribunals may solve disputes relating to EU law, as long as appropriate court control is possible. The different treatment of commercial and investment arbitrability was justified by the CJEU, quite unconvincingly as will be explained below, with a distinction between the respective sources of the arbitral power.

In this chapter, I will discuss how the intensity of the control that courts may exercise on arbitral awards may have an impact on the courts' willingness to accept

1. As a consequence of the growing criticism, two working groups of the UNCITRAL are discussing improvements to commercial arbitration (Working Group II) and to investment arbitration (Wokring Group III).
2. Case C-284/16 *Slovak Republic v. Achmea BV*.

arbitrability of disputes. This applies particularly to the court control on the award's compatibility with public policy (*ordre public*).

The thesis of this chapter is that courts may independently evaluate whether the award is compatible with public policy. This should be sufficient to prevent that confidence in arbitration is eroded. At the same time, this does not mean that courts shall be able to revise arbitral awards with regard to the merits.

The opposite attitude is to postulate that courts may not independently evaluate public policy issues but are bound by the evaluation of those issues that was made by the arbitral tribunal. This would mean that the courts are expected to delegate the question of public policy to arbitral tribunals. Such an attitude contributes to the growing suspicion against arbitration and may result in restricting the scope of what disputes are arbitrable.

Assuming that the courts owe deference to the arbitral tribunal's evaluation of the public policy issues might seem to be the most arbitration-friendly position, but it ends up damaging arbitration. Likewise, permitting independent court evaluation of the public policy issues seems to be a position hostile to arbitration, but it preserves a larger scope of arbitrability.

## §12.02 COURT CONTROL

Courts may deal with arbitral awards in two contexts: at the initiative of the losing party, they may set aside an award; at the initiative of the winning party, they may enforce the award.

### [A] Sources

The body which controls the validity or the enforceability of an award derives its jurisdiction from the applicable law.

In case of challenge to the award's validity, the applicable law is the arbitration law prevailing in the place of arbitration. This also applies to the relatively large part of investment disputes which is carried out under arbitration rules that are not designed specifically for investment arbitration, such as the UNCITRAL Arbitration Rules, the Rules of the Stockholm Chamber of Commerce (SCC) or the Arbitration Rules International Chamber of Commerce (ICC). These investment disputes will be subject to the regime applicable to commercial arbitration. For investment arbitration that is carried out under the ICSID Convention,[3] annulment of awards is regulated in Article 52 of the convention itself, without reference to national law.

3. Convention on the Settlement of Investment Disputes between States and Nationals of Other States (adopted 18 Mar. 1965, entered into force 14 Oct. 1966) UNTS 575 (ICSID Convention or Washington Convention).

In case of enforcement of an award, the applicable law is, in the 161 countries which have ratified it, the New York Convention.[4] For investment arbitration that is carried out under the ICSID Convention, enforcement of awards is regulated in the convention itself, which creates in Article 54 an obligation to enforce the award as if it was a final court decision rendered in that state.

National arbitration law differs from country to country; therefore the court's process in case of challenge of the award's validity needs to be analysed on the basis of the national law that is applicable in the specific case. For the sake of simplicity, however, we will assume here that the national arbitration law corresponds to the UNCITRAL Model Law, as it does, more or less literally, in the eighty countries that are considered to be 'Model Law countries'.[5]

The court's powers, to the extent that is relevant here, are equivalent in the New York Convention and in the Model Law.[6] Therefore, the analysis can be made without distinguishing between court control carried out in connection with challenge to the award's validity and court control carried out in connection with enforcement of the award. It should be emphasized, however, that if the law applicable in a specific case does not belong to a Model Law country, or if it implements the Model Law with some discrepancies from the original, it will be necessary to verify whether the law applicable to annulment has diverging regulation.

The criteria contained in the New York Convention and the Model Law largely correspond to the criteria contained in Article 52 of the ICSID Convention. These criteria are the following.

An award rendered by an arbitral tribunal whose jurisdiction did not rest on a valid and binding arbitration agreement is not valid[7] and not enforceable.[8] An award rendered as a result of a proceeding that did not give each of the parties the possibility to present its case is not valid[9] and not enforceable.[10] An award rendered in excess of the jurisdiction granted on the arbitral tribunal is not valid[11] and not enforceable.[12] An award rendered by an arbitral tribunal that was not constituted in accordance with the parties' agreement or the applicable law, or as a result of proceedings that did not comply with the parties' agreement or the applicable procedural rules is not valid[13] and

4. Convention on the Recognition and Enforcement of Foreign Arbitral Awards (adopted 10 Jun. 1958, entered into force 7 Jun. 1959) UNTS 330 (New York Convention). For an updated status, *see* https://uncitral.un.org/en/texts/arbitration/conventions/foreign_arbitral_awards/status2.
5. UNCITRAL, 1985 Model Law on International Commercial Arbitration, revised in 2006 http://www.uncitral.org/pdf/english/texts/arbitration/ml-arb/07-86998_Ebook.pdf. For an updated status, *see* http://www.uncitral.org/uncitral/en/uncitral_texts/arbitration/1985Model_arbitration_status.html.
6. This correspondence is intentional, *see* Gary Born, *International Commercial Arbitration* 2nd ed. (Alphen aan den Rijn, Kluwer Law International 2014), pp. 3186, 3340; Giuditta Cordero-Moss, *International Commercial Contracts* (Cambridge University Press 2014), p. 224.
7. Article 34(2)(a)(i) of the Model Law; Art. 52(1)(a) and (b) of the ICSID Convention.
8. Article 36(1)(a)(i) of the Model Law; Art. V(1)(a) of the New York Convention; Arts 25 and 26 of the ICSID Convention.
9. Article 34(2)(a)(ii) of the Model Law; Art. 52(1)(d) and (e) of the ICSID Convention.
10. Article 36(1)(a)(ii) of the Model Law; Art. V(1)(b) of the New York Convention.
11. Article 34(2)(a)(iii) of the Model Law; Art. 52(1)(b) of the ICSID Convention.
12. Article 36(1)(a)(iii) of the Model Law; Art. V(1)(c) of the New York Convention.
13. Article 34(2)(a)(iv) of the Model Law; Art. 52(1)(a) and (c) of the ICSID Convention.

not enforceable.[14] An award rendered on a non-arbitrable subject matter is not valid[15] and not enforceable.[16] An award infringing fundamental principles (public policy) is not valid[17] and not enforceable.[18] In addition, in the New York Convention and in the UNCITRAL Model Law, there is a rule on public policy which covers not only the procedural public policy but also the substantive public policy. While the ICSID Convention does not mention public policy as a ground to annul an award, it has a specific rule on the necessity that the award be reasoned. Regarding enforcement, ICSID awards are subject to the same regime as final court decisions in the enforcement country. To the extent the enforcement country has a public policy exception, therefore, it will also apply to ICSID awards.

### [B] Court Control Is Not an Appeal

A glance at the abovementioned provisions shows that judicial control is not meant to be an appeal: setting aside or refusing enforcement of an award cannot be based on the sole circumstance that the award contains errors in fact or errors in law. It is only issues relating to the parties' consent to arbitrate or to fairness of the proceedings that can trigger annulment or refusal of enforcement – in addition to the issues of public policy and arbitrability.

Judicial control, therefore, is not the same as a review of the award on the merits, neither in respect of the assessment of facts nor in respect of the application of law. The direct consequence of this limitation of judicial control is that an award is final and binding, even if it contains errors of fact or errors of law. This is the basis upon which the system of arbitration, as we know it today, rests: international conventions, national laws, courts of law, legal doctrine and practitioners support the aim that arbitration is to be an effective and efficient means of dispute resolution. To achieve this aim, they widely recognize that awards must be final and binding. Effectiveness and efficiency of arbitration are important principles of arbitration law, and at the origin of the widespread arbitration-friendly attitude that has characterized legislation and case law in the past decades.

In respect of the public policy exception, the distinction between public policy review and appeal on the merits is founded on the very narrow scope of what can be deemed to infringe public policy. As will be seen below, an error in the application of the law does not qualify as public policy infringement. While the wrong application of the law may contribute to the award conflicting with public policy, it is certainly not a sufficient condition to set aside or refuse to enforce the award on this basis.

Erroneous application of the law is not even a relevant theme in the public policy review: the appropriate theme is whether the recognition or enforcement of the award

14. Article 36(1)(a)(iv) of the Model Law; Art. V(1)(d) of the New York Convention.
15. Article 34(2)(b)(i) of the Model Law; Art. 52(1)(b) of the ICSID Convention.
16. Article 36(1)(b)(i) of the Model Law; Art. V(2)(a) of the New York Convention; Arts 25 and 26 of the ICSID Convention.
17. Article 34(2)(b)(ii) of the Model Law; Art. 52(1)(d) of the ICSID Convention, with respect to procedural public policy.
18. Article 36(1)(b)(ii) of the Model Law and Art. V(2)(b) of the New York Convention.

would result in a serious breach of fundamental socio-economic principles in the court's socio-economic system. There may, of course, be overlapping between these two themes: but we should not lose sight of what the proper purpose of court review is: ensuring that the award does not infringe important principles – not ensuring that the award applies the law accurately.

## §12.03 ARBITRABILITY

One of the grounds for setting aside an award or refusing its enforcement is that the dispute may not be solved by arbitration. There is no autonomous standard for arbitrability. The New York Convention specifies, in Article V(2)(a), that arbitrability is determined under national law. Likewise, the Model Law specifies, in Articles 34(2)(b)(i) and 36(2)(b)(i), that the standard for arbitrability is determined by the national law of the court. Hence, it is up to the national legislator or to the courts to determine whether a certain type of dispute may be solved by arbitration or not.

### [A] Arbitrability and Court Control

As was mentioned above, one of the pillars of the institution of arbitration is that arbitral awards are final and are not subject to any form of appeal on the merits – be it on the evaluation of evidence and assessment of the facts, or on the application of the law. The tribunal's autonomy in determining and applying substantive law is a fundamental feature of arbitration.

However, there is a growing mistrust against this autonomy.

In commercial arbitration, some domestic courts have recently denied the arbitrability of disputes on commercial agency contracts out of a fear that the important policies of agency law may not be accurately applied.[19] In investment arbitration, concerns are voiced, among others, about the ability of arbitrators to understand public interest issues.[20]

As I have explained elsewhere,[21] the scope of arbitrability is linked to the degree of control that the court may exercise on the award.

Thirty years ago, the famous *Mitsubishi* decision[22] opened an era of arbitration-friendliness and permitted arbitrability of disputes relating to competition law. Until that time, disputes involving competition law were among those considered to involve too important and general interests to be arbitrable. The condition under which *Mitsubishi* extended the scope of arbitrability was that courts be permitted to give a

19. *See*, for references, footnotes 24–28 below.
20. Report of Working Group III (Investor-State Dispute Settlement Reform) on the work of its thirty-fifth session (New York, 23–27 Apr. 2017), A/CN.9/935, paras 82–88; Report of Working Group III (Investor-State Dispute Settlement Reform) on the work of thirty-sixth session (Vienna, 29 Oct. 2018–2 Nov. 2018), A/CN.9/964, paras 64–108.
21. Giuditta Cordero-Moss, 'Mitsubishi: Balancing Arbitrability and Court Control', in Horatia Muir Watt, Lucia Bíziková, Agatha Brandão de Oliveira and Diego Fernández Arroyo (eds), *Global Private International Law, Adjudication Without Frontiers* (Elgar 2019), 82–91.
22. *Mitsubishi Motors Corp. v. Soler Chrysler-Plymouth, Inc.*, 473 U.S. 614, 628 (1985).

'second look' on the accurate application of the law – notably, in the occasion of court control and, in particular, through the rule on public policy.

A similar opening was made by the CJEU with *Eco Swiss*.[23]

This approach permits the courts to review the determination of whether important policies (such as, in these cases, competition law) are applicable, as well as their application – as long as the interests at issue are such that they qualify to fall into the realm of public policy, and for the only purpose of verifying whether these interests were seriously infringed. The large scope of arbitrability, therefore, is directly linked to the existence of judicial control over the awards, albeit a restricted control.

The *Mitsubishi* decision introduced an era of constant expansion for arbitrability. The pendulum, however, seems today to be swinging towards a more restrictive approach. Courts in EU states such as Austria,[24] Belgium,[25] Germany[26] and England[27] have already denied arbitrability[28] of disputes regarding contracts of commercial agency. EU agency law is deemed to be necessary for the achievement of the internal market. Hence, these courts have affirmed that disputes concerning commercial agency should be decided by courts of EU Member States: choosing a court outside the EU, or choosing arbitration, may endanger the effective enforcement of EU law.

Moreover, the *Achmea* decision, discussed further below, denied arbitrability of investment disputes relating to EU law.

### [B] Arbitrability and the Arbitral Tribunal's Independence from the Parties' Agreement

The legitimacy of arbitration is threatened by the fear that arbitration may become a mechanism by which the parties circumvent the application of important policies reflected in overriding mandatory rules such as competition law. By exercising their party autonomy, the parties may choose a governing law that permits them to avoid these rules. The fear is that arbitral tribunals, feeling bound by the parties' choice of law, lend themselves to the circumvention of important policies.

Arbitral tribunals may in fact fear that, if they consider these policies notwithstanding the parties' agreement on a different law, they may exceed their power and thus render an invalid and unenforceable award.

23. Case C-126/97, *Eco Swiss China Time Ltd. v. Benneton Int'l NV*, 1999 E.C.R. I-3079.
24. OGH 1.3.2017, 5ob 72/16y, Ecolex 520 (2017).
25. Cour de Cassation, 16.11.2006, PAS. 2006, I, No. 11; Cour de Cassation, 14.1.2010, PAS. 2010, I, No. 12; Cour de Cassation, 3.11.2011 PAS. 2011, I, No. 1.
26. Bundesgerichtshof, 5.9.2012, *Neue juristische Wochenschrift* (2012).
27. *Accentuate Limited v. Asigra Inc.* [2009] EWHC (QB) 2655.
28. Or they deny the recognition of a contractual choice of forum in favour of a court not located within the EU, such as was the case for the German decision referred to in footnote 26 above. This responds to the same rationale, i.e., that matters relating to commercial agency shall be decided by courts located in the EU in order to ensure a uniform application of EU law. Therefore, it can be expected that the same courts would also deny arbitrability if the contract contained an arbitration clause.

As I have discussed elsewhere,[29] the fear that courts may, in the name of excess of power, set aside or refuse enforcement of an award as a consequence of the tribunal's independent selection or application of the law, is ill-founded. While there are nuances particular to each legal system, most arbitration laws give the tribunal the power to make its own, independent legal reasoning. What the principle of due process requires in many systems, however, is that the tribunal informs the parties of its legal considerations, so that the parties are given the possibility to comment or present new evidence that becomes relevant in view of the tribunal's legal reasoning.[30]

There seems to be a growing awareness in the arbitration community of the necessity to ensure that the award gives due consideration to the law applicable to the merits.[31] Coupled with the courts' possibility to take a second look at awards to ensure that fundamental principles are not violated, this should be a sufficient basis to ensure the arbitration-friendly attitude opened by *Mitsubishi* – even though the second look is not a perfect system.[32]

Ambitions to enhance the autonomy of arbitration by restricting court control over awards may turn out to be counterproductive. Fears about the accuracy with which arbitral tribunals apply the law may affect the scope of arbitrability. Likewise, the scope of arbitrability is linked to the intensity of judicial control, as will be discussed below.

## §12.04 PUBLIC POLICY: THE INTENSITY OF JUDICIAL CONTROL

One of the grounds for setting aside an award or refusing its enforcement is that the award conflicts with public policy. There is no autonomous standard for public policy. The New York Convention specifies, in Article V(2)(b), that the relevant public policy is that of the court. Likewise, the Model Law specifies, in Articles 34(2)(b)(ii) and 36(2)(b)(ii), that the standard for public policy is determined in accordance with the court's principles. Although the specific content of public policy is national, there is an autonomous interpretation of the criteria for defining public policy, as will be seen below.

29. Giuditta Cordero-Moss, 'The Arbitral Tribunal's Power in Respect of the Parties' Pleadings as a Limit to Party Autonomy (on Jura Novit Curia and Related Issues)', in Franco Ferrari (ed.), *Limits to Party Autonomy in International Commercial Arbitration* (Juris 2016), 289–330; Giuditta Cordero-Moss, 'EU Overriding Mandatory Provisions and the Law Applicable to the Merits', in Franco Ferrari (ed.), *The Impact of EU Law on International Commercial Arbitration* (Juris 2017), 317–349. For a comparative analysis of this issue in 14 national jurisdictions, as well as in international law, *see* Giuditta Cordero-Moss and Franco Ferrari (eds), *Iura Novit Curia in International Arbitration* (Juris 2018), with general report by Giuditta Cordero-Moss (463–487).
30. For a description of due process requirements in this context *see* Cordero-Moss and Ferrari, *Iura novit curia in international arbitration*, cit.
31. Luca Radicati di Brozolo, 'Mandatory Rules and International Arbitration' (2012) 23 *Am. Rev. Int'l Arb.* 49, 66ff.
32. Massimo Benedettelli, '"Communitarization" of International Arbitration: A New Spectre Haunting Europe?' (2011) 73(4) *Arbitration Int'l* 583, 597; William Park, 'Private Adjudicators and the Public Interest: The Expanding Scope of International Arbitration' (1986) 12 *Brook. J. Int'l L.* 642.

### [A] Public Policy Review and Accurate Application of the Law

It is only serious breaches of fundamental principles that justify setting aside or refusing enforcement of an award on the basis of public policy.[33] The mere fact that the law was applied wrongly is not a sufficient basis to apply the public policy exception.

The scope of what may qualify as an infringement of public policy, therefore, is narrow. This is necessary to prevent that the public policy exception becomes a channel to review the award on the merits. Hence, review of the compatibility of an award with public policy is not the same as an appeal, because the review is not directed at evaluating whether the law was applied correctly. The review is meant to verify whether upholding or enforcing the award would seriously infringe fundamental principles. The threshold and the parameters in a public policy review are different from those of an appeal.

In his opinion in *Genentech*,[34] the Advocate General (AG) to the CJEU seemed to assume that public policy may be applied to any and all violations of competition law, given that the *Eco Swiss* decision had determined that competition law is of fundamental importance in the EU legal order. This, however, is not a correct assumption. That competition law may be deemed to be part of public policy does not mean that any and all violations of competition law infringe public policy. The CJEU has repeatedly stated that only serious violations of competition law lead to infringement of public policy, for example, in *Renault* and *Diageo*.[35]

The above is the result of balancing between the interest in maintaining the autonomy and efficiency of arbitration, on the one hand, and the interest in ensuring that fundamental principles are safeguarded, on the other hand. The narrow scope of the public policy review should be deemed sufficient to prevent that court control exceeds its borders and becomes an appeal on the merits.

However, as will be explained below, under the so-called minimalist theory, courts shall act under an additional restraint: if the arbitral tribunal has evaluated the issue of public policy, according to this theory, the court shall owe deference to the tribunal's evaluation. This may deprive judicial control of efficacy, which in turn may have negative effects on arbitrability.

33. Born, *International Commercial Arbitration*, cit., 3312, 3647; Cordero-Moss, *International Commercial Contracts*, cit., 246ff. *See also* Giuditta Cordero-Moss, 'Article 5 (2) (b), Public Policy', in Herbert Kronke, Dirk Otto, Patricia Nacimiento and Nicola Christine Port (eds), *Recognition and Enforcement of Foreign Arbitral Awards: A Global Commentary on the New York Convention*, 2nd ed. (Wolters Kluwer).
34. Case C-567/14 (*Genentech*), AG Opinion, paras 70–72.
35. Cases C-38/98 (*Renault*) and C-68/13 (*Diageo*). These decisions were rendered in connection with recognition and enforcement of foreign court decisions under, respectively, the 1968 Brussels Convention on Jurisdiction and the Enforcement of Judgments in Civil and Commercial Matters, and under the Brussels I Regulation (EC) No. 44/2001. More extensively, *see* Giuditta Cordero-Moss, 'Inherent Powers and Competition Law' (2017) 6(2) *Eur. Int'l Arb. Rev.* 69–94, 79f.

### [B] Maximalist and Minimalist Approach

Elsewhere, I have discussed the different theories regarding the intensity of court control in respect of the award's conformity with public policy and commented the dichotomy between minimalist and maximalist theory.[36] Briefly, the minimalist theory postulates that courts are bound by the evaluation the arbitral tribunal made of the award's compliance with public policy; according to the maximalist theory, courts may independently verify whether the award infringes public policy.

The CJEU has so far not taken an explicit stance on which theory is compatible with EU law – although, as will be discussed below, the AG has repeatedly argued that the minimalist theory is not acceptable. However, for commercial arbitration, the CJEU in *Achmea*[37] has tacitly supported the maximalist approach. The CJEU assumed that a uniform interpretation of EU law may be ensured thanks to the control that courts of Member States exercise over arbitral awards. If the CJEU owed deference to the arbitral tribunal's evaluation, this assumption would not be possible to make. Hence, the CJEU assumed the maximalist approach. For investment arbitration, the CJEU took a different position in *Achmea*, as will be discussed in section §12.05 below.

The Bundesgerichtshof (BGH), in its referral of *Achmea* to the CJEU,[38] as well as the AG in the opinion for *Achmea*,[39] endorsed the maximalist theory. The BGH and the AG assumed that the controlling court of the Member State shall be entitled to independently evaluate whether the award is compatible with fundamental principles of EU law. This would mean that, since the controlling Member State court may submit requests for preliminary rulings, court control on awards would ensure uniformity of interpretation of EU law also in arbitration – at least as long as serious breaches of fundamental principles are concerned. This maximalist approach is in accordance with the abovementioned *Mitsubishi* and *Eco Swiss* approaches. Arbitrability of disputes concerning EU law is acceptable because of the possibility to exercise court control on the awards.

The minimalist approach, on the contrary, assumes that Member State courts shall owe deference to the arbitral tribunal's evaluation made in the award.[40] If the arbitral tribunal has evaluated the public policy issue, this evaluation will have to be accepted by the court. The minimalist approach was criticized by the AG in the already mentioned *Genentech*. The AG affirmed that the minimalist approach would deprive court control of its meaning and would not be compatible with EU law. This is because having to accept the arbitral tribunal's evaluation effectively means delegating the matter to the arbitral tribunal. As arbitral tribunals may not request preliminary rulings

36. Cordero-Moss, 'Inherent Powers', cit.; Cordero-Moss, 'Mitsubishi: Balancing Arbitrability and Court Control', cit.
37. Case C-284/16 (*Achmea*).
38. Bundesgerichtshof, 3 Mar. 2016, I ZB 2/1.
39. Case C-284/16 (*Achmea*), Opinion of AG Wathelet., paras 251–260.
40. Radicati di Brozolo, 'Mandatory Rules and International Arbitration', cit.; *see also*, criticising this approach, Christophe Seraglini and Jérôme Ortscheidt, *Droit de l'arbitrage interne et international*, Domat Montchrestien, 2013, para. 982.

under Article 267 of the TFEU, the uniformity of the interpretation of EU law would not be not ensured.[41]

Notwithstanding that the AG had several times brought up the relationship between court control and the compatibility of (commercial) arbitration with EU law,[42] the CJEU had, prior to *Achmea*, never expressed an opinion on the matter. It had, however, tacitly accepted that (commercial) disputes relating to EU law may be arbitrable, as pointed out by the AG in the *Achmea* opinion.[43] The CJEU seems in *Achmea*, indirectly and as an obiter dictum, to endorse the AG's opinion that commercial disputes regarding the interpretation of EU law may be subject to arbitration, as court control permits the court to review the interpretation of EU law made by the tribunal and, by requesting preliminary rulings, to ensure uniformity of the interpretation of EU law.[44]Thus, the CJEU seems to endorse the maximalist theory.

However, as will be discussed in section §12.05 below, the CJEU has denied arbitrability of investment disputes based on intra-EU treaties, based on the lack of an effective method to control the uniform application of EU law.[45] The decision is based on an unconvincing distinction between commercial and investment arbitration.

That the distinction between commercial and investment arbitration is unconvincing, gives reason to fear that the distinction may be abandoned. Abandoning the distinction may have two possible outcomes: either the CJEU accepts the arbitrability of investment disputes (which is unlikely) or it expands the inarbitrability also to commercial disputes.

As was mentioned above, national courts in various EU Member States have already taken a very restrictive approach to arbitrability of disputes relating to commercial agency.

In such a climate of mistrust against arbitration, it does not seem that arbitration can be promoted by insisting on a minimalist approach to court control - quite the contrary.

In fact, in the context of corruption and economic crime, the minimalist theory seems to have been abandoned in its country of origin, France.[46]

---

41. Case C-567/14 *Genentech v. Hoechst and Sanofi-Aventis Deutschland*, Opinion of AG Wathelet.
42. In addition to the already mentioned opinions in the *Genentech* and the *Achmea* case, that were both rendered by Whatelet, *see also* Case C-352/13 *CDC Hydrogen Peroxide v. Evonik Degussa and Others*, Opinion of AG Jääskinen.
43. Case C-284/16 (*Achmea*), AG Opinion para. 243.
44. Case C-284/16 (*Achmea*), para. 54.
45. Case C-284/16 (*Achmea*).
46. *See*, in the areas of corruption and money laundering: Cour d'appel de Paris, 4.11.2014, nr. 13/10256; Cour d'appel de Paris, 25.11.2014, nr. 13/1333; Cour d'appel de Paris, 7.4.2015, nr. 14/00480; Cour d'appel de Paris, 14.4.2015, nr. 14/07043; Cour d'appel de Paris, 21.2.2017, nr. 15/01650; Cour d'appel de Paris, 16.1.2018, nr. 15/21703. *Contra, see* Cour d'appel de Paris, 20.1.2015, nr. 13/20318; Cour d'appel de Paris, 24.2.2015, nr. 13/23404. In the area of procedural fairness, *see* Cour d'appel de Paris, 8.11.2016, nr. 13/12002.

## §12.05 *ACHMEA'S* DISTINCTION BETWEEN COMMERCIAL AND INVESTMENT ARBITRATION

The specific nature of investment disputes may require considerations that are not generally made in commercial disputes, in particular, due to the public interests involved in investment arbitration. However, it should be remembered that a considerable part of investment disputes is carried out under the rules applicable to commercial arbitration. From a procedural point of view and from the point of view of court control, investment disputes resolved under the rules for commercial arbitration do not differ from regular commercial disputes.[47]

A basis for distinguishing between commercial and investment arbitration is asserted by the CJEU in *Achmea*. This basis for distinction is not convincing.

The CJEU's reasoning in *Achmea* starts recalling the principles of mutual trust and of sincere cooperation between EU Member States. According to Article 19 of the TFEU, these principles are preserved by the judicial system established under Article 267 of the TFEU.[48] According to this provision, courts of Member States have to make a request for preliminary rulings to the CJEU whenever interpretation of EU law is necessary to render a decision on a given dispute. This ensures consistency and uniformity of EU law. The system of preliminary rulings is available to Member State courts. The CJEU has repeatedly[49] rejected requests of preliminary rulings submitted by commercial arbitral tribunals, as these are not deemed to be courts in the sense of Article 267 of the TFEU. For investment tribunals, the AG suggested, in the opinion to *Achmea*,[50] that a different approach should be taken. According to the AG, investment tribunals are courts in the meaning of Article 267 of the TFEU and can submit requests for preliminary ruling. In the AG's opinion, therefore, investment tribunals are part of the judicial system that ensures a uniform interpretation of EU law. The CJEU, however, rejected this suggestion and considered investment tribunals in line with commercial tribunals with respect to the possibility to submit a preliminary ruling.[51] Both commercial and investment arbitration, therefore, are excluded from the possibility of requesting preliminary rulings under Article 267 of the TFEU.

As regards the consequences of this exclusion, however, the CJEU distinguishes the two types of arbitration. It is this distinction that is of interest here.

As was mentioned in section §12.04 above, the CJEU has so far indirectly accepted the arbitrability of commercial disputes involving EU law. However, the CJEU in *Achmea* affirms that this approach may not be applied to investment arbitration.

47. Affirming that legitimacy issues shall be taken into consideration both in investment and in commercial arbitration, *see also* Diego P. Fernández Arroyo, 'Nothing Is for Free: The Prices to Pay for *Arbitrabilizing* Legal Disputes', in Loïc Cadiet, Burkard Hess, Marta Requejo Isidro (eds), *Privatizing Dispute Resolution* (Nomos 2019), 617–646, 632 ff.
48. Case C-284/16 (*Achmea*), paras 34–37.
49. The Opinion rendered by Advocate Generale Wathelet in the *Achmea* case refers to the following cases: *Nordsee* (C-102/81), *Rich* (C190/89), *Eco Swiss* (C-126/97), *Denuit and Cordenier* (C-125/04), *Mostaza Claro* (C-168/05), *Allianz and Generali Assicurazioni Generali* (C-185/07), *Gazprom* (C-536/13), *Genentech* (C-567/14).
50. Case C-284/16 (*Achmea*), AG Opinion, paras 100–131.
51. Case C-284/16 (*Achmea*), paras 43–49.

In paragraph 55, the CJEU affirms that: 'While [commercial arbitration proceedings] originate in the freely expressed wishes of the parties, [investment arbitration proceedings] derive from a treaty by which Member States agree to remove from the jurisdiction of their own courts, and hence from the system of judicial remedies which the second subparagraph of Article 19(1) TEU requires them to establish in the fields covered by EU law [...], disputes which may concern the application or interpretation of EU law.'

The CJEU, therefore, does not accept that court control is sufficient, for investment arbitration, to ensure a uniform interpretation of EU law. The CJEU thus relies on an alleged difference between the freely expressed wishes of the parties in commercial proceedings and the removal of jurisdiction based on a treaty in investment arbitration. Moreover, the CJEU examines the arbitration agreement upon which the *Achmea* dispute was based, contained in the Bilateral Investment Treaty (BIT) between the Slovak Republic and the Netherlands. The CJEU points out that the arbitration agreement provided that the award would be final,[52] that the tribunal would apply its own procedure[53] and, by choosing the seat, would be able to determine which procedural law would govern the proceedings,[54] and that court control over the award is restricted.[55]

On the basis of these characteristics, the CJEU affirms that, contrary to its practice in the field of commercial arbitration, it cannot consider investment arbitration as a mechanism for dispute resolution that ensures a uniform interpretation of EU law. Therefore, arbitration agreements contained in investment treaties (the CJEU mentions only intra-EU treaties, but the CJEU's logic seems applicable to any treaties) are not compatible with EU law.[56]

As a result of this ruling, the BGH annulled the award rendered in *Achmea*.[57]

## §12.06 IS THE DISTINCTION CONVINCING?

The characteristics listed by the CJEU and that led to the conclusion that investment arbitration, unlike commercial arbitration, is not compatible with EU law, are the following.

The award is final; the tribunal applies its own procedure and, by choosing the seat, is able to determine which procedural law governs; courts' possibility to control the award is restricted. With regard to this latter, the CJEU also mentions that commercial arbitration agreements are freely entered into between the parties, whereas investment arbitration is based on treaties removing jurisdiction from state courts and thus from the special judicial system provided for in Article 267 of the TFEU.

52. *Ibid.*, para. 51.
53. *Ibid.*
54. *Ibid.*
55. *Ibid.*, para. 53.
56. *Ibid.*, paras 55 and 56.
57. BGH I ZB 2/15, 31 Oct. 2018.

A glance at these characteristics shows that they apply equally to investment and to commercial arbitration.

In particular, in *Achmea*, the arbitral tribunal was subject to the UNCITRAL Arbitration Rules. The UNCITRAL Arbitration Rules apply to ad hoc arbitral proceedings. They are originally meant to be applied to arbitral proceedings solving commercial disputes. However, they can also be applied to investment disputes. Also arbitration rules issued by institutions such as the SCC, the ICC or the London Court of International Arbitration (LCIA) are originally meant to be applied to commercial disputes but can equally be applied to investment disputes if the basis for jurisdiction makes reference to them.

Arbitral proceedings subject to UNCITRAL Arbitration Rules, like all arbitral proceedings subject to institutional arbitration rules such as the SCC, the ICC or the LCIA, are governed by the same regime irrespective of whether they concern a commercial or an investment dispute. They will be subject to the parties' agreement, to the chosen arbitration rules and to the arbitration law of the country where the tribunal has its seat.

In the BIT that gave rise to *Achmea*, the seat of the arbitral tribunal was not pre-determined. This, however, is not a characteristic exclusive to investment arbitration. There are many commercial arbitration agreements that do not specify the seat of arbitration. That the seat shall be specified is not a condition for an arbitration agreement to be valid.[58] That arbitral proceedings are subject to the arbitration law of the seat, even though the seat was not chosen by the parties, has been accepted by the European Court of Human Rights.[59]

Among the consequences of the common procedural regime to which commercial and investment disputes are subject is that awards are subject to the same court control irrespective of whether they are rendered in a commercial or in an investment dispute.

A distinction should be made for investment awards under the ICSID Convention. These awards are rendered under the special regime of the ICSID Convention, and not under the abovementioned procedural rules that also apply to commercial arbitration. ICSID awards are not subject to annulment proceedings before the courts of the country in which the tribunal had its seat[60] and are not enforced under the New York Convention. As already mentioned, this latter difference does not necessarily mean that the regime, for what is relevant here, is structurally different from awards rendered under rules applicable to commercial arbitration. According to the ICSID Convention,[61] awards shall be enforced as if they were final judgments rendered in the country of enforcement. To the extent the enforcement court has, in respect of domestic judgments, the possibility to evaluate whether enforcement would be compatible with public policy, there is therefore a possibility to exercise court control also when

58. For example, it is not a requirement for validity of the arbitration agreement under Art. II of the New York Convention.
59. *Tabbane v. Switzerland*, para. 31.
60. ICSID awards may be annulled by an ad hoc committee under Art. 52 of the ICSID Convention.
61. ICSID Convention, Art. 54.

enforcing ICSID awards. However, because ICSID arbitration has a different regime than investment arbitration that is carried out under UNCITRAL Rules or under other rules also applicable to commercial arbitration, the AG affirms in the Achmea opinion that choice of ICSID arbitration should be avoided.[62]

For all other investment awards that are not rendered under the ICSID convention, the AG points out that the procedural characteristics are the same as in commercial arbitration. In particular, court control can be exercised in the same way on commercial and on investment awards.[63]

In this particular context, the reasoning made by the AG is compelling. There appear to be no reasons for distinguishing between commercial and investment awards in this respect. Certainly there is in the applicable sources no expressed basis for treating court control on investment awards differently from court control on commercial awards, as long as both types of award are rendered under the same arbitration rules and arbitration laws. The very circumstance that the Achmea award was challenged before, and eventually annulled by, national courts in Germany, where the arbitral tribunal had its seat, is one of many examples that investment awards are subject to the same court control as commercial awards, when they are rendered under the same arbitration regime.

Particular attention should be devoted here to the argument made by the CJEU according to which commercial awards are based on an arbitration agreement freely entered into by the parties, whereas investment awards are based on a treaty by which the Member State removes jurisdiction on the dispute from its own courts.

As was seen above, the CJEU seems to accept that, for commercial arbitration, court control is a sufficient means to ensure a uniform interpretation of EU law – because the controlling court may request preliminary rulings under Article 267 of the TFEU. The CJEU emphasizes, however, that investment arbitration is based on treaties according to which the state removes jurisdiction over the dispute from its courts, and thus from the justice system that, under Article 267 of the TFEU, is meant to ensure a uniform interpretation of EU law.

In my opinion, it is doubtful that this distinction from commercial arbitration has any bearing on the matter. The CJEU's reasoning may be split into four elements that are examined below.

*First,* it is not exclusive to investment disputes that arbitration is based on the removal of jurisdiction from the host state's courts. Also commercial arbitration is based on the removal of jurisdiction from state courts: according to Article II of the New York Convention, for example, a court must decline jurisdiction if it is seized with a dispute that falls within the scope of an arbitration agreement. Thus, commercial awards are also based on the removal of jurisdiction from state courts.

*Second,* it is not exclusive to investment arbitration that arbitration may be removed from the justice system provided for by Article 267 of the TFEU: under some arbitration laws, parties may waive their right to challenge the validity of the award. If they do so, courts will not have the possibility to evaluate the award's compliance with

62. Case C-284/16 (*Achmea*), AG Opinion, para. 253.
63. *Ibid.*, paras 244–250.

fundamental principles of EU law. Moreover, if the parties to a commercial dispute choose a country outside of the EU as seat for the arbitral tribunal, courts of Member States will not have jurisdiction to annul the award. This also applies if the parties have not chosen a seat, and the (commercial) arbitral tribunal chooses a seat outside the EU. Furthermore, if the winning party enforces the award outside of the EU, the courts of Member States will not have jurisdiction to control the award in the enforcement phase either. Thus, commercial awards may also be rendered outside of the system established by Article 267 of the TFEU.

*Third,* it is not exclusive to investment arbitration that the arbitration agreement is based on a treaty. Arbitration law is mainly based on domestic statutes or case law, but the 161 countries who have ratified the New York Convention have entered into a public international law commitment to ensure that, i.a., their courts decline jurisdiction if a dispute is covered by an arbitration agreement. They also have committed themselves to ensure that their courts enforce foreign arbitral awards, save for the restricted control mentioned above. Thus, also, commercial arbitration is based on a treaty.

All this is equivalent to saying that commercial arbitration is based on a treaty by which Member States agree to remove from the jurisdiction of their own court's disputes which may concern the application or interpretation of EU law. As was seen above, if the seat and the place of enforcement are outside of the EU, the treaty also leads to removing these disputes from the system of judicial remedies which the second subparagraph of Article 19(1) TEU requires them to establish in the fields covered by EU law. This description of commercial arbitration is equal to the description of investment arbitration quoted above and used by the CJEU to describe investment arbitration and to substantiate the distinction between commercial and investment arbitration.[64] In other words, as just shown, the description applies equally to commercial and to investment arbitration. Hence, this is not a basis for distinguishing between the two types of arbitration.

*Finally,* it is not exclusive to commercial arbitration that the arbitration agreement is based on the parties' free will. The system of investment arbitration provides that the host state in a treaty, in a domestic investment statute, in a concession agreement or otherwise, gives investors an open offer to arbitrate.[65] If the investor initiates an arbitration, it is deemed to have accepted the offer. The investor is not obliged to initiate an arbitration: usually, the investor is free to pursue its rights before any national courts having jurisdiction. If the investor brings a claim before a national court, it will be deemed not to have (yet) accepted the open offer to arbitrate. Hence, courts will not have lost their jurisdiction. The arbitration agreement, therefore, is also based on the parties' free will in investment arbitration: the state's free will is embodied in the state's open offer to arbitrate, and the investor's free will is embodied in the commencement of arbitral proceedings, that can be construed as an acceptance of the

64. Case C-284/16 (*Achmea*), para. 55.
65. Jan Paulsson, 'Arbitration Without Privity' (1995) 10 *ICSID Rev. – Foreign Inv. LJ* 232, 234; Christoph Schreuer et al., *The ICSID Convention: A Commentary* 2nd ed. (Cambridge University Press 2009), paras 195–205.

offer. Also in investment arbitration, the arbitration agreement is based on the meeting of the parties' will.

The analysis made above shows that the CJEU in *Achmea* does not provide a proper basis for distinguishing between the two types of arbitration.

## §12.07 CONCLUDING REMARKS

To continue enjoying the friendly framework from which it has benefitted in the past forty years, arbitration also henceforth must show that it is capable of deserving the confidence of the legal systems.

Insisting on its unlimited autonomy, for example, insisting on the minimalist theory according to which courts owe deference to the public policy evaluations made in the award, deprives court control of any significance. This does not seem to be a productive route to gain confidence. To the contrary, it may provoke the opposite reaction and lead to arbitrability being restricted. It should be kept in mind that the scope of arbitrability is determined under national law. The threshold for determining that a dispute is not arbitrable, therefore, is easier to lower than if the standard were international. As we have seen above, courts in a number of states have already shown a restrictive approach to arbitrability.

Some may be reluctant to supporting the maximalist theory, out of fear that it would be equivalent to allowing an appeal against the award. This is a misunderstanding.

The maximalist approach permits a meaningful court control but does not mean that courts review the award on the merits. The court will make its own, independent evaluation of whether the award is compatible with fundamental principles. However, this is not the same as second-guessing the arbitral tribunal's evaluation of the facts or application of the law. The court and the tribunal may have a different opinion as to the infringement of fundamental principles, but this is a different theme from what the court would evaluate if it was revising the award on the merits. The court's opinion on how the facts should have been evaluated or the law should have been applied is not relevant. If the award contains errors, but the errors do not reach the high threshold required to breach public policy, the court may not set aside or refuse enforcement of the award. If the errors lead to a serious breach of fundamental principles, the court may set aside or refuse enforcement of the award because the award breaches public policy – not because the award misjudged the facts or applied the law wrongly.

It has been suggested,[66] in the context of the minimalist theory, that it should be possible to exercise court control by examining, in some detail, the reasoning of the award. Only in exceptional cases, such as when the award has no reasons, or the award did not consider the applicability of public policy rules, should the court be allowed to go further and examine the parties' pleadings or the evidence produced in the arbitral proceedings or, in extreme cases, to launch a full-fledged investigation. I can subscribe to this scale of court control intensity, with one addition: in order to safeguard the

66. Radicati di Brozolo, 'Mandatory Rules and International Arbitration', cit., 63f.

efficacy of the public policy rule, I would add that the court may go further and examine the pleadings and the evidence also when the court does not find the award's reasoning convincing. With this addition, the intensity of court control corresponds to the criteria laid down by the maximalist theory.

The narrow scope of the public policy exception permits preserving the difference between public policy review and review on the merits. This should be of comfort to those who are worried about the autonomy of arbitration.

The very same narrow scope, however, may give reason to question whether court control meets the high standard for arbitrability of investment disputes set in *Achmea*. If the CJEU seeks a mechanism by which uniform application of EU law is ensured in every detail, the public policy review is not the appropriate means. The public policy exception may be triggered only when the application of EU law is such that it seriously infringes EU fundamental principles. It could be argued, therefore, that the public policy review is not sufficient to meet the high standard postulated in *Achmea*.

However, it seems questionable that the uniformity standard in *Achmea* is as high as requiring full uniformity also in the details. As was seen above, according to the CJEU, court decisions that infringe competition law are enforceable under the Brussels Convention and under the Brussels I Regulation on the recognition and enforcement of civil decisions, as long as the infringements are not so serious that they conflict with public policy. Hence, non-uniform application of EU law does not seem to be inacceptable, as long as it is below the threshold of public policy.

If this is so for court decisions, there seem to be no reasons for having a different standard for arbitral awards. Admittedly, arbitral tribunals have no competence to refer to the CJEU questions for preliminary rulings. While it is true that arbitral tribunal are thereby deprived of the possibility to obtain the CJEU's view on the application of EU law, it does not mean that the dispute will be deprived of this possibility. If the award is subject to court control in an EU Member State, the court will have the possibility to request a preliminary ruling in the context of the public policy review.[67] Precisely this was recently done by the Swedish Supreme Court.[68] This will put the court decision on an arbitral award in the same situation as a court decision on the enforcement of a civil decision of another Member State under the Brussels Convention or the Brussels I Regulation. As seen above, the CJEU accepts the enforceability, under these instruments, of decisions that apply competition law wrongly, as long as they do not breach public policy. The same standard should apply to arbitral awards. Court control under the maximalist theory, therefore, is sufficient to safeguard the uniform application of EU law in the sense of the CJEU.

Court control according to the maximalist theory, in summary, permits to meet a balance between opposing interests: (i) it preserves the autonomy of arbitration,

67. Case C-567/14 (*Genentech*), AG Opinion, paras 59–62. The AG refers here to commercial arbitration. The same AG Wathelet expressed, in the *Achmea* case, the opinion that in investment arbitration the arbitral tribunal is entitled to refer questions to the CJEU, *see* footnote 50. This opinion, however, was not followed by the Court.

68. *Republic of Poland v. PL Holding*, Case No. T 1569-19.

thanks to the restricted scope of the public policy exception; (ii) it ensures the safeguard of the legal system's fundamental principles, thanks to the court's independent evaluation of the public policy issue; and (iii) it permits to ensure a uniform application of EU law, thanks to the court's possibility to request a preliminary ruling.

This balance seems to be a condition for maintaining the wide scope of arbitrability that was introduced by the *Mitsubishi* decision. Insisting on the minimalist approach to court control, on the contrary, will contribute to reversing the era of arbitration-friendliness that was initiated by *Mitsubishi*.

CHAPTER 13

# Sovereign Immunity from Execution of Foreign Arbitral Awards: Sweden's Liberal and Pragmatic Contribution

*Ylli Dautaj*

## §13.01 INTRODUCTION

The plea of sovereign immunity can be invoked by a State in order to prevent a foreign court from either exercising its jurisdiction to hear a case against the state or to attach and execute against its property. In other words, it functions as a procedural shield available only to States, whereby the substantive issues at hand cannot be addressed by the foreign court if the plea is successfully invoked.

Courts have struggled with the plea of sovereign immunity for many years, but yet several issues remain unresolved.[1] One largely unresolved issue is that of immunity from execution, and hence it has been described as "the last fortress, the last bastion of [sovereign] immunity."[2] This chapter will discuss the defense of sovereign immunity from execution of foreign arbitral awards in the Swedish context. This will include some discussion on attachment, which can also be a post-judgment measure of constraint. This seemingly technical and narrowly defined question will, however, underscore a much greater debate on the theory of sovereign immunity and the scope, extent, and degree of qualifying the general rule of immunity.[3]

1. Kaj Hobér, *Selected Writings on Investment Treaty Arbitration*, 497 (Lund: Studentlitteratur AB, 2013).
2. *Yearbook of International Law Commission Commentary*, Art. 18, paras. 1, 208 (United Nations, 1986).
3. The law of sovereign immunity—regardless of adhering to the absolute or restrictive theory of immunity—provides that absolute immunity is the rule. The restrictive theory then enumerates exceptions to the rule, e.g., based on commercial activity. *See*, e.g., James Crawford, *Brownlie's Principles of Public International Law*, 489 (8th ed., Oxford: Oxford University Press, 2012);

While the issue of immunity from execution remains largely unresolved, the Swedish experience has neither been a regressive nor a silent one. Quite the opposite, Swedish courts have contributed to the development of the law of sovereign immunity in a liberal and progressive manner. That said, a recent decision from the Svea Court of Appeal has presented some deviation from the Swedish contribution thus far, and it is hoped that the regressive decision will soon be reversed in the Supreme Court.[4] The author is convinced that global commerce, trade, and investment will be richer if foreign and international courts accommodate the Swedish experience as a best practice of public international law and transnational adjudication. This chapter seeks to disseminate this contribution to the international legal community, while simultaneously making the point that Swedish courts should keep faithful to its liberal and pragmatic ethos.

In a Swedish case from 2011 regarding execution of State property, the Swedish Supreme Court *inter alia* (a) accepted parts of the 2004 United Nations Convention on Jurisdictional Immunities of States and Their Property (UNCSI) as a codification of customary international law, and (b) treated the purpose test liberally by reasoning pragmatically on the property of "mixed-use" (i.e., commercial and governmental).[5] In this case, the State was not able to shield its property. As a result, the State was held accountable in accordance with the decision in the arbitral award, which was both enforced and executed. The Court endorsed the ends as well as the means of international arbitration between investors and host States. The Court exercised its coercive powers in a situation where the State for no legitimate reasons had both decided to default on its voluntarily and freely entertained agreement to protect foreign investments and to arbitrate any grievance stemming from such protection.[6] This case represents neither an embarrassment nor an infringement on that sovereign's dignity, independence or equality. On the contrary, it manifests that a State is sovereign enough to engage in international affairs as a private actor.

---

Foreign Sovereign Immunities Act 1976; State Immunity Act 1978; the 2004 United Nations Convention on Jurisdictional Immunities of States and Their Property; and *Germany v. Italy: Greece Intervening*, Jurisdictional Immunities of the State, Judgment of February 3, ICJ Reports 2012.

4. *See The Republic of Kazakhstan and the National Bank of Kazakhstan v. Stati, Ascom, et al* ÖÄ 7709-19 (June 17, 2020).
5. *Sedelmayer v. The Russian Federation*, Swedish Supreme Court Case No. Ö 170-10 (reported in NJA 2011 p. 475). *See also* a recent District Court judgment with a similar reasoning, i.e., *Stockholm District Court*, T 10498-17, 21 (Kazakhstan making the point that "the Supreme Court has declared in NJA 2011 p. 475 that the [UNCSI] to large extent is a codification of international customary law.").
6. For a recent and good reasoning making a pro-arbitration point *vis-á-vis* enforcement and immunity, *see Eiser Infrastructure Ltd v. Kingdom of Spain* [2020] FCA 157, para. 179 ("It was thus apparently the intention of the parties to the ECT to create rights in favour of private investors capable of enforcement in consensual arbitration against one or other state parties to the ECT [...] and that, therefore, [i]n that regard, it has agreed to the terms of the Investment Convention which provide, amongst other things, that a Centre award is binding on the parties and is not subject to any appeal or any other remedy except those provided for in the [ICSID Convention Art 53], that Contacting States (including Australia) are obliged to 'recognise and enforce the pecuniary obligations imposed' by the award 'as if it were a final judgment of a court in that state'.").

This chapter makes the point that Sweden—together with other arbitration friendly jurisdictions—should remain a driving force in shaping the law on sovereign immunity from execution of foreign arbitral awards. These arbitration friendly jurisdictions should not give in to regressive sentiments stemming from investor-state arbitration backlash or political pressure. Thus far, Swedish courts have exercised an overall pro-arbitration approach. This has been manifested in the courts' pragmatic decision-making, e.g., with respect to back-end supervision of award enforcement.

However, the International Court of Justice (ICJ) remains best placed to interpret and consolidate the overall framework on immunity from execution when the opportunity arises.[7] In the author's view, the ICJ should exercise its jurisdiction to strengthen the currency of liberal and pragmatic municipal decisional law by forming certain principles of state practice as customary international law. The ICJ did some good work in this respect in its famous 2012 *Jurisdictional Immunities* case.[8] That said, the debate on the evolution of the law is on-going and the Swedish contribution as a politically neutral country with an independent judiciary will remain important.

## §13.02 SOVEREIGN IMMUNITY: SOURCES AND THEORY

The law on immunity is one of the classic branches of public international law.[9] The law on sovereign immunity has evolved separately from other areas of immunity, e.g., diplomatic immunity or immunity for international organizations. In addition, the law on sovereign immunity has evolved differently depending on the context, e.g., arbitration, human rights violations, torts. Sovereign immunity operates on twin bases as: (1) immunity *ratione materiae* (i.e., a direct inference from the equality and independence of states), and (2) immunity *ratione personae* (i.e., foreign state officials should not be subject to host state jurisdiction—the personal or functional level).[10] Here, we are concerned only with the former. Moreover, it should be said that the law on immunity is a procedural plea and does in no way exonerate legal liability per se.

Sovereign immunity has been described as "a rule of international law that facilitates the performance of public functions by the state and its representatives by preventing them from being sued or prosecuted in foreign courts."[11] Put differently, "[i]ts rationale is to promote the functioning of all governments by protecting states

7. Depending on your preference of judicial methodology and attitude, i.e., whether ICJ judges should be pro-active or restrained, one could also make the case for further elaboration in *obiter dicta*. *See* Pieter Kooijmans, *The ICJ in the 21st Century: Judicial Restraint, Judicial Activism, or Proactive Judicial Policy*, 27 International and Comparative Law Quarterly 741–753 (2007), Vera Gowlland-Debbas, "*The Role of the International Court of Justice in the Development of the Contemporary Law of Treaties*" in Christian Tams and James Sloan (eds.), *The Development of International Law by the International Court of Justice* (1st ed., Oxford: Oxford University Press 2013).
8. *Germany v. Italy: Greece Intervening*, Jurisdictional Immunities of the State, Judgment of February 3, ICJ Reports 2012.
9. Jan Klabbers, *An Introduction to International Institutional Law*, 139 (2nd ed., Cambridge: Cambridge University Press 2009).
10. *See* Crawford, *supra* n. 3, at 487.
11. *Ibid.*

from the burden of defending litigation abroad."[12] Therefore, it has been described as a protection that enables states "to carry out their functions effectively."[13] In practice, absolute immunity seems to be a default international rule of law that has been subjected to municipal procedural exceptions due to contextual realities.[14]

The law on sovereign immunity is a branch of public international law. Therefore, the sources are, generally speaking, to be found in Article 38(1) of the Statute of the ICJ.[15] Because a multilateral framework is lacking, the law has primarily developed through domestic decisional law (and in parts of the world through legislation). It has been noted that "[i]mmunity exists as a rule of international law, but its application depends substantially on the law and procedural rules of the forum."[16] As a result of the lack of a harmonized legal framework, many States engaged in discussions in order to reach consensus on the application and interpretation of the law. This eventually culminated in a multilateral treaty, namely, with the adoption of the 2004 UNCSI.[17] The UNCSI has not yet entered into force. However, given the fact that the convention has been adopted by several influential States (including Sweden) and was essentially produced as a verbatim result of the International Law Commission (ILC), it has largely been treated as a codification of customary international law. Thus, "the starting point for any discussion of the international law relating to [sovereign] immunity is now the

12. Julian D.M. Lew, Loukas A. Mistelis & Stefan Kröll, *International Comparative Commercial Arbitration*, 744 (Kluwer Law International, 2003).
13. Hazel Fox & Philippa Webb, *The Law of State Immunity* (3rd ed., Oxford: Oxford University Press, 2013).
14. *See*, e.g., Crawford, *supra* n. 3, at 489; Foreign Sovereign Immunities Act 1976; State Immunity Act 1978; the 2004 United Nations Convention on Jurisdictional Immunities of States and Their Property; and *Germany v. Italy: Greece Intervening*, Jurisdictional Immunities of the State, Judgment of February 3, ICJ Reports 2012.
15. Article 38 of the Statute of the International Court of Justice (adopted on April 18, 1946) ("1. The Court, whose function is to decide in accordance with international law such disputes as are submitted to it, shall apply: (a) international conventions, whether general or particular, establishing rules expressly recognized by the contesting states; (b) international custom, as evidence of a general practice accepted as law; (c) the general principles of law recognized by civilized nations; (d) subject to the provisions of Article 59, judicial decisions and the teachings of the most highly qualified publicists of the various nations, as subsidiary means for the determination of rules of law. 2. This provision shall not prejudice the power of the Court to decide a case *ex aequo et bono*, if the parties agree thereto."), www.icj-cij.org/en/statute.
16. Crawford, *supra* n. 3.
17. The convention will take effect and enter into binding force when ratified by thirty countries. This is not likely to happen anytime soon. To this day (May 22, 2019) fourteen have signed but not ratified the Convention; including Belgium, China, India, Russia, and the U.K. twenty-two States have ratified the Convention, including Austria, France, Iran, Italy, Japan, Saudi Arabia, Sweden, and Switzerland. The United States have neither signed nor ratified the Convention, https://treaties.un.org/Pages/ViewDetails.aspx?src = IND&mtdsg_no = III-13&chapter = 3&lang = en. Some of these states have traditionally been opposed to restrictive immunity, e.g., China, India, and Russia. Furthermore, two earlier treaties deal with sovereign immunity (one in a narrow context and the other limited to members of the Council of Europe); that is, the Brussels Convention for the Unification of Certain rules Relating to the Immunity of State-Owned Vessels (adopted on April 10, 1926, additional protocol added on May 24, 1934) and the European Convention on State Immunity (adopted on May 1972) (ECSI).

text of that convention."[18] Other sources of significance include decisions of international tribunals and municipal courts[19] and scholarly work.

Absolute immunity has been replaced in most parts of the world, especially with respect to immunity from jurisdiction (alternatively "adjudication" or "suit"). The theory on restrictive immunity is based on a distinction of State acts as either (1) an exercise of sovereign authority (*acta iuree imperii*) or (2) an act that a private person may perform (*acta iuree gestionis*). Conclusively, States should not be treated differently when acting as private parties. This distinction rests and is firmly entrenched on the concept of "commerciality."[20] Nowadays, further exceptions are increasingly being carved-out from the general rule of immunity from jurisdiction as well as execution.

At the inception of the restrictive phase on immunity, a debate emerged, namely, whether commerciality should be determined on the basis of the "nature of the act" (the nature approach) or on the basis of the "purpose of the act" (the purpose approach).[21] The nature approach has gained most traction and is the dominant position. In other words, if the act is commercial in nature (or an act under the private law sphere), the state's immunity should be limited even if there is an alleged public purpose. However, despite being rejected in the context of immunity from jurisdiction, the purpose test unfortunately surfaces as the main test for elaborating a limitation on sovereign immunity from execution.[22] Finally, some States add a nexus requirement, i.e., a minimum connection between the territory and the commercial act or between the territory and the host-State where the property is located.[23]

This chapter focuses on immunity from execution. An illustration of the general rule on immunity from execution and exceptions that have received a general

18. Fox & Webb, *supra* n. 13. *See*, e.g., *Germany v. Italy: Greece Intervening*, Jurisdictional Immunities of the State, Judgment of February 3, ICJ Reports 2012 (the Court held *inter alia* that parts of the Convention were a codification of customary international law). *Sedelmayer v. The Russian Federation*, Swedish Supreme Court Case No. Ö 170-10 (reported in NJA 2011 p. 475) (where the court relied on the 2004 Convention as constituting in part customary international law).
19. Primarily from the International Court of Justice; *see*, e.g., *Democratic Republic of the Congo v. Belgium*, Arrest Warrant, Judgment of February 14, ICJ Reports 2002; *Germany v. Italy: Greece Intervening*, Jurisdictional Immunities of the State, Judgment of February 3, ICJ Reports 2012; and *Islamic Republic of Iran v. United States*, Certain Iranian Assets, Judgment of February 13, 2019 (preliminary objections), ICJ Reports 2019.
20. There is no red-line between what is a commercial activity and what is not. The court must draw a distinction on a case-by-case basis unless the activity or transaction falls in a "straight-jacket," such as a sale of goods. *See* Xiaodong Yang, *State Immunity in International Law*, 77 (Cambridge: Cambridge University Press 2012), where the author stated that: "all that the current instrument on State immunity say is, in essence, that 'a commercial activity is a commercial activity'. This is pure tautology. In most cases, therefore, the courts are left to their own devices; and an examination of the relevant case law reveals a picture of great variety and complexity." It is equally difficult to understand what is a governmental, non-commercial activity.
21. One could add a "context approach." *See Ibid.*, at 85. Some judges have found difficulty in favoring a distinction and have instead searched for an answer in the totality of the circumstances.
22. Ylli Dautaj, *Enforcing Arbitral Awards Against States and the Defence of Sovereign Immunity from Execution*, 16(3) Manchester Journal of International Economic Law (2019).
23. *See*, e.g., U.S. section 1605(a)(2) of The Foreign Sovereign Immunities Act of 1976 (FSIA), Pub. L. No. 94-583, 90 Stat. 2891 (codified in scattered sections of 28 U.S.C.).

consensus worldwide can be found in the UNCSI.[24] More specifically, in Articles 19 (post-judgment), 20 (effect of consent to jurisdiction to measures of constraint), and 21 (specific categories of property (considered immune)). The articles read as follows:

**Article 19**
**State immunity from post-judgment measures of constraint**

No post-judgment measures of constraint, such as attachment, arrest or execution, against property of a State may be taken in connection with a proceeding before a court of another State unless and except to the extent that:

(a) the State has expressly consented to the taking of such measures as indicated:
  (i) by international agreement;
  (ii) by an arbitration agreement or in a written contract; or
  (iii) by a declaration before the court or by a written communication after a dispute between the parties has arisen; or
(b) the State has allocated or earmarked property for the satisfaction of the claim which is the object of that proceeding; or
(c) it has been established that the property is specifically in use or intended for use by the State for other than government non-commercial purposes and is in the territory of the State of the forum, provided that post-judgment measures of constraint may only be taken against property that has a connection with the entity against which the proceeding was directed.

**Article 20**
**Effect of consent to jurisdiction to measures of constraint**

Where consent to the measures of constraint is required under articles 18 and 19, consent to the exercise of jurisdiction under article 7 shall not imply consent to the taking of measures of constraint.

**Article 21**
**Specific categories of property**

1. The following categories, in particular, of property of a State shall not be considered as property specifically in use or intended for use by the State for other than government non-commercial purposes under article 19, subparagraph (c):
   (a) property, including any bank account, which is used or intended for use in the performance of the functions of the diplomatic mission of the State or its consular posts, special missions, missions to international organizations or delegations to organs of international organizations or to international conferences;
   (b) property of a military character or used or intended for use in the performance of military functions;
   (c) property of the central bank or other monetary authority of the State;
   (d) property forming part of the cultural heritage of the State or part of its archives and not placed or intended to be placed on sale;
   (e) property forming part of an exhibition of objects of scientific, cultural or historical interest and not placed or intended to be placed on sale.
2. Paragraph 1 is without prejudice to article 18 and article 19, subparagraphs (a) and (b).

24. For a proper understanding of its content it is necessary to read the legislative history; that is, the International Law Commission and the Working Group of the United Nations General assembly, Sixth Committee. The ILC submitted its "draft" to the UN in 1991.

Article 19 presents three exceptions to immunity from execution, and Article 21 lists five categories of property as immune from execution *ipso facto*. As mentioned, the UNCSI has not yet entered into force, but it is said to, at least partially, represent customary international law. Moreover, the UNCSI indeed represents a measure of common ground among widely diverse jurisdictions.[25] It would be an outright denial to not accept the fact that the UNCSI has entrenched the move toward a restrictive theory on immunity also for execution purposes.

One must also proceed with a caution and cynicism. It is evidently the case that the evolution of restrictive immunity has not been as prevalent with respect to measures of constraint.[26] The doctrine on immunity from execution allows for certain qualification to the general rule of immunity. However, the doctrinal development has grown apart from the evolution seen with respect to immunity from jurisdiction. An expert on sovereign immunity wrote that:

> An examination of relevant State practice shows that, even though, as a general rule, preventive measures and measures of forced execution against foreign States and their property are permitted, such measures are subject to a number of conditions and limitations. First, a clear distinction has been drawn between immunity from the adjudicative process and immunity from measures of constraint [...]. [...] Secondly, the "purpose" test, much discredited in the context of adjudicative jurisdiction, resurfaces as a determinative factor in the context of measures of constraint. Generally speaking, the property of a foreign State enjoys immunity from attachment, arrest and execution when it is used for sovereign or public purposes, but not when it is used for commercial purposes. Thirdly, the territorial nexus requirement is adhered to even more strictly in the process of enforcement and execution of judgments against foreign State property. Finally, certain categories of property still enjoy absolute immunity, even where the foreign State has expressly waived its immunity from execution.[27]

It is partly for these reasons that the law on sovereign immunity remains largely unresolved. This chapter will not solve the issues, but it will illustrate how the Swedish courts have generated decisional law that could be consolidated as state practice representing customary international law in the context of immunity from execution from foreign arbitral awards.

25. *See*, e.g., *Germany v. Italy: Greece Intervening*, Jurisdictional Immunities of the State, Judgment of February 3, ICJ Reports 2012 (the Court held *inter alia* that parts of the Convention were a codification of customary international law). *Sedelmayer v. The Russian Federation*, Swedish Supreme Court Case No. Ö 170-10 (reported in NJA 2011 p. 475) (where the court relied on the 2004 Convention as constituting in part customary international law).
26. Measures of constraint "encompass the full variety of pre- and post-judgment measures available in national legal systems"; among other things, injunctions, attachment, and execution. *See* Crawford, *supra* n. 3, at 1,962. *See also* Yang, *supra* n. 20, at 343 (Cambridge University Press 2012) ("'Measures of constraint' is a generic term covering both interlocutory, interim or pre-trial measures prior to final judgments and the execution or enforcement of judgments. In the context of State immunity, these are coercive or enforcement measures taken by the court either to restrain the foreign State in the disposition of its property, normally in the form of interlocutory injunctions, or otherwise to attach, arrest or seize the property of the foreign State.").
27. *Ibid.*

## §13.03 THE INTERNATIONAL COURT OF JUSTICE

As mentioned already, the law on sovereign immunity has developed almost predominantly through municipal decisional law. At the same time, these courts know that they are constrained by other developments in public international law. Nowadays, the general rule of sovereign immunity is cemented as one of the customary international laws. Whether, when, and how to qualify the general rule of sovereign immunity is, therefore, also a matter of customary international law. Incidentally, the exceptions to the general rule will play out in municipal decisional law and legislative amendments first, and only thereafter be interpreted, consolidated, and crystallized by the ICJ.

In the well-known 2012 decision *Germany v. Italy (Greece Intervening)*, the ICJ interpreted and partly consolidated customary international law with respect to immunity from jurisdiction and indirectly the law on immunity from execution.[28] This case is better known as the "Jurisdictional Immunities Case." Unsurprisingly, much of the ICJ's decision was based on a reflection of liberal and pragmatic municipal decisional law, legislative action, scholarly work, and the UNCSI. The ICJ observed, *inter alia*, that: (1) immunity from jurisdiction had been "adopted as a general rule of customary international law solidly rooted in the current practice of States";[29] (2) there is a distinction between proceedings for the recognition and enforcement, on the one hand, and the execution of a foreign judgment on the other;[30] and (3) parts of Article 19 of the UNCSI (on immunity from execution) represent customary international law.[31] However, the vagueness in the majority opinion did not prove all that helpful with respect to the debate on immunity from execution. It was vague in the way that it did not really address the issue of immunity from execution head-on. The law on immunity from execution remains an unchartered territory and one in a state of flux, let alone in the context of enforcing foreign arbitral awards.

The ICJ only briefly discussed immunity from execution and mentioned that, even though not yet in force, the UNCSI "provides a comprehensive regime of rules covering immunity from adjudication and [execution] of a state."[32] As such, the court felt free to refer to Article 19 of the UNCSI, in general, and Article 19(c), in particular. Although the ICJ was careful to not endorse the article as a mandatory manifestation of customary international law, it "shaped, by reference to that article's exception (c), the standards to be applied by a third state's court in proceedings for recognition of a

28. *See* Roger O'Keefe, "*Jurisdictional Immunities*" in Christian Tams and James Sloan (eds.), *The Development of International Law by the International Court of Justice* 111–115 (Oxford: Oxford University Press 2013).
29. Jurisdictional Immunities of the State *(Germany v. Italy: Greece Intervening)*, Judgment of February 3, 2012, para. 26, where the Court observed this by citing International Law Commission Yearbook of 1980.
30. *Ibid.*, at 128 and 130.
31. The Court did not find it necessary to determine whether the entirety of Article 19 reflects current customary international law. *Ibid.*, at 117–118. But the ICJ seems to have made a serious mistake in closing off additional discussion on implied waiver from execution. The court seems to have created a caveat by stating that this reflected only "current" customary international law, and therefore the discussion may remain open.
32. Fox & Webb, *supra* n. 13, at 47.

judgment given against a foreign state in the national court of another state."[33] Thus, in a kind of back-handed endorsement of the treaty, the court crystallized and consolidated the law as written in the convention, holding that:

> When the United Nations Convention was being drafted, these provisions gave rise to long and difficult discussions. The Court considers that it is unnecessary for purposes of the present case for it to decide whether all aspects of Article 19 reflect current customary international law.
>
> [...]
>
> Indeed, it suffices for the Court to find that there is at least one condition that has to be satisfied before any measure of constraint may be taken against property belonging to a foreign State: that the property in question must be in use for an activity not pursuing government non-commercial purposes, or that the State which owns the property has expressly consented to the taking of a measure of constraint, or that that State has allocated the property in question for the satisfaction of a judicial claim.[34]

The court then held that the property in dispute was clearly in use for sovereign functions, namely, for cultural exchanges between Germany and Italy.[35] Put slightly differently, the property enjoyed immunity because it was used for governmental non-commercial *purposes* "regardless of the validity of the judgment on which it was based."[36] In so holding, the ICJ appears to have solidly acknowledged the "commercial purposes exception" as forming part of customary international law. Naturally, because it was not required to discuss the entirety of the UNCSI, the court remained silent on whether *all* aspects of Article 19 reflect current customary international law. One could have wished for more in obiter dictum but, on the other hand, as the saying goes: "if you stand for everything, you stand for nothing." At the same time, it was perhaps slow in endorsing the entirety of Article 19 as that may have given some States the indication that other articles would be treated as customary international law, too. That is hardly the case.

In a dispute between *Iran v. United States* from 2019 (on-going), the ICJ was again presented with a singular opportunity to clarify a great deal of the law of sovereign immunity and perhaps to further crystallize or consolidate customary international law with respect to immunity from execution.[37] Two scholars rightly

33. *Ibid.*
34. *Jurisdictional Immunities*, at paras. 117 and 118 (citations omitted).
35. *Ibid.*, at para. 119. Going even further, the ICJ may have indirectly recognized Article 21 (1)(d) of the UNCSI in that the property forms "part of the cultural heritage of the State" and is "not placed or intended to be placed on sale."
36. *See* Fox & Webb, *supra* n. 13, at 51.
37. The case stems from the United States having taken several direct and indirect measures against Iran for its alleged support of groups labelled as "terrorist organizations" and for other, related violations of human rights. To effectuate this position, the United States has created an exception to the jurisdictional immunity for States that allegedly are "sponsors of terrorism." The USA has blocked certain Iranian assets and property and made these assets available for attachment and execution. By way of both legislative and executive action the USA has provided victims of terrorism with a judicial forum to remedy their grievances. In most cases, these actions have led to claims that are essentially in the form of either restoration or reparation. As expected, these measures have been challenged by Iran in USA courts and before the ICJ. Many

commented that "a range of questions might arise that the 2012 *Jurisdictional Immunities* case has left unanswered" and that the court would be in a position to *inter alia* "shed light on matters such as the exact regime relating to the property of central banks," in particular between the stricter provisions of the UNCSI and those of more "liberal" state practice.[38] The ICJ was not forced to reach any conclusion on those issues due to a successful jurisdictional challenge. The court also turned down the opportunity to elaborate further in obiter dictum.

As expressly mentioned in 2012, the language in Article 19 of the UNCSI provides for a general rule of immunity under customary international law. To what extent the exceptions form part of customary international law is less certain. Additionally, five categories are listed as immune *ipso facto* in Article 21, including "property of the central bank or other monetary authority of the State." Whether these exceptions form part of customary international law is debatable.[39] If it does, the property of a central bank enjoys virtually absolute immunity categorically, because the exception is not qualified by governmental non-commercial use or for property used within a central bank's traditional functions. As of today, we are not even sure whether Article 19(c) of UNCSI makes the *nexus* requirement an obligation pursuant to customary international law, let alone that Article 21(c) would represent customary international law.

## §13.04 SOVEREIGN IMMUNITY IN SWEDEN

There is no legislation on sovereign immunity in Sweden.[40] Thus, the Swedish law on sovereign immunity remains non-statutory. As a result, the rules are to be extracted from customary international law, which entails an analysis of decisional law (municipal and international) and views expressed in renowned scholarly work.[41] As mentioned already, there is no multilateral treaty in force yet, but Sweden did ratify the UNCSI and, as the ICJ has done,[42] the Swedish Supreme Court has emphatically endorsed parts of the convention as a codification of customary international law.[43]

The liberal and pragmatic Swedish attitude seem partly to be reflected in the willingness of the courts—the Supreme Court in particular, but also the courts of

of the USA-based court judgments have resulted in default judgments in favor of the claimants because Iran refused to participate in the proceedings.

38. Philipp Janig & Sara Mansour Fallah, *Certain Iranian Assets: The Limits of Anti-terrorism Measures in Light of State Immunity and Standards of Treatment*, 59 German Yearbook of International Law (2016).
39. *Ibid.*, "Yet, again, judicial as well as legislative State practice so far have been reluctant to award special protection to property of a central bank. Only a limited number of States enacted legislation as to that effect. Thus, the customary nature of this provision is 'contentious', and courts usually apply the general rules to property of the central bank as well."
40. Ove Bring, Said Mahmoudi, & Pål Wrange, I *Sverige och Folkrätten* 97 (2011).
41. *See* Kaj Hobér, *International Commercial Arbitration in Sweden*, 21 (Oxford: Oxford University Press, 2011). Ove Bring, Said Mahmoudi & Pål Wrange, *Sverige och Folkrätten*, 97 (2011).
42. Jurisdictional Immunities of the State *(Germany v. Italy: Greece Intervening)*, Judgment, (2012), I.C.J, ¶ 26 (Feb 3) and *Islamic Republic of Iran v. United States*, Certain Iranian Assets, Judgment of February 13, 2019 (preliminary objections), ICJ Reports 2019.
43. *See Sedelmayer v. The Russian Federation*, Swedish Supreme Court Case No. Ö 170-10 (reported in NJA 2011 p. 475).

appeal and the district courts—to entertain a comparative legal approach vis-á-vis the rule of sovereign immunity. This comparative pragmatism can be traced back to 1942 and the decision in *The Charente*.[44] The Supreme Court held that:

> [I]t is of utmost importance that the principle of sovereign immunity is recognized without any modifications, or with only minor modifications, by most countries, including such major and highly culturally developed nations, which are close to Sweden, such as Germany, France and the United Kingdom, as well as the United States. Having regard to the significance of the problem to international commerce it cannot be assumed, unless compelling reasons are presented—which in fact are entirely missing—that Swedish law takes a different position on the principle as such of recognition of sovereign immunity.[45]

This decision may appear to endorse a doctrine of absolute sovereign immunity, especially since the United States (U.S.) subscribed to the restrictive doctrine on immunity first in 1956, the U.K. in 1977, France in 1969, and Germany in 1963 but definitely in 1972. However, what is progressive is not the holding itself, but rather the reasoning.[46] Post-*Charente*, it was a generally accepted view that Swedish courts adopted the globally prevailing doctrine—including modifications—on sovereign immunity as those of "culturally aligned" states.[47]

The court positioned itself in the world of legal governance.[48] Thus, implicitly the Swedish Supreme Court already in 1942 recognized that the law on sovereign immunity can best—or only—be understood through the lens of a comparative legal methodology and was not to be considered in isolation of historical, political, economic, cultural, and legal evolution. In a word, the Swedish Supreme Court implicitly took a decidedly liberal and pragmatic position, namely, that international commerce, trade, and investment, will dictate the evolution of the doctrine as reflected in major trading nations that adhere to liberal capitalism and a liberal democratic world order. In fact, this rationale proved instrumental as the developed world transitioned from the doctrine of absolute to restrictive immunity.[49] In other words, Swedish courts have increasingly and incrementally held that immunity from suit (and to a lesser extent,

---

44. NJA 1942, para. 65.
45. *The Charente*, NJA 1942 para. 65, at 74–75; Hobér, *supra* n. 41, at 21 (For another Supreme Court case entrenching the old and more rigid doctrine of sovereign immunity, *see Åke Beckman v. People's Republic of China* NJA 1957 195.).
46. Letter from Jack B. Tate, Acting Legal Adviser, Dept. of State, to Acting Attorney General Philip B. Perlman (May 19, 1952), reprinted in 26 Dept. State Bull. (1952) (US); *The Philippine Admiral* [1977] AC 373, 401–402 (actions in rem), *Trendtex Trading Corporation v. The Central Bank of Nigeria* [1977] QB 529 (actions in personam), and *I Congreso del Partido* [1983] 1 AC 244 (UK); *Administration v. Société Levant*, France (1969) 52 ILR 315; *Englander v. Statni*, France (1969) 52 ILR 335; *Société v. Chaussois*, France (1969) 65 ILR 44, 45–46 (France); and (Germany).
47. *See* Hobér, *supra* n. 41, at 21; Ove Bring, Said Mahmoudi & Pål Wrange, *sverige och folkrätten*, 99 (2011).
48. From a non-legal standpoint—especially considering the political element of the doctrine pre-1970s—it is important to note that Sweden started endorsing and embracing a move towards a liberal democratic order with a fully integrated market economy system. This kind of reasoning proved instrumental for Swedish prosperity.
49. It has been said that "[t]he history of the law of [sovereign] immunity is the history of the triumph of the doctrine of restrictive immunity over that of absolute immunity." Yang, *supra* n. 20, at 6.

immunity from execution) for commercial or private law dealings (or property) is not compatible with modern trade, commerce, and investment.[50] This transition has happened gradually and really took off from the 1970s and onwards.[51]

Given the contextual reality in 1942, the reasoning and sound approach taken in *The Charente* is to be applauded.[52] This kind of Swedish judicial pragmatism echoes as clear and loud today as it did then. Issues and challenges in international commerce, trade, and investments have changed and so has the role of the sovereign in the twenty-first century. *The Charente* rationale is not outdated, it treats the law on sovereign immunity in Sweden as a living non-statutory rule of law. Hobér duly noted that:

> The significance of [the rationale in *The Charente* is that,] in the view of the [Swedish Supreme Court,] Swedish law should be adopted—and presumably changed, if need be—to developments in law in other countries which from a political, legislative, and cultural point of view are similar to Sweden.[53]

Today, almost eighty years later, one of the major issues pertaining to the general rule of sovereign immunity is whether the otherwise rather elaborate exceptions to it also extend to immunity from execution of foreign arbitral awards.[54] This issue is a prevalent one due to the distinction between immunity from jurisdiction and immunity from enforcement.[55] Because immunity is treated narrower in the context of execution compared to that of jurisdiction, it has rightly been pointed out to be "the last fortress, the last bastion of [sovereign] immunity."[56] While immunity from jurisdiction attracts a lot of attention *inter alia* in the human rights context, it remains uncontroversial in the arbitration context. The same is not true for immunity from execution.

Another area that surprisingly has proved to be controversial in the arbitration context is the distinction between "enforcement" and "execution."[57] Sometimes states invoke immunity from execution in order to avoid enforcement of an arbitral award. A clear distinction should be made between recognition, enforcement, and execution (*see* further below in V(c)(ii)).

50. *See*, e.g., *Kuwait Airways v. Iraqi Airways Co* [1995] 1 WLR 1147, 1171 (HL) (*per* Lord Mustill, "[t]he rationale of the common law doctrine of the restricted immunity, of which section 3 is the counterpart, is that where the sovereign chooses to doff his robes and descend into the market place he must take the rough with the smooth, and having condescended to engage in mundane commercial activities he must also condescend to submit himself to an adjudication in a foreign court on whether he has in the course of those activities undertaken obligations which he has failed to fulfil.").
51. Fox & Webb, *supra* n. 13, at 321.
52. For an interesting discussion on the case, *see* V.V. Veeder, "*A Swedish-British Story. The 'Charente' on State Immunity*" in Eric Bylander, Anna Jonsson Cornell and Jakob Ragnwaldh (eds.), *Forward! Вперёд! Framåt! Essays in Honor of Prof Dr Kaj Hobér* (Iustus Förlag 2019).
53. Hobér, *supra* n. 41, at 21.
54. *Ibid.*, at 22. *See* Dautaj, *supra* n. 22.
55. *See* Jurisdictional Immunities of the State *(Germany v. Italy: Greece Intervening)*, Judgment, (2012), I.C.J. Feb 3).
56. International Law Commission Commentary to Art. 18, para. 1.
57. *See Micula and others v. Romania* [2020] UKSC 5 and *Eiser Infrastructure Ltd v. Kingdom of Spain* [2020] FCA 157.

From a practical standpoint, it is unequivocally the case that Sweden will not alone set the global agenda on whether and how to qualify the general rule of immunity from execution from foreign arbitral awards. That said, the courts will continue to act as a leading architect in elaborating a sustainable transnational enforcement framework by consolidating pragmatic and liberal efforts reflected in foreign decisional law and renowned scholarly work. The Swedish approach, thus far, transcend nationalism, idiosyncrasy, and parochialism. As will be shown in this chapter, the Swedish experience represents a best practice that could serve as guidance to foreign courts, legislators, and the ICJ. A minor caveat is the recent regressive decision from the Svea Court of Appeal, which will likely be the subject for appeal to the Supreme Court, which should grant *a certiori*.[58]

### [A] Decisional Law

In a surprising decision from 1999, the Swedish Supreme Court held that Iceland enjoyed immunity from execution with respect to a contract that had both a public and private law character.[59] The Swedish Supreme Court followed the lines of the Court of Appeal, which had in turn affirmed the district court's decision, where it had concluded that: (1) the contract had both a public law and private law character; (2) both parties were public law entities, (3) the contract was concluded ancillary to specifically designated cooperation between the Nordic states, and (4) the contract *ipso facto* had a public law character.[60] For the reasons mentioned, Iceland was granted immunity.[61] The Swedish Supreme Court tuned in by first recognizing the doctrine of restrictive immunity. However, then it embarked upon determining whether the action was indeed commercial in *nature*. It did so by, *inter alia*, referring to the *nature* of the act and the *purpose* of the act.[62] The court highlighted that it is controversial whether it is the form of activity or the nature of the activity that is to be given emphasis.[63] The court suggested that, because there was no binding decisional law on this point, each individual case demands an overall assessment of all the circumstances.[64] In this case, due to the public nature of the agreement and the intergovernmental agreement between the Nordic states, Iceland was considered to enjoy immunity for what the court characterized as "public acts."[65]

58. *The Republic of Kazakhstan and the National Bank of Kazakhstan v. Stati, Ascom, et al* ÖÄ 7709-19 (juni 17, 2020).
59. *Västerås kommun v. Republic of* Iceland NJA 1999 821. Hobér, *supra* n. 41, at 22–23.
60. The Swedish District Courts (especially Nacka) and the Court of Appeal, too, are usually pragmatic *vis-á-vis* transnational adjudication and often renders very sensible and sound judgments.
61. *See* Hobér, *supra* n. 41, at 24.
62. *Ibid.*
63. Ove Bring, Said Mahmoudi & Pål Wrange, *Sverige och folkrätten*, 101 (Norstedts Juridik AB 2011).
64. *Ibid.*, it should be noted that a "totality of circumstances approach" is indeed a good device (or tool) in the context of deciding whether to grant, condition, or withhold immunity.
65. NJA 1999, 821–825. Hobér, *supra* n. 41, at 24.

It can be said that the court indeed followed its de facto regressive and conservative holding in *The Charente*, but it also disregarded the more liberal and pragmatic reasoning which should have retained its precedential value and ethos some fifty years later. In this regard, Hobér has written that:

> Given, in particular, the nature of the Contract, its purpose, as well as the intention of the parties, an appropriate application of the restrictive immunity would—and probably should—have resulted in a denial of sovereign immunity. The Supreme Court seems to have given too much weight to the fact that both parties to the contract were public entities.[66]

It remains a mystery and very unfortunate that the court decided to undercut its otherwise sound and rational commercial approach when confronted with mixed agreements. In 1999 the courts were well aware of the distinction between sovereign and commercial acts.[67]

It would be comfortable to analyze Sweden's more recent decisional law and completely reject the 1999 decision as a thing of the past. From a historical context that would be unwise and even an intellectually lazy approach. The decision unfortunately reflects and underscores the underlying tension of the doctrine *ipso facto*, namely, the fact that despite the present majority adherence to restrictive immunity, "sovereignty nonetheless remains an obdurate obstacle to adjudicatory civilization."[68] More than that, it reflects the hard-felt truth that even liberal, pragmatic, and commercially oriented states will defer to sovereignty at times where the political pressure may be too strenuous. The decision also reflects the ad hoc nature—and instances of regression—of the evolution of the law on sovereign immunity. Thus, the decision actually underscores great practical and theoretical concerns, viz.: (1) the constant fear of either ad hoc set-backs or, more systematically, that the pendulum will swing back to absolute immunity or near absolute immunity; and (2) whether concepts such as equality, dignity, independence appropriately can justify the rule of immunity or its exceptions. It seems that much of the decisional law globally (regardless of developed/underdeveloped, capitalist/socialist, or any other sharp difference) rests primarily on political concerns and policy objectives. It is submitted that this lack of a firmly entrenched theoretical framework leaves global merchants in limbo in its practical consequences. Bring, Mahmoudi, and Wrange have written that:

> The Supreme Court's decision in [the *Västerås kommun v. Republic of Iceland* of 1999] goes to show that the court decides to neglect the commercial character and purpose of the agreement (to purchase services in exchange for compensation), despite being aware of the distinction between *acta jure imperii* and *acta jure gestionis* and the criterion that are available in order to separate the two from each other. The Supreme Court [was] instead satisfied with the fact that both parties

66. Hobér, *supra* n. 41, at 24.
67. *See* Bring, Mahmoudi & Wrange, *supra* n. 63.
68. Thomas E. Carbonneau, *The Law and Practice of Arbitration*, 545 (JurisNet, 2020).

> [were] public law entities, and thus grant[ed] Iceland immunity. This is an implicit application of the old-fashioned principle on absolute immunity.[69]

However, the surprising decision from 1999 was partly remedied by the Swedish Supreme Court's decision in *Bostadsrättsföreningen Villagatan 13 v. Kingdom of Belgium*.[70] In that case, the court reversed and remanded the decision of the district court (that had been affirmed by the Court of Appeal), in which it had been held that Belgium enjoyed immunity vis-á-vis a declaratory judgment for a lease contract to be used by the Belgian Embassy, in which the Embassy undertook to refurbish the apartment and bear the costs thereof.[71] The court endorsed the principle of restrictive immunity by referring to the 2004 UN Convention.[72] The court went on to discuss how to characterize an act as either sovereign or commercial—it focused on the *nature* of the act, "adding that sometimes also the purpose of the act should be taken into account."[73] Despite Belgium trying to argue that the premises were going to be used as an embassy, the Swedish Supreme Court characterized the contract as commercial (it was a private law setting) and one that could have been entered into by private law entities, too.[74] This case demonstrates the semi-consistency in the Swedish decisional law vis-á-vis sovereign immunity. On this topic, Hobér highlighted that:

> [T]he approach taken by the Supreme Court with respect to immunity from jurisdiction of courts is in line with the approaches of other countries which subscribe to the theory of restrictive immunity. The reasoning in [*Bostadsrätts-föreningen Villagatan 13*] very much echoes the approach taken in the [...] *Charente*, viz, Swedish law should adapt to developments in the leading trading nations.[75]

Going forward, it should come as no surprise that Swedish courts will continue to closely monitor and follow the approaches taken by the leading trading nations, including but not limited to England, U.S., France, and Germany. Meanwhile, it is evident that Swedish courts are rightly treating UNCSI as a stepping-stone for further analysis and indeed as constituting in part a codification of customary international law. Additionally, Swedish courts have and will continue to contribute to developing the law of sovereign immunity. For good reasons, other States should look at the Swedish jurisdiction in order to adapt to the developments in this jurisdiction.

A few broader-perspective take-aways merit close attention. First, Sweden is the financial, political, and cultural center of Scandinavia. As a corollary, Sweden has a large embassy community, museums and other exhibitions, and significant foreign investments are made in the Swedish stock market and elsewhere. These factors

69. Ove Bring, Said Mahmoudi & Pål Wrange, *sverige och folkrätten*, 101 (2011) (Translated from Swedish). Translated from Swedish.
70. NJA 2009 p. 95, Case No. Ö 2753-07.
71. *See* Hobér, *supra* n. 41, at 24–25. Moreover, the Supreme Court made a distinction between state immunity and diplomatic immunity; the latter which was raised by Belgium as a potential issue. *See* Bring, Mahmoudi & Wrange, *supra* n. 63.
72. NJA 2009 p. 95, Case No. Ö 2753-07.
73. Hobér, *supra* n. 41, at 25. Case No. Ö 2753-07, 5–7.
74. Hobér, *supra* n. 41, at 25.
75. *Ibid.*, 26.

combined with Sweden being a robust pro-arbitration jurisdiction means that investors will continue to try to enforce awards against States in Sweden. Second, as a form of "anchoring state," the neighboring Scandinavian countries should keep track of—and perhaps even adopt a similar approach as—the Swedish courts vis-á-vis public international law, in general, and the enforcement of foreign judgments and arbitral awards, in particular. Finally, Sweden is a neutral participant in global affairs and has rightly earned a reputation for having a highly developed rule of law country. Thus, the Swedish courts' decisional law has enjoyed a strong currency globally and its legal community has a reputable standing among its peers. In a word, Sweden has—and will continue to—significantly contributed to developing the framework of transnational adjudication. In this role, the courts have assumed a great responsibility to live up to.

## §13.05 SOVEREIGN IMMUNITY AND ARBITRATION

There is no need to delve deep into immunity from jurisdiction in the arbitration context, apart from the ancillary jurisdictional issue that has been at the forefront of the debate again, namely, municipal courts' jurisdiction in the *sensu stricto* enforcement phase (which does not deal with attachment nor execution).[76] There is a generally held view that an arbitration clause constitutes a waiver of immunity from jurisdiction for the arbitral process. In a word, the restrictive theory on immunity was complimented by the implied waiver doctrine.[77] In the arbitration context, the crux of the matter for the waiver debate has been, firstly, whether this jurisdictional waiver extends to municipal courts jurisdiction to enforce the award, and secondarily but more controversial and intrusive, whether the waiver extends to immunity from execution. From a practical point of view, the more relevant debate has focused on what kind of property is considered to be used for a "commercial purpose." Put colloquially, what property or assets can be attached and executed pursuant to the restrictive theory of immunity from execution?

Enforcing foreign arbitral awards happens primarily pursuant to the enforcement regime established by *New York Convention* or the *ICSID Convention*. "Both conventions are widely adopted and followed in letter as well as in spirit."[78] The enforcement framework can well be represented as the "edifice of trust upon which the international arbitration system rests."[79] As learned arbitration scholars put it:

> Unless parties can be sure that at the end of arbitration proceedings they will be able to enforce the award, if not complied with voluntarily, an award in their favour will be only a pyrrhic victory. Further, the high degree of voluntary

76. *See Micula and others v. Romania* [2020] UKSC 5; *Eiser Infrastructure Ltd v. Kingdom of Spain* [2020] FCA 157; and *Stati, Ascom, et al v. The Republic of Kazakhstan*, Stockholm District Court T 10498-17 2.
77. Where legislation is provided for, the waiver doctrine is mostly codified as one of the exceptions.
78. Dautaj, *supra* n. 22.
79. The New York Convention has been held to be 'the pillar on which the edifice of international arbitration rests.' J. Gillis Wetter, *The Present Status of the International Court of Arbitration in the ICC: An Appraisal*, 1(1) The American Review of International Arbitration 91–107 (1990). Dautaj, *supra* n. 22.

compliance is due to there being an effective system for the enforcement of awards in case of non-compliance.[80]

"Put simply, the international arbitral framework has elaborated a transnational legal order that transcends municipal barriers, parochiality, and idiosyncrasy"[81] and at times it is the role of municipal courts to guarantee that the last link of international arbitration does not remain the weakest.[82] On this positive note it remains perplexing that neither of the two enforcement conventions deals effectively with sovereign immunity. In fact, the ICSID Convention makes this explicit, i.e., Article 54(3) reads in part that "execution of the award shall be governed by the laws concerning the execution" of judgments in the state where execution is sought, while Article 55 reiterates that for sovereign immunities nothing in the *ICSID Convention* should be construed as derogating from municipal laws on the matter.

An award-creditor should be aware of the simple fact that "recognition and enforcement of awards is in the coercive power of the court" and that sovereign immunity could potentially present itself as a barrier.[83] Counsel should advice clients to carefully take into account several factors when seeking to enforce an award, such as whether the courts' outlook is likely to be internationalist or parochial and whether the attitude of the forum State with respect to sovereign immunity is liberal and pragmatic.[84] In this respect, Fox and Webb write that:

> A debtor [state] determined not to honor his commercial obligations can always use the law to delay, if not to evade, his liability[;] but these cases [of invoking immunity from execution] additionally illustrate that, beyond the inevitable differences which arise between trading parties, the complexity of the current law of [sovereign] immunity from enforcement offers a debtor state additional methods of denying [the award-]creditor execution in satisfaction of a valid award obtained in respect of a commercial transaction.[85]

Delaying or obstructing voluntary compliance with an arbitral award is a powerful tool/right that a host State can (ab)use unilaterally either as a tactic to avoid responsibility or as a strategy to renegotiate the quantum. It is an inequality of arms that has the potential to detrimentally hurt investors—in particular small and medium enterprises. The defense of sovereign immunity can indeed manifest itself as a barrier and an obstacle to the mission of achieving the ideals of international arbitration. It can be said that "sovereign immunity remains a significant obstacle to obtaining forced satisfaction of [foreign arbitral] awards against states."[86]

80. Lew, Mistelis & Kröll, *supra* n. 12, at 688.
81. Dautaj, *supra* n. 22.
82. *Ibid.*
83. Lew, Mistelis & Kröll, *supra* n. 12, at 689.
84. Nigel Blackaby, *Redfern and Hunter on International Arbitration*, 513 (New York: Oxford University Press, 2009).
85. Fox & Webb, *supra* n. 13, at 536. *See*, e.g., *Sedelmayer v. The Russian Federation*, Swedish Supreme Court Case No. Ö 170-10 (reported in NJA 2011 p. 475) (the creditor eventually was finally able to attach Russian assets after seventeen years).
86. Philippe Fouchard, *Fouchard, Gaillard, Goldman on International Commercial Arbitration*, 377 (The Hague; Boston: Kluwer Law International, 1999).

### [A] Arbitration in Sweden

Sweden has earned the highest possible reputation as a jurisdiction with a strong rule of law and a neutral liberal democracy that embraces capitalism. Thus, the Swedish jurisdiction has the right ingredients to perform as a world-leading pro-arbitration jurisdiction. It is submitted that the Swedish courts' consistently commercially sound, liberal, and pragmatic decisional law has led the way in that direction.[87] Swedish courts have made sure that the last link of the arbitral legal order remains effective. Arbitral awards in Sweden are truly treated as final, binding, and directly enforceable. The Swedish jurisdiction makes little distinction between international commercial arbitration awards and investment treaty arbitration awards. One should add that part of the Swedish arbitration success story is attributed to the Arbitration Institute of the Stockholm Chamber of Commerce (SCC), which is one of the major service providers for institutional arbitration and competes globally for arbitration business. Leading scholars rightly noted that:

> Sweden has a modern arbitration law and a very well-functioning legal system. A long tradition of arbitration practice gives it the foundation to offer not just reliable, but also a responsive, arbitration service. This is also reflected when it comes to recognition and enforcement of foreign arbitral awards.[88]

It is unequivocally the case that Sweden has provided the global arbitration community with a perfect balance between institutional arbitration services, a robust arbitration legal framework, and a highly pro-arbitration supervisory and enforcing judicial function.[89]

### [B] Sovereign Immunity from Jurisdiction in Sweden

Generally speaking, a valid arbitration clause constitutes a waiver of sovereign immunity from jurisdiction. However, this was not always the case; for example, in *Tekno-Pharma AB v. State of Iran*,[90] the court addressed the validity and scope implied waiver. Tekno-Pharma had an arbitration agreement with Iran. Despite this, Iran invoked immunity from jurisdiction. The Swedish Supreme Court confirmed the Court of Appeal's holding that it did not "consider the arbitration clause [...] to be equivalent to an express waiver of immunity."[91] Today, however, it is a generally held view among leading Swedish scholars and practitioners that a State cannot plead immunity from jurisdiction when the parties have agreed to submit any future or existing dispute

87. *See* Ulf Franke, Annette Magnusson & Joel Dahlquist, *Arbitrating for Peace: How Arbitration Made a Difference* (Kluwer Law International 2015), One could add SU ICAL and now UU ITAP.
88. Ulf Franke, et al, *International Arbitration in Sweden: A Practitioner's Guide*, 296 (Kluwer Law International;, 2013).
89. The court rejects enforcement in very few cases. *See Compilation of enforcement decisions of the Court of Appeal (2000-2012)* in *Ibid.*, at 300–302.
90. NJA 1972 C No. 434.
91. *Ibid.* Hobér, *supra* n. 41, at 29.

to arbitration.[92] In a word, where the state has signed an arbitration agreement, it is considered to have waived its immunity from jurisdiction.

A more controversial matter, but equally one that should have been as firmly entrenched as a matter of law, is that of immunity from jurisdiction *of* the enforcing court. The Swedish courts have been pragmatic in this perspective for decades. In *LIAMCO v. State of Libya*,[93] the Court of Appeal held that Libya did not enjoy immunity from the jurisdiction of the Swedish courts ancillary to arbitration (namely in the enforcement phase). As is mostly the case thanks to the New York Convention and the ICSID Convention, arbitral awards are considered to be as enforceable as a court judgment. In *LIAMCO*, the majority of the court held that:

> By accepting the arbitration clause contained in [...] the concession agreements[,] Libya—which otherwise in its capacity as a sovereign state enjoys extensive rights to immunity from the jurisdiction of the courts of Sweden—must be deemed to have waived its right to invoke immunity.[94]

Because the case was settled shortly following Libya's appeal, the case never reached the docket of the Swedish Supreme Court. But it is very likely that the Swedish Supreme Court would have aligned.

Surprisingly, this distinction between immunity from jurisdiction *over* the arbitral tribunal and the enforcing court has been at the forefront of the debate. Incidentally, this debate highlights the complexity of the distinction between *sensu stricto* enforcement and post-judgment measures of constraint, such as attachment and execution.[95]

The distinction between immunity from jurisdiction and immunity from execution still presents theoretical as well as practical obstacles. In 2018, the Republic of Kazakhstan invoked that it enjoyed immunity from jurisdiction of Swedish courts with respect to proceedings that it considered were not strictly about enforcement but rather about the creation of an enforceable title, which is considered to be a separate legal procedure.[96] The Stockholm District Court, however, disagreed and held that "[i]mmunity from the jurisdiction and immunity from enforcement are two different concepts, which are to be examined separately."[97] Further, the district court reasoned that:

> The case before the District Court concerns only attachment; when the decision is rendered, the case is closed. Against this background, it is difficult to see how this case should be categorized if not as an enforcement matter in the sense that the Supreme Court obviously refers to. It would be unreasonable to examine the question about immunity from the jurisdiction separately in a case as the one at

92. *See*, e.g., Franke, Magnusson & Dahlquist, *supra* n. 87.
93. Case No. Ö 261/79 (1980). *See also* Jan Paulson, *Sweden: Court of Appeals of Svea Judgment Concerning Recognition and Enforcement of Arbitral Awards*, 20(4) International Legal Materials (1981).
94. 20 ILM (1981) 895–896; Hobér, *supra* n. 41, at 30.
95. *See Micula and others v. Romania* [2020] UKSC 5 and *Eiser Infrastructure Ltd v. Kingdom of Spain* [2020] FCA 157.
96. *Stati, Ascom, et al v. The Republic of Kazakhstan*, Stockholm District Court T 10498-17 22.
97. *Stati, Ascom, et al v. The Republic of Kazakhstan*, Stockholm District Court T 10498-17 21 (referring both to the headings in the UNCSI and the Government Bill 2008:09:204 79).

> hand, but not when the Enforcement Authority's subsequent enforcement decision is appealed to court.[98]

At this stage, the matter was essentially one of making a judgment of the arbitral award, namely turning it into an enforceable title. The procedure at hand was one of declaring property attachable, i.e., "sequestration" (sw: "Kvarstad"). It is argued that Kazakhstan conflated enforcement jurisdiction with execution. This procedure was clearly a matter ancillary or incidental to enforcement but not one that deals with execution. It was thus, as the Court rightly noted, an "enforcement matter against property of a foreign state."[99]

As is the routine practice in Sweden, the Swedish Enforcement Agency (Kronofogden) makes the decision on execution, but it first needs an enforceable title in order to execute against property. In Sweden, an arbitral award cannot be enforced without giving the opposing party the opportunity to comment on it. It is subsequent to the Enforcement Agency's final decision with respect to execution that the debtor-State can challenge the decision on the basis of immunity from execution or perhaps other post-judgment measures of constraint, such as attachment of specific (not generic) property.

Kazakhstan also invoked immunity from post-judgment measures of constraint pursuant to Articles 19(c) and 21(c) of the UNCSI before the Stockholm District Court. It is argued that the Court should have closed this discussion by holding that Kazakhstan had clearly and unmistakably waived its immunity from jurisdiction, which includes any jurisdiction matter ancillary or incidental to the arbitral procedure, such as making a judgment of the arbitral award by creating an enforceable title. There was no need to discuss Article 19(c) or 21(c) of the UNCSI any further at this stage. The Stockholm District Court did not attach specific property.[100] The plea of immunity from post-judgment measures of constraint—attachment and execution—should have been presented only to the Nacka District Court when challenging the Enforcement Agency's decision vis-á-vis execution. Put simply, there was no need to consider whether the property indicated was of the nature stated in Article 19. In fact, the Court rightly noted that:

> The requirements set out in article 19 will be examined in the subsequent enforcement proceedings in relation to the specific property which the Enforcement Authority intends to seize and the parties will be provided the opportunity to comment further with regard to this.[101]

The matter eventually came back to the Enforcement Agency. The agency, with an enforceable title at its disposal, then directed enforcement (execution) measures against several assets allegedly located in Sweden.

And this lends us to the crux of this chapter, namely, immunity from execution of foreign arbitral awards. At the end of the day, despite the "procedural ping-pong" and

98. *Stati, Ascom, et al v. The Republic of Kazakhstan*, Stockholm District Court T 10498-17 22.
99. *Ibid.*, 23.
100. *See* Chapter 15 section 1 of the Code of Judicial Procedure.
101. *Stati, Ascom, et al v. The Republic of Kazakhstan*, Stockholm District Court T 10498-17 24.

temporary enforcement success, an arbitral award remains a piece of paper without coercive force.[102] And because it is not the role of the arbitral tribunal to guarantee the ends of arbitration, the role of municipal courts often turns into the last and most important link of the arbitral procedure.[103]

### [C] Sovereign Immunity from Execution (and Attachment) of Arbitral Awards in Sweden

The two exceptions to the general rule of immunity from execution that becomes relevant in the arbitration context are "*waivers*" and "*property used for a commercial purpose.*" However, if the UNCSI is subscribed to in its fullest extent, some property of the State will be treated as categorically immune *ipso facto* pursuant to Article 21 of the convention.

There is a generally held view that a waiver from jurisdiction does not translate into a waiver of immunity from execution.[104] Albeit an important academic topic for discourse, any such debate will for now remain theoretical and *de lege ferenda* at best. Thus, an award-creditor must rely on the commercial purpose test, which makes things way more difficult. One of the outstanding sub-issues of immunity from execution is to determine what property or which assets are considered to be in use for a "commercial purpose." In this light, the Swedish courts have proved to endorse and embrace a liberal and pragmatic point of view. However, the recent application of Article 21 of the UNCSI as constituting customary international law is cumbersome to fit into the previous Swedish practice.[105]

It must also be noted that any interference with immunity from execution is traditionally considered a greater infringement with State sovereignty than simply

102. This is a simplified point of view and merits a bigger contextualization; that is, the award has commercial value despite the temporary lack of compliance. Immunity does not equal impunity and the investor can go on for an asset-hunt (indefinitely), the award can be sold, third-party funders can assist, etc. *See* Loukas A. Mistelis, *Award as an Investment: The Value of an Arbitral Award or the Cost of Non-enforcement*, 28(1) ICSID Review 64–87 (2013). *See also* Franz J. Sedelmayer, *Welcome to Putingrad* (Welcome to Putingrad LLC, 2017). *See also* IA Reporter, Damien Charlotin, *Looking Back: German Investor, Franz Sedelmayer, Was Early-Adopter of Investment Treaty Arbitration, but Had to Engage in Decade-Long Assets Hunt Against Russia*, https://www.iareporter.com/articles/looking-back-german-investor-franz-sedelmayer-was-early-adopter-of-investment-treaty-arbitration-but-had-to-engage-in-decade-long-assets-hunt/.

103. *See*, e.g., *Eiser Infrastructure Ltd v. Kingdom of Spain* [2020] FCA 157 para. 63 (" The arbitrators, whose jurisdiction arises from the consent of the parties, do not have powers of coercion in relation to property—their decisions can only have that effect through the means of enforcement by judgment of a court and then execution.").

104. Crawford, *supra* n. 3, at 1961. The most notable exception to this presumption was presented in France, in *Creighton v. Qatar* Case (Court of Cassation, 2000) the Court held that the arbitration agreement constituted a waiver for purposes of execution, too. *See* Crawford, *supra* n. 3, at 503 ("[I]t is well established that the regimes governing immunity from adjudicative jurisdiction and immunity from execution are separate.").

105. *See The Republic of Kazakhstan and the National Bank of Kazakhstan v. Stati, Ascom, et al* ÖÄ 7709-19 (juni 17, 2020).

rejecting immunity from jurisdiction.[106] It has been said that the restrictive immunity theory (discussed in section §13.02 above) has not received the same breakthrough in customary international law with respect to immunity from execution.[107]

### *[1] Commercial Activity Exception*

The issues pertaining to sovereign immunity from execution of foreign arbitral awards came to test before the Swedish Supreme Court in a case between Mr. Sedelmayer and the Russian Federation (*Sedelmayer v. The Russian Federation*).[108] In this case, Mr. Sedelmayer had won an investment treaty arbitration against the Russian Federation. Russia was not keen on complying voluntarily. As a result, he had to engage in an "asset-hunt," tracing Russian assets to execute the award against in various jurisdictions. Subsequent to a long search for commercial assets, he was successful with real estate in Cologne, Germany, and then sought to execute against real estate also in Sweden.

The issue at hand was whether a property owned by the Russian Federation was used for commercial purposes (i.e., *jure gestionis*) or sovereign purposes (i.e., *jure imperii*). In other words, the question culminated in whether Mr. Sedelmayer could enforce and execute an arbitral award or whether the Russian Federation could invoke the plea of sovereign immunity in order to shield its property.

The Swedish Supreme Court duly noted that the real estate had mixed uses as it was partly resided by diplomatic staff; or put differently, was used for diplomatic purposes. However, ultimately the court concluded that the property was mainly used for "non-official," non-governmental purposes. The fact of the matter was that apartments in this large complex were sublet for rental purposes. Consequently, the Swedish Supreme Court held that Russia could not be shielded from enforcement by virtue of sovereign immunity.

Apart from the pro-investor decision itself, this case had broader implications on the overall law of sovereign immunity. First, the Swedish Supreme Court interpreted the UNCSI as a stepping-stone. The Court pointed to the fact that Sweden had ratified convention and that parts of it could be viewed as a codification of customary international law.[109] Second, the Court "broke from the traditional commercial/noncommercial dichotomy and held that state-owned property used for noncommercial uses may not be immune from attachment."[110] This distinction was itself a major step in the right direction, but the fact that it was taken despite the "mixed-use" of the property and despite the Vienna Convention on Diplomatic Relations was a strong signal to the legal community that the Swedish jurisdiction has endorsed and embraced transnational adjudication as a mechanism, indeed a vehicle,

106. *Ibid.*, at p. 7.
107. *Ibid.*, at p. 9.
108. Swedish Supreme Court Case No. Ö 170-10 (reported in NJA 2011 p. 475). For a good analysis, *see* Pål Wrange, *Sedelmayer v. Russian Federation*, 106(2) American Journal of International Law (2012).
109. *Ibid.*, at 12.
110. *Ibid.*, at 21–23 (unofficial translation).

that enables cross-border business and holds the participants accountable to their undertakings and obligations. *Pacta sunt servanda* was given increased standing and currency.[111] Going forward, if a debtor State has property with mixed uses, but predominantly for commercial use, the plea of immunity may not suffice to obstruct enforcement.[112]

As important *The Sedelmayer* may be, it reflects the Swedish position and echoes the *rationale* elaborated already in *The Charente*. The Swedish Court may have taken an additional step; that is, not "only" did it align with "highly culturally developed nations" but it acted as an architect in developing the law of sovereign immunity. The objective but liberal and pragmatic stance on the otherwise controversial "mixed-use" question was in a league of its own and should be firmly entrenched as a best practice to be followed by other courts and subsequently crystallized as a matter of customary international law.

In Sweden, the sovereign is treated as having exchanged absolute or near absolute immunity for the benefits of honest participation in the global market. In the new global legal order, promises are made and international arbitration makes sure that they are kept. Ultimately, however, it will continue to be municipal courts that bear the responsibility of securing that the last link of the arbitral legal order will not be the weakest. Pro-arbitration Swedish courts have helped legitimize this new global institutional order by unqualified and unequivocal support for the enforcement of a transnational rule of law. *Sedelmayer* was not a deviation from the norm, and it reflects the very spirit of the Swedish approach vis-á-vis sovereign immunity. The reasoning and decision reflect a pattern established as far back as in *The Charente* and Sweden's positioning as a world center for business and arbitration.

The rationale in *The Charente*, shining bright in the cases of *LIAMCO* and *Sedelmayer*, is a testament to the Swedish position with respect to the law on sovereign immunity vis-á-vis international arbitration. And unless the pendulum swings back,[113] the trend seems to go further in this commercially pragmatic direction.

In 2017, award-creditors sought to enforce an arbitral award against the Republic of Kazakhstan in Sweden.[114] In 2018, the Stockholm District Court ordered, as a conservatory measure, the sequestration of property belonging to Kazakhstan for the amount sufficient to cover the outstanding debt of roughly USD 500 million.[115] The

---

111. *See* Hobér, *supra* n. 41, at 30; 20 ILM (1981) 895–896 ("The principle or immunity should not, in a case like this, be allowed to keep fundamental principles of contract law from being applied. I therefore take the view that execution of the arbitral award should be allowed.").
112. *See* Franke, *supra* n. 88 ("In such case, the different purposes must be considered collectively and an assessment made whether they are of a qualified nature, thus covered by state immunity from enforcement.").
113. Which is per se a common and reoccurring legal feature. It should be noted that a minority in *LIAMCO v. State of Libya* sided with language from *Tekno-Pharma AB v. State of Iran*, in which the court took the opposite approach *vis-á-vis* arbitration clauses constituting implied waivers (*see* above).
114. This award had been rendered by an SCC Tribunal in 2013. In 2014, Kazakhstan applied to the Court of Appeal to set aside the award. It was unsuccessful. In 2017, Kazakhstan requested the Supreme Court to reopen the case based on alleged miscarriage of justice. The request was rejected.
115. *Stati, Ascom, et al v. The Republic of Kazakhstan*, Stockholm District Court T 10498-17 2.

court concluded that it was an enforcement matter against the property of a foreign State and that the issue of immunity from jurisdiction "should not be examined separately."[116] Both parties referred to *The Sedelmayer* and to the UNCSI as binding law, reinstating the importance of treating the latter as a stepping-stone for further analysis. Kazakhstan invoked immunity against post-judgment measures of constraint. The Court could have rejected Kazakhstan's invoking of Articles 19(c) and 21 of the UNCSI on the basis that the arbitration clause is a waiver of enforcement jurisdiction, but it did not.

First and foremost, Kazakhstan argued that the property did not belong to it and that it was not located in Sweden.[117] Moreover, Kazakhstan argued that the property (shares, subscription rights, share dividend, etc.) were used for a non-commercial *purpose*.[118] Additionally, Kazakhstan made the case that even if the property was considered to belong to Kazakhstan, it was "property of the central bank or other monetary authority of the State," and thus immune. The applicants noted that the *nexus* questions are subject to the subsequent enforcement proceedings, but went on to make the case that the property belongs to Kazakhstan, is used for other than governmental non-commercial purposes, and that it is indeed located in Sweden. The Stockholm District Court held that "there is no immunity that would hinder enforcement" and that there was no hindrance for attachment for the same reason because: (1) the property belongs to Kazakhstan, (2) the property is exclusively used or intended to be used for other than governmental non-commercial purposes, and (3) the property is located in Sweden.[119] The Stockholm District Court rejected Kazakhstan's argument that the matter is not one of enforcement. The Court reasoned that a matter of a conservatory measure, i.e., the sequestration, was to be considered an enforcement matter as had been clarified by the Supreme Court.

When the Stockholm District Court had rendered its decision on sequestration of generic assets corresponding to the outstanding debt amount, the Enforcement Authority decided to direct enforcement measures against specific assets, including property allegedly belonging to the debtor State's National Bank (central bank). The State and its National Bank challenged the decision in the Nacka District Court, invoking immunity from execution. The Nacka District Court rejected the appeal and dismissed "the matters from further action with respect to the decisions on enforcement of sequestration."[120] The Court held:

116. *Stati, Ascom, et al v. The Republic of Kazakhstan*, Stockholm District Court T 10498-17 23.
117. *See* The "*nexus*" requirement in Article 19 (c) of the UNCSI, "[...] and is in the territory of the State of the forum, provided that post-judgment measures of constraint may only be taken against property that has a connection with the entity against which the proceeding was directed."
118. *Stati, Ascom, et al v. The Republic of Kazakhstan*, Stockholm District Court T 10498-17 13: "The purpose of the holding of the shares is to stabilize the social and economic development of Kazakhstan. This is a sovereign act and the property is therefore subject to immunity under Article 19."
119. *Stati, Ascom, et al v. The Republic of Kazakhstan*, Stockholm District Court T 10498-17 24–26.
120. *The Republic of Kazakhstan and The National Bank of Kazakhstan v. Stati, Ascom, et al*, Nacka District Court (Procedural Order, July 5, 2019) p. 3.

> In sum, the District Court concludes that the appellants have not established that the purpose of the holding of the property is of such qualified nature by belonging to the Central Bank under the Convention or otherwise. None of the circumstances invoked by the appellants entails that the property is immune against measures of constraint.[121]

In short, given the available information about the property at hand, the Nacka District Court decided that (i) the property is located in Sweden; (ii) the property belong to Kazakhstan; and (iii) that there is no impediment to enforcement due to sovereign immunity.[122] The case was then challenged to the Svea Court of Appeal, which reversed the decision on 17 June 2020 (*see* section §13.05[C][2] below) by focusing on the heightened element of sensitivity.

The Stockholm and Nacka District Courts followed the ethos in *The Charente* and *Sedelmayer*, but the Svea Court of Appeal seems to have gone in the opposite, and more regressive, direction. Several similar proceedings between the same parties are also on-going in, *inter alia*, England and Belgium. Those courts may benefit from the Swedish contribution to the law on sovereign immunity from execution of foreign arbitral awards; but first, the Supreme Court should realign the case law with the liberal and pragmatic spirit that used to represent the Swedish position.

### *[2] Property Immune* **Ipso Facto** *(Diplomatic Property and Central Bank Property)*

As mentioned in section §13.02 above, certain property is considered categorically immune *ipso facto* pursuant to Article 21 of the UNCSI. In *Sedelmayer*, the Court referenced to Article 21 once and quickly concluded that the property may be used for various purposes.[123] The Court then highlighted the difficulty in mixed-use situations.[124] Finally, the Court concluded that the property was not "to a substantial part used for the official purposes of the Russian Federation."[125] The Swedish contribution was thus one of pragmatism and in sync with furthering the ideals of a liberal doctrine of sovereign immunity.

Recently, however, Kazakhstan and the National Bank challenged the decision from Nacka District Court's decision to reject the plea of immunity (*see* section §13.05[C][1] above). Kazakhstan and its National Bank claimed that the attached property (i) does not belong to Kazakhstan; (ii) is not located in Sweden; (iii) is protected by sovereign immunity; and (iv) cannot be executed due to ordre public. The Svea Court of Appeal started with the plea of immunity from execution, and for the

121. *The Republic of Kazakhstan and The National Bank of Kazakhstan v. Stati, Ascom, et al*, Nacka District Court (Procedural Order, July 5, 2019) p. 3.
122. *The Republic of Kazakhstan and The National Bank of Kazakhstan v. Stati, Ascom, et al*, Nacka District Court (Procedural Order, July 5, 2019) p. 3.
123. *Sedelmayer v. The Russian Federation*, Swedish Supreme Court Case no. Ö 170-10 (reported in NJA 2011 p. 475), paras. 14–15.
124. *Sedelmayer v. The Russian Federation*, Swedish Supreme Court Case no. Ö 170-10 (reported in NJA 2011 p. 475), para. 16.
125. *Sedelmayer v. The Russian Federation*, Swedish Supreme Court Case no. Ö 170-10 (reported in NJA 2011 p. 475), para. 23.

sake of its analysis presumed that the property belongs to Kazakhstan and that it is located in Sweden.

The Court reached the final conclusion that the attached property is absolutely immune because it constitutes central bank property, and such property is categorically immune *ipso facto* pursuant to Article 21(c) of the UNCSI. Thus, the Court held that Kazakhstan and the National Bank enjoyed immunity pursuant to Article 21(c), and therefore, that there is no need to analyze Article 19(c) of the UNCSI any further. As a result, because the said property enjoys immunity, it cannot be executed and the on-going procedure at the Enforcement Agency must be stopped.[126]

The Court rightly noted that prior case law has referenced to the UNCSI as partly codifying customary international law.[127] The Court also noted—as it should—that each provision of the UNCSI cannot automatically be treated as customary international law.[128] It is argued that the Court was right to treat the UNCSI as a starting point for further inquiry, but it should not treat each and every provision as a codification of customary international law. Especially not such provisions that were clearly agreed upon as a concession between liberal and conservative States in an attempt to reach multilateral consensus between divergent views. The fact of the matter is that state practice is divergent on whether central banks enjoy virtually absolute immunity with respect to attachment and execution of its property. Some states' legislation provides near absolute immunity from execution of central bank property (which seems to be in line with the UNCSI); other States protect central bank property only when it is used for central bank functions or for governmental purposes; and a third category of states provides no special protection at all.[129] Sweden could have endorsed the middle-ground approach and reasoned in light of the ethos in *Sedelmayer*.

Furthermore, the Court rightly noted that an examination of international customary international law is called for.[130] Unfortunately, the Court does not seem to have engaged in an analysis of what level of protection customary international law mandates, and instead surprisingly outright treated Article 21(c) of the UNCSI as a codification of customary international law. Article 21(c) offers essentially absolute immunity to central bank property by treating such as categorically immune *ipso facto*. As mentioned, the alternative viewpoint would be to treat the immunity question as in *Sedelmayer* and in the District Court of the aforementioned case, i.e., determine whether the specific property is used, in the first step, solely for commercial purposes, and in the second step (if necessary), if the use is predominantly for commercial or governmental purposes. Notwithstanding this, such interpretation would not align

126. *The Republic of Kazakhstan and the National Bank of Kazakhstan v. Stati, Ascom, et al* ÖÄ 7709-19 (juni 17, 2020), p. 26.
127. *The Republic of Kazakhstan and the National Bank of Kazakhstan v. Stati, Ascom, et al* ÖÄ 7709-19 (juni 17, 2020), p. 9 (citing NJA 2009 section 905 and NJA 2011 section 475).
128. *The Republic of Kazakhstan and the National Bank of Kazakhstan v. Stati, Ascom, et al* ÖÄ 7709-19 (juni 17, 2020), p. 9.
129. Ingrid Wuerth, *"Immunity from Execution of Central Bank Assets"* in Tom Ruys and Nicolas Angelet (eds.), *Cambridge Handbook on Immunities and International Law*, 266 (Cambridge: Cambridge University Press; 2019).
130. *The Republic of Kazakhstan and the National Bank of Kazakhstan v. Stati, Ascom, et al* ÖÄ 7709-19 (juni 17, 2020), p. 13.

with the language of the provision. However, whether the provision should have been the only focal point is the crux of the matter; that is, the Court should first have determined whether Article 21(c) of the UNCI does represent customary international law. Only thereafter should the Court have proceeded with the textual inquiry. The Court circumvented a threshold issue, and thus the result may have been flawed.

An interpretation of Article 21(c) based on the Vienna Convention on the Law of Treaties (VCLT) makes it clear that a categorical application is mandated. This becomes evident when comparing the protection offered to other types of property under the same article, which allows for an analysis of the particular use and functions. An alternative interpretation would be to read the provision in light of Article 2(1)(b)(iii), which makes a reference to "acts in the exercise of sovereign authority of the state." According to this author, the strongest argument in favor of a categorical application was that presented by Professor Wrange in his expert testimony, namely, that the structure of Article 21 is such that another specifically protected property has language qualifying the *ipso facto* protection (i.e., by its functions), while subsection (c) does not.[131] A limitation in (c) that central bank property specifically protected should be used for "central bank" functions or used for governmental purposes is non-existent. The other main point validating a categorical interpretation is that the purpose of Article 21 is to provide an additional set of protection, otherwise it would have been futile per se.[132] This position gets reinstated by the governmental bill to the Swedish ratification of the UNCSI; that is, the property in Article 21 by its very nature is such that it is presumed to be used or intended to be used exclusively for governmental purposes, without any commercial purposes whatsoever.[133] For the reasons mentioned, the interpretation of the UNCSI was likely not flawed per se, even if the alternative interpretation lending itself toward a functional application was equally compelling.

What is even more perplexing is that when all was said and done, the Court nevertheless qualified the now de facto rule of absolute immunity in this context by stating that it may not be ruled out that situations may appear in which a property of a central bank may not enjoy immunity pursuant to Article 21(c). This purported position is indeed mutually exclusive from the categorical approach endorsed. This can only mean one thing, namely, that a textual interpretation in accordance with Article 21(c) should not lend itself toward a categorical application where the result would render the outcome manifestly absurd or unreasonable.[134]

Thus, the Court should have started the analysis backwards by answering two threshold questions: (1) whether Article 21(c) should be treated as customary international law, and (2) whether this is a situation where the functions are so separate from the ordinary functions of a central bank that a grant of immunity would be

131. *The Republic of Kazakhstan and the National Bank of Kazakhstan v. Stati, Ascom, et al* ÖÄ 7709-19 (juni 17, 2020), p. 20.
132. *See The Republic of Kazakhstan and the National Bank of Kazakhstan v. Stati, Ascom, et al* ÖÄ 7709-19 (juni 17, 2020), p. 21.
133. Govt. Bill 2008/09:204, p. 82.
134. *The Republic of Kazakhstan and the National Bank of Kazakhstan v. Stati, Ascom, et al* ÖÄ 7709-19 (juni 17, 2020), pp. 23–24.

manifestly absurd or unreasonable. It is the firm opinion of this author that (1) Article 21(c) does not represent customary international law, and (2) that the functions of the National Bank with respect to the property under dispute was so clearly separate from the ordinary functions of a central bank that a grant of immunity was manifestly absurd and definitely unreasonable. However, the Court should not have side-stepped the full analysis necessary. The ICJ made it emphatically clear that the UNCSI only constitutes a codification of customary international law in part. It is this author's opinion that Article 21(c) does not represent a codification of customary international law and that the Swedish practice should not endorse the more regressive of divergent state practices.

To summarize the case, the Court had to determine (1) whether the National Bank is a central bank pursuant to Article 21(c); (2) whether the property belongs to the National Bank; and (3) whether the Article 21(c) should be applied categorically or functionally.[135] The Court concluded that the National Bank—given its nature and function—constitutes a central bank pursuant to Article 21 of the UNCSI, and, furthermore, that the property belongs to the National Bank in the manner prescribed in Article 21.[136] With respect to the third issue, the Court reasoned that a categorical application lends Kazakhstan immunity, while a functional application mandates a position on whether the property is used for governmental non-commercial purposes or not. Based on this, the Court concluded that the property is immune *ipso facto* because the article supposedly mandates a categorical application. The Court reached its decision on the basis of treaty interpretation in accordance with the VCLT.

### *[3] Implied Waiver Doctrine*

In Sweden, a valid arbitration clause constitutes a waiver of sovereign immunity from jurisdiction. Whether this should extend to immunity from execution was for long a debated issue.[137] Nowadays, it is almost a firmly established view that an arbitration clause should not be treated as a waiver of immunity from execution. Whether an arbitration clause constitutes a waiver of immunity from enforcement jurisdiction is more cumbersome to discern. Enforcement jurisdiction does not include post-judgment measures of constraint such as attachment and execution. Such is a matter to be treated separately.

In the 2018 case between an award creditor and the Republic of Kazakhstan, the latter argued that the district court "has to declare its position regarding the question about immunity from jurisdiction of the courts of another state" prior to addressing immunity from post-judgment measures of constraint.[138] As outlined above, the Stockholm District Court rejected this argument. It is this author's opinion that the

135. *The Republic of Kazakhstan and the National Bank of Kazakhstan v. Stati, Ascom, et al* ÖÄ 7709-19 (juni 17, 2020), pp. 14–15.
136. *The Republic of Kazakhstan and the National Bank of Kazakhstan v. Stati, Ascom, et al* ÖÄ 7709-19 (juni 17, 2020), p. 18.
137. *See* Franke, *supra* n. 88.
138. *Stati, Ascom, et al v. The Republic of Kazakhstan*, Stockholm District Court case No. T 10498-17 12.

court could have taken yet another step. The court had an opportunity to make clear that an arbitration clause constitutes a waiver from immunity vis-á-vis jurisdiction, including enforcement jurisdiction (as opposed to execution) in municipal courts. There was no need to elaborate on Articles 19 and 21 of the UNCSI at the stage of attaching generic assets, i.e., turning the award into an enforceable title. The elaboration of a robust waiver doctrine would make it clear that States can only invoke immunity from *execution* and that such immunity would only encompass property that is clearly used for governmental purposes. The burden of proof should be on the State in proving that the property is used for governmental purposes exclusively or majorly.

In theory, the Svea Court of Appeal could have elaborated a full-fetched double-waiver doctrine, namely, holding that an arbitration clause constitutes a waiver of immunity from execution, too, in non-ICSID arbitration. The investors argued that Kazakhstan was obliged to comply with the arbitral award pursuant to Energy Charter Treaty (ECT) Article 26(8):

> The awards of arbitration, which may include an award of interest, shall be final and binding upon the parties to the dispute. [...] Each Contracting Party shall carry out without delay any such award and shall make provision for the effective enforcement in its Area of such awards.

The investors argued that the invoking of sovereign immunity was a means to undercut the enforcement, and therefore was an attempt to circumvent its treaty obligations. The investors essentially alleged that the treatment of immunity as a shield in circumventing its obligations was an "abuse of rights," namely, a procedural tool disposed to avoid complying with the award. However, the argument falls flat on its face because immunity is treated as a procedural plea and it does not imply impunity. A misuse of rights (or privileges rather) is thus, as the Court noted, incompatible with the rules on sovereign immunity.

However, the parties could at least have made the argument that Article 26 of the ECT constitutes an implied waiver of immunity from execution. It is true that the double waiver doctrine is not fashionable nowadays, but at least it would force the court to reconsider its important role as the last link in effectuating a transnational dispute resolution regime that has brought the rule of law to all corners of the world. Political concerns and policy objectives of yesterday may—and probably will—eventually be reconsidered. At least this author remains hopeful that the Swedish jurisdiction will in a not too distant time resume where the French Court took off (and eventually capitulated).[139]

That said, one should not be too wishful or naive with requests that are not yet ripe for reconsideration, even in the most pro-arbitration jurisdictions. The regressive outcome in the Svea Court of Appeal may itself prove to be a testimony to the fact that pendulums swing in both directions. The fact of the matter is that we live in an era of investor-state backlash, where political concerns and policy objectives sometimes

139. *Creighton v. Qatar* (July 6, 2000). Cf *Noga and Republic of Cameroon v. Winslow Bank & Trust Paris Court of Appeals on August 10, 2000* and Loi n° 2016-1691 relative à la transparence, à la lutte contre la corruption et à la modernisation de la vie économique, 9 December 2016 ("The Sapin 2 law").

interfere with legal logic and equal accountability for all parties to a dispute. But, as mentioned, pendulums do swing and proponents of the double waiver doctrine should not waste an opportunity to make their voices heard loud and clear. Come the day for an honest reconsideration of the double waiver doctrine, it is likely that one of the main reasons for justifying the doctrine will be that rogue states have for too long been abusing their procedural privileges to circumvent ancient principles of legal wisdom, such as *pacta sunt servanda.*

Sweden has the potential to be the leading architect among other "developed nations, which are close to Sweden."[140] Therefore, this author hopes that the day will come where an arbitration clause is finally treated as a waiver of immunity from execution, with the exception only for certain specifically outlined property, which is used for governmental purposes and fulfills the functions of the institution it seeks to protect (e.g., diplomatic property or pure central bank property). Given the Swedish experience and contribution to this area of law, it is not unlikely that the Swedish courts will pave that way. But first, the Supreme Court has to reclaim the liberal and pragmatic Swedish position by rejecting the reasoning in and perhaps reverse the holding of the Svea Court of Appeal in *The Republic of Kazakhstan and the National Bank of Kazakhstan v. Stati, Ascom, et al.*

## §13.06 CONCLUDING REMARKS

Sweden has since long embraced the international trend toward a restrictive doctrine of immunity. Moreover, Swedish courts have given effect to the general rule of immunity as forming part of customary international law, which is now firmly entrenched since the ICJ decision from 2012. As is the case under the doctrine of restrictive immunity, the general rule is qualified by several exceptions.[141] What the exceptions are and how they operate in practice remain unclear. The UNCSI has provided some guidance, especially making it unequivocal that there is an overall consensus that certain exceptions should be approved at the execution stage as well as at the adjudicative stage. The UNCSI is not yet binding but it partly represents a codification of customary international law. As a result, municipal courts are still rather free to carve-out further exceptions or to navigate the scope, degree, and extent of the exceptions in the yet to be entered into force convention. Thus, the law and legal theory on sovereign immunity keeps on posing hard questions relating to, *inter alia*, statutory or treaty interpretation, the justification for the law, the lack of uniformity, and the desire for removal of legal barriers. Moreover, it throws up sensitive debates on various political, legal, historic, and cultural issues—e.g., whether and why economically and politically influential Western countries have been the leaders in elaborating the doctrine on sovereign immunity, despite it being a public international law concept.

140. As expressed in *The Charente* NJA 1942 65, at 74–75.

141. *See*, e.g., Crawford, *supra* n. 3, at 489; Foreign Sovereign Immunities Act 1976; State Immunity Act 1978; the 2004 United Nations Convention on Jurisdictional Immunities of States and Their Property; and *Germany v. Italy: Greece Intervening*, Jurisdictional Immunities of the State, Judgment of February 3, ICJ Reports 2012.

In the author's view, the final arbiter of defining the law on sovereign immunity should be the ICJ. As the main judicial branch of public international law, the ICJ has a natural standing to consolidate, crystallize, and interpret public international law. When cases reach the court, the judges will be tasked with orienting the maze of foreign decisional law, legislative developments, and scholarly work, only to embrace some of it. The ICJ should take into account the best state practices from all over the world. In that task, the Swedish jurisdiction has a unique voice by the fact that it is a neutral country that belongs to a legal tradition that constitutes a kind of mixture of common and civil legal families. ICJ judges should look to Sweden for guidance. Moreover, the rarity of cases reaching the ICJ means that municipal courts must engage in a comparative legal methodology by looking at foreign decisional law to fill the gaps. This is especially so in the arbitration context. The Swedish contribution will be helpful to any court that seeks to align with a legally and commercially sensible pro-arbitration doctrine of sovereign immunity.

The Swedish experience and contribution demonstrate a liberal and pragmatic approach to the law. The approach squarely resonates with liberal capitalism and liberal democracy. Conclusively, if a court decides to endorse a balanced pro-business doctrine of sovereign immunity, the Swedish decisional law in this area should be highlighted and strenuously praised. Especially in the arbitration context where Swedish courts have been architects of an unequivocal pro-arbitration policy. Put simply, Swedish courts do not shy away from enforcing arbitral awards against States.

Furthermore, from a philosophical standpoint, it can be argued that Swedish courts have understood their role in legal civilization. The courts have assumed their duty to assist and supervise a new global legal order by being active, pragmatic and progressive participants of the system. The development started with *The Charente* and has continued that path with only minor deviations. Sweden early on undertook a leading position as architect of a pro-arbitral legal order and has kept true to that promise ever since.[142]

*Sedelmayer* is the decision that shines the brightest. The decision is to be applauded. It will likely be cemented as one of the Swedish Supreme Court's greatest arbitration legacies. The decision leaves us with two main take-aways, i.e., (1) the courts treat the UNCSI as a manifestation of customary international law, and thus a stepping-stone for further analysis on the law of sovereign immunity; and (2) the courts interpret the convention through the lens of liberal, pro-business pragmatism. In a word, in *Sedelmayer*, the Swedish Supreme Court started off by analyzing the UNCSI only to fill the gaps by reasoning pragmatically vis-á-vis property used for "mixed

142. With the exception of the decision in *The Republic of Kazakhstan and the National Bank of Kazakhstan v. Stati, Ascom, et al* ÖÄ 7709-19 (juni 17, 2020). The investor has been on an asset-hunt ever since the arbitral award was rendered on December 19, 2013. Subsequent to the Court decision in *The Republic of Kazakhstan and The National Bank of Kazakhstan v. Stati, Ascom, et al*, Nacka District Court (Procedural Order, July 5, 2019), Anatolie Stati, CEO and shareholder of Ascom Group, said that "We welcome the latest judgment of Nacka District Court, which confirms the pro arbitration policy adopted by Swedish courts." Hopefully the Supreme Court can revive the Swedish pro-arbitration policy *vis-á-vis* immunity from execution.

purposes." It is likely that the Swedish courts will continue to engage in defining the contours of the law of sovereign immunity, viz., to determine when and how the general rule of immunity should be qualified.

One large caveat remains lurking in the Swedish horizon, namely the recent decision by the Svea Court of Appeal in *The Republic of Kazakhstan and the National Bank of Kazakhstan v. Stati, Ascom, et al.*[143] It is hoped that the Supreme Court will eventually redirect the case law to reflect the ethos previously endorsed. It was perplexing to see that the Svea Court of Appeal, without proper justification, decided to disregard a discussion on divergent state practice and instead outright treating Article 21(c) as *de lege lata*. Unless the Supreme Court overturns the decision or the reasoning in it, Sweden's latest contribution to the law on sovereign immunity would risk endorsing the vision of the proponents of absolute immunity. That would indeed be a surprise and a regret.

143. *The Republic of Kazakhstan and the National Bank of Kazakhstan v. Stati, Ascom, et al* ÖÄ 7709-19 (juni 17, 2020).

CHAPTER 14

# Approaches to Arbitrators' Liability: Immunity or Liability?

*Sarah Schæffer*[*]

## §14.01 INTRODUCTION

The global economy has turned arbitration into a big business.[1] Historically, arbitration was a special honour rather than a profession, and the arbitrator's fees were merely of nominal character.[2] In the past few decades, there has been a notable change in the use of arbitration as a dispute resolution mechanism. The increasing number of international commercial disputes has led to a growth in demand for arbitration and consequently a professionalisation of arbitration as a business activity.[3]

Arbitration has become more complex and time-consuming, often leading to significant arbitration costs, including arbitrator fees and costs.[4] One of the effects of this changing nature of arbitration has been an increase in the parties' expectations to the arbitrator and the fulfilment of the arbitrator's task. Since the parties place their trust and confidence in the arbitrator, the expectations to his/her skills, experience and integrity are often considerably high. In the event the arbitrator negligently or

* The article is based on the author's dissertation 'Approaches to Arbitrators' Liability – A Study of Theory and Practice' submitted as part of her LL.M. studies at Queen Mary University at London 2018/2019 under the supervision of Professor Loukas A Mistelis. The article has been published in a slightly different version in the Danish journal 'Erhvervsjuridisk Tidsskrift' (April 2020) adding a Danish perspective on the topic.

1. Julian D M Lew (ed.), *The Immunity of Arbitrators*, 1 (Lloyd's of London Press Ldt 1990).
2. Tamara Oyre, *Professional Liability and Judicial Immunity* 64 Arbitration 45 (1998).
3. Lew (*supra* n. 1) 1.
4. Jason Yat Sen Li, *Arbitral Immunity: A Profession Comes of Age* 64 Arbitration 51, 55 citing Mustill & Boyd (1998).

fraudulently disregards his/her duties, not only the confidence in the arbitrator will be lost, but the parties might sustain significant economic loss.[5]

The available remedies in case of such arbitrator misconduct are generally limited to the removal of the arbitrator, vacating the award, and potential criminal liability in case of extreme misbehaviour. As none of these sanctions gives any account to economic losses or damages suffered by an aggrieved party, such redress is often considered inadequate or ill-suited. Prompted by the high economic risks at stake in arbitration, civil liability claims against arbitrators have emerged in recent years.

Arbitrator liability is, however, controversial and subject to various opinions among legislators, national courts and commentators as to the existence, legal basis and scope of such liability.[6] The contentiousness of this legal area originates from the hybrid nature of the relationship between the parties and the arbitrator; the latter being a contract partner as well as a private judge. The judicial nature of the arbitrator's profession has led to the controversial question of whether arbitrators should be immune from liability?

At this point, there are no international binding instruments that regulate arbitrators' liability.[7] Hence, the question is determined solely by local lawmakers and national courts from different legal systems.

The use of local applicable conflict-of-law rules is resulting in divergent approaches.[8] The inevitable result is uncertainty for all parties involved in the arbitration process, as the consequences of a potential future lawsuit against the arbitrator are unknown. While some jurisdictions have dealt with this issue through legislation or case law – other jurisdictions have not provided a clear approach to arbitrator liability.

Despite the existence of various divergent approaches prompted by the use of local applicable conflict-of-law rules, there seems to be a general movement from an absolute immunity to a qualified immunity (or limited liability) norm. The magnitude of the move seems to depend on whether the jurisdiction is regulated by civil or common law.[9] However, the commonality in recent developments in case law is, that arbitrators *can* be liable to the parties under certain circumstances.

In view of the above, this chapter seeks to identify the underlying considerations for and against arbitrators' liability. Further, the aim is to examine the different approaches to arbitrators' liability and the legal bases for these approaches, using various jurisdictions as examples, and to provide a recommendation on the preferred approach to arbitrators' liability.

5. Christian Hausmaninger, *Civil Liability of Arbitrators – Comparative Analysis and Proposals for Reform*, 7 J. Int'l Arb. 7, 8 (1990).
6. Susan D Franck, *The Liability of International Arbitrators: A Comparative Analysis and Proposal for Qualified Immunity*, 20 N.Y. Sch. J. Int'l. & Comp. L. 1, 2–3 (2000).
7. Neither the UNCITRAL Model Law on International Commercial Arbitration, 2006 ('Model Law') or the Convention on the Recognition and Enforcement of Foreign Arbitral Awards, 1958 regulate this matter. *See* Franck I, *supra* n. 6, at 3 and Hausmaninger, *supra* n. 5, at 8.
8. Since the potential liability often depends on the law of the arbitration seat. *See*, e.g., Franck I *supra* n. 6, at 49–53.
9. The US standing out from the crowd as the only jurisdiction providing the arbitrator with nearly absolute immunity except from situations where the arbitrator lacks jurisdiction or where the misconduct does not relate to his/her judicial acts. *See*, e.g., Franck I *supra* n. 6, at 31–32.

## §14.02 THE STATUS OF THE ARBITRATOR

Determining the *status of the arbitrator* aims at defining the legal relationship between the arbitrator and the parties, and, thus, concerns the source of the arbitrator's rights and obligations in relation to the parties. For this reason, the determination of the arbitrator's status is paramount for questions concerning liability and immunity.[10] As the majority of arbitration laws and rules do not regulate the relationship between arbitrators and the parties, different theories have been suggested by national courts and legal commentators for defining the status of the arbitrator.[11]

The most widely recognised theory, particularly among civil law jurisdictions, is that the status of the arbitrator is based on a contractual relationship with the parties ('*Contractual Status Approach*').[12] According to the Contractual Status Approach, the arbitrator's liability is based on the terms of the appointment as arbitrator, including agreed arbitration rules and terms of payment of arbitrator fees and costs, and not the adjudicatory function which the arbitrator performs.[13] The applicable rules of contract law will therefore be determining for the arbitrator's liability.[14] Consequently, the arbitrator incurs liability for breach of contract[15] in the event of documented faults committed during the arbitration proceedings, which violate the terms of the appointment.[16] However, the Contractual Status Approach does not necessarily exclude liability on legal principles that are non-contractual. Thus, the arbitrator might - despite the contractual relationship with the parties - be held liable on the basis of national rules of tort law at the seat of arbitration if (s)he fails to demonstrate the expected level of care and skill following from his/her profession.[17]

The main alternative theory to the Contractual Status Approach is based on the adjudicatory function performed by the arbitrator rather than the contract with the parties ('*Functional Status Approach*').[18] The Functional Status Approach rests on the supposed analogical relationship between the arbitrator and the judge.[19] Central for this theory, which typically attracts support from common law jurisdictions, is that

10. Gary B Born, *International Commercial Arbitration*, 1963 (2nd ed, Kluwer 2014).
11. Born, *supra* n. 100, at 1967.
12. Julian D M Lew, Loukas A Mistelis and Stefan M Kröll, *Comparative International Commercial Arbitration*, 276 (Kluwer 2003); Patrik Schöldström, *The Arbitrator's Mandate*, 27 (Stiftelsen Skrifter utgivna av Juridiska fakulteten vid Stockholms universitet 1998). This approach is coined the 'Contractual Status Approach' by the author and will be used throughout this chapter.
13. Franck I, *supra* n. 6, at 7.
14. Franz T Schwarz and Christian W Konrad, *The Vienna Rules: A Commentary on International Arbitration in Austria*, 178 (Kluwer 2009).
15. Absent an explicit provision in the agreement or applicable arbitration rules.
16. Emmanuel Gaillard and John Savage (eds), *Fouchard Gaillard Goldman on International Commercial Arbitration*, 1144 (Kluwer 1999); Franck I, *supra* n. 6, at 5.
17. Franck I, *supra* n. 6, at 10.
18. Hausmaninger, *supra* n. 5, at 16. This approach is coined the 'Functional Status Approach' by the author and will be used throughout this chapter.
19. Dario Alessi, *Enforcing Arbitrator's Obligations: Rethinking International Commercial Arbitrators' Liability* 31 J.Int'l Arb. 735, 742 (2014).

arbitrators are involved in the administration of justice just as state court judges.[20] The status of the arbitrator is therefore 'quasi-judicial' in nature, meaning that the arbitrator's obligations and rights, similar to those of state judges, are founded in national law.[21] Contrary to the Contractual Status Approach, the legal basis for arbitrator liability is tort in common law and damages in civil law. However, given the perception that arbitrators are exercising a function comparable to that of state court judges, advocates of this theory have suggested that arbitrators enjoy the same immunity from liability as judges (judicial immunity).[22]

Although the adjudicative function of the arbitrator undoubtedly has an important influence on the status of the arbitrator, arbitrators differ from judges in fundamental ways.[23] A central distinction is the mandate; the arbitrator derives his authority from the parties while judges derive their jurisdiction from the state.[24] Furthermore, arbitrators and judges differ in respect of how they are remunerated and selected. While parties are in control of the appointment procedure of arbitrators and solely responsible to pay their fees, judges are randomly assigned to cases and their salaries are paid by the state.[25] Judges and arbitrators also differ in terms of their administrative functions. Whereas judges are strictly bound by rules of civil procedure and evidence, arbitrators often have the discretion, subject to the parties' agreement, to decide on the applicable rules of the procedure.[26] Finally, as correctly pointed out by *Born,* a range of aspects of the arbitrator's rights and duties[27] can only be explained by a contract between the arbitrator and the parties, and the functional approach does not provide sufficient legal basis for those.[28]

As a result of the fundamental differences between judges and arbitrators, especially the source of their adjudicative power and authority (*public versus private nature*), it would in the author's opinion be erroneous to characterise the status of the arbitrator as strictly functional.

Nevertheless, due to the hybrid nature of arbitration, neither a traditional contractual approach nor a strict functional approach seems to fit for defining the status of the arbitrator. As correctly argued by some commentators, the better view is that the legal basis for the arbitrator's relationship with the parties derives from both theories ('*Hybrid Status Approach*').[29] This Hybrid Status Approach classifies the arbitrator's

20. Stefan Riegler and Martin Platte, *Chapter II: The Arbitrator – Arbitrators' Liability,* 108 in Christian Klausegger and others (eds), *Austrian Arbitration Yearbook 2007* (Manz'sche Verlags- und Universitätsbuchhandlung 2007).
21. Jeffrey Waincymer, *Procedure and Evidence in International Arbitration,* 72 (Kluwer 2012).
22. Schwarz and Konrad, *supra* n. 144, at 178.
23. Susan D Franck, *The Role of International Arbitrators,* 12 ILSA J Int'l L 499, 504 (2006); Franck I, *supra* n. 6, at 24; Hausmaninger, *supra* n. 5, at 17.
24. Franck II, *supra* n. 233, at 508.
25. Franck II, *supra* n. 233, at 508; Alessi, *supra* n. 19, at 745.
26. *See* Franck II, *supra* n. 233, at 512.
27. For example, the arbitrator's remuneration and other terms of engagement.
28. Born, *supra* n. 100, at 1973. *See also* the courts comments on this point in *Baar v. Tigerman,* 140 Cal. App. 3d 979, 189 Cal. Rptr. 834, 835 (1983).
29. For a supportive view *see,* e.g., Schöldström, *supra* n. 122, at 28. *See* however Dario Alessi who advocates for a strict contractual approach Alessi, *supra* n. 19, at 735–784. This approach is coined the 'Hybrid Status Approach' by the author and will be used throughout this chapter.

status as a sui generis contract,[30] which provides a unique set of rights and duties of the arbitrator.[31] Thus, the Hybrid Status Approach recognises the function of the arbitrator as dual and views the arbitrator as both a service provider and a private judge ('quasi-judicial'). The effect is that the arbitrator's rights and obligations are derived from the terms of appointment, national/international law, and from rules applicable to state judges to the extent necessary to protect the arbitrator's impartial and independent judgment of the dispute.[32]

## §14.03 THE ARBITRATOR'S OBLIGATIONS TO THE PARTIES

Arbitrators have several duties originating from the contract, institutional rules, national law and ethical duties; some of them both contractual and general in nature.[33]

The main obligation of the arbitrator is to *finally settle the dispute between the parties*. The finality aspect of this obligation implies that the arbitrator must render a valid award not open to challenges. From this duty follows that the arbitrator should conduct the arbitral procedure in a way which does not compromise the validity of the award, e.g., review all issues submitted by the parties, refrain from exceeding his/her authority/jurisdiction, treat the parties fairly and equally, etc.[34]

By accepting to act as an arbitrator, the arbitrator is obliged to *resolve the parties' dispute*.[35] This duty is only fulfilled if the arbitrator renders an award or the parties settle the case.[36] Thus, any resignation without a good cause is a violation of the arbitrator's obligations to the parties. In the event of any undue resignation, the parties risk a considerable loss of resources (time and money) already invested in the arbitration, as proceedings may have to be repeated and/or will be delayed.[37]

One of the essential obligations of the arbitrator is to *be and stay independent and impartial*. This obligation continues to exist after the appointment stage throughout the arbitral proceedings.[38] The obligation requires the arbitrator to be unbiased and to be free of personal, contractual, institutional or any other relationship that would compromise his/her impartiality and independence.[39] These personal obligations imply a pre-contractual and continuing contractual duty[40] to disclose all relevant facts, which might, in the eyes of the parties, affect his/her impartiality or independence.

The arbitrator shall *conduct the arbitration in a fair, equal, diligent and expeditious manner*.

30. Rather than an agent contract or a contract for the provision of services.
31. Fouchard, *supra* n. 166, at 607; Oyre, *supra* n. 2, at 45.
32. Born, *supra* n. 100, at 1979; Assif Salahuddin, *Should Arbitrators Be Immune from Liability?* 33 Arb Intl 571, 578 (2017); Hausmaninger, *supra* n. 5, at 22.
33. Salahuddin, *supra* n. 322, at 578; Fouchard, *supra* n. 166, at 609–610.
34. For example, English Arbitration Act 1996 (EAA) s. 33. *See* Born, *supra* n. 100, at 1986–1987; Lew et al., *supra* n. 122, at 280.
35. Born, *supra* n. 100, at 2008.
36. Lew et al., *supra* n. 122, at 281.
37. *Ibid.*
38. Lew et al., *supra* n. 122, at 282; Born, *supra* n. 100, at 1988.
39. Born, *supra* n. 100, at 1989.
40. Based on the general duty of good faith in bargains. *See, e.g.*, Alessi, *supra* n. 19, at 778.

Finally, the arbitrator is under a duty to *keep the arbitration confidential* in order to preserve the private nature of arbitration.[41]

## §14.04 *IMMUNITY VERSUS LIABILITY*

Immunity for arbitrators originates from the concept of 'Judicial Immunity' according to which judges cannot be held liable for their judicial acts.[42] While judges tend to enjoy absolute immunity from civil claims in common law countries,[43] no such concept exists in civil law jurisdictions, where liability is at least a theoretical possibility.[44]

### [A] Arbitrator Immunity

According to one school of thought, who favours the Functional Status Approach, it is argued that immunity should be extended to arbitrators in order to protect their impartiality and independence (arbitrator immunity).[45] Thus, acts related to the *adjudicatory function*, in other words, the decision-making process, will be covered by arbitrator immunity, unless they represent a manifest disregard of the law.[46] Hence, arbitrators will be immune from, e.g., lawsuits based on wrongful application of legal principles, unjustified reliance on facts of the case or arbitrary conclusions based on submitted evidence in the arbitration.[47]

Various justifications for arbitrator immunity have been proposed by commentators, legislators and courts.[48] One of the primary reasons for immunity is to protect arbitrators' integrity and independence.[49] The rationale is that arbitrators should not fear being threatened, harassed or sued by unsatisfied parties to the arbitration, as this would risk affecting the arbitrator's decision-making.[50] Another argument is that arbitrator immunity preserves the finality of the award by preventing unsuccessful parties from attempting to re-litigate the case by bringing legal action against the

41. For example, LCIA Rules Art. 30 and Arts 34 and 35 of the Rules of Arbitration Procedure adopted by the Danish Institute of Arbitration. *See also* Lew et al., *supra* n. 122, at 283; Born, *supra* n. 100, at 2003–2004.
42. Franck I, *supra* n. 6, at 16; Martin Domke, *The Arbitrator's Immunity from Liability: A Comparative Survey*, 3 Toledo L. Rev. 99 (1971).
43. For example, US. *See also* Hausmaninger, *supra* n. 5, at 9–14.
44. Franck I, *supra* n. 6, at 17; Hausmaninger, *supra* n. 5, at 13.
45. *See also Hoosac Tunnel Dock & Elevator Co v. O'Brien*, 137 Mass 424, 426 (1884): 'An Arbitrator is a quasi-judicial officer exercising judicial functions. There is as much reason in his case for protecting and insuring his impartiality, independence, and freedom from undue influences, as in the case of a judge or juror.'
46. Hausmaninger, *supra* n. 5, at 47. As regards the common-law test applied in respect of the determination whether an act falls within the decision-making process and thereby covered by immunity *see* Franck I, *supra* n. 6, at 18–23 incl. note 208.
47. Domke, *supra* n. 422, at 101.
48. For example, *Sutcliffe v. Thackrah* [1974] AC 727 (HL) 736 (Lord Reid), 744 (Lord Morris).
49. Hausmaninger, *supra* n. 5, at 17; Domke, *supra* n. 422, at 99; Schöldström, *supra* n. 122, at 339.
50. Franck I, *supra* n. 6, at 28.

arbitrator.[51] Additionally, it has been argued that the number of skilled arbitrators willing to accept assignments as arbitrators would be considerably reduced without immunity as protection.[52] Such effect is alleged to adversely affect the quality of arbitration.[53]

### [B] Arbitrator Liability

Critics of the concept arbitrator immunity, supportive of the Contractual Status Approach, generally claim that arbitrators should be liable for any type of misconduct, including acts related to the arbitrator's quasi-judicial role.[54] The typical arguments for this approach are as follows.

First, immunity encourages arbitrators to act carelessly as misconduct will not be penalised. Second, in contrast to judges, there are no disciplinary sanctions available against arbitrators. Third, arbitration should not favour finality of the award rather than individual justice.[55] Finally, critics have suggested that the alternative remedies against arbitrators do not sufficiently compensate the parties for their economic loss caused by the arbitrator's misconduct.[56]

### [C] Qualified Immunity/Limited Liability

The two schools presented above – i.e., arbitrator immunity and arbitrator liability – represent two ends of a spectrum, a concept of full immunity on the one side; and on the other, a concept of full liability (provided that the misconduct reaches a certain level of seriousness). Originating from the Hybrid Status Approach, there are, however, various types of qualified immunity/limited liability in between, which to some extent recognise liability for arbitrators but exempts some types of actions from liability.[57]

In fact, the majority of jurisdictions agree that absolute immunity is undesirable.[58] The reason is first of all that, in situations of serious misconduct of the arbitrator, the parties should have the opportunity to be indemnified for the financial loss caused by the arbitrator.[59] In such cases, the parties, which remunerate the arbitrator, should not bear the economic risk of the arbitrator's negligent failure to meet his/her obligations.

---

51. Lord Justice Saville and others, *Departmental Advisory Committee on Arbitration Law 1996 Report on the Arbitration Bill*, 13(3) Arb Intl 275–316, para. 132 (1997); Franck I, *supra* n. 6, at 28–29; Andrew I Okekeifere, *The Parties' Rights Against a Dilatory or Unskilled Arbitrator*, 15 J. Int'l Arb. 129, 139 (1998). For a critical view *see* Schöldström, *supra* n. 122, at 336.
52. Hausmaninger, *supra* n. 5, at 16.
53. Franck I, *supra* n. 6, at 29.
54. Alessi, *supra* n. 19; Schöldström, *supra* n. 122, at 340.
55. Salahuddin, *supra* n. 322, at 577; Franck I, *supra* n. 6, at 30.
56. Franck I, *supra* n. 6, at 30.
57. *Ibid.*, 31.
58. With the US being one of the only extreme jurisdictions providing for absolute immunity for acts related to the decision-making process. *See* Franck I, *supra* n. 6, at 31–32.
59. Schöldström, *supra* n. 122, at 340.

Second, absolute immunity might influence the arbitrators' conduct adversely during the arbitration as absolute immunity has the potential to remove his/her incentive to act fairly and professionally. A complete lack of responsibility for misconduct may potentially foster carelessness, irresponsibility and even recklessness. It is, however, unlikely that the effect of a total absence of sanctions would be as profound as set out above. Assumedly, the average arbitrator will have many reasons for conducting him/herself in a professional manner. Arguably, the primary rationale for acting professional is not the existence of sanctions, but other reasons, such as the desire to further his/her own brand in order to get reappointments. Another contributing factor could be a sort of 'pride' in the profession as arbitrator, i.e., a desire, which is not prompted by financial or reputational reasons, to perform professionally and render an arbitral award of high quality. Thus, clear incentives exist for any serious arbitrator to conduct the proceedings in a manner which comes across as fair and reasonable to the parties.

In addition, the radical difference between court litigation and arbitration has also been highlighted in support of arbitrator liability. While appeal proceedings are likely to address and correct any errors in the first judgment, including abuse of immunity and misconduct, arbitral awards are generally subject to a very limited review. This supports that arbitrators, in situations of serious misconduct, should be susceptible to liability. Otherwise, parties may be deterred from choosing arbitration as their dispute resolution method as they perceive the system as unjust and unpredictable.[60] There is, however, room for challenging this line of reasoning as situations of serious misconduct in most jurisdictions will enable a successful challenge of the award. Thus, the possibility to set aside the award functions as a safety valve against abuse of immunity and cases of serious misconduct of the arbitrator. However, successfully setting aside the award does not compensate the parties for the potential economic loss related to the arbitration proceedings not being successfully completed.

On the other hand, supporters of the qualified immunity standard acknowledge that the arbitrator, whose assignment is to decide the parties' dispute in a neutral and objective manner, should be granted protection in his/her decision-making. Such point of view is indeed eligible. If arbitrators could face liability for every breach of contract or every negligent act during the arbitration process, regardless of the nature of the breach/misconduct, it would be impossible to preserve the arbitrator's integrity and independence. Furthermore, it would disturb the arbitration process. A scenario, where it became the norm that parties commenced legal action against the arbitrators in the event of an unsuccessful outcome of the arbitration, would potentially lead to the risk of affecting the arbitrators' independent judgement. This fear of repercussions could lead to unfounded decisions, depriving the parties one of the fundamental features of a judicial process.[61]

60. Hausmaninger. *supra* n. 5, at 33.
61. Franck I. *supra* n. 6, at 54.

## §14.05 DIFFERENT JURISDICTIONAL APPROACHES

### [A] Arbitrators' Liability Regulated in National Arbitration Acts

A number of jurisdictions have chosen to actively deal with the subject of arbitrator immunity/liability by passing national legislation. The national arbitration statutes generally either grant arbitrators specified immunities (the '*Negative Approach*') or provide liability for arbitrators in specific circumstances (the '*Affirmative Approach*').[62]

#### *[1] United Kingdom*

The United Kingdom has granted arbitrators immunity on a statutory level through section 29(1) of the English Arbitration Act 1996 (EAA).[63] This mandatory provision provides an arbitrator with general immunity for any act or omission in the discharge or purported discharge of his/her functions as arbitrator unless the act or omission is shown to have been in bad faith.[64]

In line with the common law tradition, section 29(1) EAA provides arbitrators with a high level of protection by granting them a broad form of immunity, although not absolute. The scope of the provision is the 'functions as arbitrator' and there is no distinction between acts related to the arbitrator's decision-making and other functions of the arbitrator task.[65] As stated in section 29(1), the immunity does not extend to cases where the arbitrator has acted in bad faith.[66] Seen from a civil law perspective, the immunity standard in section 29(1) is too protective as it provides immunity for acts of gross negligence.[67] The underlying considerations of arbitrator immunity do not support an approach where arbitrators are immune from civil actions in such situations. Thus, the quasi-judicial nature of the arbitrator far from justifies that he/she seriously ignores his/her duties to the parties and the general duty to act with care and skill in conducting the arbitration process. Furthermore, the immunity standard is too broad and should, in the author's opinion, be restricted to acts falling within the adjudicatory function of the arbitrator leaving him susceptible to liability for breach of contract. Based on a textual interpretation of section 29(1) it could, nevertheless, be argued that there is room for a conclusion where the arbitrator's failure to disclose and

62. Born, *supra* n. 100, at 2028.
63. Arbitration Act 1996.
64. Similar provisions can be found in s. 25 of the Singapore International Arbitration Act 2012 and s. 73 of the Scotland Arbitration Act 2010.
65. One important exception to this rule is s. 29(3) which exempts liability incurred due to the arbitrator's unreasonable resignation from immunity.
66. About this notion *see* DAC Report, *supra* n. 511, at para. 134 incl. the reference to *Melton Medes Ltd v. Securities and Investment Board* [1995] 3 All ER 880 and Lord Fraser of Carmyllie during the Grand Committee on the arbitration bill, HL Deb 28 February 1995, vol. 569, col CWH7.
67. In support of the contention that the notion bad faith does not include acts of gross negligence *see* Matthew Rasmussen, *Overextending Immunity: Arbitral Institutional Liability in the United States, England, and France*, 26 Fordham Int'l L.J. 1824, 1856 (note 190) (2003).

the failure to act at all falls outside the scope of the immunity (functions as arbitrator).[68]

### *[2] Spain*

Article 21(1) of the Spanish Arbitration Act (SAA)[69] establishes that arbitrators, who do not faithfully fulfil the task entrusted to them, can be considered professionally liable for their conduct, if their actions were carried out with bad faith, recklessness or wilful misconduct.[70] Additionally, Article 37(2) SAA, concerning the time limit for issuing an award, provides basis for a potential liability of arbitrators who fail to comply with the statutory time limits.

Both provisions establish a legal basis for the arbitrator's liability and, concurrently, raise several questions regarding the scope of applicability.[71] One of the questions is which liability standard that applies to the liability regime in Article 21(1) SAA. This issue became one of the main issues for the Spanish Supreme Court in the recent and well-reasoned *Puma* decision.[72]

The case arose out of an ad hoc arbitration seated in Spain between the claimant, 'Studio 2000', and the respondent, 'Puma', resulting in an award ordering Puma to pay Studio 2000 EUR 98.19 million. The award was signed by the arbitrator appointed by Studio 2000 and the chairman, but not by the arbitrator appointed by Puma, who had no knowledge of the award having been issued. Based on that the arbitral tribunal had deliberated, voted, and issued the award without the participation of the third arbitrator, the award was set aside at the request of Puma.[73] Under Spanish law, this amounted to a breach of the principle of collegiality and constituted a violation of the right of defence and in turn a violation of public policy.[74] After the award was set aside,[75] Puma initiated professional liability actions against the two arbitrators, claiming the fees and costs paid by Puma to both arbitrators plus interests. Puma succeeded in all three court instances and was awarded EUR 750,000 per arbitrator.

One of the key issues for the Spanish Supreme Court was whether the arbitrators' conduct met the requirement of recklessness in Article 21(1) SAA. Studio 2000 argued that the assessment of recklessness should not only be based on whether the arbitrators have acted with gross negligence but also include an analysis of the intent of the

68. Van Vechten Veeder and Ricky H Diwan, *National Report for England*, 34, in Jan Paulsson and Lise Bosman (eds), *ICCA International Handbook on Commercial Arbitration* (supp 98, Kluwer 2018); Schöldström, *supra* n. 122, at 71.
69. Spanish Arbitration Act 60/2003 of 23 December 2003.
70. Similar approaches in Portuguese Voluntary Arbitration Act 2011, Art. 9 and Peruvian Arbitration Act (Legislative Decree 1071 of 2008), Art. 32.
71. A more detailed analysis of these questions is included in the authors dissertation, *supra* n. *.
72. Supreme Court Civil Chamber, Judgment 102/2017 of 15 February 2017.
73. Provincial Court of Madrid, Judgment 200/2011 of 10 June 2011.
74. SAA Art. 41(1)(f).
75. Regional Appeals Court (Audiencia Provincial) of Madrid, Judgment of 10 June 2011.

arbitrators. In this regard, the court found that recklessness should not be assessed subjectively. In other words, the assessment is independent of the arbitrators' intent and instead based on an objective evaluation of what is deemed a professional standard. In addition, the court stated that:

> Recklessness is equal to an inexcusable negligence, with a manifest and serious error, without justification, that is not linked to the annulment of the award, but to a perilous action on the part of those who know their office and should have respected it in the interest of those who entrusted them to carry out the arbitration.[76]

Additionally, the court clarified that arbitrators can only be liable in cases where the conduct is intended to cause harm or amounts to gross negligence, engaging in conduct which is 'extraordinary or unforeseen conduct that is beyond the good judgment of anybody'.[77]

Applying this standard, the court found that the arbitrators' conduct of deliberately excluding the Puma-appointed arbitrator from the deliberations and voting of the matter amounted to a reckless violation of the fundamental principles of collegiality and contradiction, which resulted in personal liability for the arbitrators.[78]

The Spanish Supreme Court's decision constitutes an authority for the position that the liability threshold in Article 21(1) SAA is gross negligence, and that the assessment is based on a *bonus pater* approach. In this regard, *Puma* confirms the liability standard laid down in a former Spanish Supreme Court decision,[79] which established that arbitrators are susceptible to liability for substantive errors in the award.[80] Based on the reasoning of the court, the successful setting aside of the award seems to be a prerequisite for the finding of liability.[81] Furthermore, *Puma* recognises liability for the arbitrator's breach of fundamental principles in the arbitral process without being restricted to clear breaches of procedural rules following from the applicable law and rules. As *Puma* concerned the deliberations of the arbitral tribunal, it touched upon one of the central adjudicatory obligations of the arbitrator. Arguably, the same high liability threshold does not apply to acts and omissions which are not adjudicatory in nature, but which rather relate to case management.

76. B. Cremades & Asociados *Unofficial Translation of the Supreme Court Judgment Dated February 15, 2017*, pp. 7-8, 2nd chapter, subsec. 3, para. 1, https://www.cremades.com/pics/contenido/7729b459e44f750f4ee0e6fe7d8e3c3e_398872_1.pdf (accessed 14 May 2020).
77. Unofficial translation, *supra* n. 766.
78. The arbitrators being fully aware that the third arbitrator was travelling and did not summon him to the meeting where the outcome of the award was agreed. In other words, it was gross negligence to confuse the provision of SAA Art. 37(3), which allows the majority to render an award, with the fundamental principle of collegiality.
79. Supreme Court Civil Chamber, Judgment 429/2009 of 22 June 2009.
80. The case involved a calculation error in the award. *See also* Bernardo M Cremades Román and David J A Cairns, *National Report for Spain,)*, International Handbook on Commercial Arbitration (2018), *supra* n. 688, at 15.
81. Unofficial translation, *supra* n. 766, at pp. 7-8, subsec. 3, para. 1.

#### [3] *Austria*

The Austrian approach is dual in nature as it is based on the specific arbitral liability regime in the Austrian Code of Civil Procedure (ACCP) as well as the general contract/tort law regime.

According to section 594(4) of the ACCP,[82] an arbitrator is liable to the parties in cases where he negligently refuses to act or does so with unreasonable delay.[83] For breaches which do not amount to the arbitrator's non-fulfilment or delay, the Austrian Supreme Court has found that the general rules of contractual liability and tort law applies.[84] Thus, the arbitrator's liability arising from failure to make a correct award or to comply with the arbitration procedure applicable to the specific case is governed by the general rules of the law of damages.[85]

As for the cases falling outside the scope of section 594(4) ACCP, case law has set forth two prerequisites for arbitrator liability, which was recently confirmed by the Austrian Supreme Court, and that restricts the liability of arbitrators to exceptional circumstances.[86] First, a successful challenge of the arbitral award leading to either annulment or non-recognition is necessary in order to succeed with a liability claim against the arbitrator.[87] Under Austrian law, an award can generally not be contested because of any mistake in law or wrongful evaluation or essential defects in the proceedings.[88] As a result, the arbitrator is generally accountable for intentional infringement of the principles and rules pertaining to arbitral proceedings, but the arbitrator will be liable for damage only when his action leads to the inoperability of the award.[89] The second prerequisite for arbitrator liability laid down by Austrian case law is that the arbitrator's misconduct shall amount to intentional harm or gross negligence.[90] Gross negligence has by Austrian commentators been defined as 'negligence so severe that a diligent person would never act like this in the circumstances'.[91] The approach laid down by Austrian courts therefore shows that arbitrators in fact enjoy a high degree of protection.

82. The predecessor was s. 584(2).
83. Schwarz and Konrad, *supra* n. 144, at 181. Examples of such conduct is the total failure to render an award or at least with unacceptable delay.
84. OGH 17 October 1928, ZBl 1929/79.
85. Schwarz and Konrad, *supra* n. 144, at 183.
86. OGH 17 October 1928, ZBl 1929/79; OGH 6 June 2005, JBl 2005, 800/9 Ob 126/04a; OGH 28 February 2008, 8 Ob 4/08h; OGH 22 March 2016, 5 Ob 30/16x.
87. For example, OGH 6 June 2005, JBl 2005, 800/9 Ob 126/04a and OGH 22 March 2016, 5 Ob 30/16x.
88. OGH, 17 October 1928, ZBl 1929/79.
89. Schwarz and Konrad, *supra* n. 144, at 183–184.
90. Stefan Riegler and Martin Platte, *Chapter II: The Arbitrator – Arbitrators' Liability*, 120 in Christian Klausegger and others (eds), *Austrian Arbitration Yearbook 2007* (Manz'sche Verlags- und Universitätsbuchhandlung 2007). *See also* Nigel Blackaby and others, *Redfern and Hunter on International Arbitration*, 323 (6th ed., OUP 2016).
91. Schwarz and Konrad, *supra* n. 144, at 183 incl. note 28. This prerequisite of gross negligence is argued also to apply to liability under s. 594(4), cf. Riegler and Platte, *supra* n. 900, at 119.

### [B] Arbitrators' Liability Without Statutory Guidance

In contrast to jurisdictions which have statutory provisions regulating the existence and scope of arbitrator liability/immunity, a range of countries have refrained from addressing the issue on a statutory level and left it to the national courts. Finland, the Netherlands and France, which lack statutory provisions on arbitrator liability, provide some recent and interesting examples of national court approaches.

#### *[1] The Finnish Supreme Court in* 'Ruola Family'

By its decision in *Ruola Family,*[92] the Supreme Court of Finland ruled on the question of arbitrators' liability for the first time.

After the rendering of an award, the claimant was made aware that the chairman, both before and during the arbitral proceedings, had acted as legal consultant to the respondent by providing them legal opinions.[93] This information was not disclosed during the arbitration. On this ground, the award was challenged and was later set aside by the Helsinki Court of Appeal,[94] which found that the chairman had been disqualified to act as an arbitrator in the case and thereby had exceeded his authority.[95] Based on the annulment of the award, the claimant filed a civil claim for damages[96] against the chairman to recover the loss caused by his misconduct as they had to re-arbitrate the case in order to obtain a decision in the matter.

The case went all the way to the Finnish Supreme Court, which overturned the decisions of the two lower courts and held the chairman responsible for the financial loss suffered by the claimant.[97] Contrary to the lower courts, the Supreme Court held that the relationship between the parties and the chairman was comparable to a contractual relationship, and that the question of liability therefore should be decided according to the rules of contract law instead of tort. However, the court did state that, in order to preserve the independence and integrity of arbitrators, they are only susceptible to liability in *exceptional circumstances*. Only in situations of clear procedural faults or negligence displayed by the arbitrator there will be a basis for liability.[98] As for the chairman's conduct, the court found that the chairman should have disclosed his consultancy role to the claimant during the arbitration. When assessing whether this failure to disclose was negligent, the court attached considerable importance to four expert opinions provided to the respondent *during* the arbitration for

92. Supreme Court, Judgment of 31 January 2005, KKO 2005:14.
93. The legal opinions had been provided to the respondent, two banks who were the sole owners of the respondent and subsidiaries of the respondent.
94. Judgment of 10 October 1997.
95. Section 41(1) of The Finnish Arbitration Act.
96. EUR 166,725.70.
97. The ruling remained final but the amount of compensation was returned to the district court to be decided.
98. Jan Waselius and Tanja Meinander, *The Ruola Family v. X, The Supreme Court of Finland, 2005:14, 31 January 2005*, in *A Contribution by the ITA Board of Reporters* (Kluwer).

which he had charged EUR 38,010.47.[99] The Finnish Supreme Court found that the chairman should have foreseen how his consulting work, for which he received substantial remuneration, would appear in the eyes of the claimant. Taking due account of the chairman's education, experience and substantial remuneration for his consulting work, the court found that he should have foreseen that his consultancy work was likely to give rise to justifiable doubts about his impartiality and independence.

This case touches upon the relationship between the parties and the arbitrator and considers which type of misconduct can lead to liability for an arbitrator under Finish law. The judgment also raises an important question regarding the required standard of liability. While the lower courts, which based the liability assessment on rules of tort, found that the negligence was only minor, the Finnish Supreme Court does not address the question. The court seems to have deliberately left out a discussion on the liability standard (slight or gross negligence) by only referring to 'negligence'. One could argue that the Finnish Supreme Court's express restriction of arbitrator liability to 'exceptional circumstances' supports a high threshold of liability amounting to acts of intentional misconduct and gross negligence.[100] This view is in accordance with liability standards laid down in other civil law jurisdictions. This interpretation is, however, difficult to reconcile with the court's finding that clear procedural faults or negligence displayed by the arbitrator can provide a potential basis for liability. The same applies to the court's reasoning related to the specific misconduct of the chairman which does not extend to an account for gross negligence. An alternative interpretation of the judgment is that the court deliberately refrained to set out a liability threshold of gross negligence as the misconduct related to a 'contractual' duty rather than the arbitrator's adjudicatory function. If one acknowledges the latter interpretation, the judgment leaves open whether an arbitrator can be liable for acts and omissions based on breaches of its adjudicatory duties under Finish law, and if so, which liability/immunity standard should be applied.

### *[2] The 'Greenworld Standard' in the Netherlands*

The Dutch Supreme Court has ruled on the standard and scope for arbitrators' liability in two landmark cases.[101] The first case was *Greenworld*[102] which laid down the standard for arbitrators' liability in a dispute regarding the tribunal's competence to rule on its own jurisdiction.[103] The Dutch Supreme Court confirmed that arbitrators can

99. Gustaf Möller, *The Finnish Supreme Court and the Liability of Arbitrators* 23 J. Int'l Arb. 95, at 98 (2006). The expert opinions were provided to the two banks who were the sole owners of the respondent.
100. *See* Born, *supra* n. 100, at 2032–2033 who categorises the Finnish approach as a 'relatively broad arbitrator immunity, subject to exceptions for fraud or similar intentional misconduct'.
101. Supreme Court, 4 December 2009, ECLI:NL:HR:2009:BJ7834, NJ 2011/131 (Greenworld) and Supreme Court, 30 September 2016, ECLI:NL:HR:2016:2215 (Qnow).
102. Greenworld, *supra* n. 1011.
103. The appeal to the Dutch Supreme Court failed after the claim was dismissed in the two lower instances.

incur liability for wrongful acts as a quasi-judicial, but only if they 'in relation to the annulled award, intentionally or knowingly acted recklessly or with a gross misjudgement of what a proper fulfilment of their duties entails'.[104] In other words, the court laid down a standard of gross negligence leading to arbitrator liability only in exceptional circumstances. This would be the case when an arbitrator violates fundamental principles of law, such as impartiality and the right to a fair hearing, making the award incapable of being enforced.[105]

In a recent decision in *Qnow*,[106] the Supreme Court clarified the scope of the application of this gross negligence standard (qualified immunity). It thus confirmed that the standard not only applies in cases where the award is annulled on the basis of substantive grounds but also when the award is annulled due to a violation of purely procedural or formal requirements (the chairman's failure to have the two co-arbitrators sign the award amounted to gross negligence).

### *[3] The Status on French Case Law*

The rules on arbitrators' liability applicable in France have been outlined by French courts in a range of decisions. Examples included in the author's research[107] show that arbitrators benefit from a limited liability standard (implied immunity) in relation to the performance of judicial acts, in principle not being liable for error of judgment, factual or legal errors or for infringement of res judicata.[108] However, liability will arise in case of particularly serious breaches such as breaches caused by wilful or gross misconduct, fraud or denial of justice.

French courts have in several cases acknowledged the contractual obligations of the arbitrator to the parties and held the arbitrator liable where there is a breach of contract.[109] Such examples include the arbitrators' failure to comply with a deadline to render the award without requesting an extension of the time limit,[110] the arbitrator's failure to disclose,[111] unjustified resignation[112] and fault in the implementation or

104. Greenworld, *supra* n. 1011, para. 3.6.
105. Gerard Meijer and Marike M P Paulsson, *National Report for The Netherlands (2018)* International Handbook on Commercial Arbitration, *supra* n. 688), at 31.
106. Qnow, *supra* n. 1011.
107. Judgment of 13 June 1990, 1996 Rev Arb 475–476 (Tribunal de grande instance Paris) aff'd judgement of 22 May (the *Bompard* case), Judgment of 15 January 2014, No. 11-17 196 (Azran), Bull. Civ. 2014 1, no 1 (Cour de Cassation, First Civil Chamber).
108. *See also* Yves Derains and Laurence Kiffer, *National Report for France (2018)* International Handbook on Commercial Arbitration, *supra* n. 688, at 40–42; Fouchard, *supra* n. 166, at 591–592.
109. Le Club des Juristes, *Report – The Arbitrator's Liability*, 27, http://www.leclubdesjuristes.com/rapport-responsabilite-de-larbitre-disponible-anglais/, (accessed 26 March 2020).
110. Judgment of 6 December 2005, 2006 Rev Arb 126 (Cour de Cassation, First Civil Chamber).
111. Fouchard, *supra* n. 166, at 595–596 (note 179 regarding the Raoul Duval case) *See also* Juristes Report, *supra* n. 10909, at 32.
112. Fouchard, *supra* n. 166, at 620–621 incl. note 312.

conduct of the arbitral proceedings.[113] Common for this category is that liability depends on general rules of contract law and that no implied immunity is available.[114]

### [C] Summary on Jurisdictional Approaches

Based on the above selection of jurisdictional approaches to arbitrator liability, a trend towards a qualified immunity/restricted liability standard seems apparent in international arbitration practice. Divergent approaches within the large spectrum of this standard do, however, exist. As we have seen, the support for the Functional Status Approach in the United Kingdom has led to express statutory immunity for arbitrators, whereas, in Austria and other civil law countries, the adherence to the Contractual Status Approach has implied contractual liability. Yet, statutory provisions and/or case law in, e.g., Austria, Spain, Finland and France show that lawmakers/national courts to a certain extent restrict the liability in order to protect arbitrators whereby an implied qualified immunity is achieved (Hybrid Status Approach). In addition, and more uncertain, are the jurisdictions, such as Denmark and Switzerland, which so far have been completely silent on the question of arbitrators' liability and where no approach seems to have been taken, neither by legislators, nor the national courts.[115]

## §14.06 THE RECOMMENDED APPROACH TO ARBITRATORS' LIABILITY

Integrity and independence are two fundamental constituents of both court litigation and arbitration. Despite the fundamental differences between state judges and international arbitrators, the integrity and independence in the arbitration process – leading to a valid and enforceable award – can only be preserved if arbitrators are provided with some form of protection. In other words, the liability for arbitrators must to some extent be subject to restrictions.[116] Furthermore, unlimited liability would potentially lead to an abundance of lawsuits against arbitrators which would risk interfering with two of the most fundamental principles in arbitration: the finality of the award and the integrity of the arbitration process. On the other hand, arbitration will only function properly if the arbitrator is incentivised to exercise careful case management and decision-making, thereby respecting and fulfilling his/her obligations to the parties. In other words, a balance between policy and the sanctity of contract is of utmost importance.

113. *Ibid.*, 620.
114. For example, under the common law standard of Art. 1147 French Code of Civil Procedure for contractual liability.
115. For example, Denmark (Ole Spiermann, *National Report for Denmark*, International Handbook on Commercial Arbitration (2009), *supra* n. 688, at 15 and Marie-Louise Holle, *Voldgiftsdommeres erstatningsansvar i lyset af professionsansvaret*,U.2016B.43 (2016), and Switzerland (Juristes Report, *supra* n. 10909, at Annex 4, 132; Nadia Smahi, *The Arbitrator's Liability and Immunity under Swiss Law – Part II*, 35(1) ASA Bull. 67, 68 (2017).
116. *See* Salahuddin, *supra* n. 322, at 579 who disagrees with this notion. For a supportive view *see* Smahi, *supra* n. 1155, at 73–78.

### [A] Liability/Immunity Standard

The assessment of arbitrators' liability should be submitted to a distinction between adjudicatory acts (acts related to the decision-making) and those acts which, still part of the arbitrator's quasi-judicial role, are purely contractual and unrelated to the adjudicatory function ('administrative' acts and omissions).

#### *[1] Adjudicatory Acts*

Acts falling within this category relate to the arbitrator's principal obligation; the administration of justice. Hence, wrongful acts and omissions are tied to the decision-making process and typically include the arbitrator's misjudgment, errors of law, errors of fact, disregard of fundamental principles of justice, etc.

In the author's view, the need to reach an appropriate compromise between the two extremes, absolute immunity and unlimited liability, merits a restricted liability – or qualified immunity – standard as the preferred standard for arbitrators' liability for acts under this category. Misconduct related to the arbitrator's adjudicative function should therefore be protected from liability unless the act classifies as gross negligence, intentional misconduct (bad faith) or denial of justice (e.g., fraud).[117] Fixing the liability standard at this level achieves a reasonable balance between respecting the arbitrator's obligations owed to the parties and the protection of the arbitrator. The gross negligence standard should be assessed objectively and not requiring any intentional harm on the part of the arbitrator. Making arbitrator's liability subject to a fixed and objective standard allows the arbitrator to exercise control over the risk of potential liability, which, in turn, serves to preserve the integrity and independence of the arbitration process.

#### *[2] Non-adjudicatory Acts*

The liability standard for conduct falling outside the adjudicatory function of the arbitrator is more complex. Acts and omissions falling within this category are, for example, the duty to disclose, the duty to possess agreed qualifications, the duty to comply with time limits.[118] Although such obligations relate to the arbitrator's role as quasi-judicial, they derive from the contractual relationship with the parties, and the considerations supporting qualified immunity do not justify limitations of the arbitrator's liability for breach of contract. On the contrary, policy concerns support that arbitrators should be liable for acts and omissions that do not concern their administration of justice.[119]

The rather delicate question is which legal basis of liability should apply to acts falling within this category. As the assessment of breach should be based on national

117. The manifest disregard of the law is not protected by immunity. *See*, e.g., Hausmaninger, *supra* n. 5, at 47.
118. For a supportive view *see* Hausmaninger, *supra* n. 5, at 28–33.
119. Schöldström, *supra* n. 122, at 32.

contract law in each jurisdiction, it is neither possible nor appropriate to seek harmonisation in this area of liability.[120] In the author's view, the determining factor should be that the arbitrator acts with the degree of professional care, which could generally be expected from other members of the profession. In other words, an arbitrator should not be liable of damages in the event of a mere contractual breach, nor should he be protected by the high threshold applicable to misconduct in the arbitrator's adjudicatory capacity.[121]

### [B] Other Prerequisites for Liability

As is the case in a range of jurisdictions, e.g., Austria and Spain, a prerequisite for arbitrator liability should be either the premature termination of the arbitration proceedings or the successful setting aside of the award. This standard serves to avoid discrepancies between court rulings rendered on arbitrator liability and in setting aside proceedings. Furthermore, the prerequisite reinforces the finality and binding effect of arbitral awards by limiting the possibilities of parties to attempt to re-litigate the case through liability proceedings.[122] In addition, in the event of early termination or successful setting aside, any costs associated with the arbitral proceedings will always (at least to some extent) have been incurred by the parties in vain. Consequently, making arbitrator liability subject to early termination or successful setting aside proceedings seeks to limit the cases of arbitrator liability to situations where it is likely that at least one of the parties have suffered an actual loss.

### [C] Consequences of Arbitrator Liability

The divergent approaches to arbitrators' liability entail uncertainty about the consequences of arbitrators' liability. This will be discussed in the following section.

#### *[1] Damages*

When liability has been established, the question arises on how to assess the damages. Different jurisdictions tend to base the assessment of damages on principles of either contract law or tort law. Basing the assessment of damages on contract law principles is the expected method in jurisdictions of civil law tradition while, historically, common law jurisdictions have used tort law principles.[123]

One of the key issues when assessing damages is whether the scope of the arbitrator's liability should be limited to the forfeiture of fees and costs of the arbitrator,

120. While English law of obligations is based on case law and the liability for breach many civil law countries have a general civil code regulating the law of obligations providing for professional liability, often based on a standard of fault. *See*, e.g., Schöldström, *supra* n. 122, at 44 and 46.
121. *See* Fouchard, *supra* n. 166, at 621 who advocates for the French approach to distinguish between obligations of result and best effort obligations.
122. *See* Schöldström, *supra* n. 122, at 337–339 for a critical discussion of this prerequisite.
123. Waincymer, *supra* n. 211, at 357 incl. note 570.

or whether the arbitrator should also be held liable for the additional loss the party has suffered.[124]

From a civil law perspective, damages should generally entail full compensation for the harm suffered by the aggrieved party[125] to the extent the financial loss is well substantiated by evidence. Thus, the mere reimbursement of the arbitrator's fees and expenses is from a traditional civil law perspective insufficient to indemnify an aggrieved party.

A party should undoubtedly be reimbursed for the arbitration costs that have been paid, including fees and other expenses paid to the arbitrators and arbitral institution.[126] Also, counsels' fees and additional costs incurred for the unnecessary arbitral proceedings together with any travel expenses paid in vain to witnesses, experts, etc. should be reimbursed.[127] The parties should also be able to recover costs of proceedings and legal fees incurred in the challenge and liability proceedings.[128]

In addition, compensation for the loss suffered as a consequence of the award being delayed should be recoverable on the condition that the loss can be substantiated. Although the assessment of this type of damages can be hard to evaluate,[129] the assessment can be made in the same way as damages for late payment under any commercial contract.[130]

A more controversial question is whether the parties should receive compensation for the loss of the chance to win the dispute. As a rule, this type of loss should be recoverable provided that substantial evidence for the loss is submitted by the plaintiff. However, such loss might be hard to prove, and to lift the burden of proof will in some cases require an effective rehearing of the matter to determine which of the parties ought to have won the case.[131] The claim should in any event be based on the same grounds as the sum at issue in the underlying dispute as the claim should reflect the party's loss and has to be caused by the arbitrator.[132] Indeed, the claimant has not lost a chance to win if he can re-arbitrate the case after the original award has been set aside. In this scenario, the claimant will still have a chance to obtain the damages through the second arbitration.

Damages relating to the impact on the economic capacity of the aggrieved party towards third parties (e.g., bankruptcy, insolvency) or other business damage should also be recoverable.[133] In practice, it will, however, be close to impossible to establish the necessary causation for such type of loss.

124. France is an example of the latter. *See* National Report for France, *supra* n. 108, 41.
125. Alessi, *supra* n. 19, 780.
126. The damages in *Raola Family* amounted to the unnecessary fees incurred, cf. Louis Degos, *Civil Liability of Arbitrators: New Inroads on the Arbitrator's Immunity From Suit – a Worrying or Welcome Development?* IV (14) Revista Brasileira de Arbitragem, 157–162 (note 9) (2007). *See also* Fouchard, *supra* n. 166, at 596.
127. Fouchard, *supra* n. 166, at 597.
128. National Report for France, *supra* n. 108, at 41.
129. Lew et al., *supra* n. 122, at 294.
130. Waincymer, *supra* n. 211, at 357.
131. In particular, a loss will be hard to establish where the liability claim is founded on bias or improper imposition of provisional measures, cf Waincymer, *supra* n. 211, at 357.
132. Degos, *supra* n. 1266, at 162.
133. Alessi, *supra* n. 19, at 780.

### [2] Reputational Harm

Apart from the direct financial consequences resulting from liability, one of the gravest consequences for the arbitrator is the loss of reputation that could follow from his/her liability/challenge. Frequently, arbitrators are well-known and respected within their field, appointed as such, and a liability scenario could potentially have a serious impact on their future appointments. As noted by *Born* the 'loss of such reputation, through parties' complaints, removal of the arbitrator, or annulment of an award that is by far the most effective deterrent against unsatisfactory performance'.[134]

Reputational harm might lead to the arbitrator being 'blacklisted' and removed from lists of arbitrators administered by appointing authorities. Such exclusion from future appointments can follow directly from statute[135] or through policy and practice of the appointing authorities.[136] This type of sanction is likely to have an adverse effect on the career prospects of a successful arbitrator and, as a result, might cause even more severe financial damage than the damage claim he has been faced with. 'Blacklisting' should therefore be restricted to cases where liability of the arbitrator has been established by the courts.

Given the trend towards a qualified immunity standard, it is likely that we will see more cases where arbitrator liability is proven, although such cases still will be exceptional. Hence, new developments are expected in this legal area, particularly from arbitral institutions, which will urge the arbitrators to fulfil their obligations to the parties with due care and skill in an effort of limiting liability situations. A recent example is the new practice at the ICC,[137] which in an attempt to address the issue of delays in the drafting of awards has introduced new rules on timelines for the reception of drafts and fee reductions on a sliding scale up to 20% if the arbitrator fails to adhere hereto (except for exceptional circumstances).[138] Such initiatives are welcome provided that they are reasonable and do not eliminate the necessary basis for a sound effective decision-making process.

### [3] Insurance Coverage

The diversity in national approaches extends to issues concerning arbitrators' insurance coverage, or the lack of it. While, e.g., Article 21(1) of the SAA requires arbitrators to take out professional indemnity insurance, there is no such obligation under English law. The effect is that the majority of arbitrators in the United Kingdom, not covered by a professional indemnity insurance related to another profession, are not insured for legal expenses or for liability for damages stemming from their misconduct as

134. Born, *supra* n. 100, at 2013.
135. For example, the Arbitration Law of the People's Republic of China 1994, Art. 38.
136. *See* Born, *supra* n. 100, at 2016–2017 (note 333) referring to the AAA and the Milan Chamber of Commerce.
137. International Chamber of Commerce.
138. ICC, *ICC Court Announces New Policies to Foster Transparency and Ensure Greater Efficiency*, https://iccwbo.org/media-wall/news-speeches/icc-court-announces-new-policies-to-foster-transparency-and-ensure-greater-efficiency/ (accessed 26 March 2020).

arbitrators.[139] One of the principal motives for arbitrators not taking out insurance policies is, apart from the expense, the immunity arbitrators are provided as quasi-judicials by law or arbitral rules.[140]

Considering a restricted liability standard as proposed above, the question is whether arbitrators should be required to take out insurance? To the extent the insurance policy exempts coverage in situations of gross negligence and/or intent, it could be argued that insurance would be without any effect.[141] Additionally, the prospects of personal liability are limited due to the high threshold of liability (although the claims can be substantial). On the contrary, even if the arbitrator is immune from liability, he is not automatically sheltered from lawsuits which can be both time-consuming and expensive to defend. Generally, such expenses are covered by a professional indemnity insurance. Finally, to the extent arbitrators are subject to liability for breach of contract, without meeting the high liability standard of gross negligence, a professional indemnity insurance will achieve its purpose.

In the author's opinion, a requirement by law upon arbitrators to take out professional insurance cover is not desirable. This question should be left to negotiations between the professional parties and the arbitrator. This should, however, not be perceived as a recommendation that arbitrators should refrain from obtaining professional indemnity insurance. Arbitrators are professionals, who like any others offering professional services in the marketplace, should have insurance. In addition, insurance effectively mitigates the negative impact of the legal uncertainty caused by the different approaches to arbitral liability. Hence, arbitrators, who are not covered by an existing professional indemnity insurance policy,[142] which includes the conduct as arbitrator, or covered by an insurance obtained by an arbitral institution, should take out an appropriate civil liability insurance covering their potential liability as arbitrators (most advisable for all types of negligence). Given that the majority of arbitrators are lawyers covered by a professional indemnity insurance, the issue of insurance is in practice limited to situations where the insurance does not cover arbitrator's conduct or where the arbitrator is not a lawyer or other professional covered by a similar insurance.

Although *Hausmaninger* argues that the costs of the arbitrator's insurance cover for potential wrongdoing will lead to increased fees, and hence the parties in a way will become liable for the arbitrator's liability,[143] this is not distinct from other professions

139. National Report for England, *supra* n. 688, at 33.
140. María Pilar Perales Viscasillas, *Liability Insurance in Arbitration: The Emerging Spanish Market and the Impact of Mandatory Insurance Regimes*, Kluwer Arbitration Blog (8 January 2014) http://arbitrationblog.kluwerarbitration.com/2014/01/08/liability-insurance-in-arbitration-the-emerging-spanish-market-and-the-impact-of-mandatory-insurance-regimes/ (accessed 26 March 2020).
141. According to Danish law, lawyers are legally required to obtain professional indemnity insurance covering all types of negligence (s. 61 of the Bye-Laws of the Danish Bar and Law Society: https://www.advokatsamfundet.dk/Service/English/Rules/Bye-laws.aspx (accessed 26 March 2020). The insurance normally covers the lawyer's profession as an arbitrator, but not necessarily in relation to arbitrator conduct outside Denmark.
142. For example, as part of their profession as lawyers.
143. Hausmaninger, *supra* n. 5, at 22.

where professional indemnity insurance generally is taken out and should not be a determining factor.

### [D] Prospects of an International Harmonised Approach

Considering the unambiguity and lack of transparency surrounding arbitrators' liability, the delicate question is whether an international harmonisation of this legal area is desirable. Yet more importantly, if it is at all achievable?

International harmonisation of the rules on arbitrators' liability is undoubtedly desirable, as it would bring a higher level of certainty and transparency among the various stakeholders in the international arbitration field. It would indeed provide parties to the arbitration, arbitrators, arbitral institutions and national courts with an improved basis to assess the legal basis and scope of arbitrators' liability. Hence, arbitrators would have an increased transparent basis for accepting the arbitrator's task in respect of potential liability concerns and an opportunity to adjust their insurance cover accordingly. The parties would, on the contrary, be ensured that gross and flagrant misconduct was subject to sanctions and compensation and that arbitrators were held responsible for their breach of contract.

Based on the research of the predominant policy grounds in the selected common and civil law jurisdictions and the trend towards a qualified immunity standard, the proposed restricted liability standard largely seems tolerable in both legal systems. There is, however, an underlying reason why the issue of arbitrators' liability was deliberately ignored during the preparation of the UNCITRAL Model Law; that is, the different national approaches.[144] Apart from the controversial nature of the subject, an international regulation of the subject has implications for a range of contractual and liability issues.[145] The fundamental differences as to how the legal relationship between the parties and the arbitrator is perceived are deeply rooted in the distinct legal traditions which impede a harmonisation of the rules. In addition, the assessment of arbitrators' liability cannot be completely emancipated from national laws on tort, contract and damages. This will inevitably – regardless of any attempts to harmonise – preserve divergent approaches on the basis and scope of arbitral liability and the consequences of such liability. In other words, an international harmonisation does not appear practicably feasible.[146]

## §14.07 CONCLUSION

The question of arbitrators' liability does not merely relate to the arbitrator's performance of duties but touches upon the very foundation and nature of arbitration. The way the relationship between the parties and arbitrator is perceived is determining for the legal basis for potential liability or immunity. The legal relationship is hybrid in

144. Franck I, *supra* n. 6, at 33 incl. note 213.
145. Waincymer, *supra* n. 211, at 73.
146. Due to the complexity and magnitude of this subject the prospects of an international approach have not been further explored in the author's research.

nature, which entails that the arbitrator's rights and obligations are not only derived from the contract and applicable arbitration rules and laws but also by analogy from principles applicable to state judges.

Striking a balance between the benefits of immunity and the equality between the arbitrator and parties as contract partners warrants a compromise. Hence, a qualified immunity or restricted liability standard is the appropriate way to proceed, provided that 'immunity is "not" an absolute protection, but only a limitation of the liability that otherwise exists'.[147]

Among proponents of arbitrator immunity, there is a fear that the pool of arbitrators will diminish if arbitrators can be susceptible to civil lawsuits. However, this is not likely to be the effect of the proposed liability standard, as it must be assumed that arbitrators will accept appointments regardless of a potential liability, which can only be triggered by clearly unacceptable behaviour.[148] Arbitration is a fully developed profession, where arbitrators – as other service providers in other professions – take full responsibility for their actions.[149] Responsible arbitrators will not have to concern themselves with the risk of liability lawsuits.[150] In addition, the risk of civil claims based on alleged failure in the conduct of the profession is a calculated risk which the arbitrator to a certain extent can, and should, obtain insurance coverage for.[151] Insurance serves as the arbitrator's 'second line of defence' and constitutes a way of moderating the risks of arbitrator liability by filling the inherent gaps in a non-harmonised legal area.

Although we in recent years have seen a range of examples operating with a (implied) qualified immunity/limited liability standard, the diversity of liability standards in the various legal systems (*civil law versus common law*) will inevitably turn out to be a major obstacle in global harmonisation of the approach to arbitrator liability. To the extent the scope of arbitrator liability depends on national laws on tort, contract and damages – as is the case with the liability approach proposed in this chapter – international harmonisation is arguably not practicably achievable. Despite this, the international arbitration community should urge national jurisdictions to provide clear statutory rules on arbitrators' liability (qualified immunity/restricted liability), which would add a higher level of transparency and certainty to an increasingly important area of international arbitration.

147. Nadia Smahi, *The Arbitrator's Liability and Immunity under Swiss Law – Part I*, 34(4) ASA Bull. 876, 878–879 (note 11) (2016).
148. Schöldström, *supra* n. 122, at 335.
149. Including legal liability for loss caused by the arbitrator's misconduct. *See* Okekeifere, *supra* n. 511.
150. Hausmaninger, *supra* n. 5, at 39.
151. Emmanuela Truli, *Liability v. Quasi-Judicial Immunity of the Arbitrator: the Case Against Absolute Arbitral Immunity*, 17 Am. Rev. Int'l Arb. 383, 395 (2006).

CHAPTER 15

# Squeeze-Out Arbitration: A Comparative Analysis Between Finland and Sweden

*Ville Pönkä**

## §15.01 INTRODUCTION

Squeeze-out (or buyout) is a commonly recognized technique allowing the majority (or controlling) shareholder, after reaching a predetermined ownership threshold, to gain ownership of the remaining shares in that company.[1] For example, section 253 of the Delaware General Corporation Law (Title 8, Chapter 1 of the Delaware Code) provides that any entity holding more than 90% of a company may decide to take over the remaining shares by means of a short-form merger procedure. Also, the EU Takeover Directive[2] requires Member States to implement rules regarding the rights relating to squeeze-out and sell-out—laid down in Articles 15 and 16. Although the Directive concerns only listed companies, some Member States, such as Denmark, Finland and Sweden, have provided similar rights in their domestic Companies Acts that cover all types of companies including listed, "public" companies (market squeeze-out/sell-out) as well as non-listed, "closed" companies (off-market squeeze-out/sell-out).[3]

---

* I would like to thank Erik Lidman (Juridiska institutionen—Göteborgs universitet) and Gustaf Sjöberg (Juridiska institutionen—Stockholms universitet) for helping me out me with some questions regarding Swedish squeeze-out practices.

1. A squeeze-out may be executed through various strategies such as a cash-out merger, reverse stock split, two-step merger, or compulsory acquisition, which—at least in Europe—is the most commonly utilized strategy. *See*, e.g., Hyeok-Joon Rho, *New Squeeze-Out Devices as a Part of Corporate Law Reform in Korea: What Type of Device Is Required for a Developing Economy* 29 Boston University International Law Journal 41, 44 (2011).
2. Directive 2004/25/EC of the European Parliament and of the Council of April 21, 2004 on takeover bids.
3. *See* sections 69–73 of the Danish Companies Act 470/2009 (Dan. "lov om aktie- og anpartsselskaber"; DCA), Chapter 18 of the Finnish Companies Act 624/2006 (Fi. "osakeyhtiölaki"; FCA) and Chapter 22 of the Swedish Companies Act 2005:551 (Swe. "aktiebolagslag"; SCA).

Squeeze-out is a practical and multifaceted research topic; hence, it is no surprise that it has raised much interest among legal scholars.[4] For example, in 2007, Gustaf Sjöberg defended a 504-page-long doctoral thesis on "Compulsory Redemption."[5] Later in 2015, the author of this chapter published an 883-page-long post-doctoral monograph titled "Redemption of Shares. A Company Law and Contract Law Study."[6] These thick books illustrate that even if one focuses solely on an individual jurisdiction (Sjöberg on Swedish law and I on Finnish law), it is virtually impossible to discuss all squeeze-out-related issues in one paper. Therefore, the topic of this chapter has been narrowed down to focus on the similarities and differences of squeeze-out proceedings in Finland and Sweden while paying special attention to the advantages and disadvantages related to different legal solutions.

The laws of Finland and Sweden have been selected as study subjects for three reasons. First, squeeze-out proceedings in Finland and Sweden have many normative and structural similarities, but the systems are far from being identical. Hence, they provide a well-defined context for comparing how different legal solutions function under fairly similar conditions.[7] Second, the Finnish and Swedish systems are unique in the sense that squeeze-out disputes are always decided by arbitrators, not, for example, by judges or expert evaluators. Later we will call such statutory arbitration *squeeze-out arbitration*.[8] Third, in Finland and Sweden, squeeze-out proceedings are relatively common and compared to Continental European countries, takeovers of listed companies are not a rare phenomenon.[9] Furthermore, it is important to note that according to Chapter 18, section 9(2) of the Finnish Companies Act 624/2006 (FCA) arbitral awards concerning squeeze-out disputes ("squeeze-out awards") must be registered which means that plenty of information is available on squeeze-out practices.[10]

4. Squeeze-out is also a multidisciplinary topic in the sense that the determination of the squeeze-out price (i.e., the valuation of shares) is a matter of business economics and accounting, not legal dogmatics.
5. Gustaf Sjöberg, *Tvångsinlösen* (Jure 2007) (Eng. "Compulsory Redemption").
6. Ville Pönkä, *Osakkeen lunastaminen. Osakeyhtiö- ja sopimusoikeudellinen tutkimus* (Talentum 2015) (Eng. "Redemption of Shares. A Company Law and Contract Law Study").
7. The FCA and the SCA, as well as the Finnish Arbitration Act 967/1992 (Fi. "laki välimiesmenettelystä"; FAA) and the Swedish Arbitration Act 1999:116 (Swe. "lag om skiljeförfarande"; SAA) contain rather specific rules regarding the squeeze-out procedure. That said, there are jurisdictions—such as the U.K.—which lack explicit procedures for buying out minority shareholders. Reiner Kraakman et al., *The Anatomy of Corporate Law. A Comparative and Functional Approach*, 191 (3rd edn., Oxford University Press 2017).
8. To the knowledge of the author of this article, there are no other jurisdictions in which the law requires squeeze-out disputes to be decided by arbitrators. For example, in Denmark, a dispute regarding the squeeze-out price is determined by a court-appointed expert and later the expert's opinion may be brought before the court. *See* section 67(3) of the DCA.
9. *See*, e.g., Sergio Gilotta, *EU Takeover Law and the Powerful Anti-takeover Force of Supermajority* 26 Columbia Journal of European Law 1 (2019) and Erik Nerep, Per Samuelsson & Jan Andersson, *Aktiebolagslagen. En kommentar. Kapitel 17–24*, 325 (Karnov Group 2019) (Eng. "Company Law. A Commentary").
10. For example, the author of this article has analyzed all squeeze-out awards registered since 2000. A listing of these awards for the past ten years can be found at https://kauppakamari.fi/palvelut/lunastuslautakunta/lunastusmenettelyt/ (accessed September 2020). As for legal scholarship, there is one Finnish doctoral thesis concerning the valuation of minority shares

The analysis below is structured so that it will begin with a brief discussion regarding the realization of the majority shareholder's desire to redeem the minority's shares—and vice versa, the minority shareholder's desire to force the majority shareholder to acquire her/his shares (section §15.02). In other words, this section will explain why there is a need for a statutory squeeze-out (and sell-out) right as well as what the preconditions to commence squeeze-out arbitration are. Then the focus shifts to the Finnish and Swedish squeeze-out proceedings so that the legal framework, as well as each stage of the arbitration process, is explained in a comparative manner (section §15.03). Here the chapter also seeks to contest the perception of squeeze-out arbitration as being merely expert determination and not arbitration in the true meaning of the word.[11] Although squeeze-out arbitration is based on mandatory law, not on agreement, and although the tribunal's authority does not extend beyond determining the existence of the squeeze-out right and the squeeze-out price,[12] we are nevertheless talking about arbitration as the Finnish and Swedish Arbitration Acts (FAA/SAA) apply to the arbitrators as well as the proceedings before them.[13] Finally, the analysis is concluded by a brief pro et contra overview regarding the Finnish and Swedish rules including some thoughts *de lege ferenda* (section §15.04). The laws and legal practices of other countries will also be introduced, since squeeze-out is a genuinely international topic and since foreign models have influenced the development of the Finnish and Swedish buyout rules.

## §15.02 SQUEEZE-OUT RIGHT AND THE PRECONDITIONS TO COMMENCE SQUEEZE-OUT ARBITRATION

International surveys indicate that the typical threshold for squeeze-out is 90% or 95% of the shares of the target company.[14] In enterprises with such concentrated ownership structures there is an evident risk of conflict of interest between the majority shareholder and the minority shareholders escalating and even becoming unbearable. Therefore, the law must provide an efficient exit mechanism, which makes it possible

published after Sjöberg's and Pönkä's books. *See* Hanna Savolainen, *Noteeraamattoman yhtiön vähemmistöosakkeen lunastushinnan määrittäminen osakeyhtiölain 18 luvun mukaisissa lunastuksissa* (Publications of the University of Eastern Finland. Dissertations in Social Sciences and Business Studies 2018) (Eng. "Determining the Redemption Price of a Minority Share of a Private Company in Redemptions Complying with Ch. 18 of the FCA"). In addition, squeeze-out arbitration has been discussed in a few Finnish and Swedish articles, i.e., there is not much recently-published research on the topic.

11. *See*, e.g., Gustaf Möller, *Välimiesmenettelyn perusteet*, 3 (Lakimiesliiton kustannus 1997) (Eng. "Fundamentals of Arbitration"), who argues that squeeze-out arbitration is not arbitration at all.
12. Chapter 18, section 3(1) of the FCA and Chapter 22, section 5(2) of the SCA.
13. Chapter 18, section 3(2) of the FCA and Chapter 22, section 5(1) of the SCA explicate that unless otherwise prescribed by the provisions of this chapter, the provisions of the Arbitration Act (i.e., the FAA and the SAA) apply in so far as appropriate.
14. *See*, e.g., the International Bar Association's (IBA) Squeeze-out Guides, which are maintained and updated by its Corporate and M&A Law Committee. www.ibanet.org/LPD/Corporate_Law_Section/Corporate_MA_Law_Committee/squeezeout.aspx (accessed September 2020). *See also* Christoph Van der Elst & Lientje Van den Steen, *Balancing the Interests of Minority and Majority Shareholders: A Comparative Analysis of Squeeze-Out and Sell-Out Right* 6 European Company and Financial Law Review 391, 404–414 (2009).

for the majority shareholder to redeem the minority's shares. However, as courts have traditionally viewed shares as "vested rights" that cannot be taken without the owner's consent, in many jurisdictions it used to be difficult—even impossible—to force a shareholder to leave the company. The lack of an efficient buyout mechanism thus created so-called freezeout situations in which minority shareholders were able to obstruct important transactions (such as mergers), even misuse their position to harm the majority shareholder and eventually extort excessive considerations for their holdings. Therefore, jurisdictions all over the world began to develop rules allowing the majority shareholder—under certain conditions—to buy minority shareholders out.[15,16]

Even though it is often in the majority shareholder's interest to gain full ownership of the enterprise, there are situations in which the controlling entity has absolutely no reason to acquire more shares. Particularly in non-listed companies—the shares of which typically have no efficient markets[17]—minority shareholders may find themselves deadlocked in an arrangement which they cannot leave, within which they have no influence and in which they lack the protection of certain crucial minority rights that can only be utilized if one holds at least 10% of the shares of the company.[18] Hence, to protect minority shareholders from being stranded in such a position, many countries have introduced the sell-out right, which is sometimes perceived as an *ex ante* defense mechanism against possible abuses of authority.[19] That said, there are also jurisdictions in which the squeeze-out right is not "compensated" with a sell-out right. For example, this is the case in Japan where the sell-out rule was intentionally

15. *See*, e.g., Frank H. Easterbrook & Daniel R. Fischel, *The Economic Structure of Corporate Law*, 134–135 (Harvard University Press 1991) and Elliot J. Weiss, *The Law of Take Out Mergers: A Historical Perspective* 56 NYU Law Review, 624 (1981). When making references to U.S. literature it is necessary to emphasize that today the policy goals related to squeeze-out rules are quite different in the U.S. and e.g., in the EU. *See*, e.g., Gilotta, *supra* n. 9, 8–9.
16. In 1929 the U.K. was the first European country to allow a squeeze-out following a takeover offer. As for civil law jurisdictions, Sweden was among the first countries to introduce squeeze-out rules when the institution was enacted through the adaptation of the 1944 Companies Act. *See* Sjöberg, *supra* n. 5, 180–190. In Finland similar rules were introduced over three decades later in the Companies Act of 1978.
17. *See*, e.g., Mette Neville, *A Statutory Buy-Out Right in SMEs: An Important Corporate Governance Mechanism and Minority Protection?* in Mette Neville & Karsten Engsig Sørensen (eds.), *Company Law and SMEs*, 289 (Thomson Reuters 2010), who argues that shares in small- and medium-sized enterprises (SMEs) are often effectively non-transferrable and particularly in companies with incompetent management.
18. For example, according to Chapter 5, section 4 of the FCA and Chapter 7, section 13(2) of the SCA only a shareholder (or shareholders together) who owns at least 10% of all shares in the company may require an extraordinary general meeting to be held to address a specified matter.
19. *See*, e.g., Nerep, Samuelsson & Andersson, *supra* n. 9, 325 and Van der Elst & Van den Steen, *supra* n. 14, 434. Especially in SMEs a sell-out right is also necessary as shares cannot be abandoned or otherwise renounced by their holder; i.e., the shareholder is bound to her/his shares until someone (i.e., the company or another person) either takes (purchases, inherits, redeems etc.) them or the company ceases to exist. *See*, e.g., Ville Pönkä, *The Legal Nature of Cooperative Membership* 7 Journal of Entrepreneurial and Organizational Diversity 39, 46–47 (2019). In this regard a share with no markets (i.e., potential buyers) may be perceived as a perpetual, non-terminable commitment from the perspective of a minority shareholder.

discarded when the Companies Act was revised in 2014.[20] Although this may seem unfair to the minority shareholders, Sjöberg is quite right when pointing out that there is no evidence regarding the efficiency of the sell-out right. For example, in Finland and Sweden, it is highly uncommon for a minority shareholder of a listed company to commence squeeze-out arbitration, which naturally suggests that they often have no desire to exit the company.[21] In Finland this applies to non-listed companies as well; however, in Sweden during the past few years sell-out requests have become more common in private companies with one or a few minority shareholders.

As implied above, the universal justification of the squeeze-out regime is built on the assumption that a properly designed exit-mechanism facilitates efficiency-oriented societal goals: On the one hand, it ensures that dissenting minority shareholders cannot prevent companies from growing and developing and on the other, that resources will be ultimately allocated to those who value them the most. This justification is founded on another assumption suggesting that the interests of the minority shareholders (i.e., shareholders with a less than 10% or 5% holding in the company) are usually purely economic in nature (i.e., that they are merely anonymous investors) while the majority shareholder has a vested interest in the company meaning that she/he must have the option to determine its operations, strategy and future.[22]

Even though most scholars agree on this theory, there seems to be some doubt whether buyouts infringe certain constitutional rights—the protection of property rights in particular.[23] European constitutional courts have often reviewed this issue and systematically confirmed the legality of the squeeze-out regime.[24] For example, in 2007, the Federal Constitutional Court of Germany tested the principle of proportionality (Ger. "Grundsatz der Verhältnismäßigkeit") and held that it was satisfied by the squeeze-out rules.[25] More recently, in 2018 the Austrian Constitutional Court ruled that while squeeze-outs primarily serve the interests of majority shareholders, there is also a clear public interest in allowing businesses to react efficiently in a rapidly changing national and international environment.[26] All in all, it seems to be rather difficult to establish a claim against a majority shareholder's squeeze-out right on constitutional grounds and one may even argue that buyouts are not constitution-sensitive measures as long as the rules are clear and the minority shareholders are compensated fairly.[27]

20. *See*, e.g., Eiji Takahashi, *Squeeze-Out of Minority Shareholders: The Constitutionality Question* 41 Journal of Japanese Law 77, 80 (2016).
21. Pönkä, *supra* n. 6, 148 and Sjöberg, *supra* n. 5, 294–295.
22. This assumption only applies to large companies with a dispersed ownership structure. In SMEs, on the other hand, the minority shareholders may also have vested interests if they are employed by the firm, for example.
23. In Finland and Sweden this discussion has been explained thoroughly by Pönkä, *supra* n. 6, 165–183 and Sjöberg, *supra* n. 5, 245–295.
24. *See*, e.g., Christoph Van der Elst & Lientje Van den Steen, *Opportunities in the Merger and Acquisition Aftermarket: Squeezing Out and Selling Out* in Greg N. Gregoriou & Luc Renneboog (eds.), *Corporate Governance and Regulatory Impact on Mergers and Acquisitions. Research and Analysis on Activity Worldwide Since 1990*, 207 (Elsevier 2007).
25. BVerfG, NZG 2007, 587.
26. VfGH 27.6.2018, G30/2017.
27. In fact, the right to squeeze-out minority shareholders may be approached from a contractual point of view so that the squeeze-out rules are understood merely as a set of predetermined

That said, in certain situations, constitutional rights may impact the valuation of shares and particularly if the minority shareholder can show that she/he has a vested interest in the company.[28]

In Finland and Sweden, squeeze-out arbitration may be commenced if a shareholder owns—directly or indirectly (e.g., together with one or more subsidiaries)—over 90% of the shares of a company.[29] In addition, the FCA requires the majority shareholder to hold over 90% of all votes meaning that if a company has issued different classes of shares, it may not be enough that the redeemer's ownership quota exceeds 90%. In practice, this rule must be followed carefully as many Finnish listed and non-listed companies utilize non-voting and multiple-voting shares.[30]

When the preconditions for squeeze-out have been met, a shareholder may immediately request the matter be resolved by arbitrators. In other words, no pre-arbitration negotiations are required[31] and if there is doubt whether the parties can reach an agreement in a timely manner, the majority shareholder naturally has no interest in trying to settle the issue before commencing the arbitration.[32] To speed up the process further, the FCA and the Swedish Companies Act 1999:116 (SCA) provide a mechanism known as advance vesting of title which we will get back to in section §15.03[C].[33]

Rules regarding the right of squeeze-out and sell-out as well as squeeze-out arbitration are mandatory, meaning that it is not possible to adjust them in the company's by-laws.[34] As explained in section §15.01, squeeze-out proceedings in

"contract terms" which become applicable when certain conditions are met. Hence, buyout is a risk that a minority shareholder can—and should—consider before purchasing shares.

28. *See*, e.g., Finnish Supreme Court decision KKO 2012:64. Also in BVerfG, NZG 2007, 587 the court left open the question of whether it would be sufficient in a family-owned company for the law to provide only for the compensation of the property interest.
29. Chapter 18, section 1(1) of the SCA and Chapter 22, section 1(1) of the SCA.
30. This dual requirement has been criticized in the Finnish legal literature. Pönkä, *supra* n. 6, 155. On the other hand, Sjöberg is quite right when pointing out that due to non-voting and multiple-voting shares, the Swedish rules may result in an "extreme" situation in which a shareholder, whose ownership quota exceeds 90%, may not hold even the majority of the votes in that company. Sjöberg, *supra* n. 5, 466.
31. *See*, e.g., Nerep, Samuelsson & Andersson, *supra* n. 9, 348, who argue that it is enough that the majority shareholder merely explores the possibility for voluntary share acquisition.
32. As for listed companies, the squeeze-out proceeding is typically preceded by a public offer to purchase all shares of the target company. In such a situation the majority shareholder has no reason to commence post-offer negotiations with the remaining shareholders.
33. Also, it is necessary to point out that in Finland and Sweden the majority shareholder may choose which minority shareholders to squeeze-out. In other words, there is no obligation to redeem all existing shares, however, if the majority shareholder chooses to buy out only a particular shareholder, all the shares of that person must be acquired. *See*, e.g., Sten Andersson, Svante Johansson & Rolf Skog, *Aktiebolagslagen (2005:551)*, 22:6 (digital version, Norstedts Juridik 2019) (Eng. "Company Law") and Pönkä, *supra* n. 6, 579–580. In practice, it is highly uncommon to buyout only certain shareholders. Nerep, Samuelsson & Andersson, *supra* n. 9, 327.
34. *See*, e.g., Andersson, Johansson & Skog, *supra* n. 33, 22:1 and Nerep, Samuelsson & Andersson, *supra* n. 9, 326. In Sweden there has been some discussion about whether the shareholders should be allowed to agree in the company's by-laws that a squeeze-out dispute is decided by a court. This possibility was rejected as it was believed it would make the system too complicated. *See* Regeringens proposition 2004/05:85. Ny aktiebolagslag, 458–459 (Prop. 2004/05:85) (Eng. "Governmental proposal. New Companies Act"). Since then Sjöberg has revisited this problem

Finland and Sweden are always decided by arbitrators, who are appointed according to the rules laid down in the FCA and the SCA. That said, there are some instances in which the transaction resulting in the squeeze-out threshold being exceeded may be brought before judges. For example, in Finland there is a case in which a minority shareholder of a private waste management company objected to a directed share issue after which the subject of the issue—the majority shareholder—decided to commence squeeze-out arbitration. Since it was the directed share issue that had increased the majority shareholder's ownership and vote quota beyond 90%, the sole arbitrator had no choice but to suspend the arbitration proceeding until the minority shareholder's objection was decided. Eventually, five years later, the Finnish Supreme Court found the claim against the directed share issue groundless[35] after which the squeeze-out dispute could be decided.[36]

Furthermore, there has been some discussion on whether squeeze-out rules can be adjusted, even ruled out *ex ante*, in a shareholders' agreement. This question concerns small- and medium-sized enterprises (SMEs) in particular since their shareholders sometimes agree not to commence squeeze-out arbitration in any situation. In Finland and Sweden there is a mutual understanding that although such contractual arrangements are valid and binding between the parties, they have no legal effect at the company level.[37] This rule has also been explicated by the Swedish Supreme Court in 2011 when it ruled that a majority shareholder had the right to buyout the minority shareholder although it had promised in a joint venture agreement not to do so.[38] Then again, it is important to note that even though agreements prohibiting the right of squeeze-out and sell-out are not binding at the company level, they are legally enforceable in the sense that incompliance with them constitutes a breach of contract that may result in contractual liability.[39]

In Finland and Sweden, the right of squeeze-out and sell-out cover both natural persons and legal persons regardless of the shareholder's nationality.[40] Also, when commencing squeeze-out arbitration it is irrelevant how and why the squeeze-out threshold was exceeded. Then again, later during the arbitral proceeding, the minority

---

and proposed that in private companies the shareholders should have the freedom to decide how squeeze-out disputes are resolved. Gustaf Sjöberg, *Tvångsinlösenreglerna tvingande* Juridisk tidskrift vid Stockholms Universitet, 149 (2011–2012) (Eng. "Mandatory Nature of Compulsory Redemption").

35. KKO 2018:19.
36. In practice these situations are uncommon since the minority shareholders usually question the transaction leading to the squeeze-out threshold being exceeded during the arbitration proceeding, not before it.
37. *See*, e.g., Niklas Arvidsson, *Aktieägaravtal. Särskilt om besluts-och överlåtelsebindningar* (Thomson Reuters 2011) (Eng. "Shareholders' Agreement. Particularly on Decision-making and Share Transfer Commitments"), Ville Pönkä, *Osakassopimuksen tavoitteet ja voimassaolon hallinta* (Edita 2008) (Eng. "Objectives and Management of Validity of Shareholders' Agreements") and Christina Ramberg, *Aktieägaravtal i praktiken* (Norstedts Juridik 2011) (Eng. "Shareholders' Agreements in Practice").
38. NJA 2011 s. 429.
39. *See*, e.g., Andersson, Johansson & Skog, *supra* n. 33, 22:1.
40. *See*, e.g., Andersson, Johansson & Skog, *supra* n. 33, 22:5, Nerep, Samuelsson & Adestam, *supra* n. 9, 328 and Pönkä, *supra* n. 6, 577–578.

shareholders may bring up this matter and contest the majority shareholder's squeeze-out right, arguing that the squeeze-out threshold was not exceeded in a legally binding manner. For example, minority shareholders may assert that they were not offered the opportunity to redeem the transferred shares as provided in the company's by-laws or that the share transfer was forbidden in a shareholders' agreement. In addition, the transactions leading to the squeeze-out threshold being exceeded may be relevant when determining the redemption price. This issue will be discussed in section §15.03[C].

## §15.03 THE SQUEEZE-OUT PROCEEDING

### [A] Introduction

In Finland, squeeze-out proceedings are governed by Chapter 18 of the FCA and in Sweden by Chapter 22 of the SCA. In addition, domestic Arbitration Acts supplement these rules; however, since squeeze-out arbitration has many peculiarities vis-à-vis normal arbitration it is a bit unclear as to how far the FAA and the SAA are applicable when it comes to squeeze-out proceedings. The question of which provisions of the Arbitration Acts are relevant and which are overridden by squeeze-out-specific rules is ultimately a matter of statutory interpretation and something that cannot be addressed further here.[41]

Squeeze-out arbitration may be approached by dividing the process into three phases. (1) The first phase concerns the appointment of arbitrators and the so-called trustee ("appointment phase"). (2) The second phase covers the actual arbitration proceeding, which typically begins when the arbitral tribunal first contacts the parties and concludes in rendering an award ("proceeding phase"). (3) The last phase includes some miscellaneous topics such as the right to appeal against an arbitral award and the implementation of the redemption ("post-arbitration phase"). Next we will take a closer look at these phases utilizing a comparative approach.

### [B] Appointment Phase

The most significant difference between the Finnish and Swedish systems concerns the appointment of arbitrators. In Finland, squeeze-out proceedings are administered by the Redemption Board (Fi. "lunastuslautakunta") of the Finland Chamber of Commerce (FCC),[42] the main task of which is to appoint impartial and independent

41. For example, the provisions of the FCA/SCA and FAA/SAA concerning the right to appeal against an arbitral award overlap one another.
42. The Redemption Board is regulated by the Chamber of Commerce Act 878/2002 (Fi. "kauppakamarilaki"; FCCA) and Chapter 18, section 4(1) of the FCA. In addition, the FCC has issued rules (Fi. "Keskuskauppakamarin lunastuslautakunnan säännöt"), which explicate how, in practice, the Redemption Board functions. *See* https://kauppakamari.fi/palvelut/lunastuslautakunta/ (accessed September 2020). The Arbitration Rules of the FCC (2020; FAI Rules) are not applicable in squeeze-out proceedings and there has been some discussion if the Redemption Board should create its own procedural instructions. According to section 5(2) of

arbitrators with the expertise needed for the task. In addition, if several arbitrators are appointed, the Redemption Board designates a chairperson for the tribunal. Furthermore, it makes a petition for the appointment of a trustee to the district court which has jurisdiction in the area where the target company has its registered office.[43] According to Chapter 18, section 5(1) of the FCA, the Redemption Board may choose not to ask for the appointment of a trustee if it decides that the minority shareholders do not need a special representative or if the parties have agreed so. In practice, a trustee is involved in more than 90% of all squeeze-out proceedings.[44]

The work of the Redemption Board is divided into several stages. First, as soon as it has received the request to commence arbitration (i.e., to appoint arbitrators), the other parties involved (usually the minority shareholders) are given the opportunity to be heard. Next, the Redemption Board decides whether to ask for the appointment of a trustee or to proceed without one. This is an important decision since the trustee has a significant role in the squeeze-out proceeding.[45] That said, as the appointment process always takes some time[46] and as there are situations in which the minority shareholders have no genuine need for a special representative, it is appropriate for the appointment rules to allow some flexibility.

If a trustee is appointed, the Redemption Board gives her/him the opportunity to express her/his opinion regarding the appointment of arbitrators. Only then does the Redemption Board decide on the number of arbitrators and chooses suitable people for the task. As for the number of arbitrators, the main rule is three,[47] but today, it is typical for squeeze-out disputes to be decided by sole arbitrators meaning that on many occasions, the Redemption Board (and perhaps also the parties and the trustee) considers the dispute to be so simple that it can be decided by one person. However, in disputes involving many minority shareholders, significant economic interests and complex legal issues, a panel of three is often prioritized. Typically experienced attorneys, law professors and judges (including Supreme Court justices) are appointed

---

the FCCA the Redemption Board must have a secretariat, a chairperson, a vice-chairperson and five to seven other members, which all must be familiar with the "economic environment." Currently the author of this article is the chairperson of the Board.

43. The system works so that the Redemption Board proposes a particular person to be appointed as a trustee and the district court only decides whether this person is suitable for the task or not.
44. All decisions made by the Redemption Board are final; i.e., the parties have no right to appeal against the decisions it makes. Hallituksen esitys 71/2013 eduskunnalle laeiksi osakeyhtiölain 18 luvun ja kauppakamarilain 5 ja 6 §:n muuttamisesta, 11–13 (HE 71/2013) (Eng. "Governmental proposal concerning the amendment of Chapter 18 of the FCA and sections 5 and 6 of the FCCA"). That is if a decision made by the Board is appealed against, the court may not address it. KKO 2010:30.
45. In fact, a recent statistical analysis suggests that there is a relation between the appointment of a trustee and the outcome of the arbitration proceeding; i.e., the absence of a trustee may reduce the redemption price paid to the minority shareholders. Hanna Savolainen & Jani Saastamoinen, *Uskottu mies vähemmistön edunvalvojana OYL 18 luvun mukaisessa välimiesmenettelyssä* Lakimies, 931 (2016) (Eng. "Trustee of Minority Shareholders in Arbitration Proceedings Under Ch. 18 of the FCA").
46. Typically it takes a district court about twenty days to appoint a trustee. HE 71/2013, *supra* n. 44, 5.
47. Section 7 of the FAA.

as arbitrators and trustees,[48] but there has been some discussion whether also a non-lawyer could be chosen as one.[49] In practice, this is not a good idea as there is always a significant risk involved when delegating legal decision-making authority to people other than lawyers. Arbitrators and trustees often face complex procedural questions that only legal professionals have the expertise to address.

Finally, the Redemption Board reviews squeeze-out awards and thereby keeps track of squeeze-out practices. However, it does not gather feedback from the parties nor give feedback to the arbitrators unless asked. Furthermore, it must be noted that the Redemption Board has no authority vis-à-vis the arbitrators or the trustee, in other words, it cannot intervene in arbitral proceedings nor does it decide on the costs of arbitration. Hence, the legal authority of the Redemption Board is rather limited compared to the authority of the Arbitration Institute of the FCC (FAI), for example.

In Sweden, squeeze-out disputes are always decided by three arbitrators.[50] This rule is mandatory meaning that it is not possible to stipulate in the company's by-laws of the appointment of a sole arbitrator.[51] Similar to the Finnish system, the Swedish appointment process has several stages, which vary depending on who is commencing the arbitration.

The provisions of the SCA focus primarily on the situation when the majority shareholder is the party initiating the procedure. According to Chapter 22, section 6 of the SCA, if the majority shareholder wants to redeem the minority shares, she/he must submit a written request to the target company's board of directors and state her/his arbitrator. Immediately after the board has received the request it must notify the shareholders against whom a buyout claim is being brought and offer them the opportunity to choose their arbitrator (Chapter 22, section 7 of the SCA).[52] In practice, the minority shareholders are often confused by this notification as they have no knowledge of squeeze-outs or arbitration in general. Also, as most redemption proceedings involve several minority shareholders, it may be virtually impossible for them to agree on an arbitrator.[53] Therefore, it is stipulated in Chapter 22, section 8 of the SCA that if the minority shareholders do not appoint an arbitrator, the target

48. The parties (and minority shareholders in particular) quite often propose an arbitrator or argue that a particular person should not be chosen as one. The Redemption Board does not take such requests into account, and there are also situations where the parties agree on the arbitrator. In that case there is usually no reason why the Redemption Board should refuse the request.
49. *See* Ville Pönkä, *Keskuskauppakamarin lunastuslautakunnan organisaatio ja tehtävät* Defensor Legis, 158 (2016) (Eng. "The Organization and Duties of the Redemption Board"). For example, business school professors and other valuation experts have sometimes been appointed as "wingmen" to panels of three arbitrators. In Sweden there has been no practice for a long time of appointing non-lawyers as arbitrators in squeeze-out proceedings although there are no legal restrictions to do so.
50. Chapter 22, section 5 of the SCA.
51. *See*, e.g., Andersson, Johansson & Skog, *supra* n. 33, 22:5 and Nerep, Samuelsson & Andersson, *supra* n. 9, 345.
52. The notification must be published as stipulated in Chapter 22, section 7(2) of the SCA and in addition sent to those shareholders whose postal address is known to the company. The minority shareholders have two weeks to inform the company in writing whom they have chosen as their arbitrator.
53. Rolf Skog, *Rodhes Aktiebolagsrätt*, 259 (24th edn., Norstedts Juridik 2014) (Eng. "Rodhe's Company Law").

company's board must ask the Swedish Companies Registration Office (Swe. "Bolagsverket") to appoint a trustee.[54] The trustee will then choose an arbitrator on behalf of the minority shareholders (Chapter 22, section 10(1) of the SCA) and finally, the two arbitrators will choose the third member of the panel who will also act as its chair (section 13 of the SAA).

In the uncommon event that a minority shareholder decides to use her/his right of sell-out, the request to commence arbitration must be addressed directly to the majority shareholder as stipulated in section 19 of the SAA. Following this request, both parties choose one arbitrator and then the two arbitrators choose the third member of the panel who will also act as the chairperson. If for some reason a party fails to choose an arbitrator, one will be appointed by the district court upon request by a party (sections 14–15 of the SAA). In practice, this appointment system may turn out to be quite problematic if several minority shareholders request sell-out independently from one another. The Swedish law includes no rules governing such a situation, hence, it has been argued that if the parties do not agree on a joint proceeding, each claim must be addressed separately.[55] This is something that the parties should avoid since there is no point in deciding virtually identical disputes in separate proceedings. In fact, separate proceedings would only lead to unnecessary expense (which the majority shareholder is liable for[56]) and more importantly, there is a risk that the different arbitral tribunals would determine different values for the minority shares.[57]

### [C] Proceeding Phase

The proceeding phase begins immediately after the appointment of the arbitral tribunal and the trustee. This phase has many similarities with normal arbitration; for example, it typically has a preliminary hearing and information exchanging stage, a hearing stage (at which the parties submit written documents and may meet in person) and concludes in rendering an award. Due to these similarities, there is no reason to explain further the structure of squeeze-out arbitration; hence, we will next focus on the features that distinguish it from normal arbitration.

First, the number of parties has a major impact on the nature of the arbitration proceeding. It is different to administer a proceeding where the number of minority shareholders is counted in hundreds—even in thousands—compared to a squeeze-out involving only a few respondents. Squeeze-out proceedings also vary depending on the

54. The target company may propose a particular person to be appointed as a trustee, but the Companies Registration Office is not bound by the proposal. Also, as opposed to the Finnish system, the Companies Registration Office's decision may be appealed to the Stockholm District Court within three weeks after the decision was made (Chapter 31, section 3 of the SCA).
55. *See*, e.g., Andersson, Johansson & Skog, *supra* n. 33, 22:6.
56. *See* section §15.03[D].
57. In Finland there have been situations in which the minority shareholders have commenced arbitration independently of one another. For example, in 2017–2018 nine minority shareholders of a golf company (Gumböle Golf ry) decided to use their right of sell-out and as the Redemption Board did not have the authority to consolidate the proceedings, it appointed the same arbitrator to decide each case. After being appointed, the arbitrator—referring to the rules laid down in the Finnish Code of Judicial Procedure (4/1734)—chose to consolidate the proceedings.

level of activity of the parties. Sometimes the minority shareholders become highly engaged in the process,[58] and it is typical for at least some of them to be represented by lawyers and share valuation experts.[59] Such proceedings may have lengthy hearings and require a huge amount of procedural coordination. On the other hand, there are also situations in which the minority shareholders remain relatively passive and rely on the trustee to bring forth arguments supporting their claims. As for oral hearings, the Swedish custom seems to be that the parties do not meet in person; in other words, there are no preliminary or main hearings meaning that the whole process is written. In Finland, on the other hand, the arbitral tribunal typically decides to hold at least a main hearing;[60] however, there are also arbitrators who prefer the "Swedish style." For example, in 2014 when the Swedish company SSAB AB (publ) bought out the minority shareholders of the Finnish company Rautaruukki Oyj, the whole process was administered remotely even though it involved about 6,200 respondents including several active ones.

Another distinctive feature of squeeze-out arbitration is the involvement of a trustee. In practice, the primary role of the trustee is to represent the minority shareholders and to ensure that their rights are not infringed. Here the Finnish and Swedish systems differ from one another in the sense that in Finland, the trustee represents all minority shareholders regardless of their activity during the process.[61] In Sweden, on the other hand, the trustee protects the rights of "absent shareholders" (Chapter 22, section 10(1) of the SCA), hence, if a minority shareholder decides to become active during the process, she/he is no longer considered absent and her/his actions are not supervised by the trustee.[62] In practice, the Finnish system has proved to be quite complicated since trustees often find it impossible to represent active

58. Particularly in SMEs, where the shareholders often know one another and maybe even work together, the disputes may get rather personal in nature and involve matters that are not present in companies with wide and dispersed ownership structures. Furthermore, in Finland and Sweden there are certain "professional" minority shareholders, who are actively involved in many squeeze-out proceedings (and particularly those involving a listed company), who systematically make different kinds of claims and who try to have the majority shareholder cover their expenses. *See*, e.g., Swedish Supreme Court decision HD 17.3.2020 Ö 1082-19. It is likely that the minority-favoring rules regarding the liability for the costs of arbitration (which are discussed later in this section) provoke such opportunistic behavior.
59. In Finland and Sweden there are no registers or other listings of share valuation experts such as there are, e.g., in the U.K. Typically the parties buy valuation services from consulting firms and business professors.
60. According to section 30 of the FAI Rules, the arbitral tribunal must hold a case management conference and only in "exceptional situations" it may refrain from arranging one. Therefore, it is quite surprising that in most squeeze-out proceedings there is no such conference and after hearing the majority shareholder and the trustee (and in some cases also the active minority shareholders) the arbitrators merely issue a so-called instruction letter (Fi. "ohjekirje") confirming the conduct and timetable of the proceeding.
61. According to Chapter 18, section 5(3) a trustee "shall have the right and the obligation to make a case on behalf of the minority shareholders and to present evidence in support thereof in the arbitration proceedings".
62. *See*, e.g., HD 17.3.2020 Ö 1082-19. According to the legal preparatory materials of the SCA, the trustee (Swe. "god man") is comparable to a legal counsellor (Swe. "rättegångsombud") vis-à-vis the absent minority shareholders. Prop. 2004/05:85, *supra* n. 34, 818–819. *See also* NJA 2013 s. 1203 and NJA 2018 s. 994. In Finland, on the other hand, the trustee (Fi. "uskottu mies") is perceived as a special representative, a kind of a "minority-favoring referee."

minority shareholders whose claims are utterly unrealistic: As Chapter 18, section 5(3) of the FCA forbids all measures that are contrary to the measures taken by the minority shareholders, there are situations in which the trustee has to take a relatively passive role and merely stand by as the respondents plead their case.

As explained in section §15.01, the arbitral tribunal's authority does not extend beyond determining the existence of the squeeze-out right and the squeeze-out price. Share valuation is often a lengthy process and therefore, the FCA and the SCA allow so-called advance vesting of title meaning that (a) if the parties agree on the existence of a buyout right or it is otherwise clear that such a right exists and (b) if the majority shareholder provides sufficient security for the future payment of the squeeze-out price, she/he may be permitted to take possession of the minority's shares before the beginning of the actual valuation phase.[63] In most squeeze-out disputes the majority shareholder utilizes this right and if the above-mentioned conditions are met, the arbitrators typically accept her/his petition. That said, there must be virtually complete certainty over exceeding the squeeze-out threshold, since if it later turns out that the majority shareholder did not have the right to buy out the minority shareholders, it may be impossible to restore their ownership status. In Finland, the decision regarding advanced vesting of the title is made in the form of a procedural order (Fi. "käsittelyratkaisu") which may not be challenged.[64] In Sweden, on the other hand, the decision must be made in the form of a separate award which may be appealed before the Stockholm District Court.[65]

Next, the arbitral tribunal decides the squeeze-out price and the interest to be paid on it[66] as stipulated in Chapter 18, section 7 of the FCA and Chapter 22, sections 2 and 3 of the SCA. At this stage, the legal form of the target company (e.g., whether it is listed or non-listed), the transactions leading to exceeding the squeeze-out threshold and other case-specific factors play an important role. In Finland, the main rule is that the "fair price" of the share before the initiation of the arbitration proceeding serves as the basis for the determination of the redemption price. However, if the squeeze-out proceeding was preceded by a mandatory or a voluntary bid—as referred to in the Finnish Securities Markets Act 746/2012—the redemption price is determined on the basis of the offer, unless there is a "special reason" to decide otherwise.[67]

The primary valuation rule in Sweden is quite different as it requires the redemption price to correspond to the price of the share which might be expected on a

63. Chapter 18, section 6 of the FCA and Chapter 22, sections 12–14 of the SCA.
64. Pönkä, *supra* n. 6, 638.
65. Prop. 2004/05:85, *supra* n. 34, 820. Such an appeal could delay the squeeze-out proceeding, but there are no data suggesting that minority shareholders would file frivolous appeals to harm the redeemer. In fact, appeals against decisions concerning advance vesting of title are highly uncommon.
66. The rules concerning interest paid to the redemption price are nearly identical in Finland and Sweden. In Sweden interest must be paid from the date on which a party requested that the dispute be decided by arbitrators and in Finland from three weeks after the request to appoint arbitrators.
67. As for voluntary bids the rule mentioned above is applied only if the offer was accepted by holders of more than 90% of the shares to which it relates. In practice, there have been only two cases in which the arbitral tribunal found a special reason to deviate from a mandatory or voluntary bid.

sale under "normal circumstances."[68] However, if the share is traded on a Swedish or foreign exchange or other regulated markets, its redemption price must be fixed to the listed value (i.e., market price), unless "special grounds" otherwise dictate. Furthermore, if the squeeze-out proceeding was preceded by a public offer (a) to acquire all shares of the target company and (b) the offer was accepted by holders of more than 90% of the shares to which it relates, the purchase price must correspond to the offer, unless there is a special reason to decide otherwise. It needs to be emphasized that this "special rule" (Swe. "särregel") is applied only when the above-mentioned conditions are met, meaning that the redemption price of a listed share is normally determined according to the market price rule.[69] That said, the outcome of the valuation process is usually the same regardless of which rule is applied.

On many occasions share valuation is not only a lengthy process but also a highly complicated one requiring the use of a range of valuation methods that need to be adjusted to the circumstances at hand. Particularly in SMEs, share valuation involves much discretion as the "fair value" and the "value which might be expected upon a sale under normal circumstances" are rather vague objectives. Also, it is typical for the parties to establish their claims on expert opinions suggesting completely different outcomes, meaning that the arbitrators must have the expertise to assess appraisal reports critically. If the target company is listed, the dispute typically comes down to the question of whether the redemption price should be established according to the market price (or the bid price) or if there is a special reason to decide otherwise. Also, this question can turn out to be complicated if a minority shareholder or the trustee shows that the market price may not reflect the true value of the redeemed shares.

In Finland, arbitral awards play a significant role in the development of the share valuation doctrine, and it is no surprise that arbitrators often justify their decisions by referring to previous awards in similar cases. In fact, there are even awards that enjoy a type of precedent value. In Sweden, where squeeze-out awards are not published, they are nevertheless followed closely by scholars and legal practitioners.[70] Recently some awards have also raised critical debate whether certain valuation principles explicated in Swedish case[71] law are still valid and binding.[72] There are many other interesting share valuation-related topics—such as can the redemption price be

68. Similar as in Finland, the purchase price must be determined paying attention to the circumstances pertaining at the time a request for arbitration was made. However, also previous circumstances may be taken into account if there is a sound reason to do so.

69. *See*, e.g., Karl-Erik Danielsson, *Vad är det för särskilt med särregeln?* In Marianne Lundius, Ragnar Boman & Rolf Skog (eds.), *Aktie, aktiebolag, aktiemarknad: en vänbok till Johan Munck*, 104 (Corporate Governance Forum 2013) (Eng. "What is so Special about the Special Rule") and Gustaf Sjöberg, *Tvångsinlösen—särregelns tillämplighet* Juridisk tidskrift vid Stockholms Universitet 892, 902 (2011-2012) (Eng. "Compulsory Redemption—Applying the Special Rule").

70. Sjöberg, *supra* n. 5, 359.

71. *See*, e.g., NJA 1967 s. 1 ("Gimo"—case), NJA 1992 s. 872 and NJA 1996 s. 293 ("Balken I & II"—cases) and NJA 2011 s. 932 ("Old Mutual"—case).

72. *See*, e.g., Danielsson, *supra* n. 69 and Bo Svensson, *Lösenbeloppet vid tvångsinlösen av minoritetsaktier* 1 Ny Juridik 49 (2019) (Eng. "Redemption Price in Compulsory Redemption of Minority Shares").

negative so that the minority shareholders pay the redeemer[73]—but due to the demarcations of this chapter, these questions cannot be discussed further here.

Rules regarding the liability for the costs of arbitration are another peculiarity that distinguishes squeeze-out arbitration from normal arbitration. The main rule in Finland and Sweden is that the majority shareholder is liable for these costs regardless of the outcome of the dispute. Only in exceptional circumstances can the arbitrators order another shareholder to bear them in whole or in part.[74] However, the Finnish and Swedish rules differ from one another, as in Sweden, the costs of arbitration include the remuneration to the arbitrators and the trustee (i.e., the costs of the arbitration proceeding itself) as well as the costs of the other shareholder.[75] In Finland, on the other hand, the costs of arbitration refer only to procedural costs, and in most cases the arbitrators decide that the minority shareholders are liable for their own expenses.

In Sweden there is no published information regarding the costs of squeeze-out arbitration. In Finland, on the other hand, a rather comprehensive study shows that the arithmetic mean of the arbitrators' remuneration is EUR 25,000 (median EUR 13,000) when the target company is non-listed and EUR 40,000 (median EUR 27,500) when the target company is listed.[76] In both countries the arbitrators decide on the amount of their remuneration as stipulated in section 46 of the FAA and section 37 of the SAA. In addition, the arbitrators decide on the trustee's remuneration based on her/his invoice.[77]

Finally, the proceeding phase concludes in rendering an award. The award must state clearly the redemption price per share and meet the requirements laid down in the FAA and the SAA. The award must be delivered to the majority shareholder, the active/known minority shareholders and the trustee.[78] As explained above, squeeze-out awards in Finland are registered; however, there is some ambiguity whether decisions merely confirming a settlement or discontinuance are covered by this requirement.[79] In Sweden, squeeze-out awards are not public—in other words, squeeze-out awards are confidential in the same way as other arbitral

73. The Supreme Court of Finland is currently considering this option.
74. Chapter 18, section 8 of the FCA and Chapter 22, section 23 of the SCA. If the arbitrators decide that the majority shareholder alone should bear the costs of the arbitration, the minority shareholders cannot be held liable for any procedural costs even if the majority shareholder has become insolvent. *See*, e.g., NJA 2013 s. 1203.
75. The majority shareholder is always liable for her/his own costs. *See* Regeringens proposition 2006:07:70. Några aktiebolagsrättsliga frågor, 107 and 199 (Eng. "Governmental proposal. Some company law questions").
76. Ville Pönkä, *Välimiesmenettelyn kustannukset vähemmistöosakkeiden lunastusriidassa*. In Ulla-Maija Mylly, Patrik Nystörm & Tuija Viinikka (eds.), *Oikeuden ja talouden rajapinnassa. Juhlakirja Matti J. Sillanpää 60 vuotta*, 203 (Edita 2016) (Eng. "Costs of Arbitration in Squeeze-out Disputes"). As for listed companies, the arbitrators' renumerations have been increasing significantly during the past few years.
77. At least in Finland, the arbitrators sometimes disagree with the trustee on the amount of fair compensation and adjust it. *See*, e.g., Pönkä, *supra* n. 76, 206–207.
78. In addition, the arbitral award must be delivered to a passive minority shareholder if she/he requests it. Hallituksen esitys 109/2005 Eduskunnalle uudeksi osakeyhtiölainsäädännöksi, 175 (Eng. "Governmental proposal for new company legislation").
79. Then again, the law does not require squeeze-out awards to be delivered to the Redemption Board. Most arbitrators nevertheless do so.

awards—however, in practice they spread easily among those few involved in the business.[80] This may sound questionable, but squeeze-out arbitration does not involve a similar interest of confidentiality as would flow from normal arbitration.

### [D] Post-arbitration Phase

The post-arbitration phase begins after the arbitral award has been rendered. This phase covers several important actions such as surrendering the shares to the majority shareholder and registering the majority shareholder as the new owner of the shares, payment (or deposition) of the purchase price and furthermore, in Finland the trustee must notify a report of his or her activities to be registered, without delay.[81]

According to Chapter 18, section 10 of the FCA, a party and the trustee may appeal against a squeeze-out award before the district court which has jurisdiction in the area where the target company has its registered office. In turn, the decision of the district court is open to appeal directly before the Supreme Court. In Sweden, a party and the trustee may commence proceedings before the Stockholm District Court and its decision is open to appeal before the Svea Court of Appeal (Chapter 22, section 24 of the SCA).

In both countries a squeeze-out award may be challenged on formal and material grounds meaning that if a party or the trustee is dissatisfied with the redemption price (for example), the matter may be reviewed by judges.[82] The justification of such a broad right to appeal is founded on the interpretation of Article 6 of the European Convention on Human Rights (ECHR).[83] However, this interpretation is somewhat problematic in the sense that a right to appeal on material grounds means that judges, who may have no expertise in company law and share valuation, have the authority to override an arbitral award rendered by carefully selected arbitrators.[84] Finally, it must be noted that in Finland, it is unclear whether a court's ruling affects only the parties who have challenged the squeeze-out award or all minority shareholders whose shares

80. Sjöberg, *supra* n. 5, 359.
81. This registration obligation is sometimes neglected by trustees and the problem is that there is no sanction for such misconduct.
82. In practice, such appeals are relatively uncommon. *See*, e.g., HE 71/2013, *supra* n. 44, 6. Here it is important to note that in Finland and Sweden the "loser-pays" rule is applied if a minority shareholder or the trustee challenges the arbitral award and loses in court. *See*, e.g., HD 17.3.2020 Ö 1082-19. This may—at least in part—explain why such challenges are uncommon.
83. *See* HE 71/2013, *supra* n. 44, 11–12 and Regeringens proposition 1983/84:184 om ändring i aktiebolagslagen (1975:1385) m.m., 9 (Eng. "Governmental proposal on amending the Companies Act"). As for Art. 6(1) of the ECHR a distinction is made between voluntary and compulsory arbitration. *See* Guide on Article 6 of the European Convention on Human Rights (European Court of Human Rights 2019), 31. In principle, no issue is raised in the case of voluntary arbitration since it is entered into freely. However, in the case of compulsory arbitration—such as squeeze-out arbitration—the parties have no opportunity to remove their dispute from the jurisdiction of an arbitral tribunal, which consequently must afford special "guarantees"—in the case of squeeze-out arbitration a right to appeal on material grounds.
84. It may be reasonable to narrow down the right to appeal so that the court primarily examines whether the share valuation was carried out carefully and only if there are signs of negligence, the valuation could be opened up for reconsideration.

have been redeemed.[85] In Sweden the court's ruling affects all minority shareholders, but the case is most probably different in Finland—unless it is the trustee, who has appealed against the award.[86]

## §15.04 CONCLUSIONS: A PRO ET CONTRA OVERVIEW

The preconditions to commence squeeze-out arbitration as well as the different phases of the proceeding have been explained above in sections §15.02 and §15.03. Based on this analysis, it seems that in Sweden, squeeze-out arbitration bears more resemblance to normal arbitration than it does in Finland. For example, in Sweden, there is no administrative organ similar to the Redemption Board, the trustee has no role vis-à-vis the active minority shareholders and arbitral awards are not public. However, the Finnish and Swedish systems have many structural similarities when it comes to the authority of the arbitrators, rules regarding advance vesting of title and the right to appeal against an arbitral award. Also, the price determination rules have the same objective—to establish the true value of the redeemed shares—even though the wordings of the FCA and the SCA are seemingly different.[87]

It is impossible to determine which squeeze-out regime outperforms the other. However, since the Finnish and Swedish rules are applied under similar conditions, some general observations can be made. First, in Finland the pre-arbitration phase is made very easy for the parties as it is administered entirely by a third party. This means the target company has no role in the buyout process and that the parties do not need to concern themselves with finding competent and impartial arbitrators. Also, it is important to point out that squeeze-out arbitration in Finland is open to public scrutiny in the sense that decisions regarding the appointment of arbitrators, arbitral awards, and trustees' reports are always disclosed through registration.[88] Such transparency lifts the "veil of mystery" over squeeze-out arbitration (e.g., it eliminates concerns relating to the independence and impartiality of arbitrators) and facilitates the development of fair and efficient buyout practices. Furthermore, the Finnish appointment rules are more flexible as they allow the appointment of sole arbitrators. As mentioned above in section §15.03[B], the Redemption Board often takes advantage of this option and even the minority shareholders and the trustee sometimes agree that there is no need for a panel of three arbitrators.

85. Pönkä, *supra* n. 6, 722–723.

86. Manne Airaksinen, Pekka Pulkkinen & Vesa Rasinaho, *Osakeyhtiölaki II*, 637 (Alma Talent 2018) ("Companies Act II").

87. The reason for the similarities between the Finnish and Swedish systems can be traced back to Nordic legislative cooperation, which virtually ceased to exist in the early years of the 1970s. *See*, e.g., Jan Andersson, *The Making of Company Law in Scandinavia and Europe* in Holger Fleischer, Jesper Lau Hansen & Wolf-Georg Ringe (eds.), *German and Nordic Perspectives on Company Law and Capital Markets Law*, 27 (Mohr Siebeck 2016). Although company law in the Nordic countries has diverged from one another, it is still possible for a Finn to understand Swedish company law—and, of course, vice versa.

88. Although the names of the arbitrators and the trustees as well as the parties involved are published, the Redemption Board does not share information regarding the contents of its meetings. Only the minutes are disclosed.

Then again, the Swedish system is evidently more desirable when it comes to the role of the trustee. As explained in section §15.03[C], in Finland, the trustee may find her/himself in a difficult position if the minority shareholders decide to take an active role in safeguarding their own interests.[89] This issue could be fixed simply by ruling that the trustee represents absent shareholders, in other words, only those who are not reachable ("unknown shareholders") and those who choose not to take part in the proceeding. The Finnish system is also unreasonably cumbersome when it comes to the appointment of the trustee. As the court that is responsible for making the appointment decision has virtually no discretion in the matter and as the decision cannot be contested, there is no point in involving judges in the process. Therefore, the trustee should be appointed by the Redemption Board or by an authority similar to the Swedish Companies Registration Office.

Furthermore, the Swedish squeeze-out regime is more rational in the sense that all buyout-related matters involving the judicial system are concentrated in one district court (i.e., the Stockholm District Court). This may seem to be a trivial issue, but in Finland, where the FCA was amended in 2013 so that the District Court of Helsinki no longer has exclusive authority in squeeze-out matters, the number of problems related to trustee appointments has increased. These experiences suggest that the district court which has jurisdiction in the area where the target company has its registered office may not have the best knowledge of company law and arbitration.

There are also several material matters in which the Finnish and Swedish squeeze-out rules differ from one another. For example, in Sweden, the squeeze-out right covers both shares as well as warrants and convertible instruments.[90] In Finland, it depends on the terms of the instrument potentially carrying voting rights if it may be redeemed or not. As the aim of the squeeze-out right is to grant the majority shareholder the right to acquire full ownership of the target company, it would make sense to apply the threshold to all types of equity-related instruments.[91] Another difference concerns the question of whether the squeeze-out threshold should be fixed to the amount of the redeemer's shareholding (the Swedish system) or to the number of votes as well (the Finnish system). This question was addressed in section §15.02 and therefore it will not be discussed further here.

Finally, the question remains on whether arbitration is the most appropriate means of resolving squeeze-out disputes. On the one hand, arbitration offers the opportunity to determine the redemption price and to deal with questions of legal nature in the same proceeding. On the other hand, squeeze-out arbitration is a multi-phased, lengthy and a relatively expensive process and there is no doubt that in many buyouts it would make more sense to utilize independent expert determination under judicial supervision instead of full-scale arbitration. In light of the purposes of the squeeze-out (and the sell-out) right, it is virtually impossible to argue that a buyout dispute should always be decided in a particular manner.[92] However, judging by the

89. *See supra* n. 62.
90. Chapter 22, section 26 of the SCA.
91. Van der Elst & Van den Steen, *supra* n. 14, 438.
92. *Ibid.*

positive experiences in Finland and Sweden it is safe to say that arbitration is a viable alternative[93] and when taking into account the increasing popularity of alternative dispute resolution, it is a bit surprising that squeeze-out arbitration has remained such an unknown phenomenon.

93. *See* differently Sjöberg, *supra* n. 5, 470–473, who argues *de lege ferenda* that squeeze-out disputes should be decided by judges instead of arbitrators.

## STOCKHOLM ARBITRATION YEARBOOK

1. Axel Calissendorff & Patrik Schöldström (eds), *Stockholm Arbitration Yearbook 2019*, 2019 (ISBN 978-94-035-0692-0).
2. Axel Calissendorff & Patrik Schöldström (eds), *Stockholm Arbitration Yearbook 2020*, 2020 (ISBN 978-94-035-2410-8).

www.ingramcontent.com/pod-product-compliance
Lightning Source LLC
LaVergne TN
LVHW020643300926
849161LV00004B/791